MORE PRAIS

BLOOD IN THE GARDEN

"Readers need not love the Knicks—or even possess deep knowledge of professional basketball—to enjoy this book. It throbs with an insider's perspective . . . besides the vivid writing, what makes *Blood in the Garden* so successful is the depth of Mr. Herring's research, which rests on more than 200 extensive interviews."

—*The Wall Street Journal*

"Armed with behind-the-scenes knowledge culled from more than 200 interviews with players, coaches, and executives, Herring delivers a thrilling narrative that skillfully evokes the intensity and tension of pro basketball. Hoops fans will relish this riveting ride."

—*Publishers Weekly*, Starred Review

"The depth of Herring's reporting is remarkable, leading to a mix of behind-the-scenes stories and hard-core hoops talk that will be catnip to any NBA fan. We get new information on everything from the O. J. Simpson chase to those infamous Heat–Knicks brawls. The 1990s Knicks are an iconic team, and Herring's chronicle of that time is a must-have."

—Zach Lowe, NBA Senior Writer, ESPN

"With one jaw-dropping anecdote after another, Chris Herring presents the book that relentless Knicks team—and the long-suffering Knicks fan base—deserves."

—Alan Sepinwall, *New York Times* bestselling coauthor of *The Sopranos Sessions*

"Chris Herring's reporting and details make *Blood in the Garden* fascinating and incredibly easy to read. His digging and storytelling give one of the more mythical—and perhaps underappreciated—teams from the 1990s a proper treatment with an inside look worthy of our social media, 'give-us-all-the-tea' age."

—Marcus Thompson, *New York Times* bestselling author of *Golden: The Miraculous Rise of Steph Curry*

BLOOD IN THE GARDEN

THE FLAGRANT HISTORY OF THE
1990s NEW YORK KNICKS

CHRIS HERRING

ATRIA PAPERBACK

NEW YORK   LONDON   TORONTO   SYDNEY   NEW DELHI

An Imprint of Simon & Schuster, LLC
1230 Avenue of the Americas
New York, NY 10020

First Atria Paperback edition November 2024

ATRIA PAPERBACK and colophon are trademarks of Simon & Schuster, LLC

Simon & Schuster: Celebrating 100 Years of Publishing in 2024

For information about special discounts for bulk purchases, please contact Simon & Schuster Special Sales at 1-866-506-1949 or business@simonandschuster.com.

The Simon & Schuster Speakers Bureau can bring authors to your live event. For more information, or to book an event, contact the Simon & Schuster Speakers Bureau at 1-866-248-3049 or visit our website at www.simonspeakers.com.

Interior design by Jill Putorti

Manufactured in the United States of America

1 3 5 7 9 10 8 6 4 2

Library of Congress Cataloging-in-Publication Data

Names: Herring, Chris (Sports journalist), author.
Title: Blood in the Garden : the flagrant history of the 1990s New York Knicks / by Chris Herring.
Description: First Atria Books Hardcover Edition. | New York : Atria Books, [2022] | Includes bibliographical references.
Identifiers: LCCN 2021027368 (print) | LCCN 2021027369 (ebook) | ISBN 9781982132118 (Hardcover) | ISBN 9781982132125 (Paperback) | ISBN 9781982132132 (eBook)
Subjects: LCSH: New York Knickerbockers (Basketball team)—History—20th century. | Basketball players—New York (State)—New York—Interviews. | Madison Square Garden (New York, N.Y.)—History. | National Basketball Association—History—20th century. | Basketball—New York (State)—New York—History—20th century.
Classification: LCC GV885.52.N4 H47 2022 (print) | LCC GV885.52.N4 (ebook) | DDC 796.323/64097471—dc23
LC record available at https://lccn.loc.gov/2021027368
LC ebook record available at https://lccn.loc.gov/2021027369

ISBN 978-1-9821-3211-8
ISBN 978-1-9821-3212-5 (pbk)
ISBN 978-1-9821-3213-2 (ebook)

All insert photos are courtesy of Getty Images.

For Marsha and Cedric Herring,
the best parents I ever could've asked for.
All I've ever wanted is to make you proud,
and I pray I'm doing that now.
Until we meet again. I love you.

CONTENTS

PROLOGUE

There was a time, back in the spring of 1994, when bellies were perpetually full at Two Penn Plaza.

Back then, Knicks employees who worked in the Madison Square Garden corporate offices were treated to extravagant buffet lunches in the fourteenth-floor hallway—complete with lo mein, gourmet sandwiches, jalapeño cheese poppers, egg rolls, and desserts—whenever the club tallied a three-game winning streak.

The Knicks were transforming into an NBA fat cat, and one of the most feared teams in basketball. After a disappointing 39-win season in 1991, a personnel overhaul helped lift New York to 51 regular-season victories in 1992 and an Eastern Conference–best 60 triumphs in 1993. By then, the free lunches were no longer a rarity. They'd become an expectation.

Then came the mother of all buffets. In March 1994, with coach Pat Riley and the Knicks preying on one foe after another, they strung together 15 straight wins, and those celebratory lunches were held every week for five weeks in a row. It was during one of those jubilant meals that Frank Murphy, the team's business manager, decided to rain on the lunch parade.

"Just make sure to enjoy this," the executive said, "because it'll never be like this again. This is special."

To some in the room, the 54-year-old's what-goes-up-must-come-down message felt unwarranted. Murphy had said things like this before, sure. But this run—15 consecutive wins—felt different. There was a certain electricity everyone wanted to hold on to this time. "I was in my thirties, with all this optimism. And I remember telling him, 'Don't say that. It'll *always* be like this,'" says Pam Harris, then the team's marketing director. "But now, looking back, I can better appreciate what Frank was saying."

No one—not even Murphy—could have known just how steep the organization's fall would be.

The New York Knicks were among the defining teams throughout one of the NBA's golden eras. They made the playoffs in all ten years of the decade, with three conference finals showings and two trips to the NBA Finals. So the utter ruin into which New York would fall in the following two decades was inconceivable.

Coach Jeff Van Gundy abruptly resigned from the club on the morning of December 8, 2001, quietly taking with him some of the last remnants of the team's 1990s DNA. By and large, from that day he stepped down to 2021 or so, the once-proud organization had been nothing short of disastrous. Despite playing in the nation's largest market and pouring more money into its rosters than any other club, no franchise burned through more coaches, lost more games, or tallied fewer playoff series wins in that span than the Knicks.

With it having been twenty-five years the last time the Knickerbockers reached the Finals—and fifty-one years since the club's last NBA title—things had deteriorated to where fans were thrilled by the mere prospect of a functional team. Most fans would have settled for the free buffet lunch.

Yet in having to endure such lean years, fans only became more nostalgic for those nineties-era Knicks. No, those teams never tasted immortality. They were never the league's most skilled collection of players. But for what the Knicks lacked in finesse, they made up for with fight (often literally) and floor burns; grit that endeared them to countless New Yorkers. When fans looked at John Starks—who became an All-Star despite going undrafted after playing at four different colleges and leaving school at one point to work a $3.35-an-hour job bagging groceries at Safeway—they saw someone who overcame incredible odds by working tirelessly. In the blue-collar underdog Starks, countless fans saw themselves.

Those Knicks made you *feel* something. The team's fans felt pride in their hardworking players. League office executives felt the pulsating headaches that came while issuing punishments for the Knicks, whose brass-knuckles physicality was so extreme it led the NBA to alter its rulebook. New York's opponents felt the bone-rattling pain they had to endure during twelve-round bouts that doubled as basketball games.

"When I used to walk into the Garden to play the Knicks, I didn't always know if we were gonna win," former Bulls forward Horace Grant would say years later. "But I always knew we were going to bleed."

The 1990s Knicks were wildly colorful—at times, as flagrant and out of bounds off the court as they were on it. They were a brute-force version of Forrest Gump, repeatedly intertwined with historic moments, from the rise of Michael Jordan's Bulls dynasty; to the O. J. Simpson chase during the Finals in 1994; to Reggie Miller's eight-point outburst in nine seconds in 1995; to their blood feud with Riley's Miami Heat clubs. You can't tell the story of the league's most fascinating decade *without* the New York Knicks.

Despite that, it's a story that has never fully been told. But now—through hundreds of interviews with players, coaches, trainers, opponents, friends, family members, and executives in and around the team—it can be. The rivalries and rumors. The feuds and fights. The secret histories and stunning revelations.

And rest assured: no punches will be pulled. Which is just how those Knicks would like it.

BLOOD IN THE
GARDEN

SPEAKING A NEW LANGUAGE

Twenty minutes into his first practice as Knicks coach, Pat Riley looked a bit ruffled.

It was unusually muggy on the morning of October 4, 1991, in Charleston, South Carolina. Inside the team's practice gym—which lacked air-conditioning and was a sauna in the best of times—the air was stifling. Yet those pressure-cooker conditions were but a small reason why the coach appeared uncharacteristically off-center. Riley, featured on the cover of *GQ* two years earlier, had long been known for his pristine, slicked-back hair and stylish Armani threads. But now a number of the pomaded strands atop his head had popped out of place. Beads of sweat were showing through his team-issued polo. Momentarily doubled over and breathless, the 6-foot-4 Riley had his hands on his kneecaps.

At 46, he was the most accomplished coach in modern NBA history, having won four rings while leading the Showtime Lakers, a job that had allowed him to stand still on the sideline, relatively relaxed, while his clubs sped up and down the court. Which is why, on that October morning, it was such a change of pace for Riley to desperately sprint across the court to stop two Knick players from killing each other in the first basketball drill of the coach's tenure.

It had all begun with Riley splitting his team up to conduct three-on-three box-out drills. The smaller wing players headed down to the far end to work with assistants Jeff Van Gundy and Dick Harter, while the post players stayed with Riley and assistant Paul Silas. The concept was simple: coaches would launch fifteen-foot jumpers, and the six players would battle for positioning inside the paint to secure the misses.

In the group of post players, sharp-elbowed forward Xavier Mc-Daniel was dominating the exercise, albeit in a slightly underhanded fashion. As Riley's and Silas's shots ricocheted off the rim, and the muscle-bound teammates barreled into one another, McDaniel, a Knicks newcomer and a former All-Star, was quietly hooking opposing players' legs—a wily, veteran trick that often caused them to trip just before they could leap for rebounds. Doing this, McDaniel twice managed to beat camp invitee Anthony Mason to the ball. Mason wrote off McDaniel's first hook as an honest mistake. The second time, he grew agitated.

"You do that shit again, I'm gonna fuck you up!" Mason snarled, pointing in McDaniel's direction.

McDaniel, apparently undeterred by Mason's threat, then hooked the leg of rookie big man Patrick Eddie one play later, causing Eddie to tumble as McDaniel skyed for yet another board. By then, the 6-foot-7, 250-pound Mason had seen enough. No more warnings. It was time to follow through on his promise.

The bowling-ball-shouldered southpaw shuffled toward McDaniel and delivered an abrasive left fist to his jaw; a punch that reverberated so loudly players on the other end of the gym heard it. For a split second after Mason's blow, there was nothing but silence. Stunned, McDaniel briefly grabbed the side of his face, perhaps to make sure it was still intact. Then he set his sights on Mason and charged at the 24-year-old like a bull chasing a matador.

As Mason sought to backpedal toward the sideline, McDaniel rammed into him, landing a right haymaker before pulling his teammate in closer. Finally, after a few more pummeling blasts from each man, Riley and nearly a half-dozen others sprinted in to break up the altercation.

"His ass is gonna have to come back this way at some point!" McDaniel yelled while being pulled away.

It was the first time the team found Anthony Mason in the middle of things. But it wouldn't be the last.

Although Mason's cartoonishly chiseled physique stood out to everyone in the gym that day, he was a relative unknown from a basketball standpoint.

Having endured a nomadic career in which he bounced from one league to another—one part of the *world* to another—Mason was hell-bent on showing he belonged. He had spent time overseas with pro teams in Turkey and Venezuela, where bus rides to road games were so long his ass would go numb, and the planes they flew on were so small that the seats required passengers to sit sideways. He dealt with two years of language barriers, social isolation, and unfamiliar food for a mere shot at making an NBA team. Not only was this camp a chance to accomplish that goal, it was an opportunity to do it while playing in New York, where he'd grown up and played on countless outdoor courts.

So Mason, who lacked a guaranteed contract and was far from a lock to make the roster, wasn't about to be punked by McDaniel. Not with the stakes this high. He had come too close to merely become an obligatory world traveler all over again.

"Mase treated the box-out drill like it was Game Seven of the Finals," says center Tim McCormick, who helped break up the brawl.

In some ways, McDaniel was Mason's opposite. Where Mason had to wander the globe before getting his audition in Charleston, McDaniel was a South Carolina native who'd traveled all of ninety minutes for the first practice. Months earlier, the scoring-challenged Knicks traded with the Phoenix Suns for the former No. 4 overall pick, who was coming off a season in which he'd averaged 17 points and seven rebounds. The Knicks planned to make him their starting small forward. Unlike Mason, Mc-Daniel's place with the club that year was as secure as superstar Patrick Ewing's. He had nothing to prove that day in camp.

Yet McDaniel was no more willing to back down than Mason. Mc-Daniel prioritized manhood. Specifically, his own manhood. According to McDaniel's teammates in Seattle, he often walked around the Sonics' locker room fully erect after games, hanging towels on his hardened member. Also, he fought people—and he fought them constantly.

"X wanted to fight *everybody*," says Frank Brickowski, a Sonics teammate during McDaniel's rookie season. "There were certain guys in the league you didn't fuck with, and X made it known very quickly that he was one of those guys." Brickowski learned the lesson quicker than anyone. In the 1985 preseason, during McDaniel's very first practice as a professional, he abruptly dropped Brickowski with a blow to the face. A few days later, as if to prove it was nothing personal, McDaniel also drilled fellow teammate Reggie King in the face with a three-punch combination.

Then, once there were actual games, McDaniel got to fight players who *weren't* on his team. By the end of his 1985–86 rookie campaign alone, he'd been in a total of nine separate scuffles. His most enduring image came one season later, in 1987, when McDaniel, in the words of *Sports Illustrated* writer Bruce Newman, attempted "to do the neck version of the Heimlich maneuver on Wes Matthews," choking him out to the point that Matthews's eyes began rolling into the back of his head.

"I never wanted to back down and be branded a wimp," McDaniel says years later of his scroll-length NBA fight card. "And in order to get respect, sometimes that was how we had to settle things."

Fortunately for Mason and McDaniel, that way of thinking wasn't a problem for their coach, who learned the importance of toughness at the age of nine. In grade school, Riley routinely received after-school beatings from older, bigger kids at a park in Schenectady, New York. One day, a boy wielding a butcher knife chased Riley home, leaving Riley so fearful that he hid in his garage for hours after being pursued. When Pat never came to the dinner table that night, his dad fished him out from the garage and told him enough was enough. Riley's father instructed his older sons to take Pat to the park the next day.

When the older boys asked why, Riley's father said the first step in developing Pat's toughness was to face his fears head-on.

"I want you to teach him not to be afraid," he told them.

From then on, Riley not only lost his fear of fights; on some level, he grew to crave them. In 1968, on his first date with girlfriend Chris Rodstrom, Riley took her to a San Diego boxing club to watch a bout. Rodstrom wore a white dress, which turned out to be an unfortunate choice. The couple was sitting ringside, and one of the very first punches of the fight sprayed blood all over Rodstrom's outfit. When Rodstrom didn't seem too bothered by it all, the scrappy Riley told himself, "This is my kind of girl."

Two years later, they were married.

If there was value for Riley in finding a wife who could tolerate seeing a little violence, the trait would also prove valuable for Knicks fans during the Riley era. Mason and McDaniel's run-in was far from the only one to take place during the team's training camp at the College of Charleston.

Even when there weren't skirmishes, physicality defined the practices. John Starks, who was entering his second year with the Knicks that fall, recalls hearing an array of Batman-like sound effects—*POW! THWACK! BONK! ZWAP!*—as bodies collided during that initial box-out drill.

Within minutes of that practice beginning, the usually fearless guard decided he had no interest in penetrating toward the hoop once scrimmages began. "Man, I'm not going to the basket today—I'm not going in there," he told himself. Another preseason invitee, Dan O'Sullivan, described layups in that training camp as "miracles" due to the sheer assault someone would have to endure in order to get one. "You were honestly a lot better off taking a twenty-footer," O'Sullivan recalls. "At least you'd live."

It was on that first day of camp the Knicks learned that *this* was Riley. This—not Showtime—was the culture Riley wanted to establish. One that would epitomize toughness by making teams pay for having the audacity to wander into the paint. One that would put a premium on conditioning so the club would have the stamina to finish close games. One that would treat Knick players like royalty, while normalizing the notion of a nasty streak by issuing fines to players who were kind enough to help up fallen opponents.

The coach's blueprint, which he loosely explained to his players inside the practice gym's locker room that morning, would dictate how the Knicks played basketball for the better part of the next decade.

Given the team's makeup—led by Ewing, and far more established in the frontcourt than in the backcourt—there was no point in Riley trying to craft an uptempo attack like he'd employed in Los Angeles. Instead, the Knicks were uniquely positioned to exploit their advantages on the defensive end.

By the fall of 1991, the smashmouth "Bad Boys" Detroit Pistons had been dethroned after back-to-back title runs. They were aging and running out of steam. But to Riley, their ideology remained sound. And with the Knicks being younger than the Pistons, the coach figured New York could maximize its chances of beating Michael Jordan and the defending-champion Chicago Bulls by tapping into the same bloody-knuckle, back-alley defensive tactics Detroit once thrived with.

Adopting that strategy might inch up to and occasionally step over the boundaries of what the NBA allowed. But for a team that desperately needed to close the talent gap—Jordan and the Bulls had swept the Knicks the postseason before—it might help. Riley even hired Harter, an ex-Pistons assistant credited with designing tenets of Detroit's brutal attack, to implement those same defensive principles in New York.

If the club was going to wear out opponents by bludgeoning them, and wear down referees by hacking so much that they'd simply stop calling fouls, the Knicks themselves would need to be in elite shape.

The first fifteen minutes of that camp-opening practice were devoted to an "easy run," Riley's ironically named exercise that sapped players of oxygen by requiring them to dart up and down the court with their arms raised to make their breathing more shallow. Later on, each Knick would take part in "17s," which meant seventeen sideline-to-sideline runs in under a minute's time, briefly resting, then repeating the process over and over until the coach saw fit. A few players grew light-headed from the exertion and sweltering conditions in the gym, which left the floor so wet that the team was forced to move to another court during practice.

"We weighed in to start the workout, and weighed out at the end. I was nine pounds lighter after," says forward Brian Quinnett, adding that players were handed bottles of Ensure after the session to rehydrate.

Quinnett was far from the only one who'd pay a physical price during practices that year. McCormick, the backup center, was tasked with serving as a practice partner to the mean, manhandling Charles Oakley.

That tackle-dummy role would have been highly unenviable for any player, let alone an aging vet going into his eighth year, with retirement on the horizon. Like most people, McCormick valued his limbs, and wanted to keep them—something that was never a given when sparring with the likes of Oakley. Each day, the men battled on the glass and in the low post. And most days, things played out the way you'd think.

"He was just so much stronger than me, and was beating me up in drills every day," McCormick says.

The beatings weren't exactly softened by an underlying friendship, either. In fact, for months, the two men never spoke. About their families. About opponents. About anything. McCormick simply showed up, day after day, and silently got the hell beaten out of him by Oakley.

Then, one day, when he'd finally had enough of Oakley's elbows in a drill, McCormick thrust his arm back wildly with the power forward standing behind him, catching Oakley in the mouth and causing him to bleed. As Oakley walked away to find a trainer, he shot McCormick an unmistakable death stare.

"I was convinced he was gonna kill me that next day," McCormick says. "But instead, he walks up, slaps me on the back, and asks how I'm doing. I was so confused, because it was the first time he had said *anything* to me. Then, as I thought about it, I realized: Charles never really respected me until I hit him."

That bizarre blossoming of a friendship between Oakley and McCormick was emblematic of those 1990s Knicks. They often didn't need words to get their message across. Instead, they spoke volumes and fundamentally altered the makeup of the sport through their primal physicality alone.

2

THANK GOD THEY DIDN'T HAVE HAND GRENADES

The Knicks were mercifully approaching the end of yet another brutal campaign when, on March 17, 1987, it looked like they might catch a break.

Temperatures outside were wintry, between 35 and 40 degrees. Still, more than one million New Yorkers—many drunk off green beer and dressed like leprechauns—had packed the city sidewalks to take in the annual St. Patrick's Day Parade.

There had also been a fair amount of anticipation heading into that Tuesday night at Madison Square Garden. Not because of anything fans expected from their lackluster team, which carried a 20-44 mark and was in the midst of a three-game skid. More so because of New York's opponent: the lowly Denver Nuggets, who were on a seven-game losing streak of their own. Maybe, just maybe, victory-starved fans would have a shot of leaving the Garden with smiles for a change.

As ticket holders entered the arena from the cold, they were handed rolled-up, life-size posters of Patrick Ewing—it was St. *Patrick's* Day, after all—complete with tick marks for each inch of his 7-foot frame.

But it wasn't long after fans took their seats that things turned as sour as a day-old Guinness. In what should have been a fair fight between NBA welterweights, the Knicks punched like armless mannequins. New York's offense handled the basketball with the care of a drunk; on the defensive end, the Knicks hacked Denver even more than they turned the ball over. The second-year Ewing, the franchise savior, was struggling badly. Everyone in a Knicks jersey was. Midway through the third period, the Nuggets, who'd lost 13 of their last 17, were up by 27 points.

New Yorkers had never been known for their patience, and tonight would prove no exception. A chorus of boos rained down from the crowd. And then, with New York down three touchdowns and two field goals, a fan launched his Ewing poster onto the court. Which prompted another to do the same. Then another. One particularly fed-up fan, sitting courtside, ripped his poster to shreds like a rabid animal.

"This one guy took his poster, unrolled it, and stuck his head through the middle of it," recalls Knicks assistant Brendan Malone, describing an image that brings to mind Jack Nicholson in *The Shining*. "I just felt bad for Patrick, because it got really ugly that night, and [the fans] seemed to take it all out on him."

Soon, the arena's ball boys began sprinting around the hallowed hardwood, furiously picking up dozens of the posters. John Condon, the team's longtime public address announcer, all but begged the fans to stop airmailing them from the stands. "We have ten excellent athletes on the floor," he pleaded, sounding like a helpless middle-school principal trying to break up a food fight.

Eventually, the game ended with the Knicks losing by 22. After the dust settled, general manager Scotty Stirling fielded a question from a reporter about the poster-throwing episode and what it said about the team's fans. After pausing for a moment, he responded.

"Thank God," Stirling said, "they didn't have hand grenades."

The New York Knickerbockers of the early 1970s were the hoop aficionado's team of choice. The kind of team that, years later, people would brag, "*Back in my day . . .*" about. The kind of team that won a certain way.

They won with their brains. Aside from having a couple of players who'd become NBA head coaches—including Phil Jackson, an eventual

Hall of Famer—New York's roster possessed a future PhD; a Rhodes scholar who'd become a US senator and presidential candidate; and a man who could memorize vast portions of the New York City phone book in one sitting.

Those clubs possessed skill. They packed the court with players capable of hitting open jump shots. They had an abundance of talent, yet were almost balletic—defined by synchronization, savvy, and on-court selflessness. Their players relied on making the extra pass so frequently that, years later, Jackson revealed the Knicks made a point to slightly deflate basketballs just before games would start. This disadvantaged opponents when they tried to dribble and didn't get the same bounce they were accustomed to. But it helped the Knicks, who were far more interested in passing the ball than dribbling it to begin with.

To many, this share-the-wealth mentality represented basketball in its purest form—a tribute to how the sport was meant to be played. And with it, the Knicks won two world championships, in 1970 and 1973.

Yet by the time the next decade rolled around, it was abundantly clear that *those* Knicks were not *these* Knicks. "The Garden has become a tomb," *Providence Journal* reporter Bill Reynolds wrote of the arena's lack of electricity in the 1980s. "The banners immortalizing the great Knicks of the past hang from the Garden rafters and stare down accusingly, as if the current Knicks are their wastrel sons."

Since they'd won their last title, the Knicks had devolved into a special kind of awful—the type of ball club that presented endless opportunities for grade-school cut-downs.

The Knicks are so bad, they play like they don't even bother practicing.
The Knicks are so bad, they play like they're on drugs.
The Knicks are so bad, they play like they're shaving points.

And here's the kicker: at the low point of the decade, all three of those things might have been true.

The first two certainly were.

Consider the 1981–82 season. Those Knicks had plenty of talent, having brought back nearly the exact same roster from a 50-win unit the campaign before. But instead of giving coach Red Holzman a worthy send-off in his final season on the bench, they spiraled into last place, playing uninspired basketball. As the Knicks fell into an ugly midseason tailspin, it would have been fair to expect the team would hold more practice sessions to tighten things up.

Yet after a while, no one even bothered to schedule workouts. Players had simply stopped showing up for them. "The drug thing was just killing the NBA, and guys on our team had more than their fair share of that problem, too. It was causing things to fall apart," says Paul Westphal, a Hall of Fame guard who joined the Knicks late that year, near the end of his career. "To not have practices because you know guys won't even bother to come to them? It was certainly a low point in Knicks history—you can say that."

"I had a friend in the city who would call me up and say, 'Hey, man: so-and-so is up here buying drugs,'" says Butch Beard, an assistant coach with the Knicks that year. "There were things I didn't even bother telling [Holzman], because he wasn't ready to hear that. He was used to the Clyde Fraziers and Willis Reeds, who were true pros. But those early-eighties teams were wild as hell, and the city gobbled them up."

Drug use may have had a role in the alleged point-shaving, too. In the spring of 1982, the FBI began an investigation into whether three Knick players that season were fixing games as a favor to a drug dealer, who was placing five-figure bets on New York's opponents. "A source observed heavy betting toward the latter part of the season . . . on the Knicks to lose certain games. In each case, the Knicks did lose, or failed to cover the spread," reads the bureau's file. (The probe, which redacted the names of the three players in question, closed in 1986 with no arrests due to a lack of confessions and physical evidence in the case.)

There were the feuds, like when guard Darrell Walker engaged in a shouting match with coach Hubie Brown during a practice in January 1986, then staged a sit-in during the team workout in Atlanta . . . by plopping down in the middle of the lane, forcing his teammates to shoot around him.

There were the distractions, like when a few players learned that one of the coaches on the team's staff was having an extramarital affair with a woman who lived in guard Trent Tucker's apartment complex—which irked the players, who'd been criticized all year for not showing professionalism.

There were the never-ending ailments—including major ones to key players like star scorer Bernard King and big man Bill Cartwright—which led to the Knicks shattering NBA records for most team games missed due to injury. (After breaking the league-record mark in 1985, the Knicks then blew past their own record in 1986.) There was even the rock-hard court they ran on at the team's practice facility at the time—Upsala College in New Jersey—which some felt played a role in the team's struggles to stay healthy. "It was complete shit. That facility was horrible," says Butch Carter, who played in 74 games with New York in 1984 and 1985. "I hadn't played on a floor that bad since seventh or eighth grade."

And then there was simply terrible basketball. During that decade, the Knicks occasionally finished quarters with more turnovers than points. Interim coach Bob Hill once jokingly threatened to fine his players for their horrendous rebounding, and things might have worked out better for everyone if he'd actually followed through. They ranked dead last by a wide margin in defensive rebounding in 1986–87. One columnist noted that the 7-foot-1 Cartwright was somehow grabbing fewer boards per minute than 5-foot-3 Muggsy Bogues, the NBA's shortest player by three inches, to start the season.

There was Ken Bannister, a seventh-round big man forced into action due to the laundry list of centers who'd been sidelined with injuries. Bannister might have been the worst free-throw shooter to ever don a New York uniform. He once left spectators slack-jawed when he grazed the right lower corner of the backboard on an attempt in one game. And he'd go on to miss ten straight free-throw tries in another contest.

There was Kenny "Sky" Walker, the University of Kentucky All-American taken with the No. 5 overall pick in the 1986 draft, who despite his pedigree had no idea how to throw a pass without shuffling his pivot foot and committing a traveling violation. When coach Rick Pitino stopped a passing drill during training camp in October 1987 to show Walker what he was doing wrong, Walker continued repeating the mistake. Flabbergasted that a heralded second-year pro couldn't grasp the concept of a pivot foot, Pitino ended up asking one of his assistants to take Walker to a side court to teach him, literally, how a pivot foot worked.

But perhaps most baffling of all during those 1980s years was the team's management group.

From 1986 to 1990 alone, the club's executives burned through five different coaches and three general managers. And for every move that worked out (dealing Cartwright for Charles Oakley, who'd become a foundational piece), there was an equally egregious one (trading away the first-round draft pick that would yield Hall of Famer Scottie Pippen for eighth-year guard and journeyman Gerald Henderson). "There were times, in those first three years after I got season tickets, that I was glad the executives running the Knicks weren't juggling chainsaws instead of running the Knicks. Because that would have been as ugly as some of those teams played," wrote Knicks superfan Spike Lee in his memoir.

Then, for a brief moment, there was hope. In 1987, the Knicks hired the 35-year-old Pitino to be their new coach. He won 38 games his first year, 52 in his second, with the Knicks reaching the playoffs each season. The sustainability of his strategy was up for debate. (Particularly the notion to have the team run a full-court press on defense for long stretches, which can wear down players—especially veterans—over the course of an 82-game season.) But after enduring three straight years with 24 wins or fewer, everyone embraced Pitino's tenure and the playoff trips that came with it.

Well, just about everyone. Knicks general manager Al Bianchi, who felt his bosses at the Garden had forced him to hire Pitino, had his differences with the coach. Bianchi was traditional; Pitino, with his press defense and ahead-of-its-time, bombs-away offense, was unconventional. And winning wasn't enough to salvage things. "There was a basic mistrust, both ways, from the start," Pitino said back then.

Those issues, and Pitino's preference for the college game, prompted the coach to ask for, and receive, the okay to negotiate with the University of Kentucky just two seasons into his five-year deal with the Knicks.

When Pitino took the Kentucky job, Bianchi was eager to show he could win without the coach. So he installed one of Pitino's assistants, Stu Jackson, to take over. It worked for a while, with the Knicks jumping out to an Eastern Conference–best 26-10 mark to begin the 1989–90 campaign. The hot start led Garden higher-ups to reward Bianchi with a multiyear extension offer in the middle of that season.

Curiously, Bianchi opted against signing it. Not because of money, or a disagreement on vision. The real reason? "He was in the midst of a divorce. And the situation was messy, so he decided to wait so his wife wouldn't be entitled to half," says Jehudith Cohen, Bianchi's executive assistant during those years.

Just one problem: shortly after that offer, the Knicks struggled mightily, losing 20 of their last 30 games before the postseason—a tailspin so severe that the Garden's bigwigs took Bianchi's unsigned extension off the table.

Jackson and the team managed to upset the Celtics in the first round, which perhaps saved Bianchi's job. But only temporarily. He landed a one-year extension that made him little more than a lame duck. "That might as well have been my death warrant," Bianchi would say decades later.

The short extension put Bianchi on notice, which then led the general manager to put Jackson on notice. And when New York slumped to begin the 1990–91 season, Bianchi quickly ousted the second-year coach before desperately replacing him midyear with someone from the outside, in John MacLeod. The Knicks snuck into the playoffs as the No. 8 seed, but the organization was a mess. The club would be swept in the first round by Michael Jordan and the Bulls, who'd go on to earn their first NBA title that summer.

Bianchi was terminated. The Garden replaced him with Dave Checketts, a 35-year-old who, seven years earlier, had become the youngest chief executive in league history. The 6-foot-4 man of Mormon faith had spent six years running the Utah Jazz, overseeing the drafts that landed John Stockton and Karl Malone.

In taking the Knicks' job, Checketts would quickly discover how different New York City was from Salt Lake City.

*   *   *

Well before he became the Knicks president, Checketts knew whom he wanted to coach the team.

The executive had walked away from Utah in 1989, and now, two years later, was settling into a new job with NBA International, which sought to broaden the sport's popularity into other countries. Commissioner David Stern had done a lot to land Checketts in the office, signing off on a relocation payment of thousands of dollars to move Checketts and his family of eight to Connecticut. But while Stern was thrilled to have Checketts on board, Checketts himself quickly grew bored with the job.

"I missed the competition so much. It becomes a way of life. You get addicted to winning," he says.

Checketts knew he wasn't alone in having that feeling. Months earlier, Pat Riley, in search of something to do after a nine-season, four-title run with the Lakers, had taken a job as an analyst with NBC Sports.

Checketts had spoken with Riley in passing a few times for different clinics with NBA International. But after a few months, he asked the ex-coach if he'd be up for having lunch in New York City.

When the two men met at the Regency Hotel in the fall of 1990, they reminisced about the fiery seven-game Western Conference semifinal series between the Jazz and Lakers back in 1988.

"There has to be some part of you that misses that, right?" Checketts asked Riley.

Then he pivoted.

Checketts told Riley he had a good feeling he'd be offered an opportunity to take over the stumbling Knicks sometime in the future. (The Knicks had expressed interest in Checketts before, but at the time, he hadn't been interested in leaving the ascendant Jazz.) If and when it actually happened, Checketts wanted to know whether Riley would consider coming with him to take the coaching job.

Riley was noncommittal. But after the way things had unraveled with the Lakers, any situation he stepped into would require unity. "We all would need to speak with one voice," Riley said.

The use of a hypothetical "we" left Checketts feeling hopeful.

Six months later, Checketts got the nod to take over the Knicks. He orchestrated a soft landing for coach John MacLeod—as the 1990–91 season ended, he quietly reached out to Notre Dame in hopes of getting MacLeod hired there—then shifted his focus to securing Riley. But he had no idea how challenging the task of hiring him would turn out to be.

By just about any measure, Riley was a fantastic NBA coach. But no one in the history of sports had ever handed someone a longer list of demands than Riley handed Checketts.

Wanting to be the highest-paid coach in the game, given what he'd accomplished with the Lakers, was understandable. And while the idea of asking the team to pay for his new home in the area was certainly unusual, if you were going to make that exception for anyone, you'd do it for someone of Riley's caliber. Beyond that, Riley wanted the team to facilitate a book deal. With the club being owned by Paramount, he wanted a potential movie deal as well. He also asked that his team-issued polo shirts actually be manufactured by Ralph Lauren's Polo brand. And if that laundry list wasn't enough, Riley added an *actual* laundry list. He asked the organization to pay for his laundry and dry-cleaning expenses, too. (On principle alone, Checketts and the Knicks put their foot down when it came to this particular request.)

Yet the highest hurdle Riley put in front of the Knicks was one they couldn't really control. At some point in the talks, he told Checketts he'd agree to take the job only if Patrick Ewing chose to stay with the team.

Going on his sixth coach and fourth general manager in six years, Ewing was frustrated, lacking faith in the Knicks' ability to build a winner around him. Through agent David Falk, Ewing had begun threatening to use a clause in his deal that'd make him a free agent that summer.

That Ewing potentially wanted out was no small matter. The fact that the Knicks had landed him at all back in 1985—they won the NBA's first draft lottery in controversial fashion—was one of the seminal moments for the league, which was still struggling to become relevant on a national stage. Having a bankable college star who drew frequent comparisons to

Bill Russell in the nation's largest market figured to be a coup for both the growing sport and the Knicks.

Falk fully understood that, and wisely used it as leverage when negotiating Ewing's rookie contract with the team. Not only was Ewing's 10-year, $32 million agreement the richest deal in NBA history at the time; it also contained a first-of-its-kind provision that would allow Ewing to become a free agent if his pact fell outside the league's four highest-paid contracts. And with Ewing sitting at No. 4 in 1991—behind Cleveland's John "Hot Rod" Williams, Houston's Hakeem Olajuwon, and Chicago's Jordan—Falk was looking for other players whose paychecks could eclipse Ewing's.

There were indications Falk sought to have the Warriors restructure Chris Mullin's contract by moving some of the money from the back end of his deal to instead pay it in 1991–92. For Golden State, such a move would have made Mullin the fourth-highest-paid player that year, while knocking Ewing from that group. And in theory, by making Ewing a free agent, it would have allowed the Warriors an opportunity to sign him away from New York.

But when the Knicks caught wind of the alleged deal—Mullin's agent, Bill Pollak, also represented Oakley, and told the Knicks' front office—they threatened to file tampering charges and to tie the Warriors up with litigation if they moved forward with such a plan. Golden State backed down.

Still, Falk pushed ahead to free Ewing, arguing that Boston's Larry Bird, who would make $7.1 million in earnings in 1991–92, was in line to displace Ewing from the top four, making the Knicks center a free agent. Again, New York disagreed, saying Bird's base salary that season was ultimately lower than Ewing's.

The dispute posed a conundrum for Checketts. On the one hand, he had Ewing looking for an escape window and a parachute, convinced the Knicks might not ever win. On the other, the coach the Knicks desperately needed was saying he'd only come on board if the star stuck around.

In short, the Knicks executive was trying to handle a pair of delicate negotiations that, if not handled perfectly, could irreparably harm the franchise. Martin Davis, the chief executive of Paramount and de facto team owner, drove that point home in a brief conversation with Checketts.

"Dave," Davis warned him, "don't you dare fuck this up."

After ample back-and-forth with Riley and Ewing, Checketts arranged separate sit-downs with them on May 31, 1991. He would meet Riley at the Regency Hotel on the Upper East Side, then head fifteen blocks north to the Mark Hotel to speak with Ewing and Falk.

As he spoke with Riley, Checketts said there was no runway left. He told Riley he'd be holding a press conference with the media later that day—in which he'd either be introducing Riley as the team's next coach, or announcing the club had been forced to go a different route. Checketts also said he couldn't guarantee Ewing's place on the roster, meaning Riley would need to make his decision without knowing if he'd have the franchise centerpiece.

Checketts exited Riley's suite, telling him he'd leave him some time to consider his options.

A half hour later, the phone inside Checketts's hotel room rang. It was Riley.

"I just needed to find out what you were made of—to know the man I'm working for isn't willing to be pushed around. Now I know," Riley said, accepting the job.

It was the news Checketts wanted to hear, but he still had more to do. He jumped into a limo stationed in front of the hotel to see Ewing, hoping Riley's commitment would assuage the star center's concerns. It didn't. Falk and Ewing said they still planned to go to arbitration in hopes of exercising the early termination clause in the contract.

The Knicks were uneasy about going to arbitration. They felt good about their argument and the way they'd interpreted the language in Ewing's contract. Still, losing the ruling would be borderline disastrous. No matter how you sliced it, the 28-year-old was a five-time All-Star and franchise player. The club had entertained trades for him before. But few names could yield equal value in a deal. And few clubs could absorb Ewing's high salary while also staying under the salary cap.

So it was a huge win for the team when the arbitrator ruled in the Knicks' favor, saying Ewing wasn't eligible for free agency. But it didn't change the center's desire to leave the team. At least not right away.

Shortly after the ruling, Riley flew out to Washington to have a heart-to-heart with Ewing. As the men prepared to sit down inside a hotel room, Ewing handed Riley a sheet of paper. The list contained six teams—the Warriors, Blazers, Suns, Lakers, Celtics, and Bullets—Ewing said he would be content landing with. He had four years left on his deal, and didn't think he wanted to stay in New York.

Riley studied the team names on the list for a moment before focusing his attention back on Ewing. He knew the big man was frustrated. He legitimately understood his desire for a fresh start. But for Riley, everything came back to a relatively simple concept, one he'd grown familiar with in Los Angeles.

"I want you to think about something," Riley said. "Close your eyes and think of a championship parade on Broadway. Think about what that would mean to New York. And what it'd mean to you."

Ewing wasn't sold right away. But the image Riley conjured—a parade snaking its way through Manhattan, with confetti falling like rain—stayed with Ewing. And because Riley gave him something to aspire to, the conversation ultimately helped Ewing decide he should stay with the Knicks.

3

THE REINVENTION OF PAT RILEY

Pat Riley absolutely lived for soul music. More specifically, he lived for Motown music.

"My Girl," the megahit by the Temptations, had long been one of Riley's favorites. So had "This Old Heart of Mine," the 1965 track by the Isley Brothers, a tune he enjoyed so much he asked the Knicks' game-operations crew to play the song whenever he walked onto the Garden floor before each game.

Perhaps because of his love of Motown and soul, one of Riley's trademark practice drills borrowed heavily from *Soul Train*, the iconic dance television show led by baritone-voiced host Don Cornelius. Specifically, Riley replicated the "Soul Train Line," the portion of the show where dancers formed an aisle on the floor to allow people with bell-bottom pants, perfectly coiffed Afros, and platform shoes to strut toward the camera to do effortless cartwheels, shimmies, spins, and splits.

Yet where the show's version of the exercise was gleeful and smooth, Riley's was bloody and bruising.

During an early-season practice in Purchase, New York, the new Knicks coach lined six of his players on one side of the free-throw line and six on the other, telling them to throw every possible shoulder and elbow into guard Gerald Wilkins, who would try his best to somehow race through the lane unscathed.

"I'll never forget it. He puts me on the baseline and says, 'Okay, Gerald—if you run through all of them, then we ain't having practice to-morrow,'" Wilkins recalls. "Now you *know* we wanted that day off. But at the same time, those guys weren't just gonna let me through, either. They just weren't wired that way."

So Wilkins shook out his legs and stretched his neck. He took a deep breath, Riley blew his whistle, and Wilkins took off running, closing within a few feet of the first two players, both of whom were standing there ready to clock him. But in that split-second, Wilkins decided to run completely outside the line, like a running back who saw open space along the sideline.

"Right as I was gonna run through the line, I said to myself, 'Hell naw!'" Wilkins says. "Wasn't worth it."

The drill was an insight into the kind of physicality he demanded from his players, even in practices. It spoke to how a distinguished-looking, Motown-loving coach, who'd presided over a smooth attack with the Lakers, could flip the script into something violent.

Forward Kiki VanDeWeghe had to literally brace himself for prac-tices. He'd been in a car accident that broke two of his ribs the month before training camp began. So in the twilight of his career, he wore a flak jacket to protect his torso from the knocks that were sure to come from teammates.

Had the Knicks thought ahead, they might have issued flak jackets for members of the coaching staff, too.

Unsatisfied with his team's defense at one point, Riley had players take part in a help-and-recovery practice drill. He felt the Knicks were too often getting caught in no-man's-land—not quite running hard enough at perimeter shooters to alter their shots, but also not in a good enough stance to be able to stop players from driving past them into the paint. So Riley instructed his assistant coaches to serve as shooters, while the players would do their best to either close out on the shot, or at least seal off a driving lane.

On the first go-round, Anthony Mason half-heartedly rotated over on defense to get in front of assistant Bob Salmi before softly tumbling over onto the hardwood in an effort to take a charge. As Mason prepared to stand back up, Riley was furious, sensing Mason hadn't given anywhere near his full effort to defend the play.

"See! That's what I'm talking about! We don't do the things we need to do on defense!" Riley shouted. "You're playing soft! Are you seriously afraid to take a charge from Salmi?" He demanded that Mason repeat the drill.

Agitated by Riley's criticism, Mason rose to his feet. Salmi, meanwhile, walked back to the three-point line terrified, knowing Riley's criticism would only light a fire under Mason, and might send him over the edge. As they ran the drill again, Salmi this time dribbled into the paint with everything he had, knowing that sort of effort would be necessary to counter Mason's physicality. And when the play was over, there was a man on the ground, just like the first time. But unlike before, Mason was left standing.

Salmi lay on the court wincing and struggling to get back on his feet. "I tried to run him over. But I ended up bouncing off the guy," says Salmi, who, after being flattened, learned he'd fractured two ribs.

These were practice sessions on a level most had never experienced. Riley, preaching the notion of dedication, was a man whose workouts regularly ran more than three hours. Most other teams worked out for ninety minutes, or two hours, tops. A number of players contend that New York's shootarounds—held the morning of a game and designed to help players loosen up as they walk through their game plan—were more involved than other clubs' full-scale *practices*. Riley shootarounds often went two hours and were full contact. Riley had his players get their ankles taped up for the sessions, like they would for actual games.

Not everyone was a fan of this.

Forward Xavier McDaniel vividly remembers what, to him, felt like a never-ending shootaround the morning of a December 26, 1991, home game against the Spurs. "We had a three-hour workout that day, where he ran us hard," McDaniel says. "After that, I went back to the team hotel. By then, it was like 1 [p.m.] and I'm exhausted. I don't even bother showering, I'm so spent. I take a nap, and next thing I know is, I wake up, and it's six something. I'd almost overslept the game! I'd never done that in my career. Not once."

By the time McDaniel walked into the locker room at 6:45, his team-mates were already dressed and ready to take the floor, already having gone through the scouting report. And what ensued was one of the forward's worst games of the season: a 3-for-11 shooting night, with an even worse showing on defense, where he offered the resistance of an unlocked subway turnstile, allowing Sean Elliott to blow past him repeatedly. The Knicks didn't fare any better, getting blasted by 29 points in front of the Garden crowd.

Inside the locker room after the game, McDaniel made a beeline for Riley. "Shit, Pat—I'm out here playing my second game of the day because of how hard you ran us this morning!" McDaniel screeched.

Riley managed to keep the situation from boiling over by telling Mc-Daniel the locker room wasn't the right place for that conversation, and that they'd discuss the issue in his office after the coach finished address-ing the team. But behind closed doors, they clashed. McDaniel ripped the coach for his lengthy game-day workouts. Riley, in turn, called out McDaniel for not taking part in the club's mandatory weight-lifting rou-tine, for which he'd been fining McDaniel, the team's marquee offseason pickup, $5,000 a month.

The disagreement—with the player saying he'd been worked to the point of ineffectiveness, but the coach firing back that the player actually hadn't worked hard enough—spoke volumes about Riley.

In his world, there was no such thing as working too hard.

Just like it had taken only a few minutes into his first practice with the Knicks for Riley to learn what kind of team he'd have in New York, it hadn't taken long for Riley's first professional coach to sum up what he thought of the rookie back in 1967.

After having back surgery his senior year at Kentucky, Riley was struggling mightily just minutes into his first practice with the San Diego Rockets. A classic tweener, Riley often wasn't quick enough to stay in front of guards defensively, nor was he tall enough at 6-foot-4 to enjoy a size advantage on offense. All the while, Jack McMahon, who doubled

as San Diego's coach–general manager and drafted Riley, looked on from
the sideline with concern before pulling Riley aside.

"I drafted you, my job is depending on you, and that is the *worst* five
minutes of basketball I've ever seen," McMahon told him.

When Riley, a forward in college, told McMahon he'd never played
guard before, McMahon shot back, "You'd better learn."

It was an instructive moment for Riley. He had always been the best,
most athletic player on the court—aside from handling jump balls for
Kentucky, he was selected by the Dallas Cowboys as a wide receiver in
the 1967 NFL Draft—but now he was going to have to work harder than
ever to earn his keep.

So he put in the sweat equity to carve out a small role with the Rockets, scoring 7.6 points per game in sixteen minutes a night over three
seasons. When the league grew in 1970, necessitating an expansion draft,
San Diego left Riley on its unprotected list, allowing the Portland Trail
Blazers to sign him away. Months later, the Blazers turned around and
sold Riley's rights to the powerhouse Lakers—boasting the likes of Jerry
West, Wilt Chamberlain, Elgin Baylor, and Gail Goodrich—where he'd
get an even more defined role than what he'd had in San Diego. The man-
date wasn't complicated. "His number one task was to beat the hell out of
me," said West, the recipient of frequent bruises due to Riley's physicality
on defense.

For Riley, who won the 1972 title with the Lakers, the strong effort
stemmed from fear of losing his spot. He didn't know what he'd be without basketball. And given the way his father's life had crumbled after
leaving professional baseball, Riley wasn't in any rush himself to find out.

Born in upstate New York on March 20, 1945, as the youngest of Leon
and Mary Riley's six kids, Pat grew up in a strict family that was quiet and
somewhat cold, both literally and figuratively. (His mother often sat atop
the home's heat register to stay warm.) A family where a punishing pop
on the behind from the father was far more common than an affection-
ate comment. "I can't remember my father ever telling me he loved me,"
Riley said in a 2017 *ESPN The Magazine* profile. "Not much from my
mother, either."

Riley grew up in the blue-collar, industrial town of Schenectady at 58 Spruce Street, a two-story home. But the Rileys spent a decent amount of time on the road due to the patriarch's baseball career, and the travel it required. The elder Riley played as an outfielder for nineteen different minor-league clubs over twenty-two years (he sat out the 1943 season to work in a defense plant during World War II) before finally getting the chance to play in the majors in 1944. The Philadelphia Phillies called him up to the big leagues at the age of 37, just ten months before Pat was born. Lee appeared in only four games, with one hit—a double—in twelve at-bats before Philadelphia sent him back down to the minors, where he'd stay for the last few years of his career.

Lee eventually transitioned from player-managing to just managing in the Phillies' minor-league system. (He even coached a young pitcher named Tommy Lasorda, who entertained a toddling Pat in the dugout before games.) But Lee Riley lost his job in the fall of 1952, when the Phillies cut their farm system from twelve teams to nine. That same night, a despondent Riley walked into the attic of his home on Spruce Street, grabbed every bit of baseball memorabilia he could, and burned it, blazing two decades' worth of work.

The abrupt nature of how his shot at the majors ended at 44—as a player and a manager—soured him not only on the sport, but on life in general. After seeing a pair of his businesses fizzle out, he turned to heavy drinking and stormed the court during one of Pat's high school games to drunkenly confront a referee over a call that had gone against his son.

Walt Pryzbylo, the team's coach, rushed in and mercifully escorted Riley's father off the court. But Lee's fall—to go from being on the cusp of a dream to losing all sense of worth and purpose—stayed with Pat.

It was a feeling Pat wanted to stave off the best he could in his own life.

Try as he might, that feeling of emptiness came for Riley anyway.

It hit him square in the stomach just months into his retirement in 1976, when Riley attended a Lakers home game. After it ended, he made his way toward the press lounge, where writers, broadcasters, and those more closely affiliated with the team in some way could stand and mingle. But as Riley tried to head into the room, a security guard stopped him, saying former players weren't allowed in the lounge.

"I walked out of there a little crushed," said Riley, who'd thought his relationships in and around the team could endure. But even if Riley wasn't ready to cut the cord, the organization he'd played for clearly was.

Depressed and unsure what to do with his newfound abundance of time, Riley began going to State Beach every day. As the Pacific tide rolled in, he sat against a wall and wrote, filling yellow legal pads with thoughts. Maybe they could form the foundation for a book. If not, they'd merely be the ramblings of an ex-ballplayer seeking a new identity. He was open to anything. Maybe he could be a junior college coach. He thought about taking a position as a manager at a friend's clothing store, but even that opportunity fell through.

Riley's saving grace eventually came in the form of a broadcasting job. In 1977, Chick Hearn, who was twelve years into what would become a legendary sportscasting run with the Lakers, approached Riley about becoming his color analyst. Though he thought Riley sounded a bit nasal in his practice tapes, Hearn handed over what he deemed Riley's best to Lakers owner Jack Kent Cooke, who was impressed.

The $20,500-per-year gig actually marked the second time Hearn had intervened to help Riley land a job with the Lakers. After an exhibition game between the Blazers and Lakers in 1970, and at a time when Riley felt he'd be cut by Portland, he spoke with Hearn about his situation. Hearn liked Riley's hard-nosed playing style, and said he'd put in a good word with Cooke. Days later, the Lakers bought the rights to Riley's deal.

In the color job, which also required Riley to operate as the Lakers' traveling secretary, Riley developed a pair of key skills: an unmatched attention to detail, and a sense of when to chime in and when to let his partner have the floor. The latter proved useful about two years later, when the unexpected happened, and Lakers coach Jack McKinney suffered a near-fatal head injury during a cycling accident early in the 1979–80 season. It prompted the Lakers to hire Riley on as an assistant coach—a role

Riley was reluctant to accept until he was given assurances he could get his color job back once McKinney returned to the Lakers sideline.

Los Angeles was loaded with talent, touting dominant center Kareem Abdul-Jabbar, who'd already won five league MVP awards, and star rookie Earvin "Magic" Johnson, who at 6-foot-9 could handle and pass the ball in a fluid, effortless fashion no one had ever seen someone do at his size. It helped that McKinney put in place the uptempo, "Showtime" style of play that would maximize Johnson's vision and skill set, making it a far easier tactical transition for Riley and interim head coach Paul Westhead. And a number of Laker players spoke openly of their appreciation for Westhead not feeling the need to complicate the team's playbook by stubbornly putting his own stamp on things in the midst of the season.

The club took its talent and McKinney's game plan and won the NBA title in 1980 under Westhead. But the honeymoon ended when the Lakers dropped their first-round series with Houston in 1981.

Ahead of the 1981–82 season, Westhead went back to the drawing board and tried to install an offense that'd make Los Angeles better in half-court situations. Just one problem: the Lakers, and Johnson in particular, really didn't want a new offense. So eleven games into the year, Johnson told reporters he couldn't play in Westhead's system, and he wanted a trade. Which ultimately spelled the end for Westhead.

That's where Riley entered the picture. Sort of. New Lakers owner Jerry Buss tried to hand the coaching job directly to West, the former Laker great. But West didn't want it; at least not long-term. So when Buss announced the coaching change at a press conference, he bizarrely introduced West as the team's offensive captain, while saying Riley would stay on to lead the Lakers' defense. Reporters pressed Buss for clarity on the official division of labor. Then West simplified things for everyone. "I'm going to be working *for* Pat Riley," West said. "With and for . . . Because I feel in my heart that he's the head coach."

So at just 36, Riley nervously took over the team whose press lounge had been off-limits to him just a few years earlier. With a multitude of thoughts flooding his mind before his head-coaching debut against the Spurs, Riley said he had forty-five pages of notes written out for a ten-minute pregame talk for his players. But he scuttled most of it, realizing he'd be better off letting Johnson and the other players go back to the basics.

"We didn't want anybody who could come in and change the systems we had. The best coaches leave the players alone," Lakers guard Norm Nixon said. "The years I was there, Riley . . . man, he just let us play."

Riley's egoless approach yielded instant results. The aging Lakers won four championships in their first seven seasons with him, including back-to-back crowns in 1987 and 1988. They were expected to win even more, and the coach, thinking ahead to 1989, went so far as to trademark the phrase "three-peat," which would allow him to cash in on the Lakers' commercial appeal if they won a third straight trophy.

But by then, an undeniable degree of strain had developed between Riley and his players. They had grown tired of his speeches, which almost felt rooted more in the psychological than the physical; as if they were patients on a couch, as opposed to players on a court. They chafed at Riley's increased use of the media to get messages across to them. More than anything, the Lakers were agitated by what they perceived to be a massive increase in Riley's stature and ego. In seven years, Riley had gone from a co-coach Buss didn't initially trust to handle the job on his own to becoming a best-selling author, a motivational speaker who could command $20,000 per talk, and a face that would grace not only billboards, but magazine covers.

"What happened was, he made more money, commercials, and things than players did," Johnson said.

As the Lakers lost trust in their coach, their coach grew paranoid, losing trust in just about everything.

In 1990, his last year with the club, Riley began to worry that maybe the Laker Girls were somehow becoming too big a distraction in the late stages of games. So he pulled aside Mitch Chortkoff, who wrote for the *Santa Monica Evening Outlook*, hoping to plant a seed for a story about the dancers' presence, hoping it might prompt Lakers management to pull them from the sidelines more often. That same season, the coach—who'd been vocal behind closed doors about never having been honored for his coaching ability—won Coach of the Year, but then initially told John Black, the team's public relations man, he didn't feel like doing a news conference to accept the award.

He did ultimately end up doing one. "Of course he did," Black said of Riley. "But that's what it was like all year long. Every day I'd go into him with interview requests, and he was just a miserable prick."

The Lakers' joyless 63-win season came to an end with a second-round loss in five games to the Suns.

A few years later, well after he left the Lakers, Riley published a book titled *The Winner Within*, which included a chapter called "The Disease of Me." In it, he describes the affliction at length, saying a team dynamic can be undermined by an individual's belief in his or her own importance.

But regardless of how Riley took stock of the Lakers' breakup—seeing it as his fault, the players' fault, or maybe a bit of both—the experience colored the way he approached his job with the Knicks. His paranoia was still present. And it led him to ask for, and receive, broad power in terms of dictating who could and couldn't have proximity to his players.

Shortly after getting the Knicks job, Riley took steps to distance a handful of team staffers from the players. Longtime broadcasters Marv Albert and Walt "Clyde" Frazier, whose analysis was pointed at times, would no longer fly with the club. Team scouts would now have to get clearance in advance if they'd be in town and wanted to attend a practice. Pastor John Love, the longtime unofficial chaplain, recalls the Riley hire having a chilling effect with a handful of players, who felt the coach quietly objected to their pregame prayer sessions. (It wasn't an unfounded thought. Swen Nater, who played for Riley with the Lakers, says Riley noticed him reading his Bible on team flights, and that the coach expressed concern that reading it too frequently might reduce Nater's on-court aggression.) Team psychologist Frank Gardner kept his job upon Riley's arrival, but was relegated to doing predraft work with draft prospects. He was told he'd no longer work with the Knick players, even though he had prior relationships with many of them.

"I was told, 'He doesn't want any other voice in the room besides his own.' And I remember that language, specifically, because I found it to be such an interesting way of putting it," says Gardner, who was given the news by president Dave Checketts and general manager Ernie Grunfeld. (Gardner says Riley later called to share the same message. It would turn out to be the only time he and Riley spoke.)

Riley seldom got pushback on these sorts of changes. But early in his New York tenure, he made a seemingly abrupt decision to let go of a basketball operations staffer—one who was popular not only with a number of his players, but also with other members of the organization. Riley, sensing a quiet tension had built over the dismissal, decided to address it as he prepared to end practice a day or two later.

Yes, the staffer was liked by many, he acknowledged. "But sometimes in a situation, you have to shoot a hostage in the head, then look around and say, 'Who the fuck is next?'" Riley said in a serious tone.

Maniacal as it was, this was Riley's way of trying to build a foxhole, and an us-against-the-world sort of bond. And for how extreme Riley's tactics could be, he managed to earn the respect of most players, especially ones who had been with the Knicks in earlier seasons. They quickly took note of his dedication to putting key changes in place, like the team getting its own private plane. Similarly, Riley arranged to have the players put up in a Midtown Manhattan hotel on home-game days, so the athletes could relax instead of having to drive back home to the suburbs after shootarounds, then return to the city for games mere hours later.

Even when the team was in Charleston for training camp, Riley wanted things a certain way for his players. One particular night, he asked team officials to rent out Garibaldi's, an upscale Italian restaurant near the club's hotel, to hold a dinner for players, coaches, and trainers only. He gave specific instructions about how he wanted the room laid out. And upon inspecting the venue himself, Riley was just as particular, bending down to pick up a folded cloth napkin on one table.

"Then he changed the configuration of the napkin, flagged someone down, and said he wanted them arranged *that* way instead," says Ed Tapscott, the team's administrative director that year. "And I said to myself, 'Oh my God, has this guy got attention to detail or what?'"

Brian Quinnett pulled Riley aside in the New York Rangers' locker room at the Garden during the 1991–92 season, asking what he should work on in hopes of becoming a bigger part of the rotation.

Riley asked the third-year guard whether he wanted his honest answer. Quinnett said he did.

"Honestly? I think you come from a white, middle-class background, and you play like you're not hungry enough," Riley said.

The response stunned Quinnett, not only because there hadn't been that much to judge him on yet—"I wasn't even getting all that much playing time [under Riley] in preseason," he says—but also because Riley's critique felt like such a broad analysis to him. Perhaps one more rooted in Riley's own playing experience.

If Quinnett worried that Riley's comment was an omen, months later he was proven right. In February, the Knicks traded him to Dallas, which might as well have been Siberia, given how awful the Mavericks were. Yet while Quinnett felt frustrated by what he considered a rather general response from Riley, it was one of the few times—perhaps the only time—someone had accused him of not having done his homework.

Championship experience aside, Riley brought to New York a handful of ways to analyze the game more deeply than most other teams were doing at the time.

While film study wasn't a new concept in the NBA by the time Riley joined the Knicks in 1991—the notion swept through the league more during the 1980s—the coach saw enormous value in video, and was already finding ways to manipulate it to focus on specific things. His color work with Hearn in the late 1970s, where he'd watch video specialists pare down clips for television, helped give him a sense of what to ask and look for. And players in training camp were given assignments after they completed their two-a-day workouts: for each man to watch tapes of eight players they'd be tasked with guarding during the season, and then be quizzed on them the following day.

For his own purposes, Riley asked Salmi, also the team's video coordinator, to produce "late-game tapes," ones that would distill opponent's nail-biter games down to the final three or four minutes, with one offensive sequence after another. The idea, which Salmi had never heard or thought of before, allowed Riley to prepare for precisely what actions teams would be running with the game hanging in the balance.

The more specific film breakdowns represented just one of many things Salmi would now be asked to do.

His biggest undertaking that year was learning to input data into a computer to track statistics that would help Riley assess players' performances on a positional, league-wide scale. "He'd group players from 1 to 10, with a 1 being a point guard, a 5 being a center, a 6 being a backup point guard, and a 10 being a backup center," Salmi says. "And he'd have me feeding all their data—scoring, efficiency, rebounding, defense—into a spreadsheet system. Excel didn't exist yet, so I was using something called Lotus 1-2-3."

The result was an early sketch for what, fifteen years later, would essentially be known as player-efficiency rating, or PER. Among other things, Riley had Salmi track how New York performed in each player's minutes, a universal metric in today's game known as plus-minus. Assistant coaches also tallied how frequently the team boxed out, took charges, closed out on jumpers, and missed defensive rotations.

Needless to say, everyone on the staff kept busy. "Before Pat got to New York, most [assistants] would golf a time or two per week," Salmi says. "But then he takes over, and there's barely enough time in the day to get to all the stuff he's asked for."

Deep-dive work was only part of it, though. The new-look Knicks still had to go out and win. And their first two games under Riley, surprising losses to the Orlando Magic and Miami Heat—a pair of recent expansion teams—weren't very promising.

By that point, losing wasn't an uncommon result for the Knicks, who'd long teetered on the line of mediocrity. But to Riley, losing was torture. A particularly frustrating loss might prompt him to take sleeping pills to stop game sequences from replaying themselves in his head. And Riley saw an acupuncturist in Los Angeles to unknot the tension in his shoulders whenever the Lakers lost two games in a row.

After the loss to Miami that dropped the Knicks to an 0-2 start, players picked up on one of Riley's private habits when they smelled the acrid stench of cigarette smoke filtering out through his office door.

When the team met for practice two days later, players barely recognized their coach—usually pristine and clean-shaven—who had three days' worth of stubble on his face. "He was looking for answers, and you could tell it was keeping him up at night to try and find them," recalls center Tim McCormick.

Not even one week into the season, New York had reached a small fork in the road. Were the Knicks about to turn Riley into the Coach Who Never Sleeps? Or would they find the winner within?

4

KNOCK MICHAEL JORDAN TO THE FLOOR

Having been hired in March 1991, just in time to see the 39-win Knicks sneak into the playoffs and get swept by Michael Jordan and the Bulls, president Dave Checketts put several plans in motion at the end of the season.

Shortly after signing Pat Riley, Checketts arranged focus groups for season-ticket holders, speaking to a passionate group that—with attendance sputtering at just 80 percent—had begun losing patience with the club's direction. Checketts poured far more money into the team's marketing budget. (One of the staff's best ideas: a zoomed-in photo of Riley's left hand, with a Lakers championship ring on each finger, and a caption reading "He's Saving the Other Hand for New York." But Riley rejected it, and it never ran.)

Around that same time, the club hung an enormous, eight-sided jumbotron—the first of its kind—above the Garden floor. The team outsourced the task of creating music playlists for home games to Craig Balsam and Cliff Chenfeld, a pair of New York University Law School alums, and let Jesse Itzler, a 22-year-old Jewish rapper, write a catchy tune called "Go New York Go" that would serve as the Knicks anthem. (All three men parlayed their experiences with the club to get similar work from other NBA teams. And they each later became multimillionaires.)

Checketts also backed the notion of starting a Knicks dance team—an idea owner Stanley Jaffe hated so much that he began throwing notebooks in a conference room during a meeting on the subject, yelling

"Turn it off! Get this shit off my TV!" when shown an example of what the performances might look like.

Looking back, Checketts says there was a reason he chose to invest so heavily in those secondary things.

"Honestly, I thought we were going to struggle [as a team] for a little while, and I wasn't sure how long it would take us to compete," he says. "When I took the job, sometimes these massive boos would rain down, and it felt like our players hated playing at home, because our fans were so tough on them. So to me, it was a question of 'How can we distract the crowd until we really put this thing together?'"

By starting 0-2 under Riley, the Knicks hadn't done anything to mitigate Checketts's concerns. But after posting a string of stellar defensive efforts—Riley instantly approved of the John Starks–Greg Anthony bench tandem, referring to the duo as "assault"—New York recovered, building a 22-11 mark by January.

Save for Patrick Ewing, the team's offense was less than stellar; prone to droughts, indecision, and drives to the basket that prompted collisions between teammates due to the lack of spacing inside.

Xavier McDaniel was often hesitant, with coaches trying to talk him out of his habit of pump faking unnecessarily. McDaniel, who'd been acquired to serve as the team's second option, could be hit-or-miss—logging two points in a loss to Chicago one game, then scoring 37 in Boston the next night.

Surprisingly, Starks had come out of nowhere as a reserve to fill that second scorer's role. But he possessed the same hot-and-cold tendencies, albeit with a more decisive mind-set. Anthony, the lefty guard, played hard but shot unsightly jumpers that rarely went where they were supposed to. The guard's attempts were so wayward that coaches quietly played Rock, Paper, Scissors to determine which unlucky assistant would rebound for him following practices. "I was in the best shape of my life rebounding for him, because it was so hard," assistant Bob Salmi says. "With good shooters, or even decent shooters, they usually hit the front rim or the back rim, where the rebound is right there. With Greg, he'd miss and the ball's not *anywhere* near the basket. It ends up going out the door, or down the stairs. Sometimes, I'd just walk over to the rack and get another ball. Because the rack might be forty feet away, but his rebound is something like a hundred feet away, and I'm not going to chase that shit."

Yet there was another, more subtle problem with the team's offense: a handful of players felt starting point guard Mark Jackson had a tendency to play favorites in terms of where he'd go with the ball.

"He'd pass it to me, and make it seem like he was doing me some favor," guard Brian Quinnett says.

That feeling, even if blown out of proportion, had the potential to create strife. For example, Quinnett recalls Kiki VanDeWeghe making a joke with some teammates. After games, VanDeWeghe might say he was "3-for-5." But while that usually means making three shots in five tries, in this context VanDeWeghe meant how many shots he managed to *take* in the five times he touched the ball.

The takeaway was simple: VanDeWeghe was going to play somewhat selfishly, shooting as often as he possibly could, since the basketball wasn't coming his way most sequences.

By the time the Knicks made it to Oakland for their West Coast trip in late January, they had lost four of their last five contests, the team's first real rut since it had stumbled out of the gate back in November.

At the beginning of the skid, New York wasn't scoring enough in losses to Portland and Milwaukee. But in the latter two defeats, to Cleveland and Philadelphia, the defense was a sieve, surrendering an average of 113 points. For whatever reason, there was little to no cohesion to what the Knicks were doing anymore.

Riley had players unite in a hotel ballroom during a walk-through in Oakland. When they got there, players saw four round tables—with chairs surrounding each one—in different pockets of the space.

Riley assigned Charles Oakley, Ewing, Jackson, and McDaniel to sit down at the first table. He sat Starks, Anthony, and Gerald Wilkins at a second table. VanDeWeghe, Quinnett, and center Tim McCormick were at the third. Anthony Mason, Patrick Eddie, and Kennard Winchester sat at the final one.

Once they were seated the way Riley wanted, he diagnosed what he saw as a lingering problem. "We're a bunch of cliques rather than a team, and that's the way we've been playing lately," Riley said, adding that he'd arranged the groups that way because it was how the players generally split themselves up anyway.

Ewing's table marked the veterans who'd made names for themselves already, and had a sense of status. The guards at the second table had bonded over the course of the year. The third table encompassed each of the team's white players, while the fourth comprised young players trying to establish their footing.

In the meeting, Riley made clear that he didn't need the players to be best friends with each other. He just didn't want them to potentially drift or splinter as a group, either by never interacting, or by interacting in a way that could jeopardize the team. One of those concerns was the notion of gambling.

Like players on every club, the Knicks were highly competitive, wanting to win at everything. That was the case privately, with Ewing— a former No. 1 overall pick, who'd earn $125 million over his playing career—who frequently bought lottery tickets. ("I told him, 'Patrick: You've already won the lottery several times over!'" says trainer Mike Saunders.) And it was the case between teammates who'd race each other to see which player could get to the practice first, like Oakley and Jackson did in their Ford and Toyota SUVs, respectively. (Jackson ended up getting pulled over by a Purchase campus officer one time.)

And it was certainly the case when it came to card games on flights— Anthony said $50,000 games weren't uncommon—or shooting contests between players in practice. Jackson and Anthony had taken part in a five-figure shooting wager, spraying jumpers from all over the court one day after practice. When word reached Riley about how high the stakes had gotten, his concern was how it might impact the team dynamic. "How the hell do you expect someone to pass you the ball if you owe him $30,000?" Riley shouted. "That's fucking tuition for a kid!"

Whatever the reason for Riley's speech—the notion of cliques actually troubling him, or if this was merely his way of firing up the Knicks to distract them from their struggles—there was a payoff. Beginning with that game in Oakland, New York won its next five contests, and would take eight out of the next nine; a stretch that put the Knicks ahead of the Boston Celtics for first place in the Atlantic Division.

"That speech was one of the turning points of our season," Wilkins says.

If Riley sometimes laid into his players, he also made occasional efforts to repay their hard work.

Still basking in the glow of its appearance on the cover of *Sports Illustrated* one month earlier, New York was rolling in March, beating Denver on the road for a fifth-straight win to improve to 45-25.

As the Knicks prepared to travel to Seattle for their game two nights later, the team's aircraft sat on the tarmac in Denver for nearly an hour due to strong winds. The wait felt like an eternity to the giant men who were in the midst of a road trip and wanted nothing more than to collapse into their hotel beds.

When the Knicks did finally arrive in the Emerald City, their bus pulled up to the team hotel just after 2 a.m., waking a number of players who'd dozed off during the ride from the airport. As they prepared to stand to exit the bus, Riley stood toward the front of it, in the aisle. "We're going at ten tomorrow," Riley said, meaning the team would be holding practice less than eight hours later. "Make sure to get taped up."

The collective groan players unleashed could be heard 2,800 miles away back in New York. "We were so worn down," recalls Tim McCormick, the backup center. "We all figured he'd give us an off day."

After just a few hours of sleep and a brief breakfast buffet, the Knicks—dressed in their practice uniforms and ankle tape—sluggishly loaded onto the team bus for their morning workout. Yet when they arrived, they saw a huge warehouse instead of a practice court. A projector screen sat in the middle of the room. Some players figured the 10 a.m. practice had simply been scaled back to a mere film session instead—a schedule adjustment that would have been a small victory in its own way. But then Riley explained.

"You've done everything I've asked of you," Riley said. "So, we're not gonna practice today. Instead, we'll watch a movie that just came out. It's about Tim McCormick. It's called *White Men Can't Jump*."

Riley grinned as the room erupted with laughter and two servers suddenly emerged with drinks and small bags of popcorn for the players; a few of whom let out sighs of relief once they realized they'd have the day off.

To that point in the year, the Knicks had beaten all their preseason projections, and put on a show. So it was only fitting, Riley thought, that they have an opportunity to sit back and enjoy one themselves.

It was hard to debate that logic. The day after the screening, New York beat the Sonics, then finished the trip with a double-digit victory over the Blazers, who would finish the campaign with the West's best mark.

As for the Knicks, who'd reeled off nine wins in ten games, they were now a near lock to finish as the No. 2 seed in the East. With a five-game cushion over Boston and just eight games left in the regular season, New York was on autopilot, and could afford to take that stance for the last couple of weeks.

At least it seemed that way.

In what amounted to a comedy of errors, the Knicks would then:

- lose to Cleveland as Boston beat the Bulls, shrinking the division lead to four games . . .
- fall against Detroit as the Celtics took down the Cavaliers, cutting the lead to three games . . .
- falter versus the Larry Bird–less Celtics, who now held the tie-breaker, and trimmed it to two games . . .
- score a franchise-worst 61 points in a loss at Detroit, as Boston won again, making the lead one game . . .
- go scoreless over the final 3:41 at Atlanta to lose, 95–94, as the Celtics won, leaving them tied for first . . .

Scouting prospects at the Portsmouth Invitational in Virginia, members of the front office were at the Norfolk Marriott hotel bar, watching the final seconds tick off the clock against Atlanta. They looked on, stunned, as the Hawks scored the game's final 10 points to come from behind and beat New York by one. Just like that, the Knicks—who'd been in full control of their division—had now lost a five-game edge in just seven games.

Checketts processed all this, along with the Celtics' fourteen wins in fifteen outings to catch New York in the standings. Frustrated, he kicked over a nearby chair in the bar, a highly uncharacteristic reaction from the mild-mannered executive. A few seconds later, Red Holzman, the most accomplished coach in team history, who by then was serving as a consultant, gently grabbed Checketts's arm. "Let me remind you of something, Dave," Holzman said. "We're the Knicks. We're above that."

Checketts nodded, told Holzman he was right, then walked over to pick up the chair.

Picking up the Knicks after such a monumental collapse, however, would be more difficult.

Ahead of the team's regular-season finale in Milwaukee, Riley huddled with his players for a closed-door meeting. He didn't shy away from the truth: after its unthinkable late-season fall, New York no longer controlled its own destiny, and now had to rely on an unlikely outcome to win the division outright. (Boston's finale was against the Heat, who would finish tied for eighth in the East.) Riley largely put the blame on his own shoulders, saying he did more "coaxing than coaching" down the stretch, particularly once the Knicks earned their impressive road win over the Blazers. For a team that had grown used to outworking everyone, Riley said, lightening the load might have thrown the players off.

The players appreciated Riley's gesture. But they didn't like what he said next: the team would be heading back down to Charleston between the end of the regular season and the start of the playoffs. The coach thought holding another training camp would not only filter out distractions, but also help players get back to the long days and hard, physical work they'd grown accustomed to earlier in the season.

So when the buzzer sounded on the regular-season finale in Milwaukee, the Knicks walked away with their 51st victory, a twelve-win improvement from the season before. They technically earned a share of the division title, though losing a five-game lead with eight games to play—still the only team in NBA history to blow that big a lead with such little time left—wasn't exactly a candles-and-confetti occasion.

Neither was the idea of having to play an aging, highly accomplished Pistons club to start the postseason.

New York had a game plan in mind for its first-round series with the two-time champions.

On offense, the Knicks would station Ewing farther from the basket, just inside the three-point line, to force the Pistons to run greater distances if they wanted to double-team him. On defense, they'd utilize a pair of strategies: to smother guard Isiah Thomas with two defenders as soon as he dribbled around screens, and to have the Knicks' big men position themselves almost out of bounds whenever the Pistons shot jumpers. By doing that, Oakley and Ewing could back their bodies into Dennis Rodman, the league's leading rebounder, more aggressively than normal to box him out of position and keep him away from the glass.

All three ideas worked to perfection in Game 1. Taking away Detroit's ability to double-team Ewing, the big man had a breezy 24 points. Thomas never got comfortable, logging three points on 1-for-9 shooting in one of the worst games of his career. Rodman finished with a season-low four boards, fifteen fewer than his nightly average. And the Knicks blew the doors off the Pistons, 109–75, to begin the best-of-five matchup.

New York's other adjustment wasn't a game plan so much as a suggestion. Before the postseason, Riley had a two-hour sit-down with McDaniel, the team's on-again, off-again forward. "I need you to go back to being the old, Seattle version of X," the coach told him. By that, he meant going back to the player who had a well-documented mean streak—who took, rather than politely waiting for defenses to give.

After the Game 1 rout, the series tightened into a nasty, hard-fought battle, one that saw six technical fouls and one flagrant in Game 3, and then four techs and a flagrant *in the first five minutes* of Game 4. But with the help of McDaniel, who averaged better than 20 points and nine rebounds over the final four contests, the Knicks did just enough to out-muscle the Pistons in the decisive Game 5 at the Garden.

While it certainly wasn't the equivalent of the Bulls' watershed victory over Detroit in 1991, the Knicks' series win did mark a sort of changing of the guard. In beating the Pistons—who saw Chuck Daly step down after the first-round defeat, officially ending the Bad Boys—the Knicks had effectively become the new bullies on the block.

"When push came to thug, [Detroit] wanted no part of the Knicks' physical game. Call it the start of the Knicks' gory years," *Sports Illustrated*'s Bruce Newman wrote.

The Knicks' defense had been oppressive all season, delivering an NBA-high twenty flagrant fouls, including ones on consecutive plays in a January game against San Antonio, when they nearly beheaded San Antonio's David Robinson. And now they had a second-round date with the Bulls, who'd had plenty of experience with physical play. Chicago had endured it for three straight playoffs before getting past the Pistons' Jordan Rules, which were designed to dictate, through strategy and blunt force, where Jordan went with the ball.

A couple of hours before New York's Game 5 win over the Pistons, Oakley's phone rang. When he answered, he heard a familiar, southern voice on the line: that of Bulls star Scottie Pippen. The forward, a former teammate of Oakley's in Chicago, had called to wish he and the Knicks luck in the elimination contest.

Of course that could've been inferred a few ways: innocently, with Pippen merely providing support to a good friend. (Pippen had served as Oakley's rookie initially, meaning Oakley could task him with errands and playfully bully him as part of the hazing rookies receive from veterans.) It also could have been taken as a sign of how much Pippen and the Bulls simply hated the rival Pistons, and wanted them to falter. Or, depending on how cynical you are, it could have been a bit of both, with Pippen wanting the Knicks to advance because he respected Oakley, but also because he felt they were less of a threat than the Pistons.

Between the Bulls sweeping New York the postseason before—and their wins in all four regular-season meetings—the media had rendered a quick judgment. Noting that the series opened in Chicago, where the Knicks had lost seventeen in a row, the *New York Post* ran a headline reading "Knicks' Best Hope? Look Good Losing."

Riley didn't feel that way, though. In fact, he'd used the doubt in the media as a rallying cry. Dating back to the team's training camp in October, he'd had the Bulls in his sights. "Pat told us on Day One: 'Listen, we already know we're gonna have to go through Chicago,'" recalls Wilkins. "He was a champion, and he made it clear that he ain't come to New York to lose. So he instilled that confidence in us right away."

The Knicks didn't show any fear in Game 1, but they might have stirred up some in the Bulls. Less than two minutes in, Oakley bumrushed a driving Bill Cartwright and knocked him out of the air, sending the 7-footer to the floor. Fans in the Chicago Stadium crowd groaned as if they'd been clocked themselves.

Right away, Oakley's foul sent a stern message: no layups allowed. "I don't want to use the word 'fear,' but there was always this thought in your mind that they might take things too far on any given play. And thinking about that took you off your game mentally," says Will Perdue, a Bulls backup center.

With that tone set, and Ewing pouring in a game-high 34 points and 16 rebounds, the Knicks shocked just about everyone with a 94–89 road victory over Jordan and the Bulls in Game 1.

And even when Chicago got back on track to win Games 2 and 3, the Knicks felt their style of play was exacting a physical toll. In the Game 2 defeat, McDaniel's aggressive play on Pippen—who shot just 2-for-12—contributed to the Chicago forward tweaking his right ankle badly. And in the third matchup, New York again came out swinging, literally. Oakley drilled Horace Grant in the head, knocking the big man's goggles from up around his eyes to down around his mouth during the first minute of play.

It would turn out to be one of the Knicks' milder fouls of the afternoon. In the third quarter alone, New York forced three different Bulls—a bloodied Jordan (nose), Pippen (chin), and John Paxson (arm)—out of the game because they had to be bandaged by Chip Schaeffer, Chicago's trainer. The Knicks played with a sanguine mentality, almost as if they wanted to leave their opponents' blood on the Garden floor.

On the strength of McDaniel's 24 points and oppressive defense on Pippen—who shot 4-for-13 and was "thrown around like a rag doll," in the words of one columnist—New York rebounded from back-to-back losses to even the series with a Game 4 victory. "I imposed my will on him," McDaniel says now of the Pippen matchup. "Any time I got an opportunity to give him a good shot in the head, I wanted to do it."

But again, the momentum was short-lived. Back in Chicago, Jordan did as he pleased in Game 5, breaking out for 37 points, many of which came on straight-line drives to the rim. The Bulls won, 96–88, giving them a 3–2 series lead that put the Knicks on the brink of elimination.

It was going to end up being another one of those sleepless nights for Riley. How could it not be?

The same image—Jordan repeatedly gliding to the rim for scores, and looking completely unbothered while doing it—gnawed at the coach for the entirety of the flight back to New York. Riley decided he needed it to eat at his players, too. So he enlisted the help of Salmi, the team's video coordinator.

What happened next is something that remains with each of those Knicks three decades later.

As the players sat at their lockers waiting for Riley's talk before Game 6, the coach wheeled a TV and VHS machine into the middle of the room. He popped in Salmi's tape, then hit play. Footage from the prior year's postseason began playing. It was a clip of Jordan dribbling past Starks on the left wing before being met by Oakley, who'd stepped up as a help defender. Then it showed Jordan throwing a nifty hesitation move in the post with his left shoulder to fake Starks and Oakley out of frame. The clip concluded with Jordan throwing down a huge tomahawk over a helpless Ewing, who, despite being six inches taller, had instantly become a poster.

For somewhere between five and ten minutes, while his team sat in stunned silence, Riley showed that same play—with Jordan schooling three of the Knicks' best players on their home floor—displaying the lowlight on a loop. It was a *Clockwork Orange*–style aversion therapy, with Riley forcing his players to repeatedly watch their misdeed. When he finally hit the stop button, Riley paced in front of the TV to find the words he wanted to say. "This makes me sick to my stomach," he finally snarled.

"One of you is gonna step up, knock Michael Jordan to the floor, and not help him up," Riley continued. "We can't show him deference just because of who he is, or how good he is. Not anymore. You can achieve whatever you want in life, but no one—especially not Michael Jordan—is gonna give it to you. You have to *take* it. Michael isn't just gonna play poorly. You have to force him to play that way."

Even before that pregame edict, Riley had made his displeasure with the defense known. In his post-practice press conference the day before, he'd been unusually critical, saying the Knicks' efforts to keep Jordan out of the paint weren't good enough. Citing his own film review from Game 5, Riley said Jordan and his teammates had driven to the basket between 35 and 40 times, about twice as often as New York.

Word of Riley's messaging reached Jordan through the media, and the superstar seemed to have it on his mind ahead of Game 6. "If I come through [the paint] today, I expect my head to be taken off," Jordan told writers that morning, hours before Game 6. "I wish this was over. This series has been brutal."

Jordan wouldn't get his wish. Not that night, at least.

Sensing that the Knicks were prepared to take a heavy-handed approach, Jordan played passively in Game 6. After the dominant showing in the fifth game of the series, he rarely ventured toward the basket in the sixth one. Jordan treated the New York defense as if it were a game of Minesweeper. Even if he got past one defender, he tiptoed around, knowing the next man might blow him up.

His first drive toward the hoop, early in the second quarter, looked completely out of sorts. From the left wing, he dribbled twice to his right and accelerated, trying to make it past Wilkins. But as he neared the free-throw line, three players—Anthony, Oakley, and Mason—collapsed toward him. Hearing the footsteps, the superstar uncharacteristically lost the ball on his own, without a defender poking it away. The Knicks quickly cashed in on the mistake, which led to a fast break and ended with a Starks layup.

Jordan shot plenty. But 22 of his 25 shots came from outside the paint. The result, a 9-for-25 showing for 21 points, was arguably the worst shooting performance of Jordan's playoff career to that point.

New York won, 100–86, forcing a winner-take-all Game 7 that no one expected before the series.

Through the first six games of the matchup, the Knicks led the defending NBA champions in total points, rebounds, and assists. They had held the Bulls more than 20 points beneath their regular-season scoring average, and almost 30 points under their playoff scoring average, by playing an unceasingly physical brand of basketball. The Knicks had notched five flagrants—including one where Starks clotheslined Pippen to the floor—to Chicago's zero. The resurrected McDaniel was outscoring Pippen—19.3 points per game on 51 percent shooting to 15.8 points on 37 percent—with the gap widening over the last three games of the series. Even the normally stoic Jordan was beginning to look uneasy.

But as the series shifted back to Chicago for Game 7, Jordan found his footing again. On the first possession of the game, he caught the ball on the left wing, used a stutter step to leave McDaniel in the dust, then leapt for the rim before being fouled across the arm by Oakley on the way to the hoop.

As he landed back on his feet, Jordan briefly checked his lip for blood, having taken a second blow to the face from Ewing at the end of the play. But the takeaway from the sequence was simple: after settling for jumpers in Game 6, Jordan wasn't going to let the Knicks' physical play diminish his aggressiveness.

And he wasn't going to let New York's bullying style impact his teammates anymore, either.

Near the end of the first period, McDaniel and Pippen got tangled up on consecutive plays. The second got whistled as an offensive foul on

McDaniel, who threw his shoulder into Pippen's chest on a post-up. On the way back down the court, the men exchanged words, with McDaniel getting inches from Pippen's face. But before long, Jordan and Grant intervened, and Jordan turned to confront McDaniel.

The two players mashed their shaved heads against each other in what would become a lasting image from the series. McDaniel was seeking to be the irritant he'd been to Pippen all series. But Jordan, who rarely got into it with opposing players—even when he was the one being targeted—opted to push back.

"Fuck you, X! Fuck you!" Jordan shouted. Both he and McDaniel were given technical fouls.

New York kept things close through halftime, and were within three, 60–57, three minutes into the third period. But then the Knicks' wheels came off. Playing on a terrible ankle sprain, Ewing picked up his second, third, and fourth fouls in a four-minute span, forcing him to the bench. Shortly after he took a seat, Jordan made a string of jaw-dropping plays—a banked-in jumper, a steal in the backcourt, and then an incredible come-from-behind strip on McDaniel, who thought he had an easy breakaway bucket.

Much like he'd stood up for Pippen, Jordan again said enough was enough, shutting down any real chance the Knicks had of making a comeback. "Everything shifted when he got that strip," McDaniel says.

Pippen had a triple double, and Jordan scored 42 points as Chicago pulled away, 110–81, to win the series in seven.

By no means was it the Game 7 result the Knicks wanted. But to come within a game of taking down the defending champs in the first year of the new regime—under a club president who'd wanted to install on-court dancers as a distraction just in case the team struggled early on—wasn't half-bad.

It was early yet. But after years of mediocrity, the Knicks finally appeared to be building something sustainable.

5

CHALK OUTLINE

Somehow, Pat Riley either hadn't heard or understood the disclaimer.

So when the handouts made their way around the conference room table at the Madison Square Garden offices in Midtown, Riley grabbed the sheet of photo paper, analyzed it, then wore a confused look.

What he saw was unambiguous: an aerial, half-court image of the Garden floor, with the chalk outline of a human body lying in the blue painted area directly in front of the basket. The messaging was blunt: if an opposing player had the audacity to drive toward the rim against New York, he might lose his life doing it.

Beneath the image, there was a phrase. "Tough Town, Tough Team: The 1992–93 New York Knicks."

Before Riley could even fully digest the first image, another handout made the rounds. This one was just as direct as the first, featuring a Mack truck roaring through the middle of the page, coming right at the reader. "If you want to know what it's like to play the Knicks, stand here," it read. Again, beneath the image was the slogan "Tough Town, Tough Team: The 1992–93 New York Knicks."

A few of the team executives chuckled at the mock-ups, which had been presented by a visiting ad agency. But then an uncomfortable Riley spoke up. "I think maybe these go a little bit too far," he said.

That's when the presenter reiterated what Riley must have somehow missed to start the meeting: that the promotional poster ideas for the 1992–93 season were just icebreakers, and that the unusually aggressive designs—accurate as their portrayals were—would never actually see the light of day.

Still, the mock-ups illustrated something. In just one year, Riley's rough-and-tumble Knicks had developed an unmistakable identity. The marketing staff—eager to piggyback off New York's budding reputation for rugged play—wasted no time capitalizing. Looking to deter counterfeiters that season, the club began printing Knicks tickets on indestructible, synthetic paper. The change allowed the Knicks to cleverly deem their entry permits "the toughest ticket in town."

The front office was just as eager to take the next step. Operating comfortably beneath the salary cap for the first time, the Knicks saw an opportunity to add meaningful pieces to a roster that had pushed the Bulls to a seventh game. And because of how they planned to maneuver—by using the Bird rights exception, which gave teams the ability to exceed the cap to re-sign their own free agents—they knew they'd be able to bring back bruising forward Xavier McDaniel. The Knicks fully planned to make re-signing McDaniel their final roster move of the summer, once other deals were locked into place. And they told him as much.

Ironically, the prospect of bringing back McDaniel had been looking less attractive to the Knicks during the season's second half, as the forward struggled. On top of the 29-year-old's inconsistency, team doctors had questions about his knees, and urged Knicks executives not to offer him anything longer than a one-year deal. But McDaniel's strong play in the playoffs, particularly against Scottie Pippen and the Bulls, changed the front office's mindset. Now the club merely wanted to find ways to add scoring beyond McDaniel and the other starters.

The Knicks did that by trading with Dallas for four-time All-Star Rolando Blackman, a 33-year-old shooting guard, and by drafting Hubert Davis, a sharpshooting guard out of North Carolina. They then took a big swing in July, making a six-year, $17 million offer for restricted free agent Harvey Grant, 27, who'd just averaged 18 points a game. But the Bullets opted to match the offer, forcing the Knicks back to the drawing board.

Still on the hunt for another scoring forward, New York sought to orchestrate a three-team trade that would send out starting point guard Mark Jackson, a first-round pick, and a second-round pick to land power forward Charles Smith, veteran floor general Doc Rivers, and shooting guard Bo Kimble from the Clippers. The proposed trade, which also involved the Magic, had been agreed to by all three of the teams involved.

Just one problem: Stanley Roberts, the second-year center whom Orlando included in the deal, invoked his no-trade clause and blocked the transaction from being finalized in late August. Annoyed he hadn't been given a heads-up that the Magic might try to move him, Roberts held his ground. Firmly. The second-year center had played in college with Shaquille O'Neal at LSU, and was content to keep backing him up in Orlando.

So the proposed trade sat there pending; first for days, then for a week. Then for a second full week.

Meanwhile, McDaniel stewed watching it all happen. Not only had the Knicks tried to sign Grant, who played the same position. But now they were targeting another scoring forward in a trade. By early September, the process royally annoyed McDaniel, who worried that whatever free-agent money remained on the market might dry up completely in the time New York took to land another player tasked with the same offensive responsibilities. It all left McDaniel feeling like an afterthought.

After Boston came calling and offered him a deal, McDaniel phoned Patrick Ewing, who shared an agent and was his closest friend on the team. He said he badly wanted to stay with the Knicks, but also felt like New York's decision-makers weren't treating him like a priority. So McDaniel asked Ewing: what do you think I should do?

"Man, if those guys wanted to keep you, they would've done it by now," Ewing told him, perhaps not understanding that McDaniel had to be the team's final signing that summer because of how the Bird rules worked.

Taking Ewing's message to heart, McDaniel agreed to the Celtics' three-year, $6.6 million offer on September 10, 1992, three weeks before camps were set to open. The news was not well received at the Knicks practice facility in Purchase. "What the *fuck* just happened?" Riley asked rhetorically as he walked into the gym.

Assistant coach Bob Salmi recalls hearing items shatter in Riley's office; ones he assumes Riley threw in anger. "Just a bad, bad day. It was the one time I really saw Pat thrown off by something like that," Salmi says.

Dave Checketts went from being confused to being concerned. He thought he'd fully conveyed to McDaniel that the Knicks would take care of him, but that it would happen late in free agency. Checketts got chewed out over McDaniel's exit by Paramount CEO Stanley Jaffe, the de facto owner of the team.

"This is the worst day in the history of Madison Square Garden!" Jaffe furiously shouted into his phone.

A passionate Knicks fan since childhood, Jaffe had a tendency to overreact, just like he had with the idea of team dancers the year before. "It went through my mind that I might get fired over it," Checketts recalls.

There'd be no firing. But losing McDaniel did raise the stakes of completing the trade that had been stuck in neutral. Knicks general manager Ernie Grunfeld began placing regular calls to Elgin Baylor, his Clippers counterpart, asking if he could do something to sell Roberts on the idea of moving out west. Finally, after Clippers owner Donald Sterling hosted Roberts at an all-white attire party in Los Angeles, the center—wined and dined—waived his no-trade clause, allowing the deal to be finalized after a month of holdups.

Still, even with Smith and Rivers in the fold, it was fair to wonder what the loss of a player like McDaniel meant for an intensely physical club like the Knicks, who now had a massive O where their X used to be.

The moment that changed Charles Oakley's basketball career came near the end of tenth grade.

Oakley asked varsity basketball coach Loren Olson what he could improve upon for the next season. Olson replied matter-of-factly. "You need to play football," said Olson, the coach at Cleveland's John Hay High.

The 15-year-old, closer to 6-foot-3 back then, said he didn't want to play football. His passion was hoops. Then Olson issued an ultimatum: "If you don't play football, you can't play basketball," he told him.

"I meant it. Because I knew it'd make him a much better basketball player. And it did," Olson says now.

As a youngster, Oakley had an almost fragile approach to the idea of contact; something that might have stemmed from him coming up in a household with his mother and four sisters, whom he couldn't really tussle with (and one brother who was nine years older). But playing football had exactly the impact on Oakley his basketball coach hoped it would. It taught the youngster how to stop worrying and love the boom.

"He played the game of basketball with a certain amount of finesse at first. But when he started playing football, he crossed over into another realm of physicality. Like, 'Wait: I can just hit this guy, and I'm not gonna get called for a foul? I can just hit him as hard as I want to?'" says Tim McGee, a high school football teammate and longtime friend of Oakley's, who later played in the NFL.

These were the makings of Oakley, the most physical player in perhaps the NBA's most physical era. A player who'd not only lead the league in flagrants in 1992–93—he'd end up with nine, *more than fifteen teams* finished with for the year—but would also have more than twice as many as the next-closest person that season. And someone who would more than make up for whatever physicality was lost after McDaniel's exit.

Oakley possessed a strong handshake—"Like shaking hands with a cinder block," trainer Said Hamdan says—and left welts and bruises on players trying to keep him off the glass. The forward's style of play left its mark on everyone; even his own coaches at times. Take the instance in 1990, when he got into a scrap with assistant Paul Silas during a practice. "Oak was shooting free throws, and I said something to him he didn't like. He walked up on me, and I hit him," said Silas, whose playing style in the 1960s and '70s was similar to Oakley's. "Then he hit me all in my chest and whatnot. I had bruises for like two weeks."

Still, there was more to Oakley than just constantly beating the hell out of people. He had great instincts, both in rebounding and as a help defender, which allowed him to beat opposing players to certain spots on the floor, despite possessing far less leaping ability and being a full step slower than many of them. His offensive game wasn't nearly as eye-popping as he thought—"He told me several times, 'If I got as many touches as Karl Malone, I'd be an All-Star, too,'" says Stu Jackson, who coached the Knicks in 1990—but Oakley was a solid passer, and had one of the best 17-foot jumpers on the team.

Most impressive about Oakley, though, was his motor—one that imperiled people, and, in at least one case, saved them. The forward recklessly dove into the crowd to save loose balls—frequently enough to where some members of the club opted against sitting their families close to the court, fearing Oakley might barrel into them if they did.

Oakley took a similar approach toward practices. In one scrimmage, he dove for a ball that was headed out of bounds, but knocked it into the crotch of assistant Jeff Nix by accident, leaving Nix in so much pain that he made arrangements to see a urologist. The ordeal was a blessing in disguise: during the visit, the doctor found, and removed, an unrelated growth Nix hadn't been aware of. "It's always made me grateful that Oak hustled the way he did," Nix says. "He may have saved my life."

Few players did more than Oakley to stay in peak condition. He didn't start lifting weights until he began college at Virginia Union, but became obsessed soon after, and kept his routines throughout his pro career.

"I remember walking into the living room of his house in White Plains, and right there, in the middle of his living room, was this weight set, where he could do bench presses and curls," recalls Greg Butler, a Knicks center who spent two seasons as Oakley's teammate prior to Riley's arrival. "I remember thinking, 'Well, maybe he just hasn't unpacked since being traded from Chicago.' But then he had me over a few times after that, and all the equipment was still there in the living room each time."

The notion of sore muscles from hard work didn't bother Oakley. Though he spent his adolescent years in a tough part of Cleveland, Oakley's formative ones took place in small-town Alabama, where his mother sent him to stay with his grandparents after Charles's father died of a heart attack at age 35.

The young boy lived on a cotton farm in a sleepy, red-soiled town called York, about two hours southwest of Birmingham. Too small to truly help his grandfather with the field work, Charles woke up at 5 a.m. each day—never complaining—carrying water pails to his grandfather, Julius Moss, as Moss plowed the crops. And in addition to doing field work, Moss held a labor-intensive job at a nearby steel mill.

"Other people had more equipment than [my grandfather] did," Oakley said. "He didn't have a tractor or anything like that. He just had a plow. Back then, it was really tough, but he made it happen; no excuses."

Moss's clock-punching style, full of aches and pains, influenced Oakley's work mentality. It's why, to this day, Oakley himself can be found hunching over to scrub down vehicles that drive into the car washes he owns. He sees honor in doing the grunt work other people shy away from.

Despite speaking with a bit of a low mumble, Oakley established himself as a media favorite, famous for his plainspoken riddles. (One example: "Don't ask me to be a traffic cop if I can't write no tickets.") He was everyone's least favorite teammate to eat with, because meals never ended. Or never started. He often returned dishes to the chef, saying they weren't to his standards. Sometimes more than once in one sitting.

"There was always more salad *off* his plate than on it," assistant coach Brendan Malone recalls. "Even on the team flights, where we're getting first-class desserts and stuff, you'd hear him shouting, 'This isn't German chocolate cake!' I've never been around someone who's that picky with their food in my life."

Beyond those things, there was also Oakley's Starburst-like clothing palette, with suits—he owns more than two hundred, all told—in orange sherbet, cranberry, green, gold, fuchsia. There was his insistence on never wearing the same suit for a second time in a road city. And there was the time when a teammate had the same outfit on as Oakley, which prompted the big man to head right back upstairs to change.

Oakley relished the attention, and shopped meticulously for things he felt would draw it. One time, after a morning shootaround in New York, he went shopping on Madison Avenue in search of a luxury belt.

"He grabs this one belt, and asks me what I think of it. And as I'm looking at it, I'm confused. I mean, it's a nice belt, I guess. But it's just a black belt with a gold buckle, and it's $500," says David Cain, a guard who played in a couple of training camps with Riley and the Knicks. "Maybe I was the wrong person to ask, because I've never spent more than $20 on a belt. So I ask Oak: 'You know that's a $500 belt, right?'"

"I know. But when I wear it, watch everybody's reaction to it," Oakley said as they walked to the register.

Hours later, using the team bus as his fashion runway, Oakley boarded last, to ensure every player would see him. As he came down the aisle, one teammate noticed the accessory, saying, "Damn, Oak! That belt!"

Having accomplished his goal, Oakley looked straight at Cain, winked, then walked to his seat on the bus.

As much as Oakley liked to stand out, there were times when the Knicks absolutely hated that he did.

Take, for instance, the play on December 30, 1992, against the Indiana Pacers. Star guard Reggie Miller was making a hard backdoor cut into the paint when Oakley saw him sprinting toward the rim. As Miller broke open, Indiana center Rik Smits threw Miller a perfect pass that hit him in the hands.

Then *boom*.

Oakley, beating Miller to the spot, planted his feet and lowered his left shoulder, sending the beanpole of a swingman crashing to the floor. "Whoa!" Knicks announcer Marv Albert said as the collision took place.

The hit was so jarring that it even seemed to stun the officials, who were apparently too dumbfounded to call the obvious foul. And aside from the no-call, the ball clearly ricocheted off Miller's hands and went out of bounds. But the refs either didn't notice it—possible, given Oakley's hit— or simply opted to give the Pacers the ball back out of pure empathy, after being too stunned to call a foul in real time.

Pacers general manager Donnie Walsh took note of the referees' confusion. "That play was so physical, the refs had no idea what to do," he recalls. "Right then, I told myself, 'This summer, I'm getting two guys just like [Oakley].' Because players like that would immediately change the makeup of our team."

While the referees didn't take action against Oakley, league officials did two days later, when they announced a $10,000 fine against him for leveling Miller. "Oakley [stepped] in the way and popped him, the way a defensive back pops a receiver after the ball's already passed," said Rod Thorn, the league's head disciplinarian. "I think Charles Oakley has six flagrants, and we haven't even played thirty games yet."

The Knicks' reactions ranged from miffed—"Just because there's some glass in the road doesn't mean there was an accident," Oakley said—to enraged. Checketts was so angry that he reached out to David Stern and threatened to bar Thorn from the Garden, saying the NBA had shown a pattern of bias against the Knicks.

Checketts and Grunfeld felt the Knicks, who played mere blocks from NBA headquarters, were scrutinized more than any other club. Not just because of Oakley's physicality, either. The front office felt everything was under a microscope. "The NBA was our biggest season-ticket holder by far," Checketts says. "They were in the stands for our games every night, but you knew that wasn't true for anyone else."

New York had grown fed up with having its wrist slapped over trivial things, like the league warning the club for starting-lineup introductions running long by fifteen to twenty seconds. NBA officials also made a point to chide the Knicks behind the scenes—and threaten fines—for repeatedly showing certain instant-replay sequences on the jumbotron. Seeking to spare its officials unnecessary ridicule with questionable calls, the league had limitations on how many times clubs were allowed to loop foul-call sequences on the big screens. But because the Knicks were already annoyed by what they saw as nightly overpolicing, they ignored the rule altogether when they felt an egregious call had taken place.

"There was this red phone we kept courtside in case Ernie or Dave needed to reach the game-ops folks," says Bobby Goldwater, an executive who oversaw events being held at the Garden for almost twenty-five years. "And if the red phone rang right after a controversial call, you knew it was gonna be Ernie saying, 'Show [the play] again!' You'd tell him we were gonna get fined, or that we'd get in trouble. But he didn't care."

On the surface, it sounds outlandish to suggest that the NBA would be out to get its biggest market. Yet Checketts felt the league—which came under scrutiny after the controversial 1985 draft lottery, which allowed New York to land Ewing—too often bent over backward to illustrate that it wasn't showing favoritism toward the Knicks. And by the time the Oakley fine took place, Checketts was fed up.

So in January 1993, the Knicks went to NBA headquarters to hash things out. Stern and a handful of league officials sat on one side of a conference table, while Checketts, Grunfeld, and Ken Munoz, the team's general counsel, sat on the other.

Munoz felt uneasy joining them for the session once Grunfeld explained why his presence was needed: the Knicks were going to construct a Hail Mary argument in which they expressed legal concerns with the league's integrity. "I said, 'Look, guys: we can't push this,'" Munoz recalls. "But Ernie wanted to push it. He said it might be uncomfortable and embarrassing, but that we had to get this message across."

As one might expect, the sit-down went nowhere fast. Almost immediately, the Knicks raised the issue of integrity, which sent expletives flying—first from Stern, then from the Knicks' side of the table.

"This meeting is over!" Stern, a lawyer by trade, yelled minutes later.

The approach was an abrasive way to try to solve the problem. But on some level, abrasive was all the Knicks knew.

Salmi, the video coordinator, identified a key problem early in the process.

Powered by their defense—which ranked as the league's second stingiest in 1992, and was well on its way to earning the top spot in 1993—the new-look Knicks were becoming a legitimate powerhouse.

Yet conversations in the media were focused more on whether the team's style of play was dirty—the Knicks were going to lead the league in flagrants for the second consecutive season—and whether New York had the composure of a champion. The Knicks' 97 technical fouls were also an NBA high.

So Salmi made a video, featuring dozens of clips of Knicks players whining to officials, and balling up their fists at opponents. As the images scrolled, Billy Joel's "Angry Young Man" played in the background of the tape.

And he's never been able to learn from mistakes
So he can't understand why his heart always breaks
. . . And he'll go to the grave as an angry old man.

The point of the video was to show the Knicks that their legacy—as possible champions, or as nothing more than a group of angry young men—could end up being defined by their ability to keep their cool.

Still, Riley's messaging played a key role in making the Knicks as edgy as they were from night to night.

There was the time before a game when Riley told his players they didn't want to win badly enough, then abruptly dunked his head into a bucket full of ice-cold water seconds later. As the players looked on with concern for two or three minutes, wondering how long their coach could possibly hold his breath for, assistant coach Dick Harter finally pulled out a soaking Riley, who gasped for air before composing himself.

"Now *that's* how bad you should want to win—as badly as I needed that breath!" Riley said, his adrenaline still spiking.

An hour and a half before a different game, Riley asked assistant trainer Tim Walsh to run down to Gerry Cosby's, the sporting goods store across the street from the Garden, to buy him a pair of baseball spikes. When Walsh returned, Riley took the cleats, retreated into his office, and closed the door behind him.

About fifteen minutes later, with the team waiting in the locker room for Riley's pregame talk, the coach sprinted out of his office and broke into a baseball slide just in front of the players. As he came to a stop, the Knicks realized Riley was wearing cleats. "You've gotta do everything you do with your spikes high," Riley told them, meaning to be aggressive—even if it meant physical harm for the opponent at times.

Whatever Riley told his players before a November game in Detroit that year, however, lacked that spark. The Knicks trailed by 17 as they entered the locker room for halftime. And when they came back out to warm up for the third period, they had to wait: a Frisbee-catching dog named Whitney performed for the Pistons' halftime show. And just before her curtain call, she left her mark by defecating on the court.

"And with how we played tonight, we just followed suit," Riley deadpanned after the game.

The Knicks missed 15 consecutive shots, and went without a basket for an eleven-minute span between the third and fourth periods. The result was a 16-point loss to the Pistons, who had lost seven straight games.

The nature of the defeat infuriated Riley, who ridiculed the Knicks two days later during a morning shootaround. Hours before they were due to host Portland at the Garden, Riley stood near the basket and chirped at his players, repeatedly yelling, "Soft!" as each man took turns approaching the rim for layups.

"I'd bet he said it a hundred times [during that shootaround]," Rivers recalls. "He was mad."

In the minutes before taking the floor, Riley had decided he wasn't going to issue a pregame speech. Instead, he let a video from Salmi—one he'd asked the film coordinator to make—do all the talking.

For five minutes, the players watched displays full of carnage. Ones showing brutal car crashes, spliced with clips of PBS programming that illustrated bighorn rams headbutting one another for supremacy.

The Knicks saw the reel of roughness as a call to action. "I look across the room, and I see Mason, and he's just got fire coming out of his eyes," Rivers says. "You have to remember: this is after he's been calling us soft all day. Us, soft? The last thing you think when you look at our group—Oak, Mase, Patrick, Starks—is that we're soft. I just remember walking onto the floor thinking, 'Someone might *die* tonight.' That's how amped I was. You knew we were gonna win, and that Portland had no chance."

No one died. But New York beat up on the Blazers—who owned the NBA's best record—limiting them to one basket in the first five minutes and just 30 points in the first half on the way to a double-digit victory.

Riley told his players to hack opponents early and often, feeling it would pressure officials to either slow games to a crawl, or potentially desensitize them to what they were seeing. That strategy, along with the idea of protecting the paint at all costs, rubbed many the wrong way.

Nets guard Kenny Anderson, who broke his wrist in March 1993 after a hard foul from Starks, was one such case. "Guys from my neighborhood were at the game that day, and they wanted to rough John up outside the locker room as soon as the game ended. I had to tell them to stand down," Anderson recalls.

But not everyone was capable of showing restraint the way Anderson's friends did.

The Knicks' biggest shift from the 1991–92 season to the 1992–93 campaign was simple. After collecting fifty-one wins and unexpectedly pushing the Bulls to an elimination game, no one took New York lightly anymore.

By March 23, the Knicks owned the East's best record, and were still in the running for a sixty-win regular season. The Suns, New York's hosts that night, were the only NBA club who held a better record.

If the game itself wasn't juicy enough, the Phoenix media contingent, doing its best impression of New York, added an extra layer to it. The Suns had gone 0-4 combined against the Knicks, Bulls, and Cavaliers, the teams with the three best records in the East. There was a question emerging in Phoenix. Sure, the team owned the best record in basketball. But were the high-scoring Suns—led by Charles Barkley, Kevin Johnson, and Dan Majerle—tough enough to beat *tough* clubs? And if not, could they be considered a true contender?

"I think that happened a lot, where teams decided they were gonna become us," Rivers says. "Teams hear about how we're gonna come in and beat you up, and then that puts them in a spot where they feel like they have to match that toughness and physicality, and that they have to strike back at us."

So with a little more than twenty seconds left before halftime, Riv-

ers got called for an offensive foul after bumping into Johnson, much to
the Phoenix guard's delight. The two players jawed and charged at each
other before being separated by teammates and officials near the baseline. Riley even trekked from the opposite side of the floor to make sure
the matter didn't escalate, shoving away Starks, who had engaged in a
shouting match with Phoenix guard Danny Ainge.

Extracurriculars like these were a massive part of what made officiating the Knicks so challenging.

"Anytime you had the Knicks on your schedule, you'd huddle with
your crewmates and say, 'Oh boy; we're gonna have to watch this matchup
between these two guys, to make sure nothing flares up. Oh, and this
matchup. And this one, too,'" recalls Steve Javie, one of three refs that
night in Phoenix. "And before you know it, there's a number of guys you
have to worry about keeping an eye on."

That was a key part of what went wrong that night. Ed T. Rush, widely
considered one of the NBA's best referees from that era, lost track of the
heated matchup between Rivers and Johnson on the next trip down the
floor. "If I'd seen that—with Johnson initiating the whole thing, and
then the response from Doc—the whole thing probably never happens,"
Rush says, adding that he was overly focused on the final shot of the half.
"That's what I said to the league office, too, on my game report, which
took me seven hours to finish: that this thing was probably my fault."

After Rivers sped the ball down the court and handed it off to Starks
on the right wing, Johnson leveled Rivers, jolting through his upper body
and knocking the New York point guard to the ground as the buzzer
sounded. After the dirty hit, which wasn't whistled, Johnson took off for
the locker room as if nothing had happened. Rivers popped to his feet
and sprinted in pursuit of Johnson, looking for immediate payback.

Then the benches cleared, with no fewer than twenty bodies entering
the fray, along with Johnson and Rivers. Harter, the Knicks' 62-year-old
assistant, tumbled to the floor. Yet for as ugly as things had gotten, and
how much the fans at America West Arena were loving the spectacle, the
incident simmered down after about twenty-five seconds. By then, Riley
had begun escorting Rivers to the visiting locker room.

But then, guard Greg Anthony—in street clothes due to a bum ankle—decided it wasn't quite over.

Walking up from behind Johnson, the lefty uncorked an enormous left hook of a sucker punch, igniting the biggest fight the NBA had seen in years just moments after the flame had almost been put out.

Having seen the punch, Riley raced in and piled on top of Anthony, desperately trying to pull his guard away from the scene. But before Riley could, a slew of Suns players—Barkley, Majerle, and Cedric Ceballos among them—joined the melee from behind, colliding into Riley's back and inadvertently ripping his Armani pants from the right pocket down to his knee. (Trainer Mike Saunders went to the bus at halftime to fetch him a new pair.) Anthony, meanwhile, had on a bizarre pajama-pattern button-down shirt that raised the same question that could be applied to this whole matter.

What the hell was he thinking?

The 25-year-old Anthony was full of contradictions. He was legitimately a tough guy—who came to practice with a hockey helmet and his jaw wired shut the day after shattering his teeth, breaking his chin, and fracturing his mandible at UNLV in 1990—but tried too hard to be a Tough Guy. He was someone who mistakenly left a loaded gun in the Knicks' weight room after practice, but often became gun-shy when confronted about his shortcomings. Someone so calm, and such a long-term planner, that he told teams in predraft interviews he wanted to become president of the United States, but was so impulsive that he'd charge at a ref—and draw a costly technical—over a call he didn't like while down two with ten seconds left. (While Anthony never became a politician, Johnson, the man he punched, later became mayor of Sacramento.)

The whole ordeal—with one ugly shirt, two separate fights, and no fewer than fifty people involved as both instigators and peacemakers—played out over the course of a ninety-second span. When officials returned from the locker room after halftime, they ejected six players and handed out twelve techs. "It was eerie, because there were almost more coaches on the [Knicks'] bench than players after halftime," Javie recalls.

The league fined twenty-one players, and docked them almost

$300,000 collectively—unprecedented totals—while Anthony got a five-game suspension for his actions in the loss. Far more important, the fight embarrassed NBA officials, who quickly moved to strengthen league rules regarding future fights.

Anthony rarely talks about that brawl, wanting to erase the memory. But when asked about the psyche of those New York clubs, the guard sums them up perfectly. "We'd say, 'Hey, we're gonna win *something* tonight—we're either gonna win the game, or win the fight,'" he said years later.

Now, after securing sixty wins and the top seed, it was time for the Knicks to make a run at winning the title.

6

THE BUTTERFLY
AMONG THE BUFFALOES

A sweaty, agitated Charles Smith had just finished practicing with his University of Pittsburgh teammates when he made a beeline for coach Paul Evans, who was standing on the sideline.

Smith's upper body was more sore than usual, the result of being pummeled by center Steve Maslek, his workout partner in one-on-one post drills. One play after another, as Smith broke free for what looked like a basket, Maslek would whack him across the shoulder, or rake the junior's hands, even drawing blood. When Smith asked why he was doing this, Maslek said Evans had ordered him to rough up the big man.

The next step, Smith said to himself, was to get to the bottom of why Evans had issued the directive.

When he made it to Evans, Smith had a perplexed look. "You told Steve to hit me every play?" he asked.

Evans saw himself as old-school. He had just taken the job at Pitt months earlier after a successful stint at the US Naval Academy, where he'd coached David Robinson and the Midshipmen to the NCAA Tournament's Elite Eight. When Evans watched the 6-foot-10 Smith—the strides as he ran, the soft jumper out to seventeen feet, the passing ability, the length he used to alter opponents' shots—he saw bits of Robinson's game. They even showcased similar demeanors: reserved, but articulate, and capable of leading by example.

But much like Charles Oakley in high school, Smith needed to develop more toughness to play in the post. And that's why Evans told Maslek to start being more physical with his star pupil in practices. "He took it personally and felt singled out that I asked Steve to body him up," Evans says. "But the truth is, our philosophy was to do things like that with everybody. Not just him. We wanted to make them better."

Playing in the paint amid heavy contact and traffic wasn't something that came naturally for the Bridgeport, Connecticut, native. As a quick, 5-foot-10 guard, he barely made his high school team as a freshman. But that would be the last time Smith had to worry about making a cut. "I don't remember ever saying, 'I'm 6-1 or 6-2,'" Smith said of his growth spurts. "It was like, 'I'm 5-11,' and then, 'I'm 6-7.'"

Before he enjoyed the height advantage, Smith had developed good ball-handling skills for a guard—ones that then became highly impressive for a power forward or a center, once he began playing those spots. And even as Smith parlayed his skill set and newfound height into becoming one of the nation's elite high school players, he didn't become overly absorbed with the idea of someday making it to the NBA.

Despite living sixty miles from New York City, and being just hours from Boston, Smith wasn't sports obsessed. He didn't grow up with favorite players or teams, and had limited interest in the NBA as a league. This stemmed from his upbringing, with his parents encouraging him to delve into whatever activities piqued his curiosity. In addition to basketball, Smith played football and joined Warren G. Harding High's chess, library, and yearbook clubs. He took an interest in stocks and world affairs.

Smith was far from a jock. Several people described him as the sort of man they'd want their daughters to date.

"Basketball is not a twenty-four-hour conversation piece with him," Smith's father, Charles, said. The elder Smith added that he'd try to watch recordings of his son's games at Pitt with him during breaks from school, to analyze them. But Charles often didn't want to.

This isn't to say Smith wasn't concerned about his on-court performance. He was. Smith began his career with the lowly Clippers, who had won just seventeen games the season before acquiring him as the No. 3 overall pick in the 1988 draft. Smith thrived individually, averaging 19 points on 50 percent shooting over his first three seasons in Los Angeles. He notched a franchise-record-tying 52-point performance in 1990.

But the Clippers were awful, winning thirty-one games or fewer in each of those years. The pressure of being the face of a losing club wore on Smith. He began seeing a psychiatrist after losing patches of hair as a result of the stress. "Luckily, this was when the high-top was in, so I disguised it that way," Smith said.

For all Smith's anxiety, though, he rarely let it show. His even-keeled nature was notable, especially when contrasted with his teammates' personalities. "He better understood what life was all about as a young man than I did as his coach," said Reggie Warford, the assistant at Pitt who recruited him to sign there.

Smith's playing style, rooted in finesse and polish, was a total contrast from that of his teammates. Nearly all the mainstays in New York's rotation—from Oakley, to Anthony Mason, to John Starks—had extremely physical reputations. So did Doc Rivers and Greg Anthony, who had shown they weren't afraid to mix it up, and were punished for their roles in the Phoenix brawl earlier that year. Smith's predecessor, Xavier McDaniel, also embodied that rugged persona the Knicks were known for.

Then there was Smith, who didn't fit that profile. "On a team full of buffaloes, you can use a butterfly every once in a while. But I think he struggled with the fact that he was that guy," says Ed Tapscott, the team's administrative director. "Where the rest of our guys were fighters, Charles was more of a lover."

"Charles was the guy we kept trying to pull in to make him more like us," says Rivers, who'd played with Smith in Los Angeles first. "He was skilled as hell, but [the constant physicality] wasn't his style of play."

Smith's struggle to shapeshift manifested itself during his very first practice with the Knicks.

As he did with each camp-opening session, Pat Riley put his players through a grueling conditioning test in which each man had to complete "17s"—the timed sideline-to-sideline sprints—to pass. Anyone who couldn't would have to repeat them the next day. But there was a catch: the first player to finish the initial set of 17s could bypass the remaining ones, which were sure to turn the players' legs into jelly by day's end.

The possibility of only having to run the first round of sprints was a godsend for Smith, who, as a newcomer, wasn't prepared for how exhausting that first day was going to be. "He didn't show up in what I would consider good condition," Tapscott recalls. "I remember our scout, Phil Hubbard, saying, 'Look, man—it may take us a few months for us to get the Clipper out of him.' He was coming over from a team that hadn't been all that good, and maybe didn't have the best work habits."

When that first set of 17s began, a number of veteran Knicks knew what to expect and paced themselves accordingly. Smith did the opposite, and ran like his life depended on it, taking an enormous lead to start the process. But as he got farther into the set, around the fourteenth or fifteenth sequence, Smith began running out of steam, and Starks closed in on him. Starks narrowly pulled ahead on the final leg of the sprint, and Smith, knowing he'd fallen behind, made a last-ditch effort by diving headfirst through the sideline.

Yet it was all for naught. Riley deemed Starks the winner, meaning he, not Smith, would get the free pass.

Smith, on the other hand, would get only a minute or so to catch his breath for his next round of 17s.

Not surprisingly, the recovery period was nowhere near long enough for Smith to compose himself. He finished dead last among camp invites by nearly a full minute during the second go-round. The results got uglier and uglier from there, with a wobbly-legged Smith eventually unable to run straight anymore.

It reached a point where Smith was so spent that Riley—normally the take-no-prisoners type—softly grabbed the forward and called off his remaining 17s, recognizing Smith couldn't finish them.

Then Riley turned to his assistants, saying he'd never let someone off the hook during a conditioning drill.

"It's the only time I've actually felt bad for a guy," Riley said.

*   *   *

Absolutely no one at Market Square Arena was about to feel bad for John Starks.

Certainly not Oakley or Patrick Ewing, who, despite being co-captains and Starks's teammates, were prepared to rip the guard limb from limb. The furious bigs sandwiched Starks, then shoved him, sending Starks bouncing off their chests as if he were a pinball. Oakley then delivered a harsh slap upside Starks's head.

"What the fuck are you thinking?" Oakley shouted.

But that was just it: Starks hadn't been thinking at all.

More than anything, he was reacting—something that played right into the Pacers' game plan. Indiana's playoff scouting report for the first-round series mentioned Starks having a short fuse, saying he could be thrown off his game with enough trash-talking, which Reggie Miller just so happened to specialize in.

The frustration had been building for Starks well before that moment in the third game of the first-round series, where Oakley and Ewing confronted him. Hell, in the first forty-five seconds of Game 1, Starks grew agitated after being whistled for two fouls while guarding Miller. So by Game 3, he was on edge. Enough to where his erratic turnovers and body language prompted Ewing to pull him aside early on, urging him to focus. So had ref Jake O'Donnell, to whom Starks complained about Miller's aggressive elbows. After one such objection, O'Donnell lost his patience, shouting, "Starks, just shut up and play!"

Starks put the Knicks ahead, 59–57, with a basket in the third quarter of Game 3, a contest New York could close the series with if it earned the victory. But Starks—so high-strung that his boyish face turned bright red at one point—had become more focused on Miller than the game itself. On the way back down the floor, he verbally sparred with Miller. Then, as they got tangled up, Starks leaned in and knocked his forehead against Miller's.

The Pacers star flailed dramatically. But whether he'd worked to sell the contact was a moot point. Starks, with a second-half lead in a potential close-out game, had just headbutted the Indiana guard.

"I was so mad—I just wanted to take my fist and put it through his face," Starks said of the sequence. It would hardly be the only time Starks boiled over about Miller. (After a particularly intense regular-season game with Indiana in 1995, Starks bizarrely told a beat reporter, "I'm gonna cut [Miller's] dick off and make him eat it.") And the Game 3 head-butt obviously wasn't a fist to Miller's face.

Still, the act was enough to trigger an ejection, infuriating Ewing and Oakley, who knew losing their second-leading scorer would shift the momentum on the road. And they were right. Indiana blasted the Knicks, 59–34, the rest of the way, to easily win Game 3 and stave off elimination.

Despite the lapse in judgment, Starks's mother, Irene, took issue with Ewing shoving Starks on the court, saying not to let it happen again. Ewing understood her qualm, but felt he was justified with the push.

"Ms. Starks, if he ever does that again, I'm gonna do the exact same thing the next time," Ewing told her.

Starks had a history of getting carried away with his emotions on the court. In 1990, during his time in the Continental Basketball Association, Starks's team was on the cusp of making the postseason when he disagreed with an official's call and sprinted over to argue his case. By coming over in such a huff, though, Starks inadvertently bumped the referee, who then tossed him from the game for making contact.

It resulted in Starks drawing a suspension for the final five games of that CBA season, during which time his club narrowly missed earning a playoff spot. "I never really told him how upset I was with him over that," says George Whittaker, who coached Starks with the Cedar Rapids Silver Bullets. "I forgive him now, because I know it wasn't an intentional thing. But we missed the playoffs by one game. And then after we got out to a slow start the next season, I had a shorter leash, and ended up getting replaced as coach. But that was just John. He was really fiery, and sometimes he could just lose it a little bit for a minute or two."

Starks and the Knicks eliminated Indiana after coming back from a 14-point deficit to win Game 4. And they jumped out to another 2–0 series lead in the conference-semifinal round against the Charlotte Hornets before losing in overtime on the road in Game 3—a matchup where 24,000 fans wore white shirts and waved white cotton towels to create a more intimidating atmosphere inside Charlotte Coliseum.

After Riley got to the visiting locker room to debrief his players, he looked at the right sleeve of his slate-gray Armani jacket, which was covered with dozens of small, white fluff balls. So was his left sleeve. As he peered down, he noticed his entire ensemble—down to his shoes and tie—was blanketed with them.

"What is this *shit* on my suit?" Riley asked, as his confusion briefly halted the postgame meeting. The clingy material had apparently detached from the fans' towels. But Riley, so laser focused the entire game, hadn't noticed his need for a lint roller until after the buzzer had sounded.

The Knicks, just as locked in as Riley, brushed off the Hornets in Games 4 and 5 to take the series, which led to the conference-finals showdown everyone had expected all along: New York against Chicago.

Bulls coach Phil Jackson had done his best to ignore it. But after a while, he couldn't anymore.

His team was taking part in a morning shootaround at Madison Square Garden, one meant to be totally off-limits to everyone but Bulls personnel, given what was at stake. But there was this persistent noise.

DING! . . . DING! . . . DING! . . . DING! . . . DING!

A few men in hard hats and orange vests were standing in the arena's 300-level concourse, making obnoxiously loud alterations to pieces of steel with sledgehammers high above the court for some reason. Which had been fine—annoying, but fine—while the Bulls were merely getting loose. But now, as they were going over the particulars of their defensive scheme with assistant Johnny Bach, they actually needed some quiet.

So Jackson decided he'd had enough. Putting his pinkies in the corners of his mouth, he whistled loudly enough to be heard in suburban Connecticut. The noise, which rivaled that of the sledgehammering, immediately got the attention of the workers.

"Hey!" Jackson yelled. "We've got practice! Can you stop for a bit? You're not supposed to be here!"

There was a brief silence that hung in the arena after Jackson's request. After all, this was Phil Jackson, a man who'd coached the Bulls to two straight NBA championships, and, for those who knew their history well enough, had been a beloved member of the two Knicks championship teams in the 1970s. Beyond all that, it was a reasonable request: to give the Bulls a few uninterrupted minutes to lock in their game plan.

After a few seconds of thinking Jackson's request over, a member of the small group responded to the coach.

"Fuck you!" he shouted down to Jackson, as the men kept sledgehammering during the walk-through.

The moment—hard hats, defiant swagger, competitiveness—summed up New York City's grunge beauty in one fell swoop.

"New York is this city of eight million people, where plenty of people don't give a shit about sports. But the Knicks were somehow this unifying force that could bring everybody together," says Chris Smith, a *New York* magazine reporter who wrote features on the team during those years. "People came to the Garden straight from work—some in their suits—so there was all this added energy, because it was a spiritual release. . . . Almost like a church service. And the Garden's angles and lighting made it feel like a stage."

Knicks fans had far more reason to be excited for the Bulls matchup this time around. Unlike the year before, when New York had been a massive underdog against Chicago, the Knicks were on relatively even footing in 1993, and had finished with the superior record. They owned the No. 1 seed and home-court advantage—something that figured to help, given that the Knicks had a 25-game winning streak running at the Garden. (The national media also took great interest in the showdown. The Knicks issued more than two hundred media credentials for reporters from outside the New York and Chicago markets for the series. By contrast, just twelve writers from outside the Seattle and Phoenix markets applied for credentials to cover the Western Conference Finals.)

Arguably no player sounded more confident heading into the series than Starks, who warned, "Buckle up, and get all the women and children outta the room."

His confidence was well placed. Capitalizing on the fact that the 6-foot-2 B. J. Armstrong was guarding him rather than the 6-foot-6 Michael Jordan, Starks hit four triples in the final period of Game 1, finishing with 25 points on 14 shots. He also held Jordan scoreless over the final six minutes, and limited the world's best player to 25 points on an inefficient 10-for-27 from the field.

Starks's solid two-way play helped the Knicks take Game 1 of the series, 98–90.

The second game played out similarly, with Starks forcing Jordan into ghastly 12-for-32 shooting for 36 points. Then with about fifty seconds to play, and New York up, 91–88, Starks had the ball in his hands with a chance to sledgehammer the Bulls into a 2–0 series deficit.

Starks had always been one to try to put exclamation points on things when he saw an opening. Back in 1990, when he was a mere camp invitee and a long shot to make New York's roster, he told himself he needed to make a huge play during the team's final workout to leave a lasting impression. So when the time came—with Starks pushing the ball on a fast break, and Ewing back to defend the basket—Starks elevated with everything he had, seeking to put down a dunk for the ages.

Instead, Ewing did what those Knicks would become known for: knocking the overly ambitious offensive player—nine inches shorter and sixty pounds lighter—to the floor. So Starks never finished the dunk. And making matters worse, he badly twisted his knee. But the injury was a blessing in disguise for Starks. Because an injured player couldn't be cut at that point in camp, Starks had to be kept on the roster through at least the end of December that year. And by then, with the Knicks being thin at the guard position, they decided it made sense to keep him on the team and develop his game. So in that way, the dunk attempt paid off.

While he hadn't been able to put an exclamation point on that 1990 training camp, he was able to put one on Game 2 against the Bulls. With Armstrong and Bill Cartwright assuming he'd use a Ewing screen to drive to his left, the right baseline opened for Starks like a Midtown street with an ambulance roaring down it. Starks gathered just outside the paint, leapt, and, despite being a righty, put the ball in his left hand. Forward Horace Grant came over to defend the play, but had a bad ankle, and didn't jump as quickly as Starks did. On the backside of the play, Jordan entered the frame late, attempting to back up Grant, whom Starks easily barreled through before slamming the ball through the cylinder.

As he came back down to earth, Starks twirled around, then retreated on defense as the Knicks took a five-point lead. The Bulls called timeout, and the Garden roared louder than it had in perhaps twenty years.

Starks finished with just 12 points that night. But his nine assists were more than the Bulls' starting five combined, and he'd again forced Jordan into an off night—nothing short of remarkable considering the Bulls had passed on an opportunity to land Starks three years earlier. Jerry Krause, Chicago's general manager, had considered signing Starks back in 1990 before the Knicks pulled the trigger, but ultimately declined.

"We've found through trial and error that it's not smart to have young backups," Krause said. "[Jordan] generally eats those kids up so bad in practice that he destroys them."

But two games into the series, one the Knicks now led 2–0, it was Starks eating the Bulls alive.

The Knicks' best chance to do away with the two-time defending champs might have come in Game 3.

Yes, the contest was at the raucous Chicago Stadium. But things were tense for the Bulls—Jordan in particular—after the New York Times published a bombshell report: Jordan had been out gambling in Atlantic City late the night before Game 2. And with the harsh spotlight trained directly on him, Jordan shot an uncharacteristically awful 3-for-18 in Game 3, marking the third straight game that New York had held him in check.

Yet little else went right for the Knicks. Starks, so composed in those first two games, got ejected midway through the fourth, when New York already trailed by 23 points. The club committed 20 turnovers and laid an egg on a night when Jordan struggled, blowing an opportunity. "If we'd been ready to snatch that game, maybe we go up 3–0. Instead, it's 2–1," assistant Jeff Van Gundy says. "Then Game 4 happens."

The Knicks' worst fears were realized in Game 4, when Jordan ignited for 54 points to help Chicago even the series, 2–2. His performance laid the groundwork for a massive showdown at the Garden for Game 5.

Dating back to Charles Smith's first practice as a Knick, Pat Riley was already concerned about the player's fit with the rest of the group.

Given that he had Oakley and Ewing at power forward and center, the coach had envisioned Smith joining the starting lineup as the team's small forward. But beyond Smith's poor conditioning that day, Riley wondered about Smith's toughness. In speaking to reporters, he wondered whether Smith could downshift and make the transition to play on the wing. That same week, Riley told Greg Brittenham, the team's strength and conditioning coach, he wanted him to help Smith go from 260 pounds to about 245—weight loss that would make him more capable of staying with wings like Scottie Pippen.

The adjustment of going from the post to the wing challenged Smith. Similarly, going from a No. 1 or No. 2 option to being a third option in the Knicks' crowded scheme wasn't easy. He didn't get set plays called for him, and instead was expected to play within the flow of whatever was happening. Smith had moments when it seemed like he'd taken one step forward (shooting 47 percent and averaging 15 points, seven rebounds, and four assists in the month of December) only to then take two steps back (36 percent, averaging 11 points, four boards, and less than one assist in January). Coaches, like Atlanta's Bob Weiss, sometimes even instructed their players to leave Smith open unless he was directly underneath the basket.

It left Riley wondering if Smith was what, or who, he wanted. He made that concern known months before Smith was set to become a free agent. "Pat wasn't sold at all on paying him," Dave Checketts says.

Checketts felt differently. Scarred by the year before, when de facto owner Stanley Jaffe chewed him out for losing Xavier McDaniel for nothing in free agency, the president determined he wasn't letting Smith walk. It also helped that Smith had a strong finish to the regular season, allowing the front office to feel better about entering into long-term contract negotiations with the forward's agent as the playoffs began.

For a team that had lost its grip on things, New York felt comfortable heading into Game 5. After all, the series was still tied. The Knicks would be at home, where they'd gone an NBA-best 37-4 during the regular season. Including the playoffs, the club had won twenty-seven straight at the Garden. And dating back to the 1991–92 campaign, New York owned a six-game winning streak against Jordan and the Bulls at home.

The Knicks began Game 5 on fire, scoring on their first ten possessions. But after seesawing with the Bulls for forty-seven and a half minutes, New York trailed by one, 95–94, with 28.8 seconds remaining.

When Starks caught the inbound pass and dribbled into the play that would be remembered for decades, it was the same call—a right-wing pick-and-roll between him and Ewing—the Knicks used when Starks threw down the thunderous jam to end Game 2. After getting the screen from Ewing, Starks had a glimmer of daylight in the corner, faking Jordan into the air before passing to Ewing, who was off-balance as he made the catch. The 7-footer, twenty-two feet from the hoop with Stacey King defending, awkwardly dribbled between his legs and drove left before colliding with King, which caused both men to fall over.

Just before Ewing tumbled, he desperately shoveled a pass to Smith, who had run into the painted area to crash the glass when it looked like Starks might launch the corner jumper. But now Smith had the ball in his hands, standing two feet from glory and on the cusp of making all those bruising practice drills at Pitt—where Maslek intentionally scratched, clawed, and beat on him—completely worthwhile.

All Smith had to do was bend his knees, lock the ball into his hands tightly, and elevate high enough to drop the ball in with power. But in split-second moments like this, where a play breaks down and defenders collapse into the paint, instincts take over. And Smith's instincts had always skewed more toward finesse than power.

With four Bulls surrounding him, Smith went up quickly with his right hand, only to be denied by Grant, who knocked the ball into the air.

Smith recovered the rock, then saw three Bulls looking to swat him.

He hesitated before trying again. But in pump faking before going back up, Smith allowed Jordan the opportunity to swipe at the ball—which he did, knocking the ball loose on Smith's second effort.

Jordan backed away suddenly, perhaps to avoid drawing a foul on the strip. So Smith got the ball a third time, this one perhaps being his cleanest look at the hoop—finally without a mass of limbs in his way. But again, he prioritized going quickly and beating defenders to the punch instead of slamming the ball home with authority. And Pippen—an ace defender who was two inches shorter than Smith, but owned the wingspan of an adult condor—caught Smith's third try from behind, blocking it.

Smith miraculously came up with the ball a fourth time. Yet the outcome would be precisely the same: another quick attempt, another Pippen rejection.

The sequence—like watching a halfback get turned away inches from the goal line on four straight plays, only more surreal, because all four tries occurred over a seven-second span—ended with Jordan nabbing the ball and flinging it to Armstrong, who'd streaked down the court for a layup as the clock hit zeroes.

As the buzzer sounded and Armstrong's make funneled through the rim, Smith was there to collect the ball from the most heartbreaking loss in Knicks history. The arena was church-silent as Smith spiked the basketball into the Garden floor, sending it twenty feet high as Jordan and his teammates joyously sprinted off the court. They acted as if the basketball gods might change their minds if the Bulls stuck around to savor their 97–94 win any longer.

"Like, let's not even shower. Let's just get on the bus now, because we had no business winning that," Perdue recalls.

Smith, meanwhile, looked to be on the verge of tears, and in utter disbelief.

Doc Rivers describes the Game 5 loss in very specific terms. "It felt like the sudden death of a family member who was perfectly healthy," Rivers said. "I'm not saying that losing a game is as bad as someone dropping dead. But I'm accurately describing the feeling."

The pain was so excruciating during his hour-long drive home from the Garden that Rivers stopped at a gas station—not to get gas, but because he needed fresh air. When he got there, he spotted teammate Herb Williams at the station, too, and noticed the backup had his head in his hands, clearly agonizing over the loss.

When Rivers got back on the road, he passed a vehicle on the side of the highway that had been pulled over by a police car, its red and blue lights still flashing. As Rivers slowed down and craned his neck to peer out his window, he recognized Smith as the man who'd been stopped, putting the rotten cherry on top of what had already been one of the toughest days of Smith's life.

Any worthwhile recap of the Game 5 loss, which put the Knicks behind 3–2 in the series, will indicate a ton of things went wrong aside from Smith's sequence. New York gave up 14 second-chance points, and got outrebounded 48–37—the one time in the series Chicago beat the Knicks on the glass. The club's 20-for-35 showing at the line was its worst of the year; regular season or playoffs.

But make no mistake: to this day, Smith's sequence holds a painful, singular place in the hearts of the Knicks and their fans alike.

"Maybe this is the defining moment of this team's life," Riley told writers as the team prepared to fly to Chicago.

If the Knicks placed blame on Smith for the loss, they certainly didn't show it in the aftermath of the contest. Interestingly, Smith and the club agreed in principle to a long-term deal—seven years, $26 million—ahead of Game 6 in Chicago, before he could become an unrestricted free agent that summer.

Smith and New York fought in Game 6, but ultimately came up short again, losing both the contest and the series. It marked the Knicks' third straight elimination at the hands of the Bulls, who would go on to win their third title in a row.

A number of people from that Knicks club, including Riley himself, believe the 1993 group was the franchise's best to suit up during that era. "We had a championship team. We really did. That year, I thought our team was better than anybody else in the league," Riley said. "We just could not get past MJ."

From his days leading the Lakers, Riley knew what it was to enjoy a dominant run at the top. Now he was on the other side of the fence, privately worrying whether New York, firmly entrenched in Jordan's shadow, would ever catch a break. At 30, Jordan appeared well positioned to block the Knicks' path to the Finals for years to come.

7

DAYLIGHT

Sometime during the 1993 offseason, Pat Riley and his family flew to Wailea, the picturesque Maui resort community known for its crescent-shaped beaches and pristine golf courses, for a late-summer vacation.

One morning in the middle of their trip, Riley got a call in his presidential suite from the front desk manager, who had a hint of urgency and regret in his voice. The manager's message was simple: due to an unforeseen situation, he needed Riley and his family to move elsewhere.

Riley was both confused and annoyed. For one, he'd paid extremely good money for the suite, enough to where there weren't supposed to be these kinds of inconveniences. He couldn't get a straight answer about what—or better yet, who—required the Rileys to move on such short notice.

After a short back-and-forth, Riley relented. The manager assured him hotel employees would come relocate the family's things into their next suite to help speed the process along.

Unable to stay in their own room, but needing to wait on the next one, the Rileys decided to head down to the resort's pool area to pass the time. While down there, Riley craned his neck every few minutes to look up at his departed presidential suite. He wanted to see who had bumped him.

It didn't take long for him to get his answer. As his children took a swim, Riley turned speechless as he saw the doors to the suite's balcony fly open. Michael Jordan, of all people, had been handed the suite, and was now sporting a comfy bathrobe, peering down at Riley, blissfully waving to the coach.

The scene illustrated reality for Riley, the Knicks, and twenty-five other teams in the league at the time. Jordan, fresh off his third straight NBA title with the Bulls, was on top, standing where everyone else wanted to be.

Which is why, on Tuesday, October 5, 1993, Patrick Ewing picked up his phone to call David Falk. That afternoon, reports began swirling that Jordan would announce his retirement from basketball just three months after the murder of his father.

By then, Ewing wasn't wondering whether the reports were accurate. With a press conference slated for the following day, he knew they were. Ewing wanted to know why he was only now hearing about it.

"You couldn't give me a heads-up?" Ewing asked Falk, who represented both him and Jordan.

"I promised Michael," Falk told him.

Regardless of how or when Ewing and the Knicks learned of Jordan's shocking plans, the subtext was clear. With the game's greatest player gone, New York's path to a title had become easier. "It helps us," Doc Rivers told reporters. "Nobody's said it out loud, but I'm sure almost everybody felt it."

Jordan's exit, announced two days before NBA training camps opened on October 8, had no impact on how the Knicks prepared for the 1993–94 season. Even before Jordan's announcement, Riley told his players they would be opening camp in Charleston at 12:01 a.m., the first allowable moment. It was meant to show that New York wanted to be the first team to set foot on the court that season, and the last club to leave it.

Staying on the court was about to become more challenging for at least one player, though.

In the offseason, the first of many rule changes directed at teams like the Knicks was implemented—including a point system for flagrant fouls, and subsequent suspensions if a player exceeded it. So now, Charles Oakley, who'd finished with more than twice as many flagrants as the next-closest player a year earlier, would have to sit out a game if he racked up more than five flagrant points. And judging from camp, it seemed Oakley's hyperphysicality might require fine-tuning to avoid a suspension.

During one scrimmage, the power forward stepped in front of a driving Charles Smith and elbowed him in the mouth, knocking one of Smith's teeth onto the floor, in an effort to protect the rim. Similarly, but less violently, free-agent newcomer Anthony Bonner got a taste of what it was like to grapple with Oakley during one of his first practices. As Bonner walked away from the workout with a bloody, busted lip and a bloodshot eye, Rivers smiled at him, patted him on the shoulder, and said, "Welcome, Anthony."

If there were kinks for New York to work out in the early going, they didn't show to begin the 1993–94 season. Despite spending twenty-nine of their first forty-two workdays on the road—and spending nearly as many days in the state of Texas as they had at the Garden in that span—the Knicks reeled off wins in their first seven games. Along with the Houston Rockets, they were one of the league's last two teams to remain unbeaten.

Still, a handful of issues threatened to hold the Knicks back, even as they became one of the clear favorites to win an NBA championship.

Certain players—backup Tony Campbell in particular—were griping about roles, which Riley had no tolerance for. Annoyed by complaints during the first week of camp, the coach issued a warning: bitching about a lack of playing time on this team will be the quickest way to ensure you get traded elsewhere. Riley also told each of his players exactly where they stood on the depth chart, just so there would be no confusion.

Then there was Starks, who became an All-Star in 1994, but could go from being completely frigid one game (4-for-21 in a loss to the Jazz) to scorched earth (a 37-point showing in which he tied an NBA record with seven threes in a win over Miami) the next. And when it wasn't Starks's inconsistency that tripped things up, it was the team's tendency to be too predictable on both offense and defense.

Consider one January game, in which the Knicks trailed by one to the lowly Sixers with just over a minute left. Riley called timeout to draw up a play. On the opposing sideline, Philadelphia guard Jeff Hornacek told teammates he was going to cheat the action by banking on the likelihood that New York would have Starks dump the ball into Ewing on the block.

"I'm gonna go for the steal as soon as [Starks] throws it into him," Hornacek said in the Sixers huddle.

When that very scenario played out, Hornacek secured both a steal and a Sixers win. One day later, a number of Knicks were quoted anonymously, complaining about the lack of diversity within the New York offense, which saw 47 of its 86 shots taken by Ewing and Starks in the defeat.

Too often, the Knicks didn't have a consistent scoring option beyond those two players—a glaring issue in contests where the opponent had a star center capable of taking Ewing out of rhythm. That had been the case against the Rockets, who carried a perfect 14-0 mark into the Garden, when the Knicks repeatedly pounded the ball into Ewing despite his inability to find good looks against Hakeem Olajuwon.

Starks eventually picked up the slack, finishing with 35 despite a Jekyll-and-Hyde showing, in which he missed twelve of his first fourteen attempts. But Ewing had gone cold by the second half, missing all twelve of his tries after the break to finish the game 4-for-20. Olajuwon outscored Ewing 16–0 in the third quarter. And it didn't help that the New York bench—scoreless in the first half—was virtually nonexistent. The fans at the Garden booed the effort, which wasn't nearly enough to take down the Rockets, who, by sailing to their fifteenth win, had tied the NBA record for consecutive victories to start a season.

But staying healthy proved to be the biggest challenge for the Knicks midway through that campaign.

Fresh off getting his seven-year deal over the summer, Charles Smith played in that December game against Houston. But his forgettable stat line—two points on 0-for-5 shooting, two fouls, and a rebound in twenty-four minutes—suggested something might be wrong. And there was. His left knee, which he'd had offseason arthroscopic surgery on just months earlier, was now bothering him so much he could no longer play. A December MRI identified damaged cartilage, prompting Smith to undergo another knee cleanout, one that sidelined him for six weeks.

Yet even after that period of rehab, Smith had a difficult time getting comfortable with the knee. He returned to the lineup in late January but began complaining of constant soreness again within weeks. And things only got worse.

When Smith's soreness forced him to sit out of practices again so soon after his return, his teammates—the same ones who playfully teased him about growing out his hair, calling him everything from Dr. J to Angela Davis and Shaft—began whispering, saying they felt Smith was either faking injury or dramatizing the extent to which he was hurt. They had no clue Smith was beginning to develop chronic knee problems.

"Is he at it again?" one player often asked the team's trainers whenever Smith missed a practice that year.

On some level, this was one of the downsides of having a Ford-tough roster like New York's, with so many players who were willing to play through just about anything. Because so many of the players in the rotation *had* played through intense pain and significant injuries before, they lacked sympathy for those who weren't wired that way. And Riley's apparent perception of Smith didn't seem to help much.

As Riley used the locker room blackboard to lay out X's and O's for his players before one game, Smith—who was going to miss that night's contest with what had become an arthritic left knee—walked in, wearing the suit he planned to sport on the bench. When Smith strolled in, Riley stopped writing.

"Charles, if you could give me one minute tonight—just one—to win a championship, could you do it?" Riley asked Smith in front of his teammates. Smith wore a surprised look, but said he could.

"Then what in the hell are you doing in that suit?" Riley asked as the room fell awkwardly silent. Not knowing exactly what to do, Smith went to his locker to throw on his uniform as Riley resumed writing.

Though he said nothing in the moment, Smith, who'd long sought to win over his coach and shed his ugly-duckling feathers to better fit in with his more physical teammates, felt wounded by Riley's comment.

"Charles was pissed [about that]," says Brig Owens, Smith's agent. "He wanted to win, like anyone else. As a coach, you don't question how bad your guys are hurt. They're putting it on the line the best they can."

"I saw the aftereffects of that stuff in San Antonio, where he just wasn't the same guy," says Will Perdue, both an opponent and a teammate of Smith's in later years. "Guys in New York told me about how Riley just constantly rode his ass—to the point that he was almost crying. And unfortunately for [Charles], I think Riley just pushed him too hard to be something he wasn't. In a way, I sort of think he broke him."

Riley wasn't a coach who concerned himself with pacing. Rest days weren't a consideration. Every game was a battle, and every battle had to be won. "He had this stab-or-be-stabbed mentality that made you wonder why he hadn't gone into the military," says Mike Wise, a beat reporter for the New York Times.

Riley got maximum effort out of the Knicks, who suddenly were a contender. But constantly flooring the gas pedal brought about physical consequences. "I remember when I got traded to the Knicks, I was in the gym working out at UCLA with Magic [Johnson] and [James] Worthy. They immediately said, 'You're in trouble, bro,'" Rivers recalls. "They both loved Riles. But they said the intensity of his workouts was going to kill me and kill my career. They said, 'Your career is done.'"

Rivers, then 32 years old, lived on the tip of that double-edged sword. As a late-career player, he desperately wanted to win that elusive title. But he'd also been hampered by injuries throughout his time in the league. Both ambitions—winning a ring and staying healthy—were dealt horrible blows during a December game, in which Rivers came down on his left leg awkwardly, tearing his anterior cruciate ligament.

Losing Rivers, the starting point guard, was a tough pill to swallow. Aside from the team already being decimated—they held a practice session with just six healthy players at one point that month—the drop-off from Rivers to backup Greg Anthony was considerable, both in terms of leadership and skill. And because Anthony was the only other point guard on the roster, Starks had to act as a floor general far more often during his minutes, taking him out of his comfort zone as a perimeter shooter.

It didn't take long for the front office to determine the starting role was too much for Anthony. In New York's third contest without Rivers, against the Nets, Anthony struggled to stay with guard Kenny Anderson, who maneuvered around him for a pair of game-sealing scores late to win it for New Jersey.

As Anthony got dressed and was preparing to speak with reporters in the locker room after the defeat, he couldn't find his belt—fitting, given how Anderson undressed the guard's shortcomings. Aside from dicing Anthony with his offense, Anderson also left the poor-shooting Anthony wide open on defense, messing with his head in the process.

If the Knicks didn't upgrade at point guard, they were going to be at a nightly disadvantage there. So they swung a deal for Dallas guard Derek Harper, a respected, well-rounded veteran who was languishing away with the Mavericks, who'd won just twice in their first 27 games. Harper had been a target for New York even before Rivers went down. So to land him in a time of need—especially for a disgruntled Campbell and what would be a late first-round pick—seemed worth it.

Like with Smith, though, there would be a painful transition period for Harper. It was an initiation of sorts for the 32-year-old. (In at least one case, he was literally initiated by Oakley and Bonner, who roughed him up with a surprise attack on an elevator during a trip to Boston.) There were times when Harper felt like a rookie again, despite it being his eleventh season as a professional.

In his very first practice as a Knick, Harper was preparing to reach down for a loose ball during a scrimmage. Before he could grab it, two other players, Oakley and Anthony Mason, had already dived onto the floor for it, beating him to the punch. It was a wake-up call for Harper, who'd played on a losing team for four straight years, but now saw the desperate level of intensity the Knicks played with—even during practice.

Having Harper helped right away, given how shorthanded New York had been at point guard. Starks could focus on scoring again as opposed to facilitating. And though Anthony remained the starter, Harper's presence meant Riley didn't have to stick with a less experienced point guard for entire quarters anymore.

Still, even with the smarts and the depth Harper brought to the team's rotation, he wasn't really playing all that well to begin his tenure in New York. Through his first four outings, he shot just under 24 percent from the floor. As he walked over to the bench to sub out of one of those first games, a fan sitting behind the team's bench at the Garden shouted, "Hey, Harper, how fucking long is it going to take you?"

He wasn't the only one wondering. At a practice shortly after that game, Riley had his players sit against the wall as he gave them an honest characterization of how he saw things going. He didn't mince words when it came time to sum up Harper's stint.

"Harp, we didn't trade for you to do *this* shit," Riley said as he read off Harper's ghastly stats. "I know what you can do, because you did it against me when I coached in LA. But this is *not* what we expected."

"I couldn't say shit," Harper recalls. "All I could do was look at him and listen to him put me in check."

After the dressing-down, assistant coach Jeff Van Gundy pulled Harper aside and offered to stay long after workouts if he wanted to put up extra shots each day. "If you wanna shoot, I'll be a fucking rebound machine for you," Van Gundy told him. Harper tried not to think so much about where he fit in, and began playing more off his point-guard instincts rather than getting bogged down by the playbook.

Soon, Harper's numbers off the bench improved—even as the club seemed to stagnate. At 36-15 and with the best mark in the East, the Knicks were in the midst of a very good season.

Yet something still felt a bit off.

*   *   *

At one time, Knicks scout Phil Hubbard had been excited to come into town for team practices.

As someone who spent the vast majority of his time on the road, Hubbard rarely got opportunities to be with his coworkers, or chances to watch the team at work, behind the scenes. Sure, he found it strange that he couldn't merely show up to watch the sessions, since Riley wouldn't allow that, and wanted advance notice. Nonetheless, watching someone of Riley's ilk run the team's workouts would be amazing, Hubbard figured.

But as Hubbard watched the practices, he found himself looking down at his watch. Not because Riley was boring. Not because Hubbard had somewhere to be. Hubbard just kept wondering when, if ever, New York was going to run some drills that focused on offense. "After a while," he says, "I told myself I didn't need to go see practices anymore. Each time I went, it was always the same thing as the day before. Defense."

At times, the Knicks very much looked like a team that didn't work enough on their offense.

One of those times, in the last week of February 1994, they had an embarrassing showing against Seattle, in which they scored 33 first-half points and shot just under 29 percent from the field. Ewing settled for jumpers, and missed his first fourteen attempts in what would turn out to be a double-digit loss at the Garden. Riley, clearly frustrated, said the defeat was perhaps New York's worst game in his three years as coach.

The next outing was no better. The Rockets had no trouble holding the Knicks down on offense, either, cruising to a 20-point victory while limiting New York to just 73 points. The game after that was an improvement, with 94 points on 50 percent shooting in Denver. But the result was the same, with the Knicks falling for a third time in a row. And their trip to Phoenix would end in failure, too, with just six New York players entering the scoring column in a 92–78 loss, one that marked the seventh straight time the Knicks had been held beneath the century mark. Even more problematic than the team's obvious scoring issues? The losing skid, now up to four games, was the longest of Riley's tenure as Knicks coach.

Earlier in the West Coast trip, trainer Mike Saunders had gone out of his way to ask Riley whether it might be wise to ease up on the Knicks. The players were shooting even more poorly than usual, and seemed to be pressing more with each game. Riley responded to Saunders with a question of his own.

"What do you do when you have severe bleeding?" Riley rhetorically asked the trainer. "You apply direct pressure."

It was Riley's way of saying he was going to continue flooring the gas pedal, the way he usually did.

But after declining Saunders's suggestion, Riley watched the Knicks deliver that listless, 78-point showing against the Suns, which forced him to rethink his hard-charging approach.

As he sat on the Knicks' Sacramento-bound plane, Riley wondered if it might be time for a detour.

8

THIRTY-SIX HOURS IN RENO

Third-string guard Corey Gaines was glued to the world outside his window as the team plane began descending.

The impulse to peer out and see for miles—especially out west, where the weathered deserts are vast and the contrasting snowcapped mountain ranges abundant—was understandable. Especially for the Knicks, who had grown accustomed to the skyscraper-filled concrete jungle of New York City.

But on this day, Gaines wasn't using his aircraft window to take in the spectacle. As someone who'd grown up in Los Angeles and played college ball in California, he'd already flown over the region countless times. In this instance, Gaines was peering out his window because he didn't know where the hell he was.

Moments before, one of the pilots had come over the intercom to say he would be landing the plane in a few minutes, which prompted Gaines to check his watch. There was no way the flight could have made it to Sacramento that quickly from Phoenix—they would have been arriving thirty minutes faster than usual.

Anthony Bonner was confused, too. Before joining the Knicks that year, the forward spent three seasons in Sacramento. Yet nothing about his surroundings felt familiar as the aircraft continued to descend. Bonner voiced that thought to his Knicks teammates, who had grown curious—and, in some cases, concerned—about what might happen once the plane touched down. Patrick Ewing—his mouth agape, his eyes wide with apprehension—looked the most distressed.

The uneasiness stemmed from the Knicks' play leading up to that trip to Sacramento. For the first time, New York had lost four games in a row under Pat Riley, who'd been pushing the team harder and harder in practices over the course of the skid, as if the team could be violently shaken back into rhythm.

So the players panicked, fearing this detour—wherever it was—might be a new way for Riley to test them. That was Gaines's concern as the plane flew by an enormous mountain before landing.

"I'm thinking, 'Is he taking us to run up this mountain in the middle of a desert or something? Are we on some army base? Maybe like Area 51, where he can do whatever he wants, and no one'll ever know, because we're off the grid?'" Gaines recalls. "I just knew we weren't where we were supposed to be."

As the plane neared the airport, though, things came into clearer focus. A number of casinos were visible in the distance. Not nearly enough for it to be Las Vegas. But Greg Anthony, a Nevada native, felt comfortable surmising the club was in his home state.

When the flight finally touched down, Ewing breathed a deep sigh of relief. Others did, too. There were plenty of other planes on the tarmac, meaning the Knicks were still in civilization.

What the players didn't know yet, even as they'd landed at Reno-Tahoe International Airport, was *why* they were here, as opposed to Sacramento. And Riley, who'd made a spur-of-the-moment choice to ask the pilots to change their plan as they were taking off, was still playing it close to the vest. It wasn't until the team arrived at the Peppermill Casino and Hotel in limousines that everything began making sense.

"We're gonna take time off from basketball," Riley said as players looked on. "For the next thirty-six hours, I ask one thing: that we eat together, party together, and have fun together. Don't talk about basketball. Do what a group that loves each other would do. Have fun. But just do it together."

*   *   *

As players entered the casino with enormous smiles, they walked to the cashier's booth where they'd each get $500 worth of gaming chips, courtesy of their coach's $10,000 act of generosity. It was a bizarre scene, resembling a parent giving a child tokens to play at Chuck E. Cheese—only this was Riley, the most accomplished coach of his generation, handing over thousands of dollars' worth of gambling currency to a team of six- and seven-foot-tall millionaires. "They all had their hands out," Riley said.

As the players took off for their hotel rooms to put down their things, assistant Jeff Van Gundy pulled aside point guard Derek Harper.

"There's a good chance Pat is going to put you in the starting lineup next game," Van Gundy told him.

Harper's demeanor changed immediately. "I walked over and cashed my chips in. Just pocketed the money," Harper recalls. He wanted to keep a levelheaded mentality for the trip since he'd be taking the reins as the team's on-court leader once the Knicks got back to business.

So after running up to his room, Harper came back down, grabbed a couple glasses of wine, and tagged along for a while with teammates who were completely unaware of the upcoming lineup change.

John Starks was one of them. In vintage Starks fashion, he blew through his $500 in chips in less than an hour before spending some of his own money to try to turn his luck around. He eventually developed a hot streak the next day—one so scorching that the Knicks almost left for Sacramento without him.

When trainer and traveling secretary Mike Saunders took attendance on the team bus, he realized Starks was the only person missing. "I go back in the casino, and I find him hunched over a craps table," Saunders recalls. "I tell him, 'We have to go *now*. The bus is literally out here waiting for you.' And he responds by saying, 'But Mike, I'm winning!' I had to physically drag him away from the table. I honestly don't know that he ever saw his room the whole time we were there."

When the thirty-six-hour exhalation ended, New York held a shootaround to prep for the Kings. Riley explained he was changing the starting lineup, lifting Greg Anthony, Charles Smith, and Starks, swapping them out in favor of Harper, Bonner, and second-year shooting guard Hubert Davis.

Unsurprisingly, the starters who got moved to the bench weren't thrilled. Smith was New York's third-leading scorer and had just signed a seven-year deal. Starks, the team's second option, had just played in the All-Star Game weeks earlier. Yet there was no discussion of why the change was happening. And from where Riley sat, there didn't need to be. The Knicks' struggles were an obvious enough reason.

Plus, Riley had softened the blow by giving them free time in Reno. "It was a gutsy thing he did," Bonner said of Riley swapping out two of his top scorers from a lineup that had trouble scoring. "He took out the nuts and bolts of what worked before, and replaced them with ones that emphasized ball movement."

Whatever the aim, and whether a result of strategy or a placebo effect, the Knicks got back on track instantly, beating Sacramento, 100–88, to snap their four-game skid. With the victory, New York would begin another streak, holding eight straight foes under the 90-point mark, becoming the first club since 1954—the year the shot clock was introduced—to do so. That stifling span marked the club's most dominant defensive stretch of Riley's tenure in New York; impressive for a team that would lead the NBA in defense for three consecutive years.

Even after New York saw its streak of holding opponents under 90 snapped—allowing 91 points to Boston, in a Knicks victory—Riley urged his players to stay hungry. To raise the stakes, Riley again came out of his own pocket, saying he would pay $100 for every charge one of his defenders took during wins, and that he'd double that payout with each additional victory. By the end of March, after New York had gone a perfect 14-0 for the month, and had won five straight since Riley issued his charge challenge, the payout per charge drawn had increased to a whopping $1,600.

It wasn't the kind of money that figured to change the way rugged, highly compensated players like Ewing or Charles Oakley played. But for an end-of-the-bench contributor like Eric Anderson, the cash-drenched carrot was an obvious influence in the closing minutes of a blowout win at home over Miami.

"Pat puts him in with four minutes left, and he's running around, throwing his body in front of anyone that's moving. Just the funniest thing," Van Gundy said. "He drew two charges while he was out there."

The Knicks earned their fifteenth win in a row, matching the NBA season-high the Rockets set to open the campaign. And Anderson earned $3,200—slightly more than he earned per game that year—in bonuses for drawing charges. Not bad for four minutes of work.

After the fifteen-game win streak came to a close, Riley sent Dave Checketts an invoice for the $10,000 he spent for the players to gamble in Reno.

The coach knew the trip was unorthodox, as was his choice to front his players gambling money. But he also figured that the cost—the cost of winning, really—was reasonable, since it got the Knicks out of a rut.

Checketts agreed, and said that'd be no problem. But then weeks went by. Then several months. Riley still hadn't gotten his money—partly because, according to Checketts, no one at the Garden knew how to officially label the expense, which would be subject to the scrutiny of shareholders of a publicly traded company.

The delay annoyed Riley. Much like his initial negotiations with the club back in 1991, he wanted to know his boss would always do what it took to promote the idea of winning. The amount of money wasn't nearly as consequential to the coach as the principle itself. Riley had done something in the name of winning. But in his mind, the organization wasn't as prompt in valuing the concept as much as he did.

"He never forgot it. That stuck in his craw," Checketts says of the delayed reimbursement. "If I knew what I know now, I would've just paid him back myself. Everything with Pat was black or white. In or out."

Checketts picked up on just how deeply Riley believed in being on the same page within months of working with him. During the team's first training camp in Charleston, in 1991, Checketts and Riley were having lunch when Checketts's cell phone rang, interrupting the talk. It was his wife, Deborah, who was about to buy a Chevy Suburban sport-utility vehicle, and wanted her husband's input on color.

Deborah had all but decided on the color green, and asked her husband if he was okay with that option. He was, and told her that would be a perfectly fine choice. But then Riley, who was sitting next to Checketts and had listened in enough to know the couple was choosing a color for a new vehicle, butted in.

"What are you talking about? She can't buy a green car, Dave. Green is the Celtics," Riley said, referring to the team that had served as the archrival of his Showtime Lakers during the 1980s.

Checketts laughed, before realizing Riley's facial expression hadn't changed.

"I'm dead serious," Riley said.

So Checketts, still on the phone with his wife, told her she couldn't get a green Suburban.

When Deborah asked what other colors were available, the car salesman suggested red. So she asked Checketts how he felt about red. Again, Checketts was fine with that option. Again, Riley wasn't.

"What? Red is the Bulls," said Riley, almost annoyed Checketts would even ask his take on the color.

Checketts relented. "Don't come home with anything but a blue one," he told his wife, before hanging up.

This was how Riley was wired. You were either all the way in on supporting his vision—down to the color of your car—or you weren't.

Toward the end of that 1993–94 regular season, Riley had determined Anthony Mason wasn't all-in.

The coach wanted to assess what he had to work with just days before the playoffs were set to begin, and was giving extended playing time to Charles Smith, who'd recently returned to the lineup after missing three weeks with more knee troubles. The Knicks had lost Starks for the remainder of the regular season to a leg injury, and didn't want to rely on him too heavily once he returned in the playoffs. So Riley, thinking Smith's offense might take on added importance soon, sat Mason on the bench for the entire second half of a narrow loss to the Atlanta Hawks.

"We needed scoring," said Riley, explaining that he wanted to jump-start Smith, who'd drawn boos from the Garden crowd while finishing with 6 points on 2-of-8 shooting. It was a lackluster showing in an important game, which ultimately resulted in Atlanta earning the tiebreaker for the top seed over the Knicks.

"We needed offense? That's what [Riley] said?" Mason asked when speaking to reporters after the game.

Clearly frustrated, Mason avoided offering an opinion on Riley's comment immediately after the game. But the next day after practice, Mason had an entire dissertation prepared in response to his coach's suggestion that Smith was better on offense. "That's his opinion. He has his opinion, and we have ours," Mason said with three regular-season games left to play.

"Offense is a mix of a lot of things. It starts with stopping your man and getting the rebound and outletting the ball—I do that well. I thought offense was somebody who could pass out of the post and hit the open man when he's doubled. I do all that stuff well. So when you say who's the best offensive player, you mix all that up together. I think [Riley] just defines offense a different way than I define it."

Riley was a successful basketball coach, not a neologist for Merriam-Webster. And after hearing of Mason's comments, the coach suspended him—the first time he'd ever taken such action—indefinitely for conduct detrimental to the team.

Riley informed Mason of the decision in front of all his teammates during their morning shootaround. "We're trying to get the team ready in every way, shape, and form. Everybody has to declare: you're either in, or you're out," Riley told reporters.

Riley's issues with Mason's individuality had been simmering well before that, though. Even Harper, a relative newcomer, had picked up on the undercurrent within a month or so of joining the club.

Playing in Atlanta, the Knicks had just secured a rebound, and were coming down the floor to start their possession. But Harper, the floor general, struggled to take charge. Instead, Mason dominated the ball to start the sequence, dribbling between his legs before dumping a pass into the post that resulted in a miss. The play was so disjointed Riley called timeout once the Knicks got the ball back on the next play.

As the players walked to the sideline to hear from Riley, Harper told Mason to give up the ball in the future so he could organize an actual play as the team's point guard. In response, Mason snarled.

"What the fuck are you talking about?" Mason shouted at Harper, in full view of Riley and the rest of his teammates on the bench. "You aren't gonna do anything with it if I give you the ball anyway!"

After watching the exchange, Riley questioned Harper. "Harp, are you in charge of this shit or not?"

Harper held his tongue. But he wanted to fire back at Riley, who'd somehow questioned his leadership instead of Mason's behavior.

"He's putting the onus on me to not argue with [Mason] on the floor. But I'm thinking, 'Shit, it's not my job to handle him,'" Harper says. "'Y'all built the monster, and were dealing with this before I even got here!'"

Once Riley finally took the step of holding him accountable, Mason grew enraged. His agent, Don Cronson, recalls it all vividly. He was in Arizona for the week, scouting top-end college players at the Phoenix Desert Classic, when the suspension came down.

"Mase calls me, and he's just *screeching*. Every other word out of his mouth was 'fuck.' *Fuck this. Fuck them*," Cronson says. "I just told him to lay low. I'd never heard Mase this angry before. And I tell him: 'Mase, don't go to the practice facility, since they told you to stay away. Just let the thing blow over.'"

But Mason, a habitual line-stepper, opted to poke the bear. He attended the Knicks' game that night at the Garden as a spectator, high-fiving fans while sitting in the 300 level and wearing a New York Rangers jersey. His presence drew enough attention that television cameras spotlighted him in the fourth quarter.

Knicks players knew something unusual was taking place in the crowd due to the outbursts from fans sitting in the arena's upper deck, who were thrilled to be in the presence of the suspended southpaw. "I thought there was a fight in the stands at first," said Davis, the shooting guard.

The Knicks beat the Sixers like a drum that night, 130–82. But now the glare of the New York City media figured to shine even brighter on the situation involving Mason, which only made Riley angrier.

Somehow not realizing this—or realizing it, and pushing his luck a little bit more—Mason showed up at the team facility a day or two later to work out. Riley was notified, and took the step of phoning Mason. "Don't you get it? You're banned! You're barred! You're not part of this organization!" Riley screamed.

As he said it, a dumbfounded Mason hung up the phone, only now realizing how deep the standoff was.

All the while, Cronson was left trying to clean up what had quickly become an explosive situation. "I spent time talking with Checketts about it, trying to smooth things over. And he's okay," Cronson says. "But he's telling me that Pat is so angry that he doesn't even want to put Anthony on the playoff roster."

As jarring as that possibility was, Checketts had vowed to Riley upon hiring him: he would never override his coach's decisions when it came to the roster. So he felt he couldn't go back on his word in a key moment like this. Instead, Checketts took a middle ground. He got on a call with Riley and Ernie Grunfeld a half hour before the 3 p.m. roster deadline, knowing Grunfeld would be more vocal in trying to change Riley's mind.

Grunfeld, who rarely got worked up, delivered a passionate plea, saying the team would be losing its best defender—and perhaps its best rebounder, and one of its best playmakers—if Mason wasn't added to the postseason roster. "You can't leave him off, Pat," Grunfeld said. "We'll have no chance if you do."

After hearing from his bosses, who were still on the phone waiting for a final answer, Riley sat silently, thinking about what he wanted to do. Like Checketts and Grunfeld, he obviously knew how much value Mason carried, and that the team was better with the forward on the floor. But he didn't know whether he could tolerate one of his players challenging his decision-making so loudly and openly in the media.

The more Riley tried to understand Mason, the more he found himself at a complete loss. What was it about Mason that so desperately needed to challenge authority? And where did that trait come from?

9

THE ENIGMATIC LIFE
OF ANTHONY MASON

Anthony Mason's face was completely contorted. Almost cartoonishly so, as if he were wearing an abstract, Picasso version of his actual face.

Moments earlier, Nico Childs, Mason's Tennessee State teammate, had hopped off the bench and jogged over from the sideline to sub in for him.

"Coach told you to come get *me*?" Mason asked, as his look of incredulity transformed into a death stare aimed directly at coach Larry Reid.

To Mason—the team's star, who averaged 38 minutes a night that season—it didn't matter that he'd just committed a sloppy, showboat-style turnover. By the time he reached the sideline, he was in a rage. Shouting. Gesturing wildly with his hands. And, in the words of one teammate, "dogcussing" his coach, calling him a "faggot" in front of the team and the 3,200 fans present.

When Mason finally sat down, at the far end of the bench, the forward had tears in his eyes.

As usual, he had his reasons. Not only was it Senior Night for the 1988 squad, making it Mason's last home game as a college player. It was also the first time his mother had been able to make the trip from New York to see him play in person. To be subbed out midway through the second half, with her finally in the stands? That was more than enough provocation to send Mason on a roller coaster of emotions. And apparently Reid agreed; he soon put Mason back in the game.

It had, after all, become something of a routine at Tennessee State to work around Mason's indiscretions.

For a handful of his teammates, the brash New Yorker's antics—swaggering through the Nashville campus, referring to southerners as "country bump-kins" while wearing a fat gold chain that spelled out ANTHONY—were an acquired taste. During the first week of his sophomore year alone, Mason burned, almost literally, through two different roommates.

Each of those roommates, who were basketball teammates of Mason's, had approached the coaching staff within days of moving in, saying they'd tried, but just couldn't live with him. He was weird. Specifically, they complained that Mason had an odd fascination with lighting matches, then flicking them at whoever was around. In desperation, one of the coaches asked center George Lester if he'd share his dorm room with Mason. Lester agreed.

But it wasn't long before trouble found Mason again.

"I just remember coming home from a party on campus, and walking into the dorm and seeing that these two guys were about to fight Mase in a two-on-one sort of thing," Lester says. "So I had his back, stopped the fight from happening, and he and I just kind of hit it off after that."

It was far from the last time the program would have to close ranks around Mason. Like the time Mason's coaches had to convince Tennessee State administrators not to kick him off the team after he got caught sneaking into the girls-only Mary Wilson Hall dormitory three separate times. (The coaches argued that he'd endured a challenging childhood—involving physical abuse—and said taking away Mason's chance to play would have a harsh impact on his future. In turn, administrators opted to give him a reprieve.)

Or the time a state trooper, who'd pulled over a 17-year-old Mason for driving 90 miles per hour—30 more than the limit—decided against taking the youngster in for booking because the officer was friendly with folks at Tennessee State. Or the many times TSU staffers let Mason borrow their vehicles—a violation of NCAA rules—despite knowing he wasn't very good at driving. (He once crashed teammate Judon Roper's car into a hydrant at a nearby Kroger while on a grocery run.)

"He could not drive, man. It was like putting a kid behind the steering wheel," says Lester, adding that Mason once called him from jail as a sophomore, begging to be bailed out. He'd been taken in after a traffic stop, and wanted to go home without his coach finding out about his detainment.

Still, for all the bailing out teammates and coaches had to do during those college years, they recall just as vividly Mason's many redeeming qualities.

Chief among them: gratitude. Mason grew up poor, and experienced significant growth spurts as a teenager. His pants would often go from just long enough to several inches short in the span of a school year. He drew taunts like "Goose" for his long neck and "high-water" because of his flooding pants. His big feet were joked on constantly, as were his sneakers, which had four stripes instead of three like the Adidas brand.

When Mason arrived at Tennessee State, he learned players were required to wear a tie and a pair of dress slacks each time they played on the road. He didn't own either. Teammate Cordell Johnson—who'd been in the program a year longer, and was roughly the same height as Mason— had plenty of both, and gave him a pair of brown dress pants and a pair of black ones.

"You would've thought I was his best friend," Johnson says, adding that Mason looked to reciprocate the gesture by sharing groceries and anything else he had. "Whatever he had, you had."

One thing Mason had an abundance of—and usually wanted to share with other people—was fun, particularly at the start of each school year, before basketball got under way. "We'd see him when it was time for the players to take physicals, and then we wouldn't see him again for a while," laughed Wayne Bell, the longtime trainer at Tennessee State.

One night during his sophomore year, Mason attended a campus bonfire with some friends. Sensing he had the attention of multiple women present, he urged one of them to go talk and dance with his roommate, Lester, who'd come along with him.

"Pretty soon it turned into 'Give my roommate your number!'" Lester recalls. "The funny thing is, me and the girl from that party have been married for twenty-eight years now."

Mason, too, would establish a relationship with the woman he talked to at that party: fellow Tennessee State student Monica Bryant, who immediately caught his eye during that fall of 1985.

The two of them, merely friends at that point, walked toward Mason's team bus as the club prepared for a road trip. "He brought me up on the bus, and introduced me to all his teammates as his girlfriend," Bryant says. "It was a flattering thing, but I figured he was joking, because we'd just met."

But Mason wasn't joking. He and Bryant proceeded to hang out most days—Lester considered Monica a third roommate because of how often she was over—and when they couldn't, they'd talk on the phone for hours each day. The following summer, when Bryant's mother drove her to the doctor for her annual physical, Monica learned she was pregnant. "Anthony was the first call I made, and he was so excited," says Bryant, who gave birth to Anthony Jr. in January 1987.

It would be an overstatement to say the birth of Anthony Jr. prompted an outpouring of paternal instincts from Mason, who himself had just turned 20 years old a month earlier. With Monica moving back home to Memphis to care for the child, Mason was not only more than three hours away, and unable to visit regularly, but also in the midst of his junior season. (Realizing this, Mason's mother took it upon herself to phone Monica every day from New York.)

What the presence of the newborn did change was Mason's desire to play professional basketball, which had gone from mere dream to necessity. Suddenly, he needed to provide. And reaching the sport's highest level would allow him to do it.

That meant lapping teammates during offseason conditioning in the sweltering autumn heat, when players ran a timed mile. It meant waking up Lester and other teammates at all hours of the night, sometimes at 2 a.m., to ask if they'd sneak into the campus arena with him to play pickup or shoot jumpers. And it meant tirelessly working to

tighten up his ball-handling with his right hand, in hopes of prompting scouts and defenders to question which hand, if either, was Mason's
dominant one.

It all helped transform Mason from the type of player who thrived
mostly off energy plays in his first two years into one who averaged 28
points his final season. The work paid off. In 1988, he was drafted by the
Blazers with the 53rd pick.

It would be three more years, and six professional teams later, but Mason
ultimately found his way to the Knicks.

After failing to make Portland's roster, Mason journeyed to play overseas. His first stop was Istanbul, where Mason not only struggled to enjoy
the food—"I don't like to criticize another's culture, but I had to frown at
some of the squirrelly things those Turks were slurping up," he once told
New York magazine—but also found himself at odds with his coach. After
one heated altercation, Mason parted ways with the team and returned to
the US despite leading the Turkish league in points and rebounds.

Mason enjoyed Venezuela, a more secular country than Turkey, far
more—if only for his ability to speak with local women more easily.

During those foreign stints, Mason picked up a couple of valuable
basketball skills. In Turkey, an on-court casualty was a prerequisite for
an official to call a foul. (Mason himself had a pair of teeth knocked out
there without a whistle being blown.) So he grew to enjoy playing physically. By contrast, the slightest touch in Venezuela would draw a whistle.
"So I learned to play defense with my feet, and it improved my quickness," he said. That combination, possessing brute force on dancer's feet,
would define his game.

Still, there were other stops. A couple of layovers with the Nets and
Nuggets, who would each decide he was expendable. One in the Continental Basketball Association with Tulsa. And one—with the Long Island
Surf—in the United States Basketball League, which Mason dominated
to the tune of 28 points and 11 boards per game in 1990–91.

Ed Krinsky, the Surf's general manager, was so enamored by the surprising ball-handling skills Mason showed for someone his size that he suggested Knicks scout Fuzzy Levane take a look at him. Levane arrived for a game in June, and watched the forward deliver a 36-point showing.

Levane was sold. But he almost pulled the trigger a hair late.

One July day, sitting at an Italian restaurant in Manhattan alongside then-girlfriend Latifa Whitlock, Mason had just put pen to paper for a contract with an Israeli team. A pair of executives from the club were sitting across the table from the couple, and were thrilled to have Mason coming overseas. Shortly after a congratulatory handshake, Mason's cell phone rang. It was a call from the Knicks, who were interested in signing Mason to their summer-league roster.

After stepping away from the table to take the call, Mason returned with a request: would the Israeli team let him out of the deal he'd signed just minutes earlier if the situation with his hometown Knicks came to fruition?

Much to Mason's relief, the Israeli executives said they'd act in good faith and nix their contract if he and the Knicks finalized a deal. They even went on to say he would still have a spot with the foreign club if New York later decided Mason wasn't a good fit.

But that day never came. The same combination of traits that had captivated Krinsky was immediately evident to Pat Riley. The coach was in the stands in Los Angeles for one of Mason's summer-league games when, within a five-second burst, the lefty skyed for a defensive rebound, dribbled upcourt in transition, then jammed on the head of a helpless 7-footer standing in the paint.

That moment alone had been enough to convince Riley that Mason could help the Knicks, who were a far cry from the Showtime Lakers, and would need as many open-floor creators as they could possibly find.

Anthony Mason was now a Knick. And in a way, he was about to define the club.

It took all of twenty minutes at that first practice in Charleston for Mason to illustrate he wouldn't take shit from anyone—not even Xavier McDaniel.

"He's proven himself," Riley said that day, telling his veteran bigs to stand down and view Mason as a peer, despite his churlish streak and relative youth.

At that very same practice, Mason formed a reputation as someone who could scare the living daylights out of anyone—even a coach—with a five-word phrase.

It all began when the players lined up by position group to run a set of sprints within a minute's time. Any player who finished slower than that threshold would be required to run the taxing drill again the following day to pass the conditioning test.

Bob Salmi, one of the team's assistants, was timing the forwards when Mason crossed the sideline two or three ticks after the sixty-second mark. When Salmi broke the news to him, Mason snarled.

"Fuck you—I made it!" he said.

For the rest of practice, at least seven or eight more times, Mason whispered, "Fuck you—I made it!" whenever he got within a few feet of the coach. According to Salmi, it happened so many times he eventually asked Mason to stop.

Once the session concluded and the team returned to the Charleston Place Hotel, Salmi immediately approached the front desk and asked for a room change. He worried Mason might harbor an actual grudge and act on it.

As for Mason's reputation off the court, that developed almost instantly, too; at least with his teammates, who were astonished by how well he managed to function after staying out all night.

"We'd have two-a-days, drive down from the practice in Purchase to stop by his mom's in Queens, get back in the car, and would ride and meet up with his guys on the block," recalls Gary Waites, a training camp teammate in 1991 and 1992. "They're posted up drinking gin or whatever. And I don't know what to do. I'm just a rookie, but he's making me feel like part of his clique. I'm with the guys he grew up with on the streets of Queens. They're handing me liquor, and in my head I'm thinking: 'I don't want to drink—I've got practice in the morning. How do I tell this big dude to take me back to the room?'

"So finally we leave, and I'm thinking, 'Cool, we're going home.' But then he calls this girl. So then we go pick her up. And then I'm thinking, 'Okay, maybe he's bringing the girl to stay with him, and *then* we're going back to the hotel.' No! He calls a guy, who runs this seafood restaurant, and has him open up his place for us. So we have this gourmet seafood dinner at 2:30 or 3 in the morning. We get in the car, go back to Purchase. And by the time we get there, it's 4 a.m. We have to be at practice at 8! [A few hours later] I'm on the court trying to figure out how to run, I'm so tired. Yet here he is sprinting up and down the court, winning all the drills, like nothing ever happened."

If no one worked harder than Mason, it was also true that no one partied harder. From the age of 18 until he finished playing competitively at 36, Mason's work-life balance was that of a high-wire walker performing front flips without falling. But his affinity for women often threatened to throw that balance out of whack.

Just ask Nico Childs, Mason's teammate during his senior year at Tennessee State. "One night before the end of the semester, he walks up and says, 'Hey, man, come ride with me,'" says Childs. "I tell him I've got an American history exam at 8 a.m., and he says, 'You'll be all right—we're just going to see these girls, and we'll be back in a minute.'"

Childs said okay, and Mason drove them forty minutes southeast to Murfreesboro.

Asked how it played out, Childs laughs. "It was daybreak when we left Murfreesboro to come back. This dude got me home with just enough time to shower and get to my exam," he said. "Mase was a womanizer. He just wanted me there to run interference with this girl's roommate."

When asked, in 2015, why he chose to attend Tennessee State over other colleges, Mason said: "Honest reason? [The ratio] was about 8-to-1 in favor of chicks, and then you had Fisk University up the block, which was about 13-to-1, chicks. I went down there, and didn't know much about the South. Everybody's speaking and saying, 'Hey!' Each time, I'm thinking, 'Oh, she likes me!' I didn't know the South was polite, and that's just how it is there. So I probably went for the wrong reasons."

Mason didn't become any less invested in those reasons once he made it to the NBA, where the battles for the attention of the opposite gender were almost more fierce than the on-court rivalries.

"Me and him used to rib each other all the time. I'd call him ugly, and say, 'I don't know how your Herman Munster–looking ass could get women over me,'" says Patrick Eddie, a center who played his lone NBA season with the Knicks and considered Mason his best friend on the team.

"He hated when I called him that. But it put a chip on his shoulder, and for the rest of the season, he made it a point to bring home a different beautiful woman almost every night," Eddie continued. "Me, him, and Greg Anthony all lived on the penthouse floor of this apartment building in White Plains. Mase would come knock on my door at 2 a.m. every night, with a girl on his arm, just to say good night and to make sure I saw him. Who was it that said he slept with 20,000 women? Wilt? If Mase had said he'd been with just as many women, I would've believed him. Hell, I could've been his witness."

What some teammates witnessed was Mason's "sheet," a long, accordion-like piece of paper that contained the names and numbers of dozens of women. "He'd unfurl this thing, and I'd say there were easily one hundred names in there. Easily," says Waites, the Knicks' training camp invitee.

Mason was hardly shy about his exploits. A few close friends said he bragged to them about having slept with the wives of two Knicks teammates. At times, he all but stole the women his friends were courting.

Several of Mason's buddies recall him buying fifteen or twenty Sky-tel pagers for his entourage for two reasons. One, to help the group make plans from one night to the next. And secondly, to see how many numbers they could each collect. What those friends didn't know was Mason had a third reason for buying the pagers: because he bought them, he had the PIN codes for each person's device. It meant he could not only snatch the women's phone numbers for himself, but also play practical jokes on his friends because of the back-end access he had to the pagers.

"I remember getting a page from somebody who hit me up and said, 'Man, what's up with your voice mail [greeting]? You good?' I didn't know what he was talking about until I listened," says Anthony Kelly, one of Mason's childhood friends. "I listen to the voice mail, and it's [Mason's] stupid ass. He used this high-pitched voice to make me sound gay. 'I can't talk right now—I'm with my boyfriend! But leave a message.' The voice mail greeting was like five minutes long."

Whether in skirt-chasing or basketball, Mason always craved a win. Perhaps too much.

Mason had recently retired from the NBA when his second son, Antoine, graduated from junior high. After the commencement ceremony, Antoine challenged his old man to a one-on-one game to 11 points.

Antoine made up for his height disadvantage by hitting several jumpers from outside to start, taking a 5–0 lead. Then Anthony buckled down, came back, and took a 10–9 edge. Antoine got past his father with a crossover dribble and raced in for a layup that would have tied the score. But just before he could finish the play, the elder Mason—at least seven inches taller and 80 pounds heavier than Antoine—flew into the frame and clotheslined his adolescent son in the throat. "As I'm laying on the ground, holding my throat and coughing, he grabs the ball, lays it in, and says, 'Game.' And then walks in the house," he says.

Other family members, there to celebrate Antoine's graduation, looked on in stunned horror.

It simply wasn't in Anthony Mason's nature to let anyone walk away with a win at his expense. This was clear from Mason's countless bar fights, which were often instigated by someone making a throwaway comment or critique aimed in his direction. "If you say something to him, he's going to say something back. He's not gonna sit back and just say, 'All right, whatever,' " says Kelly, Mason's childhood friend.

Knicks teammate Hubert Davis learned this the hard way sometime during his rookie year, when Mason pressured him into going out for the night. Davis, straitlaced and mild-mannered as they come, went with Mason to a few bars before Mason turned to him and said he knew of an after-hours spot they could hit before heading home. But before they left,

Mason found himself in a heated back-and-forth with a man at the bar, who'd uttered something negative about the Knicks.

"We can take it outside and settle this!" Mason shouted. The man he was arguing with agreed.

Mason grabbed Davis and told him to walk out toward the alley with him, in case he needed the shooting guard to have his back. Mason then allowed the man he was quarreling with to walk outside first. There was a reason for that, though: it helped give Mason a better angle to uncork a wild sucker punch on the man.

The spectacle left Davis slack-jawed.

"Run, motherfucker, run!" Mason yelled at Davis.

The players fled in separate directions and reunited minutes later when Mason, driving in his car, saw Davis running frantically on a sidewalk.

There weren't enough first-aid kits in New York City to address the abundance of scrapes Mason had with the law. He was either arrested or sued in civil court over an alleged physical altercation five times between 1996 and 2000. Some allegations Mason saw as money grabs, and were ultimately dismissed.

In 1997, an officer threatened to sue the forward, claiming Mason hurt his shoulder while the officer was attempting to handcuff him near Times Square. But before filing a case, the policeman called one of Mason's attorneys, saying he'd hold off on a suit if the player paid him $100,000. The cop was charged with trying to shake down Mason.

A couple of incidents wore on the Knick more heavily, though. In 2000, after one run-in, Mason's son, Antoine, got suspended from elementary school for fighting a classmate who'd made light of his father's arrest.

"He told me he had to set a better example for me," Antoine recalls.

The other, which occurred in February 1998, was by far his most serious allegation. Mason was charged with statutory rape in Queens the same weekend the NBA All-Star Game was in New York. He and his cousin, William Duggins, had been at a charity basketball game in Manhattan when they met two sisters. They left the game with the sisters in limousines, and then allegedly had sex with the girls—just 14 and 15 years old at the time—at a house in Queens.

Duggins, for his part, pleaded guilty to two counts of statutory rape and endangering the welfare of a child, and ultimately served five years in prison. By contrast, Mason—who faced five hours of questioning over the incident—saw his two felony rape charges dismissed when DNA evidence failed to link him to the crime. He pleaded guilty to two misdemeanor counts of child-welfare endangerment, and was ordered to do two hundred hours of community service.

"It was one of those things where the initial charges got so much ink, in the biggest possible font. I mean, this literally took the All-Star Game off the back page of the tabloids. I still remember David Stern just screeching at me over the phone about it," says Don Cronson, Mason's agent, who bailed Mason out of a Queens lockup hours after he was brought in. "Then when the DNA evidence proved it wasn't him, two or three months later, the damage was kind of done, because the back pages had already made up their minds. And the stories that were saying it wasn't him were far less prominent in the tabloids."

Cronson said he, Dave Checketts, and Ernie Grunfeld talked repeatedly about living in fear of the 3 a.m. phone call. In politics, that equates to a commander in chief being able to keep a nation safe from sudden, overnight harm. With the Knicks, it often meant protecting Mason from himself in a city that never slept.

Checketts received such a call late one night in 1993. He knew it was important, not only because of what hour the call came in, but also which line it came in on: the second one, which was Checketts's private number, for emergencies or important team business. This call managed to check both boxes.

On the other end of the line was the Garden's head of security, Bob Russo, a former NYPD officer, who still had eyes and ears within the department. Russo had gotten wind of an incident involving Mason: the player, apparently intoxicated, was causing a disturbance at one of the city's White Castle restaurants, profanely heckling some employees between bites of miniature sandwiches.

So Russo said he'd get Mason home before police got involved, or the media got ahold of the situation.

Other times, no one was present to stave off disaster. After spending hours with friends at the Peppermint Lounge in New Jersey and downing a supersized bottle of Moët, Mason exited the club and staggered toward his white 560 Mercedes-Benz in the parking lot. Kelly, his childhood friend, had seen Mason downing copious shots of tequila in addition to the champagne, and asked if it'd be better for him to drive Mason's car.

"Nah, nah, nah—I got this," Mason told him.

Mason plopped into the driver's seat. Kelly sat directly behind him. Three others piled into the car and were jerked backward when Mason floored the gas on the way out of the parking lot. By the time they made it onto the highway to head back to New York, Mason was beginning to scare his friends, who watched as the speedometer surpassed 100 miles per hour, and cranked closer to 110.

"Slow the fuck down! You're going too fast!" Kelly told him.

"Shut the fuck up!" Mason sneered.

And then it happened: Mason clipped the back of a white van, sending his Mercedes sideways into a guardrail on the left side of the highway before it spun back toward the right. Mason's car was totaled—"It looked like the letter Z," Kelly recalled—parts of the vehicle strewn throughout the road. Somehow, no one in the car was seriously hurt. (Oddly enough, the van Mason clipped from behind never stopped.) Mason got the worst of it, as his airbag deployed and left him with a face full of blood.

Other friends of Mason's, who were in a pair of cars trailing his when the accident occurred, pulled over, loaded Mason into their vehicle, then whisked him away in an effort to keep their buddy out of legal trouble. And it worked. When police arrived, Mason's name never came up. The story never hit the papers. Instead, Corey Kelly, Anthony Kelly's younger brother, took the fall, receiving a ticket for reckless driving—and the 1,000-plus-foot skid marks the accident left on the highway.

In short, Mason was nothing if not enigmatic.

"Anthony's what I'd call an oxymoron," said Riley, who would end up placing Mason on the Knicks' playoff roster mere minutes before the deadline in 1994. "There's a bundle of contradictions about him. He's versatile, unique in that way. Maybe too unique for his own good."

Yes, Mason was at times a volatile man. But he also deeply adored his mother, Mary Mason, a bookkeeper who raised him on her own. Even as a child, he showed a willingness to do anything for her. The physical abuse he endured—and that Tennessee State coaches made mention of in an effort to keep him on the team—stemmed from him stepping in to protect his mother from a man who was violently striking her. A young Anthony, standing between the man and his mother, took the punishment instead.

Once Mason had the means, he did everything in his power to take care of his mom. He arranged for her to stay with him in Turkey to ease his transition there. And after making it to the NBA and staying there, he brought her the same 560 Benz he already had for himself. Mason made weekly late-night stops at his mother's house to leave thousands of dollars on top of her hallway dresser. He felt he could never repay his mother's kindness and support. But it didn't stop him from trying.

That love ran just as deep for his children. When Mason would receive Player of the Game honors and do postgame television interviews on the court, he would invariably conclude them by telling his young children—who he knew had stayed up to watch him play—"Go to bed!"

As those kids grew older, Mason, who seemingly hated to sleep himself, did everything he could to convince them to stay up with him. Antoine remembers his father laying into him upon realizing he had never seen any of the *Godfather* films. So Mason suggested watching the entire nine-hour trilogy right then and there, back-to-back-to-back, despite it already being 9 p.m. Antoine agreed, but began dozing off in the middle of *Godfather Part III*.

"Ah, you can't hang, huh? Fine, then. Go to sleep," Mason said, as the clock struck 5 a.m.

An hour later, the alarm sounded. "Wake up, man," Mason told his son. "It's time to go get an offseason workout in." When a groggy Antoine looked at him in disbelief, and reminded his father that he'd just gone to bed the hour before, Mason said he didn't care. "You shouldn't have stayed up watching all those movies, then! Get up! We're gonna go work out."

This was Mason: an often humorous, walking contradiction. The player some teammates and coaches feared, but couldn't help but laugh at when he flipped out his false teeth during a practice to throw off the concentration of a foul shooter. The guy who loved to be the center of attention, but, as soon as he got it—with camerapeople circling before a game, trying to get shots of his one-of-a-kind haircut—broke wind and unleashed an odor so foul it sent folks scurrying as if they'd been sprayed by a skunk.

The stench hanging over Mason's off-court issues was unsavory enough that some kept their distance from him. But he could be a charmer. One night in the midst of a trip to Atlanta during the 1993–94 season, a group of Knicks players were seated at a strip club when several writers who covered the team walked in. The players, uncomfortable with reporters seeing them there, stood up and made a beeline for the coat-check station. Only two stayed: Eric Anderson and Anthony Mason. In fact, Mason ordered a round of drinks for the beat reporters and made small talk with them before heading out with Anderson.

"Somebody pulled me aside and said, 'Listen, I don't think you know how much trouble this guy gets into, or what kind of guy he is. If you knew, you may not want him in chapel,'" said Pastor John Love, who has served as the team chaplain for the past thirty-three seasons and formed a bond with Mason. "I told the person, 'If he's a mess, he's *exactly* the kind of guy we want in chapel.'"

Indeed, Mason regularly attended chapel during his Knick years, and wore his religion on his sleeve. He began and ended many of his days with prayer, carried around an electronic Bible, and, sometimes out of the blue, would ask people if they were Christians, to see whether they held the same beliefs.

Above all else, Mason was kind when it came to making time for kids and community outreach.

At the beginning of every season, Ed Oliva, the team's manager of community programs, would go around and ask each player on the team what issue, if any, mattered most to them. For Mason, the only core member of the Knicks who was a native New Yorker, the answer was always the schools. Whether it was a basketball clinic the Knicks were conducting in a gym, or a stay-in-school talk they were giving in a classroom, Mason saw value in those interactions.

"With a lot of players, we'd ask, and they'd say they needed to think about it, or that they'd get back to us," Oliva recalls. "But with Mason, his reaction was, 'I'm all in.' He never needed to think about it." Oliva said Mason usually sought out the kids sitting in the corner of the room and sat next to them, hoping to draw them into the conversations.

Mason took pride in appearing at summer youth basketball camps, sometimes staying overnight for them, so he could spend more time helping campers hone their skills. The camps—run by Mason's high school coach and father figure, Ken Fiedler—gave out trophies to the best young players. Yet kids got used to Mason upping the ante. If there were three hundred kids attending the camp, he might dole out $300 awards to the players who managed to win the camp's free-throw and three-point shooting contests.

The soft spot he had for children was unmistakable, perhaps because he knew what it was to grow up without his father in his life. And few things—aside from making a wisecrack about him at the bar or pulling him out of a game—made Mason's blood boil like seeing athletes shun kids' autograph requests.

Mason would take ten or fifteen minutes sometimes to sign every ball, shoe, or jersey that fans held in front of him before or after a game. And he was more than happy to do it. Patrick Ewing, on the other hand, made a point not to sign autographs in public, feeling if he signed for one person that he'd have to sign for everyone. (Mason's friends say the forward griped about Ewing's autograph snubs well into his retirement.)

Appropriately enough, it was Mason's interaction with a child that helped him find peace during yet another high-strung suspension from the Knicks, in March 1995. During his punishment, Mason learned of Joey Harrell, a 12-year-old leukemia patient at Mount Sinai Hospital, who was an enormous fan of Mason and the Knicks. When Harrell came out of a medication-induced slumber, he found Mason at his bedside, clutching an autographed hat and photo. For almost thirty minutes, as Mason visited the boy, the room was brightened by Harrell's smile.

The hospital staff had weighed telling Harrell beforehand that Mason was planning to visit. They'd decided against it, worrying that something might come up and alter Mason's plans at the last moment, which would only saddle a sick child with even more sadness.

Yet Mason was there, not only handing Harrell the shoes off his feet, but providing the boy one of the high points of his young life; one that tragically would end the next day.

"Joey had his moment before he died," Harrell's aunt, Gloria, said. "We were all such big fans of [Mason]. Now we're even bigger fans. Joey used to always talk about Mason's haircuts. He really loved him."

Mason wrote Harrell's name on his sneakers for the remainder of the season.

Cronson acknowledged the timing of his client's hospital visit, saying it might have been convenient from a public relations standpoint, given that Mason was suspended. But the visit also offered a dying boy a final moment of happiness.

It was, in other words, quintessential Anthony Mason. Good or bad, craven or heartwarming, depending on how you saw him.

10

STANDING OUT IN THE CROWD

As the Knicks became a perennial power, winning 50-plus games in the 1991, 1992, and 1993 seasons, their popularity hit a new level with New Yorkers, who made tickets disappear almost instantly.

"It reached a point where we could group stuff together—concert tickets, circus tickets, anything really—and convince people to buy them, no questions asked, as long as we attached Knicks tickets to whatever it was," says marketing director Pam Harris. "They were an engine for us."

Business was so brisk, and nightly sellouts were such a foregone conclusion during the Riley era, that the club formed a season-ticket waiting list. The log of names on the wait list eventually swelled some 15,000 spots deep—an incredible number, considering the Knicks had the NBA's most expensive seats.

At one point in 1994, John F. Kennedy Jr. asked for a pair of season tickets after he and actress Daryl Hannah—who had season tickets of her own—had broken up. His request came in a nondescript envelope; one without any sort of letterhead. Still, it was flagged by front-office staffers as being high priority, and Dave Checketts gave his okay to have Kennedy placed with other VIP season-ticket holders. Yet somehow when the issue got passed along to Joel Fisher, who worked with the season-ticket department, there was a miscommunication. JFK Jr. had been stowed in the 300 level among the cheap seats.

"I remember asking [Fisher] if he'd taken care of the request, and asking what kind of seats he gave him. When he told me he'd put [JFK Jr.] in the 300s, I couldn't believe it at first. I thought he was pranking me," says Maggie McEvoy, Checketts's executive assistant. "Dave called him to apologize, and vowed to get him better seats. But to me, the funny thing is that he didn't even complain initially over those 300-level seats—he was going to take them. That's how hard it was to get tickets back then, even if you were well connected."

That tight squeeze for fans and celebrities alike factored into the Knicks' playoff opener that year. Hosting the neighboring New Jersey Nets at the Garden, New York was in the midst of a competitive, highly physical matchup, with Charles Oakley doing what he did best: drawing blood.

"The shit he did to our guys? There were times we would've been better off if he'd just held a gun to our head and mugged us," says Butch Beard, who coached New Jersey for two years during that era.

Near the end of the third quarter, Oakley jumped for a rebound, elbowing Nets All-Star Derrick Coleman in the lip. It created a bloody mess that forced Coleman to come off the floor to get stitches. There was just one problem: because of how the Knicks assigned seats in the crowded arena for staff members of opposing teams, New Jersey's team physician, Dr. John Sonzogni, was sitting all the way in the Garden's upper deck. (The Nets got a block of seats upstairs to allow their staffers to sit as a group, but didn't request a courtside one for their doctor.) Sonzogni spent minutes pleading with security before they eventually let him down to the court level.

It was a bloody stroke of luck for New York. Coleman, who'd finish with a game-high 27 points, had been dominating just enough to narrowly put the Nets ahead. But in the six game-time minutes it took Sonzogni to reach Coleman and give him five stitches, the Knicks went on a 10–0 run and never looked back.

The Knicks' 91–80 Game 1 victory over the Nets—who'd beaten New York four times that regular season—helped power them to a 3–1 series victory in the postseason's first round. And as New York closed out the last few minutes of Game 4, Knicks fans in Brendan Byrne

Arena thundered, "We Want the Bulls!" a nod to the fact that rival Chicago, fresh off sweeping the Cavs, was waiting in the next round.

Michael Jordan wasn't a Bull anymore, but that didn't mean Chicago would go away easily.

New York managed to win Game 1 and Game 2 of the series at home—just like the year before—yet the 55-win Bulls were ahead by double digits in Game 3 with about three minutes left in the first half.

It was around that time that Derek Harper grew frustrated with Chicago backup Jo Jo English, who was guarding him in a more handsy fashion than Harper felt was necessary; especially with them being away from the ball, almost thirty feet from the hoop. So Harper angrily smacked away English's hands at the top of the key as the play wore on, and Patrick Ewing drove to the rim and got fouled. But the whistle for that infraction might as well have been a boxing bell for English and Harper, who threw a haymaker at the Bulls guard.

The swing prompted English to charge at Harper, forcefully shoving the Knicks floor general back toward the scorer's table at half-court. Harper quietly possessed a herculean strength in his hands and arms and managed to take a step to his right as he was being pushed, grabbing English and suplexing him onto his back just a few feet from the fans sitting courtside along the sideline. While those two duked it out, Riley, Charles Oakley, and John Starks—who'd sprinted all the way over from the bench on the other side of the court—arrived to pull Harper away. Scottie Pippen, Horace Grant, and Phil Jackson also entered the fray, which quickly became a full-on melee, including players, assistants, and yellow-jacketed security people.

Commissioner David Stern, seated three rows up at half-court with his wife, looked on, absolutely mortified. Here were two of the league's marquee teams in a high-profile playoff game, one that had now devolved into a wrestling match. It was the exact sort of thing Stern and other league officials sought to legislate out of the sport after Greg Anthony's sucker punch started the bench-clearing brawl in Phoenix fifteen months earlier.

Stern was also bothered by the fact that the donnybrook spilled into the crowd, leading Starks and other Knicks to jaw with well-heeled fans, including the adult daughters of a Bulls minority owner. (Some fans sitting courtside jokingly wore football helmets to Game 4.) All of this would prompt Stern to take an even harder line during the offseason on rules regarding fights.

Following Harper's ejection, the Knicks fell behind by 22 points in the second half of Game 3. But they climbed all the way back to tie the score at 102 in the closing moments. They hoped to force overtime as Jackson and the Bulls drew up a final play call during a timeout with 1.8 seconds left.

Things got strange on the Chicago sideline when Jackson opted to call the play for Croatian newcomer Toni Kukoč rather than Pippen, that year's All-Star Game MVP. Pippen angrily refused to enter the game as a result of Jackson's choice. But Kukoč bailed Pippen out, swishing a 20-footer from the wing just over Anthony Mason's outstretched arm as time expired, making the series 2–1 in favor of New York.

Capitalizing on Harper's suspension—Chicago dared the errant Greg Anthony to take jumpers, and he obliged, finishing 2-for-13 from the field—the Bulls won Game 4, too, to even the series.

Riley avoided making the obvious comparisons with what had happened the previous year, when the Knicks blew their two-game series lead and watched Chicago earn a third consecutive title. But down the stretch of Game 5, the parallels were nearly impossible to ignore, even without Jordan in the picture. Just like in 1993, the Knicks were terrible at the line, hitting just 15-for-25. And just like B. J. Armstrong hit a go-ahead jumper late in Game 5 the year before, the Bulls guard did the same thing here, drilling a fifteen-footer to give Chicago an 86–85 edge with just 44 seconds left. It was déjà vu at the Garden.

Were the Knicks really about to let things slip away again?

After a failed offensive possession and a stop, Riley called timeout to draw up a play for Starks and Ewing. During the stoppage, Anthony grabbed teammate Hubert Davis by the shoulder before he took the court. "Hubert, if you've got the shot, you gotta take it," Anthony told him, explaining that the Bulls would likely double-team Ewing, which could potentially leave the second-year Davis open.

Sure enough, as Starks came around Ewing's screen with six seconds remaining, four Chicago defenders swarmed the Knicks' top-two scorers to make sure they couldn't get off a good shot. As all five Bulls sank beneath the free-throw line to guard against Starks's drive, Davis flashed to the top of the key, where he was standing all by himself when Starks turned to throw the ball his way.

Reading Starks's eyes, Pippen raced fifteen feet from the middle of the lane out to Davis, who was spotting up to shoot with about three seconds left. "It was amazing how quickly Scottie got there," Davis said.

By the time Pippen arrived, though, the guard had already let the shot go, with nearly twenty thousand spellbound fans on their feet, anticipating either heartbreak or exhilaration.

The attempt was a misfire that was slightly long and to the right, and bounced straight into the air. But before it came down, a whistle sounded. Referee Hue Hollins had called a foul, saying Pippen hit Davis on his follow-through. The reprieve launched a wave of euphoria at the Garden.

A world-class defender, Pippen was so confident in his closeout that he didn't even know what the whistle was for initially. "I'm thinking, 'What happened? Who fouled?'" said Pippen, who took a seat on the scorer's table to calm himself after the call, which gave New York an 87–86 win and a 3–2 series lead.

Over time, Hollins stood by his call. But Darrel Garretson, who also reffed that contest and served as the NBA's officiating chief in those years, deemed Hollins's foul call to be "terrible" months after the game.

"That call wasn't right, and it might've turned the series," Jackson says decades later. "But we played over our heads that season without Michael. And I think the Knicks were a better club overall than we were."

"Turned the series" might be the most accurate way to put it, since the Bulls did rebound and win Game 6 in Chicago, to tie the semifinal matchup at three games apiece. But New York won Game 7 at home, finally getting some measure of revenge on the Bulls, to advance to the Eastern Conference Finals.

The Knicks had no idea how challenging their next opponent would turn out to be, though.

Earlier that season, Pacers coach Larry Brown could see his team was transitioning.

Prior to his arrival, Indiana had been an uptempo club that ran so fast at times that it couldn't compete in the mud when it had to mix it up with more physical opponents. But upon hiring Brown, general manager Donnie Walsh sought to make the team tougher, dealing away versatile forward and fan favorite Detlef Schrempf for the defensive grit of Derrick McKey. Walsh also drafted power forward Antonio Davis, whose nasty disposition in the paint promised to toughen up the prim-and-proper ball club.

The shift was a work in progress. "I look at my guys, and they've given the effort from the first day we've been together. But they don't know how to play while grabbing, hitting, and fouling yet," Brown said following a March loss to the Knicks. "I'm not complaining, but unless we're prepared to do that same thing eventually, [the Knicks] are gonna win those sorts of games, because that's their wheelhouse."

Brown was on to something. The Pacers were still learning how to win with their new style—one that Walsh loosely fashioned after the Knicks—and ended the regular season on an eight-game winning streak.

That run continued in the playoffs, where fifth-seeded Indiana swept Shaquille O'Neal, Penny Hardaway, and the Magic in the first round before stunning the 57-win, top-seeded Hawks in six games. It would've been an impressive groove for any team, but especially one like the Pacers, who, before the 1994 postseason, had never won a playoff series in their eighteen-year NBA life span. Yet here they stood now, just four victories away from the Finals.

The Knicks owned home-court advantage and had swept the four games between the clubs during the regular season. But knowing better than to take Indiana for granted, they won Games 1 and 2 to open the series. "They're a lot like us," Ewing said. "They play hard defense. They rebound. They bang. They bump. They're a carbon copy of us. Only thing is, we're a little bit better. They're a copy; we're the real thing."

Indiana punched back in Game 3, forcing Ewing into a career-worst 0-for-10 showing in which he had more air balls (two) than points (one). After New York's 88–68 loss—which broke an NBA record for fewest points by a team in a shot-clock-era playoff game—Ewing unleashed a scream out of frustration as he left the court to head to the locker room.

And even when Ewing bounced back with 25 points and 13 rebounds in Game 4, the rest of the team's offense was anemic. The Knicks committed 26 turnovers, including four in the final two minutes, while Reggie Miller had 13 points in the fourth quarter to lift the Pacers to an 83–77 win that knotted the series at 2–2.

Then came Game 5 back at the Garden, where the Knicks looked prepared to win in a blowout.

The club jumped out to a 15–2 lead in the opening minutes, and finished the first quarter with a 12-point edge. The Knicks stayed on that trajectory, leading by as many as 16 in the second, 14 in the third, and 12 in the fourth. The Pacers, who bricked 12 of their first 15 free-throw tries, certainly weren't helping themselves. And at just 6-for-16 from the field through the first three quarters, Miller wasn't shooting particularly well, either.

To that point, no one at the Garden—man, woman, or child—was enjoying the game more than Spike Lee.

The night of May 12, 1985, has long been burned into Lee's memory.

The 28-year-old had set the evening aside for one thing, and one thing only: to watch the NBA's first-ever draft lottery, to see where his beloved, struggling Knickerbockers would be picking from the following month.

It was hardly the first time he'd prioritized the Knicks over everything else. A die-hard fan since his childhood, a 13-year-old Lee skipped his father's jazz concert that his family was heading to so he could attend Game 7 of the 1970 NBA Finals at the Garden instead. And while the draft lottery certainly wasn't the equivalent of the NBA Finals, in a way, it was. Whichever team won the lotto would get the right to draft George-town's Ewing, perhaps the most accomplished collegiate player since Lew Alcindor in the 1960s.

As a transfixed Lee grew more and more excited the higher the Knicks climbed in terms of draft position, his girlfriend, actress Cheryl Burr, interrupted, saying she urgently needed to discuss something with him.

"One second!" said Lee, who was watching the event from Burr's apartment.

Then Stern announced the Pacers had gotten the No. 2 pick, meaning, by process of elimination, that the No. 1 selection would belong to the Knicks. Lee leapt in the air, raised both arms, and shouted triumphantly. It was around that same time that Burr—tired of waiting to get Lee's at-tention—said what she'd been waiting to get off her chest. "Spike, it's over between me and you," she said.

Stunned, Lee went home and thought about what had taken place. "I considered the error of my ways. Bit my lip. Picked up the phone. Punched the digits. Swallowed my pride. Time for commitment," he said.

But rather than call Burr, he instead placed a call to the Knicks. He wanted to know how he could buy season tickets, given that Ewing would be on the roster. And when a receptionist told him tickets would go on sale at the Madison Square Garden box office at 8 a.m. the next day, Lee took no chances, arriving at the arena at 5 a.m. He was assigned seats in Section 304 that day, and has had season tickets ever since.

By 1994, the film director had formed a bond with a number of play-ers. He'd befriend them on the sideline during breaks in the action, and would invite them to an uptown soul-food joint called Shark Bar, where they could nibble on honey-dipped fried chicken. There, he'd sometimes introduce them to the likes of Denzel Washington and Halle Berry, each of whom had starred in Lee's films. At times, Lee arranged hangouts with players in hopes of securing financing for his filmmaking.

In particular, he'd developed a tight relationship with Jordan, who was one of a handful of prominent Black celebrities to help Lee cover a $5 million budget shortfall to finish *Malcolm X*. (Lee and Jordan became close after doing a number of Nike commercials together, with Lee often reprising his Mars Blackmon character—a Knicks fan who happens to love Air Jordan sneakers—from *She's Gotta Have It*.)

Reggie Miller, on the other hand, didn't have much of a relationship with Lee, good or bad. Nonetheless, because of the back-and-forth between Miller and Starks, Lee's favorite Knick, Lee reached out to Miller before the Knicks-Pacers series began. He wanted to put a friendly wager on the outcome of the series.

If New York won, Lee wanted Miller to visit incarcerated boxer Mike Tyson, who was serving a six-year prison sentence in Indiana. Miller told Lee he would, so long as Lee would put Miller's wife, Marita—who wanted to get into acting—in his next film if Indiana won. Lee agreed, and the terms of the bet were finalized.

So with the Knicks rolling through three quarters in Game 5, the trash-talking Lee was thoroughly enjoying his night. And Miller's shooting struggles gave Lee even more ammo to chirp at the Pacers star with.

But at the start of the fourth quarter, everything began to shift. In the first minute of the period, Miller hit a three from the left wing to cut the deficit to nine. "That's luck!" Lee yelled as Miller ran back on defense.

The Pacers' next possession, Miller snuck away from Hubert Davis, who got hung up on a screen during a baseline inbound pass. The result this time was a wide-open three from the right wing, which Miller knocked down, cutting New York's lead to just eight, 72–64. A teardrop floater from Pacers forward Kenny Williams made it a six-point game and prompted Riley to call for time in hopes of stopping the bleeding.

But that didn't help the Knicks' cause, either. Indiana forced a turnover—one of nine New York would commit in the fourth quarter—and Miller capitalized on the mistake by pump-faking Greg Anthony out of the way for an open 15-footer that whittled the Knicks' lead to just four, 72–68, with nine minutes left.

As Miller backpedaled to the other end of the floor, he looked over in Lee's direction, jawing at the filmmaker after connecting on a third jumper to begin the quarter. "I turned to Tonya and said, 'Are we in trouble here?'" Lee recalled saying to his wife.

He wasn't alone in wondering that. Knicks backup point guard Corey Gaines had the same sense, mostly because he'd watched Miller—his roommate for three years at UCLA—do this sort of thing before.

"I knew I wanted to be a coach someday, so I always sat next to [assistant] Jeff Van Gundy. And even in the early part of the quarter, I kept nudging Jeff, saying, 'We've got to change up how we're defending him before it's too late,'" recalls Gaines, adding that the performance reminded him of one of Miller's games in college, at Washington State, where he fed off the road crowd's chants to go on a huge scoring spree.

The difference here, though, was that Miller was feeding off a single fan: Spike Lee.

After Ewing mishandled a pass on New York's ensuing possession, Miller found himself all alone in the left corner and connected on a jumper with his foot on the three-point line. As he drew the Pacers within two, 72–70, Miller exchanged words with Lee, who poked the bear again by standing out of his courtside seat momentarily and putting his arms up, as if to say, "You can't keep this up." But Miller kept scoring.

One sequence after the Pacers tied it at 72, with the Garden crowd chanting DEE-FENSE!, Miller looked for a driving lane. But with Starks playing four feet off him, there wasn't one. No matter. Using the space Starks gave him, Miller let one fly from 27 feet, and the result was the same. Swish. Indiana led, 75–72.

"That fourth quarter felt like nails being pushed into your body slowly," recalls Knicks assistant Jeff Nix.

As the long triple went down, Miller flared his nostrils and stared a hole into Lee, who was sitting along the court on the sideline. Just moments before, Miller looked directly at Lee, held up four fingers on his right hand, put both hands around his own neck, then reached down with his left hand to grab his crotch. Miller's message might have been vulgar—"My wife was right there!" Lee said—but it was also clear. The Knicks were choking badly in the fourth, and didn't have the fortitude to close out Game 5.

Riley kept calling timeouts to stem the tide, but they didn't help. Nothing did.

By the end of the onslaught, Miller had 39 points—25 of which came in the fourth quarter, when he hit five triples and connected on eight of his 10 shot attempts. Miller and the Pacers had outscored New York by 19 in the final period to win, 93–86, at the Garden. And Indiana suddenly had a 3–2 lead in the series.

The Knicks, in turn, were about to head into enemy territory while on the brink of elimination.

The pressure was on.

Riley and his assistant coaches felt it, and toyed with the idea of installing new plays ahead of Game 6. The players certainly felt it, too, as Starks—usually one of the less vocal players—opted to call a players-only meeting in Ewing's suite to iron out defensive coverages against the sharpshooting Miller.

As the Knicks focused on schematic changes ahead of what could be their last game of the season, there was a larger, more basic question looming. Were they up to the task mentally? Aside from the fact that they'd had their hearts ripped out of their chests during Miller's one-man show at the Garden in Game 5, there was also the reality of what the Knicks would be facing during Game 6 in Indianapolis.

Heading into that must-win game at Market Square Arena, New York owned a 1-6 postseason road record, and had lost five straight away from home. The Pacers, meanwhile, were on a ten-game win streak at home, dating back to the regular season. But those facts only explained part of the Knicks' uphill battle.

For as similar as the Knicks' and Pacers' playing styles were, just about everything else about the franchises made them polar opposites, adding fuel to a soon-to-be-raging fire.

New York was bombastic, the nation's biggest market and the city that never slept. The Pacers hailed from a city known as Naptown. Both places took pride in their basketball heritage, but in much different sorts of venues. Aside from its multitude of streetball courts, New York had the Garden—perhaps the most recognizable sports venue in the world;

one where celebrities sat courtside every game. Indiana represented small-town values, with favorite son Larry Bird referred to as "the Hick from French Lick." If Texas was known for deifying high school football, Indiana wasn't far off with its love for high school basketball. The film *Hoosiers* was evidence of that. Passion for college basketball was palpable throughout the state, too.

Market Square Arena in Indianapolis had the layout and feel of a college venue, where sound could carry. And the arena's seats were right on top of the players—far more than in the league's other stadiums—which meant the Indiana fans would have even more opportunity to rile up the Knicks in enemy territory.

The atmosphere around the matchup had become inflamed, even away from the arena. J. A. Adande and Jay Mariotti, who were covering the series for the *Chicago Sun-Times*, were walking out of an Indianapolis restaurant ahead of Game 6 as Lee entered the eatery. Unsurprisingly, Pacers fans gave Lee a hard time in Indianapolis. But some were far more hostile than others, using racial epithets.

"You're nothing but a nigger anyway!" one man shouted at Lee, according to Adande.

Lee said things were just as bad in the arena, if not worse. "I've never been to a Klan rally, but at Market Square Arena that night, they could've strung me up and they probably would've been happy," he said.

As the Knicks came out of the tunnel to warm up, at least a few heard fans sitting directly above them hurl slurs at them, prompting Oakley and Mason to angrily shout their fair share of profanities back at the fans.

After a while, even the more levelheaded banter and taunting began fraying the Knicks' nerves. Members of the team's front office—Checketts, Ernie Grunfeld, Ed Tapscott, and consultant Red Holzman—ended up being seated right next to Miller's wife, who was vocal herself.

"Vociferously vocal," Tapscott says, adding that she alternated between shouting at the referees and Starks. "Ernie and Dave were next to me and were getting quite annoyed with Mrs. Miller. So in trying to come up with a solution to smooth things over, I introduced myself, and said, 'We're with the Knicks,'" Tapscott continued. "I don't know whether telling her that part helped anything. But what did help was me offering her a Life Saver. I just happened to have a bunch in my jacket pocket. So in order to ease the tension a bit, and reduce the commentary some, I'd offer her another Life Saver each time she started up. I think it helped."

What helped most, though, was Starks having a fantastic Game 6, in which he drilled five of his six attempts from deep and finished with 26 points. After a 91–91 tie, the Knicks closed the game by scoring the last seven points. Capitalizing on a few key late plays by Harper, they won, 98–91, forcing Game 7.

The hard-fought road victory armed New York with a swagger heading into Game 7. "There was a massive thud the other night from all the people jumping off the bandwagon," Riley said. "And [now] there's probably another massive thud of people jumping back on."

Feeling confident and wanting to raise the stakes ahead of the series finale, Checketts asked a favor of the league office. He requested that the Knicks be able to take possession of the Larry O'Brien Trophy, which would be awarded to the NBA champions, for a day. He wanted to display it in the locker room before Game 7, as a way to motivate his players even more.

The NBA signed off, and got New York the trophy. But Riley shot the plan down upon hearing about it. "He wanted nothing to do with it, and thought it might jinx things. So we had to hide it," Checketts said.

After trailing by 12 in the closing minutes of the third quarter in Game 7, New York rebounded, literally and figuratively, to get within striking distance. The team's best offense that night, after Ewing, stemmed from putbacks.

With thirty-five seconds to play, the Pacers held a 90–89 edge when Riley asked for time. He'd call the same play the Knicks generally ran in game-ending scenarios: a Starks-Ewing pick-and-roll in the middle of the floor. The season hung in the balance, with a score likely sending New York to its first Finals in twenty-one years, a miss meaning the Knicks would come back a day later to clean out their lockers for the summer.

Starks took the inbound from Oakley, used the high screen from Ewing at the top of the key, and took four dribbles to his right before skying toward the rim, where three Indiana defenders awaited him. He flipped up a lefty layup effort that was too strong, and bounced off the front of the rim. But before anyone else even made an attempt to leave their feet for the rebound, there was Ewing, who not only secured the miss, but also dunked it home to put the Knicks up by one. "I look up, and there's Patrick coming out of the sky," Starks said, describing the biggest play of Ewing's career.

The putback, Ewing's 10th offensive board, marked the Knicks' 28th offensive rebound on the night—an eye-popping statistic given that Indiana would finish with just 29 *total* rebounds in the deciding contest.

With 26.9 left, the Pacers still had a chance to win. They let the shot clock run down to about ten seconds, and got the ball in Miller's hands on the right elbow. But Miller, the man who couldn't miss in the Garden four days earlier, missed everything this time, shooting an air ball as Oakley closed out hard on him. Maybe this was fate after all, with the ball going out of bounds, all but sealing the victory for New York.

When the buzzer finally sounded on the Knicks' 94–90 victory in Game 7, Miller was gracious, shaking the hand of Starks before finding and embracing Lee and his wife. (Miller wept in the locker room, and has said the loss still hurts to this day.) Ewing, who had the game of his life with 24 points, 22 boards, seven assists, and five blocks, lifted his arms triumphantly before standing atop the Garden's scorer's table.

It was fitting. Having taken out a giant-killer like Indiana, the Knicks—headed to the NBA Finals—felt they were on top of the world.

"We've yet to play our best basketball," Starks said after the Game 7 win. "The pressure was on us just to get to the Finals. After what we've been through, the championship, to us, is going to be a breeze."

11

THE DREAM,
THE CHASE, AND THE NIGHTMARE

Even as an 11-year-old, John Starks had a tendency to act on impulse.

In 1976, during his first day of school as a sixth grader in Tulsa, one of his white classmates walked past and purposely knocked one of Starks's books onto the floor. When Starks asked him to pick the book up, the boy said no, and called Starks a nigger—which sent him into a rage.

"I exploded and beat the kid up," said Starks, who got sent to the principal's office over the incident.

Starks's classmate received no punishment for his role in the matter. But Starks got suspended for three days, with the principal telling him he was the one who escalated the dispute into a fight. After Starks was told to go home, he asked the principal if he could wait in the office, since it was the middle of the day, and he relied on the school bus to get to and from his classes.

"No," the man told him. "You have to leave school grounds."

So the young Starks, terrified of the whooping he'd get from his mother or grandmother if he called them to come pick him up, walked until he made it to a local bus stop. He had a little more than a dollar in his pocket to pay for the trip back home. There was just one problem: this was a new school, and Starks had never taken the city bus by himself. He didn't know how to get home. Making the challenge even greater, Starks was painfully shy, making him reluctant to ask for help.

"So I went on the hunches I had and tried to make it back on my own," Starks said.

But instead of taking the northbound bus, which would've put him on a path toward his house, he took the one that went south. Once he realized he was in no-man's-land, he reached into his pocket, pulling out most of the change he had left to take the bus in the other direction. When he walked off the bus that second time, Starks still wasn't sure where he was. He used a skyscraper, Williams Center, as a landmark of sorts and walked toward that for a while.

Starks eventually spotted a dry-cleaning shop he was familiar with, which helped him find his way back. But that childhood ordeal revealed something meaningful about Starks: he was someone who often dug his heels in and doubled down on things, even in moments when he appeared to be totally lost.

If the Knicks didn't know that already, they became painfully aware during Game 1 of the NBA Finals against the Houston Rockets. Starks hit three of his first eight shots, but then played as if there was an airtight lid on the basket for the vast majority of the second half.

He missed wide-open looks when he came off screens. He missed a transition layup. He second-guessed himself on one sequence, passing out of what should have been a floater attempt. Then, after getting the ball back at the top of the arc, he hesitated again before launching and missing a triple from the wing.

Starks angrily took a seat on the bench between Herb Williams and Corey Gaines with two minutes left in the third. "Motherfucker! God dammit!" he shouted from his chair, which he'd kicked moments before.

By that point, Starks was 3-for-14 on the night and had missed six consecutive looks. He'd miss on two more to start the fourth quarter, pushing him to 3-for-16 on eight straight misfires.

Yet New York still had a chance. Taking advantage of league MVP Hakeem Olajuwon's second-half fatigue, the Knicks sliced what had been a 12-point deficit down to three, 79–76, with two minutes left.

With time winding down and every possession critical in the low-scoring slugfest, Starks got a pass from Greg Anthony on the right wing, before briefly shedding his man with a Patrick Ewing screen. It was still early in the shot clock and Starks—just the second Knick to touch the ball on that play—hadn't so much as glanced back in Ewing's direction following the big man's pick. Starks left his feet the very millisecond he saw an opening, launching a shot from deep that would tie the contest if it went down.

The rushed offering sailed about a foot and a half to the left of the basket, missing both the backboard and the rim before bouncing past the baseline and into the crowd. After the bad misfire prompted a jubilant eruption from the Houston fans, the Rockets scored on their next two plays, all but sealing the outcome. Then Starks flung one last shot—another misfire—leaving him 3-for-18 with 10 straight misses to end Game 1, which Houston took, 85–78.

Starks had a long, frustrating walk back to the visiting locker room, and not just because he'd been unable to throw the ball into the ocean. Personal circumstances were nagging at the guard, too. He'd planned for the start of the series to be a family reunion of sorts, asking for thirty tickets each for Games 1 and 2 in Houston—a city that was a seven- or eight-hour drive for his relatives who hailed from Tulsa.

But instead of it being a joyous gathering, it was a far more somber one. Starks's great-uncle, 85-year-old Frank Tate, who'd been planning to make the trip down to Houston, passed away unexpectedly between the Game 7 victory over the Pacers and the start of the series with the Rockets. And as the Knicks held a practice the day before the series began in Houston, Starks instead flew to Tulsa for his uncle's funeral.

"I had a special relationship with my uncle. He was a man I looked up to, and a man who gave me strength," Starks said. "But [his passing] didn't have anything to do with my [Game 1] performance."

For most players, that might sound like a stretch, given the emotions that can accompany a loss of that magnitude. But in this case, there was reason to believe Starks, whose game was as streaky as it was unrefined.

*   *   *

There were countless times when Starks—going from igloo cold to volcanically hot, or vice versa—played without a conscience, and without a feel for the moment. And there was a reason for that.

Unlike most NBA players, who dominated at the high school level before going on to play major college basketball, Starks didn't have much of a formal basketball education. He only played one true year of high school ball—and was with his varsity team for all of two games—before stopping. "He basically developed himself," says Butch Fisher, who coached Starks as a high schooler. "He had this spin move he'd use to get around people and slash to the basket." Still, at 5-foot-10, he was far from a standout.

In his autobiography, Starks wrote that he left his varsity team after a dispute with his coach. Fisher didn't remember it that way at all: "He told me he couldn't play because he needed a job to help his mom at home."

Money didn't come easily for Starks's family, which comprised seven children, all raised by his single mother and grandmother. If Starks was going to go to college, he'd need help. He held out hope for the possibility of a basketball scholarship, despite being undersized and cutting short his senior season. And if a scholarship wasn't possible, he would have to cobble together grants and loans to afford it.

He ended up doing the latter at Rogers State College, where he made the basketball team's taxi squad, meaning he wouldn't suit up for games, and would only get a chance if one of the people ahead of him couldn't play. But his spot in the rotation became moot once Starks got expelled from the school and jailed for five days after he and some teammates broke into a classmate's dorm and stole his stereo.

Starks's next stop, at Northern Oklahoma, was more promising and saw him averaging 11 points midway through the season. But that run came to a halt when he and two teammates got busted by campus police for smoking marijuana in his dorm room. Starks covered for his teammates, but got kicked out as a result.

Forced out of the residence hall with nowhere to go, Starks moved in with his brother Monty. Around that time, in 1985, John began dating a woman named Jackie, whom he'd go on to marry. Needing to provide,

Starks put school on pause and took a minimum-wage, $3.35-an-hour cashier job at a Safeway grocery store.

Yet basketball still meant plenty to him. During late-night shifts, after moving to a better-paying role as a stockboy, Starks would test his athleticism by touching the 10.5-foot-high beams toward the back of the store—a challenge that both impressed his coworkers and sometimes won him small side wagers. He continued to play ball in his spare time, including a tournament in Tulsa that featured Karl Malone and Dennis Rodman, as well as some local college players, Wayman Tisdale and Anthony Bowie, who'd later make it to the NBA themselves. Starks held his own, and was named to the all-tournament team.

It helped that the 20-year-old had grown four inches, to 6-foot-2, since finishing high school. But he was also beginning to drift, looking for something. *Anything*. He tried cocaine once, but worried it might cause him to spiral if it became a habit. The thought of doing manual, low-paying work for decades pained him.

So he returned to school, this time at Tulsa Junior College, where he'd study business. The institution had no basketball program, but Starks stayed in shape by playing on an intramural team with some friends.

During one of his games, a man named Tim Bart, an assistant coach at a nearby school, quietly stood on the sidelines. He was there scouting for talent that might have slipped through the cracks, since the junior college didn't have a program of its own. On that particular day, Bart initially noticed one of Starks's teammates as a standout. Intrigued, Bart came back to scout the player a second time, and brought a fellow assistant, Ken Trickey Jr., along with him. Trickey Jr. found himself more impressed by Starks.

The men extended tryout offers to both players, telling them they'd get their school and books paid for over at Oklahoma Junior College if they made the team. Both ended up on the roster, but Starks was one of the last to make it. "Maybe our tenth- or eleventh-best player at the time," Trickey Jr. says. "It wasn't until a guy ahead of him got hurt that he got to play more. Then, he started throwing in points from everywhere."

Starks's legend began on December 13, 1986, a day he might as well have been dressed as Superman.

That was the day he married Jackie. But it was also one Oklahoma Junior College had scheduled a road game in Kansas for. (Starks arranged his wedding plans well before he got the invitation to try out for the team.) Fortunately for Starks, the forecast that weekend called for heavy snow, all but ruling out the game and the long bus ride it required.

But then the snow never came. So the game was back on. "We're rounding everybody up last minute for the bus ride, but no one could track down John," Trickey Jr. recalls.

Unable to reach Starks, the team left for its game against Coffeyville Junior College, eighty-five miles northeast of Tulsa, without him. It wasn't until just before the game, as Starks and his bride were enjoying their wedding reception, that his coach managed to get hold of him and tell him the game was still on.

"Coach, you told me we didn't have one," Starks said. "I just got married!"

"Well, we've got one," coach Ken Trickey Sr. said in response. "Do you think you can make it anyway?"

After explaining this to Jackie, and asking her blessing, Starks and his wife hopped into their Chevy Impala and raced up Highway 75—they ended up getting a speeding ticket—in an effort to make it to the game.

When Starks arrived at halftime and went from tuxedo to basketball uniform in the gym's bathroom, his school trailed by 25. But his presence, and his 22 points, turned things around. "He went off the deep end in the second half," says Trickey Jr., recalling a half-court alley-oop Starks caught and jammed in reverse.

It wasn't quite enough to earn a win—Starks's team lost by four—but breakout showings like that helped get him a scholarship to play at a fourth school: Division I Oklahoma State. The dramatic wedding-day performance also highlighted something fundamental about Starks: he wasn't afraid of carrying his team on his shoulders if he felt he needed to.

The Knicks bounced back from their 78-point showing in the opener to win Game 2 in Houston.

Starks got back on track, shooting 6-for-11, finishing with 19 points.

He wasn't alone. Every Knick who played, save for Ewing (7-for-19), hit at least 50 percent of his shots that night. The Knicks were even better on defense, where they gradually wore down Olajuwon, the Rockets' superstar, for a second straight game.

After one Finals practice, a writer saw the MVP walking gingerly and asked what was wrong. "Mason," Olajuwon said, grinning through discomfort.

But deep down, New York's defensive physicality was no laughing matter.

"Patrick could just block my jump shots," says Olajuwon, who'd battled—and come out on the losing end—against Ewing in the memorable 1984 NCAA title game between Houston and Georgetown. "But with Mason and Oakley, they'd beat up on me so much before I could even get the ball. They knew I had a height advantage and could just shoot over them if they let me catch it. So they did everything they could to take me out of my comfort zone. They just had bruiser, after bruiser, after bruiser. They wouldn't let me have anything easy."

Concerned Olajuwon might not have anything left down the stretch of a long series, coach Rudy Tomjanovich decided to tweak things after Game 2.

"We figured we couldn't keep coming straight in and throwing the ball into Hakeem on post-ups. Because if we did that, they were set to beat up on him," Tomjanovich recalls. "So we came up with an indirect way of getting him the ball, where he wouldn't have to go through that sort of punishment."

The shift in strategy—to run pick-and-rolls to the other side of the floor, and force Olajuwon's man to rotate out of position ever so slightly—didn't look like anything special. Jack Ramsay, the Hall of Fame coach and a confidant of Tomjanovich, even asked Houston's head man why the Rockets kept running a set that seemed to be fruitless. "But we were happy as hell with what we were getting," Tomjanovich says.

Saving Olajuwon's energy paid dividends for Houston late in Game 3, with forty seconds to play and the Knicks up, 88–86. Olajuwon backed down Ewing on the block before doing a pirouette to find an open teammate, Sam Cassell, outside the arc. Cassell, a rookie, moved to his left to put himself in Olajuwon's line of sight—a quiet shift that prompted Knicks veteran Derek Harper to lose track of the point guard.

"Harp never made errors or had mental lapses, but with that play, it was almost like he totally forgot he was on a basketball court for a moment. Biggest brain fart of his career, probably, and it happened at the wrong moment," says Bob Salmi, New York's video coordinator. "It was such a bad lapse that we didn't even show it in the film room, because there was nothing to analyze. What do you even say about a play like that, where someone just wanders away from the guy they're guarding?"

"I made a mistake and a bad decision," says Harper, who shined otherwise with 21 points. "Dream made a great play there, but that shot was all on me."

Cassell took advantage, hitting a three to put the Rockets up by one, 89–88, silencing the once-euphoric Garden crowd with what would prove to be the game winner.

After their 93–89 victory in New York, the Rockets now led the series, 2–1. But the Knicks won Game 4, 91–82, getting monster showings from Oakley (16 points and 20 rebounds), Harper (21 points), and Starks, who had a double-digit fourth quarter.

The trio made up for another rough showing from Ewing, who'd seen his shooting percentages plummet from 39 percent in Game 1 and 37 percent in Game 2 to 31 percent and 29 percent in Games 3 and 4, respectively. He had done an admirable job defensively on Olajuwon at times, and would even go on to break an NBA Finals record for blocked shots in a series. But Ewing's inefficiency against Olajuwon had begun prompting New York's guards to take scoring matters into their own hands a bit more than usual.

"[Starks] basically looked around and said, 'If no one else is gonna shoot, I'll shoot,'" *Daily News* beat writer Curtis Bunn says. "It's almost like the moment was too big for everybody else other than him."

At 2–2, the championship series was there for the taking.

It was also about to fly completely beneath the radar.

By the time June 17, 1994, rolled around, the phrase "Game 5" had become synonymous with "absurd" for the Knicks.

A year earlier, New York had witnessed the infamous Charles Smith sequence during a Game 5. A month earlier, Hubert Davis and the Knicks had beaten the Bulls following a controversial foul call on Scottie Pippen during a Game 5. Just two and a half weeks prior, New York watched Reggie Miller go bonkers for a 25-point fourth quarter in Game 5 as he mean-mugged Spike Lee and abruptly stole a victory.

All three of those contests had taken place at Madison Square Garden. Yet none of them were as strange as what would take place during the Game 5 on this night.

Perhaps it's easiest to explain by outlining the people who *weren't* where they were supposed to be as the Knicks were getting set to play their biggest home game in twenty-one years. Talk-show host Maury Povich had an open courtside seat next to him, because his wife, CBS News anchor Connie Chung, had to cover a breaking story. Ahmad Rashad was nowhere to be found until NBC Sports president Dick Ebersol tracked him down in the bowels of the arena, where the sideline reporter was tearing up while sitting on bales of hay that were being held there for the recent circus run. And deep into the matchup's second half, thousands of sidetracked fans were away from their seats—an unthinkable scenario, given how much was on the line in Game 5.

All three absences stemmed the same thing. Before Game 5, criminal charges had been filed against ex–football star O. J. Simpson, who'd been questioned in connection with the double murder of his wife, Nicole Brown Simpson, and Ron Goldman, a waiter who'd befriended her weeks earlier. But after the Los Angeles Police Department agreed to let Simpson turn himself in, he never showed up. Instead, he'd fled in a white Ford Bronco, and was leading police on a low-speed chase throughout Los Angeles.

So Chung was reporting the news as it was happening. Rashad, who had Simpson serve as his best man at his wedding with *The Cosby Show* star Phylicia Rashad, was crying because he'd been mentioned by name during a press conference in what many perceived to be Simpson's suicide note. And scores of Knicks fans were leaving their seats at the Garden and doing everything they could to watch the chase rather than Game 5 of the Finals.

Even some of the players were caught up with the story over the course of the contest. During a timeout huddle in the second half, Tomjanovich saw a distracted Kenny Smith having side conversations with a few of his teammates. When Tomjanovich asked the Rockets guard why he wasn't paying attention, Smith responded by mentioning Simpson's chase. Tomjanovich lit into Smith for prioritizing the spectacle.

"What are you doing?" Tomjanovich asked him. "We're in the middle of an NBA Finals game! Focus!"

But as soon as the timeout ended, Tomjanovich walked to the scorer's table and started asking for information from people who were sitting in front of courtside TV monitors. Like his players, he wanted updates on the chase. "Of course I did—I just couldn't let the players know that," Tomjanovich says with a laugh.

Bob Costas, anchoring NBC's pre- and postgame coverage of the Finals from the Garden, was just as captivated by the chase as the next person. Because of Simpson's analyst work on NBC football games, the men knew each other. "Well, I thought I knew him. But obviously I didn't know nearly as much as I thought I did," Costas says.

Costas also had no idea that Simpson was trying to phone him from the back seat of the Bronco during the pursuit.

Simpson first tried Costas's St. Louis home. Then he dialed the NBC Sports control room. "No one was there except for a tech," Costas says. Based on what Costas was told, the conversation went like this:

Simpson: Is Bob Costas there?
Technician: No, he's not.
Simpson: I have to speak with him.
Technician: He's at Madison Square Garden—he's not here.
Simpson: I have to speak with him right away.
Technician: Who's calling?
Simpson: O. J. Simpson.
Technician: Yeah, right. *Click*

Months later, in November 1994, Costas got a request from Simpson to visit him in lockup at the Los Angeles County Jail. A. C. Cowlings,

Simpson's friend and the driver of the Bronco that day, and Robert Kardashian, Simpson's friend and one of his defense lawyers, sat with Costas on the other side of the glass from the ex-football star.

"You know we tried to call you that day from the Bronco, right?" Cowlings asked Costas.

Costas was stunned. In talking with Simpson, he concluded the former star had wanted to counter what he felt was negative media coverage in the wake of the allegations. Simpson figured he could push back by speaking to an acquaintance like Costas on live television—something Costas says would have only made the chase even more historic.

At one point during that Game 5, Costas—far more interested in the chase than the game—turned around in his chair and saw hundreds of fans behind him leaning over, trying to catch a glimpse of his monitor. The game, which was set to put either the Knicks or Rockets one win away from an NBA crown, had taken a distant backseat, both inside and outside the arena.

"My editor said, 'Please write the best game story of your life, because *nobody* is watching this game,'" recalls David Steele, who covered the Knicks for *Newsday*. "There were just so many people on the concourse, watching the TVs at the concession stands. The basketball didn't matter."

The lack of eyeballs on the game frustrated a handful of key people. Certainly David Stern, who was already dealing with far lower TV ratings as a result of Michael Jordan's exit from the league the year before. Ebersol, feeling viewers could watch the chase on virtually any other channel, wasn't thrilled with NBC affiliates prioritizing the chase or using a split screen to show both events. (Oddly enough, Ebersol says Simpson was an occasional roommate of his in the 1980s. Simpson, not wanting to stay in a hotel each time he flew to New York for his work as a studio analyst, rented a room from Ebersol and a friend during those years.)

No one was more frustrated than Dave Checketts. He'd been in a good mood earlier in the day, as the New York Rangers held a parade through Midtown to celebrate winning their first Stanley Cup in fifty-four years. But now, when he needed cheering fans in their seats to help the Knicks accomplish the same goal, they were entranced by the Simpson situation. So Checketts considered having the arena switch to closed-circuit TV, which would have allowed the stadium's televisions to only show the game. If that was the case, he thought, everyone would be forced back to their seats. "But the media would have skewered me for that," says Checketts, who opted against closing off the TV feed.

Still, even with the sparse, distracted crowd, the Knicks played well in The Game Nobody Saw. Ewing finally had a breakout showing, shooting 11-for-21 for 25 points, 12 boards, and eight blocks. Starks had 11 of his 19 in the final period, giving him back-to-back games where he'd had a double-digit fourth quarter.

With their 91–84 win, the Knicks were off to Houston, up 3–2, needing just one more victory for a confetti festival of their own.

It was like a schoolteacher forcing a student to stand at the board until he finished a math problem. Except Pat Riley was the teacher, John Starks was the student, and the math problem was a bounce pass.

After Starks's first effort failed, Riley told him to try again. Then came a second effort. And a third. And a fourth. Then Riley, having seen enough, went from exasperated teacher to angry drill sergeant.

"We're not going *anyfuckingwhere* till John gets the fucking ball into Patrick!" Riley shouted during a practice in 1993, after seeing four straight Starks passes get tipped or stolen by backup Bo Kimble.

Because Kimble viewed practice as his time to shine—he saw a grand total of fifty-five minutes of playing time that year—he hounded Starks as hard as he could during team workouts in an effort to convince Riley to play him. "But Patrick, Mason, and Oak would come up to me sometimes and tap me on the shoulder and say, 'Man, just let [John] have this. We ain't trying to be here all fuckin' day,'" Kimble recalls.

Starks did many things well. He had great range, and was ahead of his time in making frequent use of the three-point line. As the Knicks' best athlete—he'd participated in the 1992 dunk contest—he was the lone guard who could put pressure on the defense by slashing to the basket.

He played much bigger defensively than his 6-foot-3 frame would suggest. (Starks was listed at 6-foot-5 during his career.)

But the beloved Knick wasn't great at throwing the ball into tight windows—especially not to Ewing, whose hands were a bit small for a center of his size. "Patrick had a lot of what we called 'double-catches'—these catches where he'd bring the ball in, but not cleanly," says Ed Tapscott.

For the most part, the connection between those two wasn't an issue in Game 6. Much like the first four games of the series, though, Ewing again struggled to find his offense. (One key mistake: he continued to shoot jumpers rather than attack the basket in the fourth despite Olajuwon being saddled with five fouls.) That meant Starks had even less reason to pass it to him than usual, and that he'd take matters into his own hands.

Starks had no problem with putting the Knicks on his back that night. He caught fire, hitting from everywhere in the fourth and scoring 16 points in that span to keep New York in it.

With just one minute left, and the Knicks down 84–82, Starks curled around a screen on the left side and tried sneaking a pass into Ewing. But Olajuwon stole it, thwarting New York's effort to tie or pull ahead. During the next stoppage in play, Starks pointed to his head, as if to say he should have known better than to force the ball to Ewing—especially with how well Starks was shooting, and how small the window was.

That miscue may have influenced Starks's decision making on the final play of the game. With 5.5 seconds to go, and Houston up 86–84, Oakley prepared to inbound the ball for a play that could win New York the title. Starks came to get it from him, then Ewing came up above the arc to set a screen on Rockets guard Vernon Maxwell—an action that forced Olajuwon, the two-time reigning Defensive Player of the Year, to switch onto Starks. As the clock dwindled to two seconds remaining, Ewing rolled toward the free-throw line and found himself wide open, something that almost never happened for him in the final seconds.

But similar to the play from moments before—or like the practice where Riley chewed him out for his inability to throw good bounce passes—Starks didn't appear to have a good angle to make the pass.

That doesn't stop Ewing from razzing Starks about the play to this day.

"I was standing at the free-throw line, running down the middle wide open, and you didn't throw it to me," Ewing reminds him. The big man began harping on it in 2003, after becoming a Rockets assistant coach. Ewing's first day on the job, he learned that the club had a huge, blown-up photo of that play from Game 6 displayed in the arena hallway.

As Starks left his feet and launched a three that could win the championship, he had confidence it was going down. He'd made six shots in a row leading up to that, and had ditched Maxwell. Between those things, and the full step he appeared to gain on Olajuwon, there was no way Starks would miss.

"I took two dribbles to my left, fired, and when it left my hand, it was money," Starks said.

As the shot hung in the air, so much else hung in the balance. Stu Crystal, a Starter brand executive, was standing in a tunnel with a bag full of Knicks World Champions hats and shirts he'd have to race onto the floor with if the shot went down. Parade planners were set to task Tiffany & Co. with making a championship trophy ice sculpture if New York prevailed. Trainer Mike Saunders, who'd all but bribed Houston to let him bring champagne into the stadium—as he got there, Rockets security staffers "confiscated" it, then sold the champagne back to him—had bottles he'd need to rush into the locker room if the Knicks won. Millions in the New York tri-state area were ready to unleash two decades' worth of euphoric shouts as the ball made its way toward the rim.

But then Starks's shot that couldn't miss came up extremely short. Olajuwon had perhaps grazed the shot with his fingernail, doing just enough to change the trajectory of Starks's jumper.

Rockets fans roared with elation as Houston tied the series at at three games apiece. They knew they'd dodged a bullet, and now could take a few days to exhale before coming back to do it all over again for a do-or-die Game 7.

On the afternoon of the seventh game, Dick Butera, a close friend of Riley's, was waiting for the elevator in the Knicks' hotel with the coach, when Riley grabbed him by the shoulder. "Well, old buddy, I know at least three people are gonna show up tonight. You, me, and John," Riley told Butera, referring to Starks.

To that point, Starks seemed like a safe bet to pull through for New York when it counted. Since the forgettable 3-for-18 showing in Game 1 after his great uncle's passing, Starks had been the Knicks' most reliable option, hitting 49 percent of his shots—and 45 percent of his threes—averaging a team-best 21 points and seven assists per contest. Most notably, he'd logged three straight double-digit fourth quarters, the first two efforts helping the Knicks to victory, with the third almost winning them a championship.

What Riley and Butera didn't know, however, was that Starks hadn't slept the night before Game 7. Or the two nights prior. From Sunday night to Wednesday, Starks—who usually could flush bad plays and let them roll off his back—hadn't been able to stop replaying the end of Game 6 in his mind. It ate away at him.

With the final two games of the series in Houston, and the long gap between contests, the restlessness was amplified for New York. As the Rockets basked in the relief of winning Game 6, they got to sleep in their own beds to prepare for the biggest showdown of their lives. By contrast, the Knicks were antsy.

"Having to stay there for three days between Game 6 and Game 7, all you're hearing on TV is 'Houston, Houston, Houston.' You basically couldn't watch TV because of it. I was turning channels like crazy," backup center Herb Williams said. "It was like, 'Look, *please* let's just play tomorrow and get this over with.' But we had to sit there for three days and think about everything. I think Riles was thinking about having us go back to New York after Game 6 for a while. I'm not sure why we didn't do that."

When the Knicks made it to the stadium early that evening, Starks and teammate Anthony Bonner met with team chaplain John Love to say a pregame prayer. With all the arena's other rooms being occupied that night, Bonner, Starks, and Love were forced to use the venue's weight room for their chapel service.

The pastor closed his eyes and thanked God for bringing the trio together. He expressed gratitude for getting the Knicks to Houston safely, and for allowing them to advance as far as they had, with a chance to win a championship still there. Love didn't believe in praying for specific game outcomes. But he asked God to keep the players safe, and to help each of them to play to the best of their abilities.

"In the grand scheme of things, it's fair to say the last part of that prayer didn't work," Love says now.

Starks had a brutal first half. His focus lacked, as he surrendered a wide-open three to Maxwell, his counterpart. Starks had three fouls prior to halftime, which forced him to the bench early. His offense wasn't pretty, either, as he shot just 1-for-5. Still, the Knicks were right there, trailing only 45–43 at half.

But if the Knicks hoped the break at halftime would calm Starks down, things didn't play out that way.

On his first try of the second half, a jumper from three-point range, the ball bounced off the backboard before coming off the rim. Minutes later, he missed again from the right side, pushing him to 1-for-7.

"Starks has had many nights like this over the course of the year, where he'll try to shoot himself back into the game after struggling, and that's been the case here tonight," NBC announcer Marv Albert said.

"I don't think there's any question that Riley is gonna stay with John Starks, even if he's 1-of-14," said Matt Guokas, Albert's partner. "This is his guy in the fourth quarter, and he'd like to get him going."

Shortly after the comment, Starks abandoned the jumper by driving to the basket and laying the ball up with his right hand before being met by Olajuwon, who swatted the offering out of the air. And after finding no success on his eighth try, Starks then surrendered a tough, fall-away basket to Maxwell.

That sequence was a microcosm. The harder Starks seemed to try, by putting his head down and barreling into the teeth of the defense, the more wayward the result. Meanwhile, Maxwell had thrown up something of a prayer, yet watched it funnel through the bottom of the net.

The players—each three-point gunners, who had tendencies to run hot and cold and fly off the handle—were mirror images of each other. For a brief time in 1988, they were training camp teammates with the Spurs. After Starks declined what he considered to be a lowball offer, San Antonio released him. "The way [the front office] saw it, John and Vernon were pretty much the same player anyway," recalls Larry Brown, who coached San Antonio that season. "They didn't feel like we needed them both."

But where Starks had essentially paralyzed himself with overthinking in the days leading up to Game 7, Maxwell took pride in how much he could accomplish without having to think.

"Me and Maxwell got drafted the same year, and were summer-league teammates," says Greg Butler, an ex-Knick who took part in a couple of Riley's New York training camps. "One day we had each other's summer-league jerseys by mistake. So I walk into Vernon's room to give him his, and his floor is just *covered* with beers. Two cases' worth, with cans scattered everywhere, empty. He was sipping on another as I walked in. But a few hours later, he drops something like thirty points that day. The guy was different."

The Knicks, down three at the end of the third period, hoped a different Starks would appear in the fourth. That he'd pull another fourth-quarter rabbit out of his hat, the way he'd done throughout the series. Yet his struggles continued. His triple from the left wing got tipped by Robert Horry, making Starks 1-for-9. A minute later from the same side of the floor, he came off a screen and fired a three that rimmed out.

At 1-for-10, Starks's boyish face looked longer than usual. His eyes began darting as he looked over to the bench. He had the same question in his mind as everyone else: was Riley going to keep Starks in the game to work through this?

Even those who never doubted Riley were second-guessing the choice to stay with him. "I wonder if maybe this would be the time for us to take a shot with [backup Rolando] Blackman," ex–Knicks coach Red Holzman said as he watched. ("It's the closest I ever heard Red come to even mildly construing a disagreement with Pat," says Tapscott, who was sitting next to Holzman during Game 7.)

The Rockets, on the other hand, were counting their blessings each time Starks took another shot.

"He's our best player right now," Houston guard Scott Brooks recalls thinking from the bench that day. "After a while, his shot looked more like a medicine ball, with how much he was struggling to shoot it. All of us on the bench—players, coaches—kept waiting, thinking Pat was going to use Blackman. Because for years [with the Mavericks], he'd just killed us, and we couldn't stop him, no matter how hard we tried."

You have to go back two and a half weeks earlier, to the moments that took place immediately after the Knicks' Game 7 victory over Indiana, to understand the Rolando Blackman dilemma, and how it might have come into play here.

The veteran Knicks, who collectively had zero rings to their name, were in an all-time great mood, having just won the biggest game of their careers to reach the NBA Finals. Riley had just congratulated them in the locker room during a postgame debrief. The next step was for them to head down to Houston.

But before they dispersed, Blackman asked Riley a question: could the players bring their wives along? After all, the Finals trip was the culmination of an immense amount of work—the Knicks had begun their season with the midnight workout on the first allowable day of training, back in October—and New York had won two grueling seven-game series to get there. So it'd be great if the wives could come, Blackman said.

Riley's answer, in front of the entire team, and right after its biggest win in twenty-one years, was a swift no.

Blackman failed to understand the logic, and pushed back, something that rarely happened with Riley.

"Why? Why can't we take our wives?" Blackman recalls asking. "They've toiled, and dealt with us being gone all year. They should be able to enjoy this, too. They've had our backs throughout this whole time."

In response, Riley simply repeated his first answer without giving a reason: wives aren't making the trip.

The tone of the exchange stunned the players—not only because they hadn't seen Riley challenged that way in front of the group in years, but also because of Riley's terse response to such a respected veteran.

About an hour later, Riley dialed Checketts's cell phone.

"I'm driving home after the Game 7 win over Indiana, and I get a call from Pat. And the entire purpose of the call was to tell me he doesn't think the wives should make the trip with us," Checketts said. "We'd *just* won the Eastern Conference. We're headed to the Finals. Most people probably take twenty-four hours to enjoy that. He said he didn't need my answer on the whole thing—just that he wanted to put the thought in my ear, and clearly state his preference."

Checketts said he disagreed with Riley, mainly because of how long it had been since the organization had made it to the Finals, and how special a feat he saw it to be. Still, he deferred to the coach, who worried family members might become a distraction if they were flown down to begin the series. ("I hired Pat for one reason: to win. And if this guy has four championship rings to my zero, and he says, 'This is what I believe in,' I'm gonna listen to that.") As a compromise, Checketts said the entire organization, plus the players' wives, would be flown down for Games 6 and 7 if the series returned to Houston.

So, as Blackman languished on the bench during Game 7 against the team he'd enjoyed his career-best scoring average against, he wondered whether the run-in with Riley over the wives came into play. His teammates had—and to this day, have—the same question. "I don't know if it caused some interior backlash, or played a role in [Riley's] choice," says Blackman, who hadn't played in the series prior to Game 7.

The drumbeat got louder with each additional Starks miss. A jumper he front-rimmed so badly that it bounced out of bounds, into the arms of a cameraman sitting along the baseline. A pull up three in transition that hit the back iron and resulted in a Houston fast break and dunk. A great look from the left corner that bounced out. The misfires left Starks 1-for-13 as the Knicks trailed, 78–71, in the fourth.

By then, other players began thinking about their own roles in Starks's performance. Doc Rivers, who'd been left off the playoff roster—but would have been physically cleared from his ACL rehab by the conference finals—couldn't help but wonder what his availability might have meant for that Game 7. Harper, who'd played so well that he'd prepared a rough outline of a speech in case he won Finals MVP, began wondering whether he should keep passing to Starks, given his teammate's arctic spell.

Starks scored on a putback that trimmed Houston's lead to 78–73. But the make would be his last.

He'd miss a wild layup attempt, dragging his count to 2-for-15. And with just under two minutes left, and Houston up 80–75, Starks closed out hard on Maxwell as the Rockets guard fired off a triple with the shot clock expiring. The ball floated right above Starks's outstretched arm before dropping through the basket, setting off a fiesta among the fans, who were now louder than they'd been all series. Houston players ran onto the court to mob Maxwell, whose bucket forced a timeout. The Rockets could all but taste their champagne.

There'd be no merciful ending for Starks, though. Seemingly just as lost as he'd been trying to get home that day from school, Starks missed his last three shots of Game 7—the last of which fell about four and a half feet short of the basket. He'd finish an unthinkable 2-for-18 from the field, and 0-for-11 from three; still among the worst performances ever in a do-or-die game for a championship.

Houston won, 90–84, taking the game and the crown in a year the Knicks felt should have been theirs.

The Knicks could hear the Rockets' celebratory screams through the visitor locker room walls.

Before Riley pulled out a cigarette in the locker room to cope with the stress of the defeat, he first spoke with his crestfallen ball club. But not a single soul remembers what was said. It was the equivalent of Charlie Brown's teacher—sounds, but not actual words. "By that point, so much stuff is rushing through your head to where it's almost like a dam breaking. And there's no way any water is coming back in," assistant coach

Jeff Nix recalls. "You're seeing him talk, but you just aren't hearing him at all."

Harper walked into the shower in his full uniform, wailing. Herb Williams kept his shower short, not wanting to linger at the arena. When the club took its bus to go back to the hotel for their "party" in Riley's suite—they'd planned one in an advance, win or lose—Williams instead opted to walk back alone.

Blackman showered for a half hour, letting the water wash away the disappointment of not getting a chance to spell Starks. "By the time I finished [the shower], I knew that was it for me in the NBA," says Blackman, who retired that offseason. (Riley called not subbing Blackman in "the biggest mistake I ever made." The coach has sent handwritten letters to Blackman over the years, but Blackman says he's never written Riley back.)

As for Starks, the player most traumatized by Game 7, he stayed in the shower for just over an hour. "We literally had to pull him out of there, because he was in there so long," assistant Jeff Van Gundy recalls.

By the time Starks finished getting dressed, just two reporters—whose deadlines had already passed—were there to speak with him. "I blame myself," Starks told them. "Everybody knows what type of person I am. They know I'm gonna take this harder than probably anyone else in here."

When Starks went back to his hotel room that night, he again failed to fall asleep. The same thing happened when he made it back to New York, too. Game 7, similar to Game 6 before, kept replaying itself in his head. His anguish and insomnia reached a point where Starks lost focus on his children at times—they would sometimes ask him a question or tell him something, yet he'd be too distracted to notice.

The season had just ended. But in a way, that night—and the wrenching nature of the loss—marked the beginning of what would become a restless, tumultuous year for the Knicks.

12

COMMITMENT ISSUES

Well before Anthony Mason became one of the Knicks' most vital players, he first had to deal with a number of trust issues.

He craved validation and reassurance, even from those closest to him. If some of his friends couldn't hang out on a given night, Mason would guilt them by asking if their plans were really more important than he was. If barber Freddy Avila couldn't scrap his schedule to put Mason at the top of his appointment list, it suddenly became a question of loyalty. "He was possessive, and always wanted to know where he stood," Avila said.

So for how much emphasis a younger Mason placed on allegiance, it was ironic that he often began conversations with women he approached by telling them a particularly bold lie.

In 1989, as he was getting to know Latifa Whitlock—someone he'd been set up with blindly, over the phone, through a friend—they made small talk before Whitlock asked what Mason did for a living.

"I'm a fry cook at McDonald's," he said, adding he hadn't worked much that summer due to a fracture in his foot—an injury he claimed was the result of a slip-and-fall he sustained while mopping the restaurant.

But neither of those details was true. Mason sustained the fracture playing professional basketball in Turkey. And there was no job at McDonald's, as a fry cook or otherwise. In reality, Mason had been waiting for his agent to strike a deal with the Nets for a spot on their training camp roster that fall.

Mason's bending of the truth was intentional, if not calculated. Like most, he wanted companionship. But he didn't want to be with someone who'd only develop an interest in him after learning he was a pro basketball player.

Nothing ultimately changed for Whitlock once she realized Mason was an athlete. Over the first five years they spent together, Whitlock stood with him through plenty. His moodiness. Mason's disinclination to mention his first child. (Whitlock learned of Mason's first son a few months into their relationship, after noticing a picture of a child on the living room wall of Mason's mother's home. Whitlock asked who the boy was. "Oh, Anthony didn't tell you?" Mason's mother responded.) His dalliances with other women.

So when Whitlock, the mother of one of his kids, was still there through it all, Mason decided it was time.

Around 3 a.m., maybe eight hours after returning from the Finals in Houston, Mason drove his pearl-white Mercedes-Benz into Queens and onto 99th Avenue, where Whitlock, their son Antoine, and Whitlock's mother lived. As Mason parked, his speakers were loud enough to startle Whitlock—and to wake the entire block. He used his cell phone to dial her, and when Whitlock picked up, Mason asked her to come outside.

Once she did, Mason pressed play on his car's CD player, and the music went from a bombastic rap track to a softer, more melodic one, in the key of B minor. By the time Whitlock made it to the car and hopped into the passenger seat, DeBarge's falsetto-filled "Share My World" was into its first verse.

"I love you," Mason said, holding a gleaming, six-carat diamond ring. "I want you to share my world."

Mason asked a tearful Whitlock if she'd marry him. When she said yes, they walked into Whitlock's mother's house to share the good news. "We had to wake them up, because of how late it was," she said.

Mason wasn't the only one with the team making a move that offseason to lock down his future. Within a few weeks of the NBA Finals loss, Dave

Checketts reached out to Pat Riley, telling him the organization wanted to reward his success as coach by negotiating a much richer contract extension.

By almost any calculation, the move was an obvious one. Riley had inherited a mediocre-at-best club—one that couldn't sell out its games and swapped out head coaches and executives the way a runway model changes outfits. Yet the culture changed swiftly. And by 1994, Riley and the Knicks had finished with or tied for the East's best record each of the past two seasons while also logging the NBA's top defense both years.

Simply establishing that smashmouth identity would've been a worthwhile improvement. But in Riley's first campaign with the club, New York took Michael Jordan and the reigning champion Bulls to a Game 7. In Year Two, the Knicks jumped out to a 2-0 conference finals lead on Chicago before narrowly faltering after the infamous Charles Smith sequence. And in Year Three, with Jordan gone, they won the East and came within a victory of being NBA champions.

Riley had two years left on his five-year contract—a deal that, with incentives, already paid him more than any other coach in the league, at about $1.5 million a year. He'd proven to be worth that and then some.

The Knicks would eventually lay out an extension offer to double Riley's salary; something they hoped would keep him in New York and give the organization stability as it sought to make the most of Ewing's latter years.

But for all the talk of a Riley extension, the 1994–95 campaign was more akin to a draining hourglass, or perhaps the fabric from an Armani garment slowly coming undone. Despite the millions of dollars that sat on Riley's desk in the form of a new deal, the bond between him and the front office was about to unravel.

On paper, the Knicks were still well positioned to make another run at an NBA championship.

As the 1994–95 season approached, Jordan, their biggest roadblock in years prior, was still out of the league, having traded his basketball shoes for baseball spikes. The Knicks' defensive system, which often resembled tackle football, was firmly established. And because the vast majority of

New York's roster remained intact, the club could theoretically pick up where it left off. Preseason oddsmakers had the Knicks tied for the second-best odds of winning it all.

But right from the start, challenges loomed.

On the team's first day of camp in Charleston, the NBA's head of operations, Rod Thorn, dropped in to meet with the Knicks. Coincidentally or not, they were Thorn's first stop on a league-wide tour to lay out several rules changes—to reduce physicality, and increase scoring—that would be taking effect that year.

Any player leaving the bench during an altercation, for any reason, would now be suspended for a game. The three-point line was moving in by almost two feet—from twenty-three feet and nine inches to twenty-two feet—which would force paint-bound rim protectors to step farther away from the goal to stop shooters who now might try their hand from the shorter distance. And hand-checking, the tool long used by defenders to impede the progress of scorers on their way to the hoop, was now being significantly curtailed.

After Thorn and the league's supervisor of officials, Darrell Garretson, finished lecturing the club on all the changes, Garretson used a VHS player to give visual examples of what wouldn't be allowed going forward. As he spoke on the elimination of hand-checking, a familiar face popped onto the screen.

"It was a highlight of me hand-checking somebody, over and over," says Derek Harper, who initially smiled at his inclusion in the video, but found it less funny as his starring role became evident. "They made me the poster child."

Harper's sentiment was shared by the club as a whole. The Knicks, who featured a low-scoring offense with a physical, pound-of-flesh style of defense, felt the new rules were aimed directly at them. The stylistic changes came just weeks after an NBA Finals that struggled ratings-wise—not having Jordan in them was certainly a factor—where neither team managed to hit the 95-point mark in any of the games. And the rules regarding fighting came just months after Harper suplexed Chicago's Jo Jo English, setting off a bench-clearing brawl that played out in front of David Stern.

For New York, which played in the mud by fouling more than any other team, these were huge changes.

"They were anti-Knick rules. I don't even think there was any doubt about that," guard Doc Rivers says. "And to [the league's] credit, the game is far prettier now because of those rules to open things up. But it was obviously aimed at us, because we did those things so much harder and better than everybody else."

Russ Granik, the NBA's deputy commissioner at the time, says he can understand how the team came to see it that way. "It might have impacted the Knicks more than the other teams, with how they played and how they were built," says Granik, adding that league officials worried, generally, that physicality would become more meaningful than talent if they didn't alter the rules. "[The changes] certainly weren't directed *at* them. But I wouldn't dismiss the idea that they impacted the Knicks more. They probably did impact New York more than any other team."

Beyond the rule changes, there was another hard reality for the Knicks: competition throughout the league was improving. The rival Pacers looked primed for a leap, having defied the odds the year before by nearly reaching the Finals, despite being the lower-seeded team in all three of their playoff series. And young, star-laden teams like the Charlotte Hornets (Alonzo Mourning and Larry Johnson) and Orlando Magic (Shaquille O'Neal and Penny Hardaway) were becoming serious contenders, too.

Those fast, youthful up-and-comers made for a stark contrast with the Knicks, who were recovering from the wear and tear of the longest postseason that any NBA team had ever experienced. They entered the 1994–95 season as the second-oldest club, behind only the Utah Jazz. Maintaining an elite level of play simply wasn't a given for New York anymore. Neither was the idea of consistently good health.

Ewing, now 32, had undergone a clean-out procedure on his right knee during the offseason, and would sit out the entire preseason to rest his balky joints. (Charles Smith, just 29, was prone to the same issues. In fact, upon learning Smith would come to camp late due to the birth of his child, Riley jokingly told him to make sure he iced the newborn's knees.)

Charles Oakley, the 31-year-old Iron Man who hadn't missed a game in almost four seasons, would complain of significant toe pain to start the year. Somewhat remarkably, six players—or half the team's roster—had undergone surgery within a twelve-month window. That included the 33-year-old Rivers, who was returning after tearing his ACL the season before.

Riley and the front office weren't oblivious to the club being long in the tooth. The coach pulled back from his usual camp schedule, having the players work out just once instead of the two-a-days they'd undergone in prior years. And in a move that ran counter to how a veteran, contending team like the Knicks usually operated, they brought in two rookies—point guard Charlie Ward and forward Monty Williams—through the draft.

New York's efforts to land the two players with the 24th and 26th picks of the first round were rooted in a simple strategy. Sensing the need for young impact players, but unwilling to part with key members of a contender to obtain them, the team's front office looked to the draft. Yet with picks near the back end of that process, Ed Tapscott, who'd taken over the club's scouting department, figured the Knicks needed to take a few big swings on high-risk, high-reward athletes.

Ward was known far better for his time on the football field, where he'd won the Heisman Trophy as a dynamic, dual-threat quarterback at Florida State. The gridiron ate into much of Ward's time in college. But when it became clear the two-sport athlete was serious about taking on basketball full-time, Tapscott was willing to take a chance on him. And he thought New York might be able to land him with a lower draft pick because of the concern some teams would have about his involvement in two sports.

Still, Tapscott's bosses weren't sold right away. "Ernie [Grunfeld] and Dave looked at me like a three-headed Hydra when I first brought him up," Tapscott says.

Grunfeld and Checketts eventually came around, and the Knicks drafted Ward at No. 26. But the risk they took with Williams, two picks earlier, was even bigger.

Williams had starred at Notre Dame, averaging more than 22 points and eight boards per game as a senior. But he'd been forced to sit out for two years after an annual physical in 1990 revealed a thickened muscle between his heart chambers, a potentially life-threatening issue known as hypertrophic cardiomyopathy.

After Williams went through an NBA Draft physical, Knicks team doctor Norm Scott determined the forward shouldn't play, given the risk his condition posed. "I talked with tons of cardiologists, and everyone was reaching the same conclusion: negative. It was the kind of thing that could result in sudden death," says Scott, who was also the president of the NBA Physicians Association at the time.

When Williams and his agent, David Falk, went into the Knicks' offices before the draft to discuss the results, they were told clearly: it's too big a risk. "We read him the Riot Act," Scott says. Even Falk sided with Scott, telling his client it didn't seem wise to go against the medical advice of so many experts.

"Look, I'm a basketball player. This is what I do. What I love. If I die doing this, so be it," Williams said.

Williams's passionate stand, almost like a scene out of a movie, stirred members of the team's front office, who'd been uneasy about the moral responsibility they'd carry if something happened. But when Williams slid on draft night, the Knicks looked at their situation, knowing they had a rare opportunity. "We might end up with a guy of unique ability in the high twenties," Tapscott explained. "So we asked: is the risk worth the reward? And we decided that it was."

After taking Williams 24th in the draft, New York began stationing an ambulance in one of the Madison Square Garden tunnels during every game due to the forward's condition. The practice was extended to other arenas when the Knicks played on the road. And eventually, it became standard protocol to have an ambulance and two defibrillators near the court in every arena, largely because of Williams.

That decision to draft Williams was fraught with risks for the organization. But the most costly, consequential gamble the Knicks ultimately made that year would turn out to be with Riley.

*   *   *

As summer turned to fall, and the leaves began to change, so, too, did the Knicks' situation.

Viacom, the corporation that just one year earlier had taken ownership of the Knicks, was now preparing to turn around and sell them in a package that also included the Rangers, the Garden, and MSG Network.

Before the corporate sale materialized, though, Riley expressed his concerns to Checketts. Much like Ewing had been through countless regime changes during his first five seasons, the Knicks were about to play for their third corporate owner in the three years since Riley had taken the job. Fair or not, the constant turnover made him uneasy.

"Pat was paranoid about so many things," Checketts says.

One example: during the 1992–93 campaign, Riley's second year in New York, one of the reporters who covered the team, *Newsday*'s Curtis Bunn, planned to write a story about the Knicks not having any Black coaches on their staff after the departure of Paul Silas the prior offseason.

Bunn, a Black man, touched base with Tapscott, the team's highest-ranking Black official, off the record before publishing anything, just hoping to get his general take on the idea. Tapscott gently encouraged Bunn to study the rest of the NBA first, to see if the Knicks were truly an outlier in that regard. (They weren't.) Tapscott then notified his bosses, Checketts and Grunfeld, that Bunn might be publishing a story on the subject.

When word reached Riley, he grew furious with Tapscott—"He basically treated him like he didn't exist," Checketts explained—thinking Tapscott must have been the one to put the story idea in the reporter's ear.

"I wanted to go to Riles and say, 'Hey, you're way off base here,'" says Tapscott, whose efforts ultimately prompted Bunn to shelve the idea. "But Riles was suspicious of management. And I was management."

So even when the Knicks loosened the purse strings for the coach, after Checketts got approval from Viacom higher-ups to open talks for a five-year contract extension in the midst of a corporate sale, Riley expressed apprehension. More money alone wouldn't be enough, he said.

With another set of owners coming in, Riley wanted assurances in case the ground continued to shift underneath him. He told Checketts he wanted to be the first coach to get ownership stake in a team, and that he wanted final say over the team's personnel. Short of that, Riley said, he'd have to give thought to announcing a plan to step down at the end of the 1994–95 season.

Checketts urged Riley not to take that step, saying such massive news could potentially hurt a sale.

It's here that Riley's and Checketts's versions of the story diverge. Riley claims Checketts promised to sign off on letting him exit his contract after the season—one year early—if the coach kept quiet about his anxieties surrounding the sale. Meanwhile, Checketts says he told the coach he'd be in far better position to lobby for a stake in the team if the Knicks were playing well—something they were more likely to do if Riley simply kept things stable. (Checketts acknowledges asking Riley to stay quiet about his apprehension around the sale, but says there were no strings attached to the request.)

The sale took place in late August, after ITT Corporation and Cablevision combined for a $1.1 billion offer for the bundle of assets, which included the Knicks. Within days of the acquisition, Rand Araskog, ITT's chief executive and, for all intents and purposes, the team's new owner, called for a board meeting. In it, he introduced himself to his high-ranking subordinates, who gathered in a ballroom at the St. Regis Hotel. After explaining that he saw himself as principled, and as someone who let the bottom line drive his decision making, Araskog asked if anyone had lingering questions about how the transition would work.

Riley, sitting to Araskog's right, was the first in the room to raise his hand. "I'm Pat Riley, the coach of the Knicks," he said, though everyone in the meeting already knew who he was. "I'm still owed $10,000."

The statement awkwardly hung in the air for five or six seconds, prompting some in attendance to squirm uncomfortably. After realizing Riley wasn't going to elaborate, Araskog mercifully responded, vowing to follow up with him privately afterward, to better understand his grievance.

Almost no one in the ballroom knew how to take the comment, or what Riley meant. But Checketts, who was promoted to Garden president shortly after the sale, recognized the complaint immediately: it was a reference to the Reno reimbursement Riley was still waiting to receive some five months after the trip. Checketts saw it as Riley testing Araskog, to gauge whether he would be willing to quickly handle whatever issues faced the team—or, in this case, Riley himself.

There were countless issues with New York early on in that 1994–95 season, though not ones Araskog could help with.

Even with a thinner, injury-plagued rotation, Riley wasn't exactly sure how to handle Rivers, who had returned fully healthy from his torn ACL. Starks had agreed to a three-year, $13 million extension to open the campaign, but couldn't stop thinking about Game 7. Through mid-December, in the throes of a career-worst slump, the guard shot 30 percent from the floor over a frigid eleven-game stretch.

The cold spell got so bad that Starks, after a 1-for-9 shooting display in a loss to Miami, decided to grab the tape from his disastrous Game 7. He'd put so much pressure on himself to erase the the nightmarish performance that watching the game, he thought, might turn things around.

"When you run from something for so long, it can catch up to you," Starks said.

Similarly, the infighting within the Knicks' locker room seemed to be catching up with them.

It was an early December meeting in Riley's office when things between the coach and Rivers exploded.

The men loudly traded expletives while disagreeing over the veteran guard's role in New York, and the argument ended with Rivers asking Riley to release him from the club. After Riley begrudgingly agreed to Rivers's request, he left him with one thought. "You're gonna be an NBA head coach someday. I know it," Riley said as Rivers prepared to walk out.

Rivers let out a loud chuckle. "Yeah, right," he said.

The other noteworthy standoff that December: Riley's two best players, Ewing and Starks, engaged in a shouting match in Atlanta after the star center declined to pass to an open Starks, drawing his ire.

When Starks yelled at the co-captain, Ewing uncharacteristically shot back at Starks, essentially telling him to know his place. The blowup was a long time coming, as Starks felt teammates had frozen him out of the offense during his slump. And while some players felt Riley extended Starks far too much grace throughout his cold spells—a couple privately called him "Riley's son"—no one felt that way following that night's loss to the Hawks.

"Who are you to ever question *anyone's* shot selection?" Riley screamed at Starks, once the team made it inside the visiting locker room. Riley even invoked Starks's Game 7 showing, saying that alone was reason to give his teammates the benefit of the doubt. "Did anybody here ever say a *word* to you about [Game 7]?"

Starks, almost in tears during the dressing-down, would be benched the following night against the Sixers.

The root of the team's frustration wasn't a mystery. Twenty-four games into the season, New York was just 12-12, and had lost five games in a row, marking the club's longest skid under Riley. It wasn't just the record that was concerning. In those twenty-four showings, the Knicks had already lost seven of them by double digits—an alarming stat, given that they'd dropped just ten such games in 82 outings the year before. They'd already lost more games by 20 (three) than they had in the entire 1993–94 campaign (two).

"The Knicks don't have the same step [anymore] because they have a few years on us," Magic guard Penny Hardaway said after his club pulverized New York by 25 points in an early December meeting.

At the conclusion of a stressful calendar year, the Knicks enjoyed an unusually long holiday break, with no games from New Year's Eve through January 3. Taking advantage of the opportunity, Riley gave his players a bit of time off from the grind. He took some time for himself, too, chartering a jet on New Year's Eve to Aspen, Colorado, to visit longtime friend and wealthy real estate developer Dick Butera.

Upon arriving, Riley had a weighty issue to discuss. "I dunno if this [situation with the Knicks] is gonna work out," Riley told Butera and other friends while at the developer's home. "I can't take this anymore—the not knowing." As Riley dropped his bombshell, Butera announced one of his own: he and a group of deep-pocketed acquaintances planned to make a run at buying the Miami Heat, who were up for sale.

The revelation spurred a conversation. "We kind of had a quiet deal with Pat, because his relationship with Checketts was getting rocky," Butera says today. "He was growing pretty unhappy in New York. So if we were able to get the team in Miami, he said he'd consider coming with us to be our coach."

Hypotheticals cycled through Riley's mind for the rest of his trip, even as Butera, a bachelor, sought to entertain the coach with a night on the town. They had dinner, then went for drinks at the Caribou Club, a posh, members-only bar in Aspen. But Riley quickly felt out of place.

He and Butera made it only a few feet from the entrance when Riley tapped him on the shoulder. The coach hadn't even taken off his full-length fur to hand it to a coat-check person. By the time he'd given the room a once-over, he'd seen enough. This venue—with dozens of men hugged up with ladies who looked like they'd been hired—wasn't his scene. "Everybody here looks desperate," he said. "Let's go."

With New York's extension offer already in front of him, Riley was far from desperate. But knowing he had a friend with a decent chance of purchasing a team may have emboldened Riley when it came to what demands he'd make of the Knicks. In January, after the Aspen trip, he sent a counteroffer to Checketts. In it, he officially asked for a stake in ownership and a promotion to team president. (These asks were in addition to the $3 million salary the Knicks were already offering.)

Checketts claims he told Riley he was fine with making him the team's president of basketball operations. But while Checketts says he was open to promoting Riley, he told the coach he didn't think an ownership stake was realistic.

Riley asked Checketts whether he could appeal to a higher authority on the matter. Checketts said yes, and set up a meeting between Riley and Araskog, the ITT chief executive, who'd become de facto owner months earlier.

When Checketts arranged the talk between the men, he gave Araskog a heads-up that Riley would likely request a 10 or 20 percent share of the Knicks as part of his extension. "Okay, Dave. That sounds difficult," Araskog recalls saying. "But if Pat wants to see me, I'm not gonna say that I *won't* see him."

Araskog says an ownership stake in the team was never truly an option for Riley. For starters, the Knicks were corporately owned—with ITT controlling 85 percent of the properties, and Cablevision owning 15 percent—a stark contrast from a team owned by one person. That would have made adding a considerable stakeholder challenging, as the companies had countless shareholders to report to each quarter. Talented as Riley was, it would have been tough cutting through the red tape to convince shareholders to reduce their own share of the pie to make it work.

Beyond that, Araskog, a West Point graduate, was floored by MSG's relatively anemic profits in 1994. The Knicks and Rangers had all but maxed out that year, reaching Game 7 of the Finals and winning the Stanley Cup, respectively. Yet the Garden and its properties generated just $12 million in profits that year, according to Checketts, a lackluster result that prompted a round of layoffs and belt tightening at MSG.

It was sometime in late January, after Checketts arranged their sit-down, when Riley walked into Araskog's office at ITT headquarters on 54th and Sixth. As usual, Riley looked elegant, dressed to the nines in a suit and tie. After shaking Araskog's hand, he sat in one of the two chairs stationed in front of the executive's desk, before placing a leather briefcase he'd brought with him on the other seat. They made small talk for twenty minutes, discussing their families, New York City, and even the Knicks' season to that point. Then, as the conversation shifted, Riley reached for his briefcase and prepared to talk shop.

"I have to discuss something with you," Riley said. Before he got another word out, Araskog stopped him.

"Pat, don't open the briefcase," Araskog said, holding up his hand to interrupt the coach. "I know what you want to discuss. Dave already told me. But it's just plain impossible. I know you may get that opportunity down the line somewhere else at some point, after this contract. And if you do, that'll be your decision. You're one of the most outstanding people in the league, so I can't in any way question what you're asking for. I just can't honor the request."

Riley pursed his lips, illustrating his disappointment. "I'm sorry to hear that. But I understand," he said. The coach declined to push the issue any further, and the meeting concluded a few minutes later.

Araskog had a strange feeling about how it went, and made a point to call Checketts that night. He wanted to know whether Checketts had spoken to Riley about how the coach saw the talk—or the lack of one.

"He didn't mind," Checketts told Araskog. "Pat kept telling me how impressed he was with your office."

"I'm not sure what he means by that," Araskog said.

It might have been nothing more than a simple, well-intentioned compliment. It could have been mere deflection, to avoid detailing the disappointment Riley felt in not being able to have the talk with Araskog. Or it could have been a dig at how immaculate a situation Araskog had, and the idea that he and the corporation could clearly afford whatever it took to satisfy Riley's requests if they truly wanted to.

Whatever he meant, Riley didn't elaborate. Nor did he truly engage the Knicks concerning his extension again that season. "He went quiet on us after that," Checketts says. "He'd only talk basketball with us."

In 1990, just before the end of Riley's tenure as the coach of the Lakers, he gathered his players in a hotel ballroom to yell at them for what they weren't doing in their playoff series with Phoenix.

The speech, which lost players more than it galvanized them, was punctuated by an angry Riley striking a mirror, which cut his right hand and spilled blood on the sleeve of his white dress shirt.

In what would turn out to be his final season with the Knicks, Riley hit his breaking point several months earlier in the campaign.

It was mid-February, the first game after the All-Star break, and the Knicks were getting drilled on the road by a Detroit club that was twelve games under .500. New York scored a season-low 12 points in the first period, then followed that up by surrendering a season-high 38 points in the second. By halftime, New York trailed by 25. And a red-faced Riley was about to show his players how fed up he was.

As he lit into the Knicks for their awful effort, Riley all but re-created that moment with the Lakers. While he wouldn't walk away with a bloody hand, he punched a hole in the visiting locker room's blackboard.

The team's play that night wasn't all that bothered Riley around that time. Butera, his friend who'd been interested in purchasing the Heat, had just been informed he wouldn't be getting the team—a letdown for Riley, who'd daydreamed about coaching there. "He'd kept telling me, 'I'll definitely come with you if you can buy the Heat,'" Butera recalls.

But even after that plan fell through, a different opportunity remained.

The same month that Carnival Cruise Lines chairman Micky Arison took over as the majority owner of the Heat, Butera and Arison had a series of calls, phone records would later show. And while it's not clear what was discussed—Butera denies Riley was the topic of conversation—it wasn't long after that Arison sought to meet Riley, whose Knicks would be in town to play the Heat soon.

On the morning of February 16, Arison, who'd grown up a Knicks fan, arrived at Miami Arena early. He waited in a corridor that led to the court, knowing Riley and his New York club would need to pass by to take the floor for their morning shootaround. When the Knicks made it there, one of the Heat's public relations employees approached with a question: would it be okay if Arison sat and watched the Knicks' workout?

Riley was fiercely competitive and private, sometimes not even letting members of his own club—let alone another team—watch sessions. So the answer was no: Arison couldn't stay for the session.

"I was curious, based on his reputation," Arison said. "The fact that he refused? I respected it."

Rather than walk away entirely, Arison stayed in the arena tunnel nearby, waiting for the shootaround to conclude. And as Riley prepared to leave with his players, the new Miami owner was standing at the exit.

He pulled Riley aside, asking if he could talk with him for a few minutes.

Arison's persistence stopped Riley in his tracks. Since he'd taken the Knicks job, Riley had been big on loyalty. The idea of being all the way in, or all the way out. He didn't believe in fraternizing with anyone outside the team.

So could Riley really agree to meet with Arison now, after a team workout, and just hours before a game?

Surprisingly, Riley nodded. Yes, he'd meet with Arison in the tunnel. But just for a few minutes.

Arison didn't need long, though. All he needed to know was that Riley was open to a conversation—one they could presumably finish at a later point.

13

WE'RE ALL A LITTLE GUILTY

Things began crumbling shortly after Pat Riley's talk with Micky Arison.

As the Knicks were enjoying the closing minutes of a breezy home win over the Heat the following night, the Madison Square Garden crowd started chanting, "We Want Charlie!"—an appeal to Riley to sub in rookie guard Charlie Ward, who hadn't seen any playing time in the previous fourteen games. With the Knicks holding a 21-point advantage, even starter Derek Harper joined in on the act, shouting along with fans from the bench.

Ward got his chance, playing the final six minutes. But in that span, the Knicks watched their lead dwindle to just seven at one point. And after the final buzzer sounded, with the Knicks having won 100–91, Riley met with the media only briefly. "I'm just going to make one statement. In my fifteen years of coaching, that's the most unprofessional attitude of a team that I've ever been around," he said before storming out. He didn't elaborate, leaving reporters puzzled by what he was even referring to.

The players, who'd grown accustomed to Riley shielding them in the media, were blindsided when writers asked them about Riley's comment minutes later. Harper seemed particularly wounded, and wondered whether the critique was aimed at his enthusiasm for Ward getting minutes late.

Other players were simply annoyed by Riley. Even if Harper and others had been a bit overly enthusiastic in that moment, so what? After all, they had won. Most Knicks considered themselves to be extremely hardworking. To be chastised over something that inconsequential felt like a petty mind game.

Even one game later, after New York beat the defending-champion Rockets, some Knicks were still annoyed by Riley's comment. "It'd be fake to say the victory puts that all aside," forward Anthony Mason said. "I'm very professional. His definition of professional and mine might be different."

Riley and Mason's differences would be on full display just weeks later, when the coach clashed with his top reserve during a third-quarter timeout against Denver. Mason, who'd already been singled out once at halftime, bristled when his coach leveled another critique at him on the sideline. Clearly not in the mood, Riley sent him to the locker room—a precursor to him issuing Mason a late-season suspension for the second consecutive year.

The team was no longer struggling on the court as it had through the first two months of the season, when the Knicks sputtered to that head-scratching 12-12 start. But nothing about the team's late-season run felt as promising as in earlier years. An 11-6 mark in March would have been impressive for most clubs. For the Knicks, who'd posted a 37-6 record in March over the prior three seasons, 11–6 felt underwhelming.

And that, itself, was a concern. Between the aging, the injuries, the close misses, and the frustration with Riley, it was becoming harder to coalesce around a common goal. "[Riley] tried to sell them on sacrificing for a championship. But it's a tougher sell each year, because we worked so hard and came up empty for two years. They've already heard that sales pitch, and got nothing out of it," ex-Knick Doc Rivers said.

As players increasingly tuned out Riley, he continued to grow more detached from the team's front office.

Assistant Jeff Van Gundy was in Riley's hotel room in Denver, reviewing a game plan a few hours before a late-season meeting with the Nuggets, when Riley's phone rang. It was Dave Checketts on the line.

"I ask Pat if he wants me to leave, and he says no. So I'm just sitting there," Van Gundy said. "You could tell that while it was respectful, there was definitely a disagreement about things. I don't know what they were. We never talked about it. But I knew just from sitting there that he wasn't happy with some things."

After taking four games to dispatch the Cleveland Cavaliers in the first round of the postseason, the Knicks were on to their conference semifinal matchup with the rival Pacers.

But unlike the year before, when Indiana surprised everyone by taking a 3–2 lead on the Knicks and almost reaching the NBA Finals, the Pacers approached this series believing they were the better team.

Still, with only 18.7 seconds remaining in Game 1, the Knicks had clearly managed to take the first contest. Up 105–99 at home, the Knicks had overcome a hobbled Ewing—11 points on 4-of-15 shooting—and the fact that they'd burned through their timeouts prematurely, after Mason and Charles Oakley asked for time while falling out of bounds to secure possessions for New York.

But no matter. The game was over. With a little more than a minute left in the contest, Pacers general manager Donnie Walsh had already left his seat to head down to the Pacers' locker room. There, he took out a cigarette, lit it, and began smoking. "I was pissed off because we hadn't played well," Walsh says.

Since the locker room had no televisions inside, Walsh had no way of seeing what happened next.

An immediate three-pointer from Reggie Miller, who'd turned and fired after catching an inbound pass, cut the Knicks' lead to three, 105–102, with 16.4 left.

A bit concerning. But no need for New York to panic. Simply getting the ball in bounds would force the Pacers to foul, meaning the Knicks would almost certainly get a chance to regain its two-possession lead.

Only it didn't happen that way. Knowing the Pacers were going to be looking for a three, Riley had Mason—arguably his most versatile defender—on the floor as opposed to Oakley, who normally would have inbounded the ball in such situations. "[Mase] was our worst inbounder," Van Gundy says.

Beyond that, Harper, the starting point guard, had been ejected earlier for getting tangled up with Antonio Davis, which left New York without its top ball handler, forcing backup Greg Anthony into action.

So now Mason stood behind the baseline, surveying the court, trying to figure out where he'd go with his inbound. Looking to his left, he saw John Starks wasn't open. Then he scanned back toward his right.

Anthony was on that side, and Mason, thinking his teammate would generate more separation, stepped forward with his right foot, preparing to pass to the reserve guard. As Mason took the step, though, Anthony began to lose his footing, thanks to a subtle push in the back from Miller.

After the game, Mason said he regretted throwing a pass at all, and that taking a five-second violation would have been the safer option. But that clarity came only with hindsight. Close to stepping over the line and committing a guaranteed violation, Mason hesitated but eventually passed to Anthony, feeling he had nowhere else to go with the ball. As he let go of it, Anthony still wasn't standing upright, or in a position to catch the ball. But Miller was—and he swiftly took advantage of the mistake.

The Pacers star got away with the shove to Anthony's back; one he acknowledged during his Hall of Fame speech years later should have been called a foul. After intercepting Mason's pass on the left wing, Miller then raced to get behind the three-point line, where he squared his shoulders to fire another triple.

Anthony was to his feet by then, and tried contesting the shot. But Anthony stood just 6 feet tall, and the 6-foot-7 Miller shot over him with ease. He drained the shot. And now the score was tied at 105.

The improbable sequence, which left the Garden stunned, took place in just a twelve-second span.

New York got a massive reprieve when Pacers forward Sam Mitchell intentionally fouled Starks, thinking Indiana was still behind. But as Starks, a 74 percent shooter, stepped to the line, he was still shellshocked by how quickly Miller had just tied the game. "I'm thinking, 'Did this dude just did [*sic*] this?'" Starks said.

Starks's first free throw rimmed out. His second was almost a foot short.

Still, all was not lost, as—miracle of miracles—Ewing managed to grab the offensive rebound after Starks's second misfire. But instead of kicking the ball out to a teammate to ensure the Knicks would get the game's final shot, Ewing abruptly launched a nine-foot fadeaway in traffic. His jumper caromed off the back iron before falling into the hands of Miller, who then got fouled.

Riley and the Knicks were in total disbelief. Around the same time, Mel Daniels, the Pacers' player-personnel director, tracked down Walsh, who was between cigarette drags in the locker room, to tell him he'd left the floor too soon, and that Miller had somehow tied the score.

"Stop fuckin' with me!" Walsh demanded, in disbelief.

By the time Walsh made it to a TV, Miller was on the line, sinking free throws to give Indiana a 107–105 advantage. The guard had single-handedly tallied eight points in less than nine seconds of game time.

On the final play, the lefty Anthony crossed over to his weaker hand before dribbling into the paint, losing his balance, and stumbling to the ground as time expired. The Pacers bounded off their bench, celebrating the comeback as if they'd already won the series. Anthony stayed on the court, laid out, looking up at the ceiling. Starks walked off with his hands on his head.

The Knicks had given away Game 1 just as much as Miller had snatched it from them.

"You lose the edge when you start losing big games, and you don't finish," Riley would say years later. "As you keep elevating, and you keep getting turned back, you do start to lose that edge."

New York bounced back by forcing 35 Indiana turnovers to take Game 2. But the Knicks' offense suffered costly droughts in the second halves of Games 3 and 4, allowing the Pacers to take a 3–1 series lead.

Facing elimination, the Knicks narrowly staved off a third straight collapse in Game 5 when Ewing drained a game-winning floater with less than two seconds left. And back in Indianapolis for Game 6, the Knicks held Miller without a basket until the fourth to win, knotting the series at three games each.

Game 7 at the Garden was the polar opposite, though. Miller, perhaps the arena's favorite villain, caught fire, scoring 29 through the first three periods. He'd be held scoreless in the final quarter, as the Knicks mounted a late comeback in their quest to reach the Eastern Conference Finals again. But Rik Smits, the 7-foot-4 Pacers center, kept Indiana afloat instead, scoring four of the club's last five baskets.

With five seconds left, and Indiana ahead 97–95, Harper whipped an inbound pass to Ewing at the arc, where he was instantly blanketed by a double team. The big man hesitated, looking for an open teammate, before turning his back to the basket. He then pivoted to his right and pounded a dribble into the hardwood, gaining enough steam not only to get into the lane, but also to split Indiana's defenders, who'd thought that Ewing would pull up for a jumper. "It was like the seas opened up," Harper says.

Ewing created a clean look at the basket. The only problem was he'd left his feet maybe one dribble too early, leaving him too far away to dunk the ball, but too close to float it in. So with an abundance of momentum, Ewing tried to finger-roll it in. But the attempt was long, and it bounced off the back iron.

So many times before, the franchise star had come through. He'd done so two contests earlier, to win Game 5. He'd cleaned up Starks's miss in Game 7 against the Pacers the year before to reach the NBA Finals. He'd been fantastic in this Game 7, too, logging 29 points, 14 boards, five assists, and four blocks.

But in the grand scheme, being an inch or two away from sending Game 7 to overtime might as well have been a mile or two. Either way, the result was the same: the Knicks had lost, ending their season. The Pacers broke into celebration on the Garden floor, just as they had after Game 1.

As the Knicks began walking off the court following the bitter defeat, members of their front office—Checketts, Ernie Grunfeld, and Ed Tapscott—looked on from a suite inside the arena. On their television feed, Tapscott noticed as cameras caught Riley pausing to turn and look at the Garden floor before heading into the locker room.

"And now many questions concerning the Knicks and this man, Pat Riley, who's in his fourth season as their head coach. Is this the end of the era?" announcer Marv Albert asked as the broadcast concluded.

That was why Riley took that long, fateful glance at the court before leaving. At that moment, just seconds after suffering a wrenching, season-ending loss, Riley knew he wouldn't be coming back.

Maybe an hour after the Knicks' season officially ended, Dick Butera's phone rang. It was Riley.

"Are you still friendly with the guy who owns the Heat?" he asked Butera.

"Yeah, I am. He's a good guy. Why?"

"Because I'm done. I'm just done," Riley responded. "All I can tell you is, I'm finished in New York."

Butera wanted more detail from his friend. The agitated tone in Riley's voice suggested something aside from the defeat itself had taken place. And Butera could hear considerable noise in the background on the other end of the call. So he asked Riley where he was calling from—especially while discussing such a potentially explosive subject. "I'm calling you from my cell phone. I'm outside the locker room," Riley said.

That struck Butera. Riley was so angry, he didn't care that he might be within earshot of other people.

When Butera asked him if anything more had happened, Riley said no—he was simply tired of dealing with Checketts, who he said had failed to follow through on certain promises to him.

"He's been lying to me this whole time," Riley said, a reference to a verbal release he claimed Checketts had agreed to in the midst of the corporate sale from the prior fall. But now, release or no release, Riley was headed for the exits, and he'd happily pack for Miami if Butera could make the situation work.

As they ended the conversation, Butera asked Riley once more if he was sure this was what he wanted. After all, the Knicks had *just* been eliminated, and this frustration could have been stemming from the high emotions of the last-second loss. Or just the tough season in general. But Riley was clear.

"Make it happen. I don't want to be here anymore," he told Butera.

Within days, Butera and Riley discussed what, generally, Riley would want to take over in Miami. After talking through that, Butera reached out to Arison in hopes of meeting to discuss the possibility.

Butera and Arison had a series of face-to-face meetings in Long Beach, California, on *Imagination*, one of Arison's cruise ships, which was set to launch later that year. Butera had made it clear Riley was open to leaving the Knicks to join the Heat under the right circumstances.

Finally, Arison asked the question: "What does he want?"

Butera didn't hesitate. "He wants $50 million for ten years," he said.

Arison laughed. No NBA coach, not even Riley, was making $3 million a year, let alone $5 million. "What does he *really* want?" the 41-year-old Arison asked. "Because you can't be serious with that."

With a straight face, Butera reiterated his stance. Riley, already the highest-paid coach in the sport at $1.5 million a season, wanted $50 million over ten years to run the show for Arison in Miami.

Arison sat still for a moment. The asking price was undoubtedly a small fortune. But paying it—and getting perhaps the best coach in basketball to take over an otherwise listless organization—could prove a worthwhile investment if Riley turned the Heat into a winning club.

After a few minutes of back-and-forth, Arison had already moved on from Riley's sky-high salary ask.

"Okay," Arison said. "What else does he want to get this done?"

Butera considered Arison's question a win. "The minute he said that, I told myself, 'That's a yes,' " he said. "Not a firm one. But enough to where I could call Pat in Connecticut to figure out what else he wanted."

Butera and Riley hammered out a list of asks that would eventually become a four-page, fourteen-point memo. In it, Riley wanted an immediate 10 percent ownership of the team and another 10 percent share over the course of his deal. He also wanted Arison to loan him money to pay taxes on the initial 10 percent stake.

He wanted complete control over Miami's basketball operations, and to be named the team president. Riley wanted Arison to purchase his sprawling homes near suburban Los Angeles and New York City. He wanted a limo service to and from games in Miami. He wanted credit cards and a $300-a-day per diem.

After Butera jotted down the list of Riley's demands, he made a quick copy of it, then took it to Los Angeles International Airport the following day for a final meeting with Arison on June 5. When he handed Arison the list at an airport bar, Arison's eyes narrowed when he saw the per diem.

"Micky was really confused by that one," Butera recalls. "He couldn't understand how someone getting a deal worth tens of millions would ask for such a nickel-and-dime sort of thing. But that's just how Pat is."

The meeting was quick, as they'd already talked over many of the details. But before going their separate ways, Butera reached for the memo when Arison stopped him. "Can I take this with me?" Arison asked.

Butera was a bit uneasy about letting the draft out of his sight. At the same time, Arison was about to put Riley in an entirely different stratosphere of wealth. It made sense that he'd want to review the details on paper. So Butera nodded, and let Arison take the memo with him.

Riley already had a foot out the door. Certain people just hadn't picked up on the signs somehow.

With Van Gundy, the dead giveaway should have been the day Riley asked him to covertly grab as many things as he possibly could from Riley's office. With assistant Bob Salmi, it should have been when Riley asked him if it'd be possible to get a set of personalized golf clubs made.

When Riley first joined the Knicks, Salmi remembered the coach damn near glaring at him after Salmi shared that he enjoyed occasionally playing golf as a way to relax. Riley, a workaholic and firm believer that golf was one of the bigger distractions among NBA assistant coaches, wasn't thrilled to hear it.

"If I'd known you played golf, I might not have hired you," Riley told him initially.

So when Riley asked Salmi about having a personalized set of clubs made after the season ended, Salmi figured he was joking. Much to Salmi's surprise, Riley was serious. He wanted to buy some golf clubs.

"I knew a lot of guys over at Callaway, so I made a couple calls. And he got the full treatment. A bag with his name on it. A brand-new set of woods. A brand-new set of irons," Salmi says. "He tells me thank you. And then three days later, he's gone, and he's leaving for Miami. I should've known something was up."

As Butera and Riley were quietly firming up things with Arison in early June, Riley's agent, Los Angeles attorney Ed Hookstratten, was more than hinting to Checketts that Riley was done in New York.

"You and Pat have gotta wind this up," Hookstratten said to Checketts during a June 7 meeting in Beverly Hills, urging him to let Riley out of his deal for a clean divorce. But Checketts wanted to talk with Riley.

When Checketts and Riley met two days later at the coach's home in Greenwich, Connecticut, Riley was noncommittal, according to Checketts. "I'm having a hard time with this loss," Riley said, referring to the Indiana series. "I'm having a hard time figuring out the extension. I'm having a hard time with all of it."

While some were completely convinced Riley had already moved on—aside from Riley's agent saying as much, Grunfeld also figured Riley was gone—Checketts felt Riley was still trying to figure out what he ultimately wanted. So Checketts backed off, thinking he needed to give Riley space to decide for himself.

One day went by. Then a second. And a third. Around then, Riley asked Van Gundy to grab his things from his office. The following day, June 13, Riley met with his assistants to inform them: he was planning to resign from the Knicks, and wanted his right-hand men to know for their own planning purposes. But he needed them to keep the news private for a few more days, as he wasn't ready to tell the front office or the media yet.

By June 15, Riley was ready. That day, Knicks general counsel Ken Munoz was in his office when a fax came through his machine. It was a letter from the law firm that Hookstratten, Riley's agent, worked for.

Riley, one of the NBA's greatest coaches, and the Knicks' best since Red Holzman, had faxed his resignation.

In the letter, Riley wrote that no team "can realize its potential when its head coach, the person most intimately involved with the players, cannot make final, critical decisions on matters bearing directly and intensely on the team, its performance and its future. . . . I consistently and repeatedly expressed my desire and need to be charged with the ultimate responsibility for all significant aspects of the ball club. I tried my best to reach an agreement on these issues. Unhappily, the gap between us could not be bridged."

And with that, the man who had taken a 39-win Knicks club and squeezed 51, 60, 57, and 55 victories out of them in four years while coming up just short of an NBA championship was officially out the door.

By the time the fax arrived and began making waves throughout the national media, Riley was at 40,000 feet on a flight to Greece, more than likely to tune out the noise of the sonic boom he'd just triggered.

It didn't take long at all for Checketts and the Knicks to put two and two together.

Within days of Riley's resignation, Arison and Heat executive Dave Wohl had been quoted in the news, saying they'd be interested in getting Riley—even if it meant handing him a contract in excess of $20 million to sign him. But because he'd resigned with a year left on his Knicks deal, Riley was still under contract in New York, meaning other clubs needed the Knicks' permission to negotiate with him first. And Miami hadn't gotten that.

As the Riley-to-Miami speculation was intensifying in the media, though, New York got hold of something important: the fourteen-point memo outlining Riley's demands from Miami. (Asked who leaked the documents to him, Checketts said he couldn't share a name. "Let's put it this way: they were Knick fans and New Yorkers, but also well connected to the prior owners in Miami, who'd sold the team to Arison," he says.)

The memo, dated June 5—ten days before Riley's resignation—gave New York the ammo it needed to file tampering charges against the Heat, who'd clearly interfered with the deal between Riley and the Knicks.

Each club argued its case before David Stern on August 4. But Checketts, wounded by the ordeal, was out for blood and had put his organization's entire collection of nine lawyers on the case.

"What bothered me most was that [Miami] took Pat's attention away from what we were doing," Checketts says. "To this day, I maintain that Pat abandoned the team by losing his focus in the middle of that season."

On September 1, just hours before Stern was set to issue a ruling on the tampering charges, the teams reached a settlement agreement. The Heat would hand over their first-round draft pick in 1996, and give the Knicks $4 million—$1 million for interfering with New York's contract with Riley, and $3 million to cover the loan the Knicks had given Riley to pay for his home in Connecticut upon accepting the job back in 1991.

With the benefit of hindsight, it's hard to debate the logic of what Riley chose to do, even if he broke a whole carton of eggs in making his omelet. His deal with the Heat wasn't handled by the book. Not even close. But it included a sizable ownership stake and would pay him $40 million over five years—far more than the $15 million over five years he would've gotten from the Knicks, who weren't giving him a stake.

Maybe the "Disease of Me," which Riley railed against in his book, had taken root in the coach himself. Or maybe it was something more.

Months later, Riley told Mark Kriegel of the New York *Daily News* that he'd grown "miserable in New York," citing the city's tabloids as a cause of his malaise. He also mentioned that coaches there rarely make it beyond three or four seasons.

"I could have seen myself ending my career in New York, even though I don't know if any coach could ever last that long there," Riley said. "I had great respect for Red Holzman, and admired the job he did. . . . He's the only coach up there in the [Garden's] rafters. I used to envision my name next to his one day."

Instead, on September 2, one day after the teams reached a settlement on the tampering issue, Riley was introduced as Miami's coach and president. His news conference on the *Imagination* cruise ship—the same one Butera met with Arison on to discuss Riley's move—was held inside a lounge called Dynasty.

Miami got what it wanted—a star coach to establish a winning culture—even if its process to land Riley wasn't fully aboveboard. "No one's clean in this affair," Butera said. "We're all at least a little guilty."

The work relationship between Dave Checketts (left) and Pat Riley had a happy beginning, as shown here at Riley's introductory press conference with the Knicks in 1991. The divorce four years later was acrimonious, paving the way for a tampering charge and a fiery rivalry between the Knicks and the Miami Heat—the team Riley left to take an ownership stake with.

No player had more of an impact on those New York teams than seven-foot tower Patrick Ewing. In college, analysts frequently compared him to defensive savant Bill Russell. But Ewing's progression on offense as a pro—which included arguably the greatest jumper from a big man at that point in history—made him a completely different type of talent. Still, with limited offense around him, Ewing was never able to lead the Knicks to the promised land.

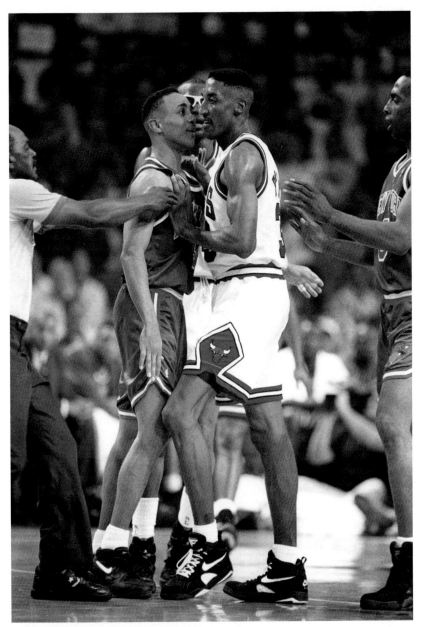

The Knicks' run of success during the 1990s was punctuated by two things: their rivalries and their refusal to back down from whoever lined up against them. In particular, their heated playoff matchups with the Bulls made for great theater each May and June. Over the years, John Starks (left) became a villain to Chicago fans because of his tendency to play over the edge.

If physicality was at the heart of what made the Knicks who they were, forward Charles Oakley was their lifeblood. Maybe the most physical player of his era, Oakley led the NBA in flagrant fouls in 1992–93 with nine—more than twice as many as the next-closest player, and more than fifteen different teams finished with that season. In part because of Oakley, the league began issuing suspensions after players accumulated a certain number of flagrant-foul points.

The most colorful Knick from those years, Anthony Mason, was rough around the edges, and one of the toughest players on the roster. But Mason—shown here with his son, Antoine—also had a certain sensitivity and vulnerability that wasn't revealed much during those years.

For how contentious the Bulls-Knicks rivalry was, Chicago generally had one thing New York did not: Michael Jordan. The teams met in the postseason five times during the decade, with the Bulls winning four of those series. The lone Knicks victory, in 1994, came at a time when Jordan—having retired that season—was out of the league. Tellingly, New York reached the NBA Finals in 1994 and 1999, immediately after Jordan's first two NBA retirements.

If there's one moment in Knicks history that lives in infamy, it's the one that took place at Madison Square Garden on June 2, 1993. That was the day forward Charles Smith—hounded by a swarm of Bulls defenders—failed to score after losing the ball four times in a four-second span while standing next to the basket in the closing seconds. Fairly or not, that play in Game 5 of the Eastern Conference Finals defined Smith's career, which was hindered by chronic knee injuries.

Dating back to his first training camp with New York in 1990, John Starks always liked the idea of dunking on someone to punctuate things. His left-handed jam to seal Game 2 of the 1993 conference finals—over Horace Grant, Michael Jordan, and the Bulls—remains a key highlight decades later. Starks says he can't go a day without a fan mentioning it to him.

The relationship between coach Pat Riley and Anthony Mason was volatile at times, with Riley suspending Mason toward the end of the year in back-to-back seasons for insubordination. Still, Riley understood the forward's unique ability on defense and even signed him with the Heat years later. After Mason passed following a heart attack at the age of forty-eight in 2015, Riley was among those who spoke at Mason's funeral.

Patrick Ewing raises his arms in triumph at the Garden moments after beating Indiana in Game 7 of the conference finals in 1994 to win the Eastern Conference crown. Ewing—who finished with 24 points, 22 rebounds, seven assists and five blocks—dunked home a John Starks miss in the closing moments to send the Knicks to the NBA Finals.

No player had a more unpredictable, mercurial game than John Starks. The guard's hot jump-shooting late in Games 4, 5, and 6 of the 1994 NBA Finals nearly won the Knicks a title. But his frigid 2-for-18 showing in the deciding Game 7 against Houston—including 0-for-11 from three-point range—played a huge role in the Knicks losing one instead.

Pacers sharpshooter Reggie Miller, whose antics and scoring outbursts in New York made him a player whom Knicks fans loved to hate, celebrates after earning a Game 7 victory at the Garden in 1995. The Indiana win ended Pat Riley's tenure with New York.

Coach Jeff Van Gundy took over the Knicks in 1996 after Pat Riley's replacement, Don Nelson, fell out of favor with the majority of the players. After a spate of signings and trades, Van Gundy oversaw a new-look roster toward the end of the decade, featuring Latrell Sprewell (left), Allan Houston, and Larry Johnson, along with an aging Patrick Ewing.

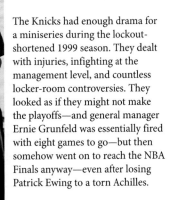

The Knicks had enough drama for a miniseries during the lockout-shortened 1999 season. They dealt with injuries, infighting at the management level, and countless locker-room controversies. They looked as if they might not make the playoffs—and general manager Ernie Grunfeld was essentially fired with eight games to go—but then somehow went on to reach the NBA Finals anyway—even after losing Patrick Ewing to a torn Achilles.

14

WHACK-A-MOLE

There may have only been light snow falling outside, but the Knicks were heading into a full-blown storm.

Aboard their team plane, players and coaches were preparing to take off from Vancouver, where they'd suffered their most embarrassing result of the young season: an 84–80 loss to the expansion Grizzlies, owners of an NBA-worst 7-30 record.

The defeat alone was frustrating enough for a team that fashioned itself a title contender. But players were also annoyed by the marching orders they'd been given by new coach Don Nelson in the final moments.

The Knicks had been down by three points with about fifteen seconds to play. But rather than draw up a play to tie the game, Nelson told his players to vie for a two-pointer, diagramming a screen-and-roll between Anthony Mason and Patrick Ewing. If it worked, the thinking went, they could then intentionally foul Vancouver and try to tie or win the game on their next possession.

Mason, Ewing, and the other players understood Nelson's logic, but didn't really agree with it. Going for two would be a great strategy if the Grizzlies let the Knicks score without any pressure. But even if New York managed a quick basket, it was undoubtedly more complicated to play the long game—to hope Vancouver missed at the line, then score on another play—than it was to simply go for the three-pointer. Especially since John Starks, who led the league in triples the season before, and Hubert Davis, who'd finished fourth in three-point percentage that year, were on the floor.

Nonetheless, the Knicks went with Nelson's design, which resulted in a tough, seventeen-foot baseline jumper from Ewing that missed. The rare Vancouver sellout crowd erupted with joy. And now the Knicks, after an ugly loss to the worst team in the association, were about to face questions from reporters about why Ewing would bother taking a two-point jumper while down by three points.

If there was one thing those Knicks didn't like, it was losing. If there were two things, it was losing, and losing to a god-awful team. And if there were three things, it was losing, losing to a god-awful team, and then having to answer for a questionable late-game call—one they didn't even agree with—after the loss.

But as Ewing and his teammates stewed over the defeat during the plane ride back east, Nelson was completely relaxed. Moments before the plane had ascended into the Vancouver sky, Nelson had given assistant coach Jeff Nix, seated across the aisle from him, a heads-up: he'd likely be dozing off for part of the flight home to New York. "If I'm sleeping when the customs agents come by, I'm putting my passport in my shirt pocket here—just grab it and hand it to the agent," Nelson instructed.

Nix figured it wouldn't come to that. After all, the team plane would have to land two separate times. Because the Knicks were flying into the domestic Westchester County Airport, they'd first need to land at Duluth International Airport in Minnesota to allow agents onto the plane to check everyone's passports. After that stop, which would likely take a half hour, the Knicks would be allowed to finish their trip home.

About three hours later, around 3 a.m., the club landed in Minnesota for what should have been a brief passport check. As customs agents opened the boarding door to enter the plane, a gust of freezing air rushed through the main cabin, prompting some players on the flight to howl with discomfort.

Nix thought either the outburst or the wave of cold air would wake Nelson. Neither of them did.

As the agents walked up and down the aisle demanding passports, Nix reached into Nelson's shirt pocket to grab his documentation. Again, he figured that might wake his boss. It didn't.

Even once the agents stepped off the plane—inviting another frigid gust of air that somehow didn't wake Nelson—the aircraft's pilot spoke over the PA system to tell everyone there'd be a significant delay. The person tasked with fueling the plane before it took off for New York was apparently nowhere to be found.

The pilot offered occasional updates over the intercom until about 5 a.m., when the team's two-hour delay finally ended. Nelson, still in the comatose position he began the flight with, slept through all of them.

Nix grew worried. "He never moved," he says. "At a certain point, I seriously thought he might be dead."

When the team landed back in Westchester a little after 8 a.m., and players began standing up to exit the plane, Nelson emerged from his slumber. He'd been out for a little more than eight hours by then.

"Wow, are we back already? What a short flight!" Nelson said earnestly.

Nix corrected his boss, saying the trip had actually taken forever. "He couldn't believe it," Nix recalls. "Somehow, he was out the whole time, oblivious to it all."

The trip from Vancouver was a microcosm of Nelson's tenure in New York. In so many ways, the 56-year-old was either unaware of—or indifferent to—just how frustrated his players were with him. And much like that flight back to New York, it took things coming to a halt for him to wake up to his reality.

It is human nature, after a bad breakup, to seek out the polar opposite in one's next relationship.

Human nature—and, apparently, the Knicks' nature.

Don Nelson couldn't have been a bigger departure from Pat Riley. Where Riley was coastal, raised in New York State before becoming a household name in Los Angeles, Nelson was a farm boy who spent his formative years in Michigan, Illinois, and Iowa. Riley was businesslike, making a point to not get too cozy with his players and bosses. Nelson would dole out bear hugs and invite folks within his work orbit for beers. The Armani-wearing Riley was tall and lithe, having graced the cover of *GQ*. The 6-foot-5 Nelson, no one's definition of lithe, often wore highly unfashionable fish ties with his suits.

Nelson's workout attire, when juxtaposed with Riley's, was the same way. "Riley's practice gear never had a single wrinkle. But Nellie would come to practice with a T-shirt, jeans, and some shoes it looked like he'd cut the grass with," says Ed Tapscott.

Fortunately, Nelson got help on the wardrobe front. Designer Tommy Hilfiger paid for the right to outfit him over the course of the season. But for how many worlds apart Nelson and Riley were as dressers and coaches, the Knicks weren't initially out to replace Riley with an anti-Riley personality.

In fact, if the team had gotten its way, Chuck Daly, who'd won two championships leading those hard-nosed Detroit Pistons clubs, would have taken over.

Well, maybe.

The hiring almost happened. Knowing the New York City media would be on the lookout for a meeting between Daly and the club, team officials had quietly arranged an interview with Daly at the St. Regis Hotel in Midtown. The Knicks handled the situation as if they were staging a scene from *Mission: Impossible* with a car service picking Daly up before whisking him to the hotel and sneaking him through a loading dock and the hotel's kitchen to avoid him being seen. Then Ernie Grunfeld and others talked for three hours with Daly, a TNT analyst at the time, about how he would lead the Knicks.

He was an appealing choice for any number of reasons. The winning pedigree. The reputation and strong relationships he'd forged with players, both in Detroit and throughout the league, as coach of the 1992 Olympic Dream Team that dominated in Barcelona. The fact that Daly had won with the brute style of defense the Knicks had borrowed from. It all seemed to fit exactly what New York needed.

Shortly after their meeting, Grunfeld extended the 64-year-old an offer to coach the club.

During his conversations with the team, Daly expressed some trepidation about taking the job. Aside from the fact that his wife, Terry, believed he should stay sidelined for the time being, Daly suggested he was a bit dismayed by the level of vitriol coming out of the city's tabloids following Riley's controversial exit. He wondered whether the media would skewer him the same way if he took the job, but didn't deliver a title.

Two days after getting the opportunity, Daly officially turned it down. "Without question, the toughest decision I have ever made," Daly said, calling it one of the best jobs in sports. "I can only say that if you were an alcoholic, and I have not been there before, it had to be the most seductive drink that's ever been placed in front of me. The Knicks were a replica of my Piston team. Everything was right about it."

So right, in fact, that Daly reached out to Grunfeld afterward to say he'd made a mistake in turning down the job.

"He turned it down, but then called back the next day—maybe forty-eight hours later—and asked, 'Is the job still open?'" says Knicks team doctor Norm Scott. "I was the Dream Team doctor, so [Chuck] and I became close. But Ernie was my source on that. He told me maybe a month or two after it happened."

Grunfeld claims it didn't quite happen that way, and that far more time had passed. "Norm's a great guy. But [Daly] told me like a year or a year and a half later that he should've taken [the job]," Grunfeld says. "Chuck was our number one guy, and the person we wanted. But he told us he just wasn't ready at the time."

Whether it was ultimately a day or a year, Grunfeld moved forward with Nelson, Riley's polar opposite.

And while Nelson came from a different school of thought, Grunfeld had begun his career playing for Nelson in Milwaukee during the late 1970s. Their history, paired with Nelson's reputation as an innovator on offense—something the scoring-challenged Knicks could certainly use—made Grunfeld more comfortable pulling the trigger on the hire. After all, Riley's stint with New York had shown a great coach could overhaul his style to fit that of his team. So there was hope Nelson could do the same.

But whatever hope the Knicks had slowly seeped out of them like the air from a three-day-old balloon.

Unlike Riley, who in his first camp with the club had gone out of his way to show players exactly how he'd use their strengths to construct the NBA's nastiest defense, Nelson focused almost solely on offense.

That wasn't unexpected. Even during his interview for the job, Nelson's first question for Grunfeld was a simple one: are you all planning to re-sign Mason in free agency? To Nelson, there was no point in beating around the bush, given how integral he saw Mason as being to his offense.

Nelson wanted Mason, who was coming off a season in which he won the Sixth Man of the Year award, to replace Charles Smith in the starting five so he could run the offense as a point forward. But that was far from the only alteration he wanted to make. Aside from moving guard Derek Harper off the ball, which would give him more opportunities to serve as a spot-up shooter, Nelson wanted lumbering power forward Charles Oakley to occasionally start the team's attack as a playmaker. He also wanted the 7-foot, 33-year-old Ewing to try his hand at quarterbacking the Knicks as a point center.

During one of the team's first practices, Nelson had Ewing work on dribbling the ball down the floor to initiate the offense. It was slow, stilted, and awkward, the way a child might look when first learning how to roller skate. But odd as it was to see the aging franchise center take over the point-guard role in practice, this sort of unorthodox idea represented much of what Nelson had become known for as a coach.

In his time with Golden State, Nelson regularly colored outside the lines with his offense, encouraging post-ups for point guard Tim Hardaway while drawing up plays to get 7-foot-7 Manute Bol open for three-pointers. On the other hand, Riley was so regimented he wouldn't accept notes and game plans from his assistants unless they were written on blue-card stock with a black pen, and slid underneath his door. (One time, Chris Brienza, a member of the Knicks' public relations team, made the mistake of knocking on Riley's door to hand him something. Minutes later, when Brienza phoned Riley's secretary, Brienza mentioned the gaffe to her. "Oh, I know," she told him. "[Pat] already called and said you knocked instead of sliding it under the door.")

Nelson was known for drawing up his plays on napkins when the inspiration struck. "He was one of the few guys I ever met who could basically replay an entire game in his head—play by play, person by person—and be right about all the details," says assistant coach Bob Salmi. "I'd go back and watch games a second time, just to see if what he was saying about a certain play was true. It always was. That's almost frightening. Mad-scientist, savant-like stuff. Like painting the Sistine Chapel."

Nelson had the sort of organization one might associate with a mad scientist. Shortly after getting the job, Nelson handed Nix the playbook he'd brought over from Golden State, asking if the assistant could go through and reorganize the pages inside the three-ring binder for him. "It was jumbled, where pages had fallen out, or were loose and out of order. But also, just the plays in there. Basketball was my life, but looking at some of his stuff was like reading Chinese. Just totally foreign stuff," Nix says.

While most Knicks in camp suggested they were open to seeing what Nelson's inverted, semi-positionless system might bring, Ewing sounded skeptical. He heard about Nelson's desire to reduce his minutes, and appreciated the coach's concern. But Ewing felt he needed to be on the floor far more often than not. The idea of an occasional fast break or two was fine, as was Mason running a possession here or there. But simply overhauling everything—especially when everything before had been based on Ewing's talent—felt like too big a departure to the big man, who in 1995–96 would make $19 million.

"I've heard a lot about us needing to run more. When Pat got here, he wanted us to run, too. [But] if you don't have the personnel to run, how are you gonna run? We're not a running team," Ewing said. "We're a post-up team. When we get the opportunity to run, we should. But I don't think we can run consistently."

It also didn't help that, in Nelson's first meeting with Ewing upon taking the job, the coach told his star pupil he felt he had room to improve as a passer. Nelson made the remark after reeling off a list of superlatives Ewing brought to the table, and offered it in a "let's figure out how to take you to the next level, so you're even more unstoppable" sort of way. Nonetheless, Ewing took some offense to it.

Even before the duo had a single game under its belt, things had already turned awkward.

Nelson joined the Knicks as the sixth-winningest coach of all time. No one doubted his ability to win, as winning had largely defined his career.

He'd won five rings with the Celtics as their clutch-shooting sixth man in the 1960s and 1970s. When he started coaching, Nelson helped relegitimize Milwaukee following Kareem Abdul-Jabbar's departure, notching seven fifty-win seasons while earning two Coach of the Year awards. He'd even turned the lowly Warriors—who'd made just one playoff run in the eleven years before his arrival—respectable again, earning another Coach of the Year and making the playoffs four times in his first six seasons there.

But the end of his run with the Warriors made it fair to wonder how Nelson would get along with players in New York.

As he joined the Knicks, Nelson's wounds were still fresh from a high-stakes standoff he'd had in Golden State with star rookie Chris Webber. Even after winning Rookie of the Year and becoming a key part of a fifty-win club in his first season, Webber despised Nelson so deeply that he exercised an opt-out in his deal, making him a free agent, and essentially forcing a trade. It was stunning, not just because of how unheard-of it was for a second-year talent to pick up and leave. There was also the fact that the Warriors had dealt *four* first-round picks—the No. 3 choice, Memphis State star Penny Hardaway, and three future selections—to the Magic for the rights to Webber, the No. 1 overall pick in the 1993 draft.

The Warriors had bet the farm on Webber just twelve months earlier.

Now he wanted out, and said Nelson was the reason why. "To the fans, I don't have anything against them. But I have no love for Don Nelson," said Webber, who would later be dealt to Washington. "This is his doing, and no one else's."

That lone season with Nelson and Webber had been a soap opera. Webber felt the coach went out of his way to play mind games, and sought to turn Webber's teammates against him. (Nelson reportedly told players that if they couldn't secure bigger contracts from the club in the future, they'd have Webber's sizable contract to blame.) Meanwhile, Nelson called Webber "about the toughest guy I ever coached," arguing that he wasn't ready to play winning basketball as a rookie.

Regardless of who was ultimately at fault, both men suffered in the short term.

Webber struggled to stay healthy with the Bullets, who made the playoffs just once in his four years there. Nelson, too, struggled to stay healthy following the Webber deal. From mid-December to early January of that 1994–95 season, the coach spent eighteen days away—five in the hospital, and thirteen at his home—with viral pneumonia, starting a spiral Golden State wouldn't recover from, even once Nelson returned.

The Warriors had entered that campaign with high hopes. Their media guide, made prior to Webber's trade demand, illustrated the team's five projected starters, all smiling, standing in full uniform on an elevator with Nelson, who was dressed as a bellhop. Nelson was reaching outside the elevator car to hit the "up" button to take Webber, Tim Hardaway, Latrell Sprewell, Chris Mullin, and Billy Owens to the next levels, which were: Division Title; Playoffs; Western Conference Finals; and NBA Finals. But with the bottom falling out of an expectation-filled year, Nelson was forced to resign midseason, at just 14-31.

The team itself took the biggest hit in the ordeal. Having dealt away future picks for a young star who was now gone, and having parted ways with the coach who'd hastened that young star's exit, the Warriors were left with incalculable collateral damage. They'd made the postseason in three of the prior four years. But in the smoldering aftermath of this dumpster fire, it would take *twelve years* for them to make it back there.

After that disastrous final year with the Warriors, it was clear Nelson needed to prove something in New York. Not that he could coach, but that he could lead and relate to modern players.

For the first few weeks of the 1995–96 season, Nelson and the Knicks looked to be in great shape.

After twelve games, the club was 10-2—a better mark than any of the Riley-led teams began with—and tied for the second-best record in the NBA. The *Houston Chronicle* had a headline claiming "Riley Is Gone, but New-Look Knicks Still Tough." One of the New York tabloids, the *Daily News*, had one praising the defense: "D-Lightful Are Don's Knicks."

On the surface, there was little reason to suspect something might be off. But underneath that surface, things were more on edge than they probably should've been.

Trade talks always carry the potential to hurt some feelings. And in the first week of play, many of the team's most prominent names—Oakley, Mason, Starks, and Smith—found themselves in the middle of a huge rumor. New York, like fifteen other NBA clubs, had laid out proposals for stud center Alonzo Mourning, who was on the market after failing to reach a long-term extension with the small-market Charlotte Hornets.

Beyond Mourning's sheer talent and his close friendship with Ewing, a fellow Georgetown alum, there was another consideration that had the Knicks interested in a deal.

"We knew [Riley] was trying to land Alonzo, and didn't want him to end up there," Checketts recalls of the pursuit. "I'd be lying if I said our feud [with Riley] wasn't a factor at the time. At a minimum, we wanted to do what we could to drive up the price that he and Miami would have to pay to get him."

New York offered Oakley and Smith first. After that was rebuffed, the club countered by making Starks, Mason, and a first-round pick available. The counter wasn't enough. Charlotte went with Riley's offer—sharpshooter Glen Rice, Matt Geiger, Khalid Reeves, and a first-round pick—giving the ex–Knicks coach his franchise cornerstone. The Hornets later said the Knicks laid out the second-best offer in the bidding war.

Aside from the early-season ego bruising, there was also the players' cool embrace of Nelson.

The club should have been in a great mood on the evening of November 16, after piecing together a 23-point victory on the road. Instead, the Knicks were sitting on their team bus, intermittently looking down at their watches and waiting to head to Oakland International Airport. Their contest had ended almost two hours earlier, yet they still hadn't left the arena, because Nelson hadn't boarded the bus.

Having exacted sweet revenge on his old club, which forced him out nine months earlier, Nelson was in no rush to exit the premises. He was in rare form, having downed five or six beers to celebrate. "He kept saying how much getting that win meant to him," one player said. "But he kinda made a fool of himself. He was stumbling around, and we ended up waiting almost an hour for him on that bus."

In some cases, players go above and beyond in showing understanding and compassion for their coaches when it comes to those sorts of emotional homecoming games. But with Nelson, someone they'd only been with for a few weeks, that camaraderie wasn't yet built. And really, how could it be?

A substitute-teacher vibe persisted. Wanting to keep his veterans rested, Nelson rarely called for practices. When he did actually hold them, the sessions deemphasized defense, and were light by the borderline-masochistic standards Riley had put in place years earlier. Riley's stamp was still on the team. Hell, Riley's name was still taped onto the TV remote Nelson used to watch game film each day.

"After an hour and a half, we'd be out of practice. Normally, [under Riley], we'd be in there practicing for two and a half or three hours," said backup center Herb Williams years later. "But that was the way Nellie was used to coaching: uptempo teams that scored a lot of points. And that's what he tried to get across to us: that if we scored, and kept our [league-best] defense the same, we would be a much better team."

Despite the Knicks' hot start to the year, some players wondered if they were succeeding *despite* Nelson's changes on offense, as opposed to succeeding because of them.

Nelson wanted his players to catch on quickly, and would give them written quizzes on his offense. For each wrong answer, players had to cough up ten dollars. During one practice, the coach walked away with $600 to give to charity after stumping them with one particularly tough exam. Assistant coaches found them hard, too.

"It was a learning curve for all of us [who'd been with Riley]. New terminology. New plays. A lot of guys out of their comfort zone, even though we were winning," Nix says. "Even for me, there'd be times I'd nod along in my head, saying I understand what he's getting at. But deep down, I'd realize I didn't know what he was talking about. And I think the players were kind of feeling like that, too, a lot of the time."

Some players were annoyed with Nelson's inconsistent approach to the rotation.

After receiving almost no playing time as a rookie, second-year guard Charlie Ward tallied 15 points and shot 60 percent in the team's season opener, easily the best showing of his young career. But after getting thirty-one minutes in that performance, he'd average just six minutes a night, including three times Nelson used him for a single minute, in the month that followed.

Smith suggested the early-season hot streak made it difficult to complain. But he also seemed to know the Knicks' fabric wasn't tight, and could come undone with the tug of a single thread.

"We're 10-2 and as a group, guys have to understand that," said Smith, who took a grin-and-bear-it approach with his inconsistent playing time as the team was winning. "But I wonder if we're all really accepting [the sacrifice]. It's tough for me to accept, so I know it's tough for other guys, too. That'll be our biggest hump: for guys to not worry about their minutes and shots. So we'll see how long it lasts."

Whatever issues existed, though, Nelson and his players were on the same page for their game on December 19, the night the Knicks would host the Heat in Riley's highly anticipated return to the Garden.

In the days leading up to the contest, MSG Network reporter Michael Kay had talked with fans in the arena to take their temperature concerning Riley's return. And while some were understanding, or said they ultimately sided with the coach over the team, most remained furious at him.

"I think he should be in jail! He didn't finish his contract with the Knicks!" one child shouted to Kay in the on-camera interview. An adult fan was slightly more diplomatic, saying, "He's a turncoat and a traitor. And we don't need him, because we're doing well without him." The traitor refrain was commonplace in the stands. One fan held a "Riley: Snake of NYC" sign. Another hoisted one reading, "Greed-ings Pat!"

Knowing the reception would be ugly, Riley brought his team to the arena for the game about a half hour later than usual. He had his players change into their uniforms before leaving their hotel instead of having them suit up in the locker room. He figured each additional minute spent inside the arena would be a distraction.

In that same vein, the Heat public relations department told writers they wouldn't be allowed in Miami's locker room for pregame interviews. Instead, the club would pay a $25,000 fine for not providing access.

The New York area got pelted with a huge snowstorm beginning that evening, resulting in fourteen inches over the course of the night. But the chorus of boos that rained down on Riley as he emerged from his dressing room to walk onto the Garden floor was as torrential as the storm itself. Rather than shy away from the jeers, Riley, dressed in a black suit and black tie, leaned into what he'd so clearly become: a supervillain.

Riley strode toward center court and lifted both arms in the air, as if he'd just been declared the winner of a prizefight. The crowd bellowed with rage, and the coach responded by waving hello to his detractors. He blew a handful of kisses, then repeatedly curled his arms inward, inviting more ridicule and disdain.

It was so out of character for Riley, who had developed such a regal, focused reputation in his years on that very sideline. At the same time, with the Garden crowd howling and worked into a lather, there was no way this moment could be focused on anything but Riley. So Riley embraced the ugliness of it.

"C'mon! C'mon!" Riley shouted, heightening the spectacle between himself and the nearly 20,000 fans. He stopped briefly to shake hands with Nelson. But the decibel-busting boos continued for nearly an entire minute, before fans transitioned to a "*Ri-ley Sucks!*" chant that rang throughout the arena. There would be a track-by-track playlist of Riley taunts that night, and this was only the beginning.

The most notable part of the night beyond that was the introduction of each team's lineups, for two reasons. First, the snakebitten Heat were without four starters, which made the Knicks' eventual 89–70 victory a foregone conclusion. Second, the difference in reception between Riley and Nelson, while not surprising, was enormous. Riley got jeered as if fans were vying for a prize to see who could boo the loudest. Nelson, never more embraced at the Garden than at that moment, got a thunderous ovation.

Under Riley, the Knicks had a strict no-fraternizing policy when it came to talking with or embracing opponents. But just before tip-off, Starks and Harper walked over to shake Riley's hand. Ewing was right behind them, and walked over to wrap his old coach in a massive hug.

New York had clear butterflies, going scoreless for more than five minutes to open the contest. But as the Knicks settled in and the Heat fell behind, Riley's voice grew hoarse from shouting to his players over the raucous crowd. A reporter, sitting close to where Riley was standing, asked the coach if he wanted a cough drop from the scorer's table to soothe his throat. He certainly sounded like he needed one.

Knowing the drops had been put there by the Knicks, Riley smiled. "You think they're safe for me?" he said, before laughing and accepting. It was perhaps the first laugh Riley had enjoyed the entire evening.

While he wouldn't necessarily need to worry about being poisoned, the way the night played out—with fans showing a visceral animosity toward Riley and his new team, and Riley embracing it—set the stage for what would become the NBA's most heated rivalry to close out the 1990s.

Unfortunately for Nelson, a victory that should have been a springboard instead turned out to be nothing more than the Knicks' high-water mark.

*   *   *

Like a whack-a-mole player without a mallet, Nelson could only watch as the problems kept popping up.

There was more bickering over shot totals. Ewing felt he needed to be the focal point of the offense, while Oakley and Mason pushed for a more equal-opportunity approach. The playing-time issue was continuing to grate on players, too, with one—athletic, multitalented guard Doug Christie—requesting a trade, while other veterans like Smith wondered aloud if they'd be moved.

The team wanted badly to trade Smith, and had been trying to since the year before. "We couldn't move him to save our souls," Checketts says. "He was a tough sell because he hadn't been able to stay healthy."

Really, though, the biggest catalyst in the team's unraveling was simple. After beating Miami, the Knicks began playing poorly, dropping four of their next five. The losses created the opening for players to air the criticisms they'd held back while they were winning, frustrating veterans who wanted the matters to stay in-house. "If there's dissension and there's a problem, you don't go to the newspaper. You talk it out," center Herb Williams said. "If I've got a problem with the guy across from me, I go to him directly. Otherwise, when it goes through three or four different channels, it comes out squash."

Days after Williams begged his teammates to stop fanning the fire, Mason poured a bucket of kerosene on it.

Following a 101–92 loss to the Blazers, Mason fielded a question concerning what the team was doing wrong. He didn't mince words. "[We] don't know what the hell we're going to do from game to game. This gets frustrating after a while," he said. His comment felt even more targeted, considering that in the closing moments of the defeat, he'd responded to a fan sitting near the bench, who'd asked Mason if the refs were to blame for the Knicks' recent struggles. Upon hearing the question, Mason shook his head.

"It wasn't them—it was that [guy] over there," Mason said, pointing in Nelson's direction.

That Mason, of all people, would air such a grievance perplexed Nelson. Perhaps Nelson and Ewing weren't going to see eye to eye, given that the offense was going through the big man far less often. And things were fraying between Nelson and Starks, as he often shortened the guard's leash—the opposite of how Riley handled his free-spirited swingman.

But Mason? In Nelson's mind, the point forward had nothing to complain about. From the day Nelson had sat down to discuss the job with Grunfeld, he said he planned to hand the keys to the offense over to Mason. And he'd followed through on that, so much so that it was increasingly annoying the franchise player.

Beyond letting Mason run the offense as a starter, Nelson also rarely took Mason off the court. In seven months, Mason had gone from being the team's sixth man, averaging thirty-two minutes per game, to now playing *forty-four minutes*. No one in the entire association—not Ewing, not the recently returned Michael Jordan, not Shaq—was getting more playing time than Mason was under Don Nelson.

Yet for how miffed Nelson was by Mason's comments, nothing could have prepared him for what would take place after the Knicks' home loss to Sacramento on January 13, 1996.

Within minutes of the defeat, the coach stepped into the locker room to make a few brief postgame remarks before heading back out to address reporters. When Nelson left to talk with the writers, a fully uniformed Mason stormed out, bounded into the hallway toward Nelson's office, and opened the door.

No one else was in the room when Mason got there, but that wasn't a problem. He hadn't come to speak with anyone anyway. He simply needed to deliver a message. Mason found a pen and angrily scrawled his thoughts on a sheet of paper, then walked out, still seething. He slammed the door behind him, and the noise was loud enough to startle assistant Jeff Van Gundy, who was in the dressing room next door.

"Who the hell was that?" Van Gundy asked Nix.

Nix had no idea, but stuck his head out to look. What he saw was a muscle-bound blur going back into the locker room. "I think it was Mase slamming Nellie's door," Nix said, unsure why the player had done it.

Minutes later, when Nelson walked back into his office, the mystery came into focus. He prepared to sit down at his desk, but first noticed the note sitting on top of it. He picked up the piece of paper and began reading.

"IF YOU FUCKIN' TAKE ME OUT OF A GAME AGAIN, I'LL KILL YOU," the note read.

Nelson brought the note into the coaches' dressing room, showing it to his assistants in disbelief.

"Nellie was miffed by the whole thing," Salmi recalls. "Both confused by it, but also trying to figure out if he needed to have genuine concern about all this. Like, 'Is this guy crazy enough to do something to me? To do something stupid?' Like, 'Do I need to check underneath my car when I go out to the parking lot?'"

Making the situation all the more strange: Mason had played thirty-eight of forty-eight minutes that night, despite being outplayed by Sacramento's Brian Grant, who had 25 points and nine rebounds.

Nelson didn't report the note to his bosses—aside from not wanting to look as if he couldn't control his players, he also relied heavily on Mason's skill set to win—but it shook him up nonetheless. The more he thought about it, the more it all made him second-guess the choice to jump back into coaching instead of enjoying his Maui vacation home. Nelson's mother, 90 at the time, had suggested sitting out a year.

"She almost died last year, and she wants me to have no stresses in life," Nelson said.

The Knicks job took a toll on Nelson's eating habits and growing waistline. In December, Hilfiger had to come back and take new suit measurements for Nelson, whose garments from the start of the year simply didn't fit him anymore.

As the fissures between Nelson and the team grew, he opted to take a laissez-faire approach toward addressing them. "I went in there with the attitude that it was a team loaded with veterans, that I could be more passive with," Nelson said. "It didn't work."

*   *   *

In the end, there were three distinct things that spelled doom for Nelson's run with the Knicks.

The first was the loss of Oakley—along with Herb Williams—to injury in the middle of February. Oakley and Williams were the two locker room leaders who *hadn't* publicly voiced any issues with Nelson. They'd served as the best shot the Knicks had of keeping everyone on the same page. But when Oakley broke his thumb after the All-Star break, it left New York without its starting power forward and best rebounder.

Days before Oakley's injury, the Knicks had also finally found a taker for Smith, dealing him and Monty Williams to San Antonio to clear millions of dollars in salary cap space for the summer of 1996. But that trade, along with one that sent Herb Williams and Christie to Toronto, sapped the club's big-man depth. New York went on to drop eight of its first ten games after Oakley's injury, which sidelined him six weeks—almost all of what was left of the season.

"Oakley was the glue to that year's team—a big key to so much of what we did," recalls assistant Don Chaney. "More importantly, I think he was Nellie's swing guy. If he could get Oak to buy into something, then Oak could convince the rest of the players. But without him, the situation just didn't work anymore."

The second problem was that by March, Starks hated Nelson, summing up the way the team felt as a whole.

At one point, well after the notion of mending fences had passed, Starks decided to speak his mind to reporters. "Everybody thought he'd be a good coach. But sometimes nightmares happen," he said.

It was a bold comment to make about Nelson, who'd been Starks's first NBA coach at Golden State. But Starks couldn't understand Nelson's zero-tolerance policy for his slow starts or shot selection. The coach even benched Starks after *making* a three against the Suns, with Nelson criticizing the shot for being out of rhythm, hurting the Knicks' game plan in the process.

The quick hooks prompted the once-conscienceless Starks to play like a man constantly looking over his shoulder. Even after the men held a half-hour meeting in late January about Starks's dwindling playing time, Nelson kept reducing his minutes. Things reached a point of no return when Nelson swapped Hubert Davis, who excelled at shooting but little else, into the starting five the following month. The move left Starks with just twelve minutes of action on some nights.

"I was trying to give him as much respect as I could and let [Starks] play his way through whatever problems he's having. I've given him every benefit of the doubt. But Hubert is the better player," Nelson said, somewhat remarkably.

The timing of the clash with one of the club's most popular players was particularly bad. Nelson already had a low approval rating in the locker room. And given that the club had just finished an 0-4 road trip out west—marking the team's worst showing on a four-game trip in ten years—fans weren't thrilled, either.

Whether it was in response to the losing streak or Nelson's harsh words for Starks, fans lustily booed the coach during starting-lineup introductions when the Knicks hosted the Warriors on March 3.

But it was the third strike against Nelson that did him in: he asked to trade Ewing, the franchise player, and somehow thought Ewing wouldn't find out about it.

Perhaps sensing the season—and the team—slipping from his grasp, Nelson approached his bosses in January with a thought. As coach of the American team at the 1994 World Basketball Championship, Nelson worked with Shaquille O'Neal, and heard through the grapevine that the young star wanted out of Orlando and into a bigger market. O'Neal would be a free agent in six months. But trading for him now, Nelson posited, would give the Knicks a head start by giving O'Neal a chance to fall in love with the city.

For Nelson, the calculus was simple. At 33, Ewing was almost ten full years older than Shaq, who was about to enter his prime. The window for building a champion around Ewing as the top option was getting increasingly narrow. "I didn't think he had very much left in the tank," Nelson said decades later in an interview with HBO's Bryant Gumbel.

Nelson had dinner with Checketts to walk him through the logic of it. "[Ewing] doesn't want to play the way I want to play," Nelson told him.

"He's too much of a low-post guy, and the game is going away from that." But Checketts, who years earlier had fought to keep Ewing in a Knicks jersey, had reservations about entertaining trade offers for a player of Ewing's stature.

"I didn't want to talk about it much, because if I gave him hope of it being possible, I knew we'd see headlines about it later," Checketts says. "I said it wasn't in the cards." Still, Nelson went a step further and met with James Dolan, who'd just become CEO of Cablevision, one of the team's corporate owners.

While Dolan also heard Nelson out, he wasn't keen on dealing Ewing away, either. It wasn't long after the coach's meetings with management and ownership that the star heard about Nelson's suggestion. "It got back to [Ewing], and once that happened, I was toast," Nelson said. The big man never confronted the coach, but "you could tell that something was different. Totally different. And we had to split after that," he added.

Nelson, whose stress and expanded waistline required Hilfiger to make a third visit with him in February to get new measurements, had grown tired of the task. During the Knicks' February 21 game in Detroit, the coach walked into the visiting locker room at halftime wearing an agitated look just before he addressed his players. "I'm tired of dealing with these damn assholes," Nelson said to no one in particular.

Forward Willie Anderson, who'd been traded to the Knicks just days earlier and had already begun picking up on the tension between Nelson and the players, said the moment was awkward. "He didn't look at us as he said it. But it was clear he was talking about us," he said. Worst of all: the players were so over Nelson by then, according to Anderson, that no one even cared enough to engage the coach's slight.

Matt Fish, a free-agent center who signed a ten-day contract with the Knicks in the midst of their turmoil, sensed the indifference, too. He recalls being thrown into the starting lineup because Ewing was sidelined with a hurt ankle, then the flu, that kept him out for a few games.

"I remember thinking, 'But how is this guy hurt if he's kicking my ass in practice?'" Fish says. "To me, it kind of felt like [Ewing] was pretending he was hurt, and that all those guys had just quit on Nellie. There's no way I should have been starting. They just quit on him."

Soon after that, with the team sitting at 34-25, Grunfeld decided to pull the plug on Nelson as well. Even with the decent record, there was no relationship between the coach and the players.

"I loved this opportunity. Ernie and Dave were first class all the way. I loved the city of New York. I loved everything except the team," Nelson said in his farewell press conference, getting in one final dig on his way out.

Decades after the flameout, it's nearly impossible to take issue with Nelson's ideas. The notion of using a big, versatile point forward like Mason is something most NBA teams seek to do now. The idea of holding lighter practice sessions and allowing older vets to rest more is embraced league-wide. Wanting to diversify the offense in hopes of having it be less reliant on post-up looks would seem obvious now, as would trading a 33-year-old Patrick Ewing for a 23-year-old star and free-agent-to-be Shaquille O'Neal.

The coach's ideology was more or less spot-on, even if players and executives—still accustomed to how things operated under Riley—lacked the stomach for it. But it was also Nelson's inability and unwillingness to communicate his vision to an old-school group that doomed his chances.

"Nellie thinks you should just know stuff sometimes, when you might not know it. So he doesn't say anything [to help]," said Christie, who scored 4 points per game in Nelson's doghouse before being traded to Toronto, where he'd average 15 points over the next three seasons. "I'm still trying to learn the game. [As a coach], you can't just say 'That's it.' Some guys may need a little more explaining."

Regardless, the Knicks were now in a free fall, coming apart at the seams. They needed a coach who could not only explain game strategy, but also return the team to its blue-collar roots established under Riley.

Fortunately for the Knicks, they wouldn't have to look very far down the bench in order to find him.

15

BACK TO BASICS

There was a distinct chill in the air, and the sun had just begun to emerge amid Rhode Island's dark autumn sky, when Stu Jackson stepped out of his car to head into his office.

Seeing the sun rise had become an almost-daily ritual for Jackson during his first year as an assistant coach and lead recruiter at Providence. He'd gotten used to arriving for work between 6:30 and 7 a.m. each day, and was almost always the first member of Rick Pitino's staff to clock in.

But at the start of Jackson's second year there, in 1986, a young assistant repeatedly beat him to the punch. So the ever-competitive Jackson began making an effort to drive to the team's practice facility progressively earlier—first 6:45, then 6:30, and eventually 6:15—each day, hoping to get there first. But no matter what time Jackson drove in, he saw the same car already comfortably parked there each time.

"At first, I was telling myself, 'Man, this guy's really industrious,'" Jackson recalls saying of Jeff Van Gundy, who'd also made a point of being the last assistant to leave the basketball offices each night.

But then by the second week—with Jackson even arriving at 6 a.m. a time or two, and still as the second coach to arrive into work—Jackson grew curious, and began doing some detective work. First, he noticed Van Gundy's car was always parked in the exact same spot each day.

Going one step further, he peered into the windows of Van Gundy's Toyota Corolla, only to find the car filled with moving boxes.

It was then that Jackson deduced how Van Gundy was the first to arrive and last to leave each day.

"The man was literally living in the office. Sleeping on the reception-area couch, with this beautiful oriental rug, using the practice facility's showers. He made the office his house!" Jackson recalled. "Rick told him: 'You've gotta move out of the office and get an apartment. That's what normal people do.'"

Van Gundy might've taken his Eat, Sleep, Breathe mentality toward the sport a bit too literally at times. But between that tireless mindset, and the six Diet Cokes per day that kept him overly caffeinated, it was unsurprising that Van Gundy was wide awake when he got a knock on his hotel room door at 8 a.m. on March 8, 1996. The droopy-eyed coach had already been up watching game film for hours by that point.

As he peered through the peephole of Room 1814 at the Philadelphia Ritz-Carlton, Van Gundy saw Ernie Grunfeld standing outside before allowing the general manager in. Grunfeld then put his hand on Van Gundy's shoulder, congratulated him, and told the longtime assistant he'd be taking over as the new coach.

The news floored the 34-year-old. In an instant, he became the league's youngest head coach by seven years. He cycled through a wave of emotions. Compassion for Don Nelson, who was a few rooms down the hall, literally packing his bags despite holding the East's fourth-best record at 34-25. Joy and nervousness as a result of the massive opportunity he'd be getting. Underlying guilt for reaching the mountaintop when so many coaches—his own father included—endured the decades-long *hired, fired, then relocate the family again* cycle at the sport's lower levels without getting a payoff anywhere near this sweet.

Truthfully, though, even with just one season of head-coaching experience—he oversaw the varsity team at McQuaid Jesuit High in Rochester, New York, in 1985—Van Gundy had more than paid his dues.

* * *

Perhaps the first true sign of Van Gundy's devotion to basketball, and starting at the bottom rungs of it if necessary, came at age 18. In 1981, he'd just finished his freshman year at Yale, one of the world's most prestigious colleges.

But then he got cut from the team during that first year of school. And once it ended, he had news for his parents. "I've decided that I'm going to transfer," he explained. His father asked where he planned to go instead.

"Menlo Junior College," he said with a straight face.

"From Yale to Menlo Junior College?" his mother asked, wondering if she'd missed something. "Are you sure?" But the younger Van Gundy was positive. "I'll have a better chance to play ball," he surmised.

So for one year, in 1982, he played at the California school for a coach who was a family friend. He transferred again the following year, this time to play for his father, Bill Van Gundy, at SUNY Brockport. But his time there would be short-lived, too. He left after one season following his father's dismissal, and ended up transferring to Nazareth College in Rochester. There, the hustle-oriented point guard played for two years, led the team to the Division III Elite Eight, and was named magna cum laude.

After four schools in five years, the whirlwind continued on the coaching side. He spent the one year running the high school program at McQuaid Jesuit, two years as an assistant at Providence, and then one season in the same capacity at Rutgers. He then joined the Knicks—who were "said to be working with Huggies to develop a disposable coach," in the words of *Washington Post* columnist Tony Kornheiser—a club that cycled through four coaches in a six-and-a-half-year span. Van Gundy found himself in limbo after one of those coaches got fired, and, in May 1991, had been temporarily assigned to handle administrative tasks for Grunfeld—a role that bored him, as it was too far removed from coaching.

As the team's junior assistant, Van Gundy held so little seniority that the club booted him from his office to give that space to Pam Harris, the newly hired marketing director. "I remember feeling bad that I didn't really get a chance to know who he was until after they'd moved him out," Harris recalls.

Simply looking for ways to pitch in at times, Van Gundy occasionally noticed one of the team's secretaries, a single mother, was forced to bring her five-year-old son to the office when she couldn't get a babysitter. Knowing she was swamped and unable to entertain the boy, Van Gundy would whisk the child away to do puzzles or play cards. "He was incredibly sweet to do that," the woman says years later.

Less than enthused with the office work, and less than sure he'd be able to stay on as an assistant after John MacLeod's dismissal, Van Gundy interviewed for a few college coaching gigs. But after Pat Riley officially agreed to replace MacLeod as the Knicks head coach, Dave Checketts asked Riley to strongly consider holding on to Van Gundy—whom Riley had never met—for a seat on his bench.

Riley quickly grew to like the 29-year-old. Much like Stu Jackson, Riley learned quickly that no one would beat Van Gundy into the office each morning. The assistant's scouting reports were consistently crisp and detailed. But more than anything, Riley appreciated the 5-foot-9 Van Gundy—who hadn't played at the pro level—and his lack of hesitation when it came to engaging the players during workouts.

Every day, Van Gundy would be on the court two hours before practices to rebound for young, developing players. And he constantly threw himself into drills to show how he wanted something done.

"One of the few things I could offer was to run around and work up a sweat each day," Van Gundy recalls. "I didn't see myself as qualified to talk with someone like Patrick about his release angle or anything."

Sometimes he pushed the players a bit more than they liked. During a practice that first year under Riley, Van Gundy repeatedly shouted at Charles Oakley, telling him he was playing soft. After the third such remark, Oakley fired the ball at Van Gundy's crotch, leaving the coach doubled over.

But those instances were few and far between compared to the countless times he'd sit and go over film with a struggling player, or offer constructive criticism on the sideline during a game. And because they'd seen firsthand how much time Van Gundy was willing to invest, the Knicks had immense respect for him.

After the 1991–92 season, Riley held individual exit interviews for his assistant coaches. As he finished his one-on-one with Van Gundy, Riley asked him whether he wanted to become a head coach someday.

A disheveled Van Gundy hemmed and hawed before eventually saying he did.

"Okay," Riley said, taking a moment to figure out how to phrase his next critique. "Well, if you want to be a head coach, you probably need to start dressing better."

Beyond that, Riley told him not to be sheepish about the fact he hadn't been an NBA player. "These guys only care about you having four qualities: that you're competent, sincere, reliable, and trustworthy," Riley told him. "If you are those four things, you can accomplish anything in this league."

The talk was a huge confidence booster for Van Gundy, whom Riley slowly began entrusting with more responsibility the following season. Specifically, when Riley felt his voice was wearing thin on his players, he'd hand the reins to Van Gundy—not top assistant Dick Harter—to let him run team workouts.

Riley's trust in Van Gundy deepened the bond between the men; enough to prompt Van Gundy to give his daughter, Mattie, the middle name "Riley" in 1995. (A trust was also formed when a compassionate Riley told Van Gundy he was fine to take the time he needed to be with his wife, Kim, following a miscarriage.)

Riley even tried, but failed to get clearance from New York's front office, to pry Van Gundy from the Knicks upon joining the Heat. "I was kind of upset about it at the time," Van Gundy recalled about Checketts's decision. Unable to take Jeff to Miami, Riley hired Jeff's brother, Stan, as an assistant instead.

"I wanted at least one Van Gundy with me," Riley said.

Jeff Van Gundy had no clue his head-coach-in-training lessons under Riley would come in handy just months after Riley's exit. But minutes after getting the job, he began putting one of those lessons to use.

*   *   *

As Van Gundy met with his players for the first time as head coach, he told them they'd be going back to the way things had been prior to Nelson's arrival. That defense would be paramount. That strong effort would be a constant. And that practices would be longer and more strenuous than they had been.

To drive the point home, the process would begin immediately, starting with that morning's shootaround—one that felt more like a full-scale practice; the same way Riley's shootarounds were.

Van Gundy hoped the extra work would tone and sharpen the Knicks' focus against the hapless Sixers, who entered the night with a league-worst 11-47 mark, and had lost eleven of their prior twelve contests.

Instead, the exact opposite happened. New York carried a six-point lead into the half against Philadelphia. But the Knicks—physically spent from the hard workout earlier in the day—imploded in the second half. They scored just 35 points after halftime to suffer a humiliating loss to the Sixers, a team New York had beaten seven straight times—including a 32-point shellacking just one month earlier.

Following the game, Sixers forward Ed Pinckney described Philadelphia's upset win as a Christmas miracle of sorts. On the flip side, Van Gundy—who, even as a child, had never been able to view wins and losses through a proportional lens—instantly began feeling sick over the Knicks' defeat. Just before the team began its bus ride back home, Mike Saunders, the club's traveling secretary, handed out cheesesteaks to everyone on board. Van Gundy was so nauseated he never bothered to touch his.

Basketball had almost always been top of mind for Van Gundy. In separate instances throughout his career, he'd run a red light, rammed into his own garage door, and crashed into another car because of his mental preoccupation with the game.

The coach did have quiet pleasures. In the offseason, he'd occasionally go to the movie theater and take in matinee showings with a tub of popcorn. A baseball fan, he'd often go to Shea Stadium with assistant Brendan Malone and buy tickets off scalpers—even after ascending to the head-coaching job—to get into Mets games. The college history major made a point to visit Babe Ruth's burial site one muggy day.

"He's a totally relaxed guy during the offseason, once he's away from the court," says Malone, who made the trip to Ruth's Hawthorne, New York, grave site with Van Gundy.

But this—losing to the worst team in the sport—was the total opposite of a relaxing day in the offseason. Ratcheting up the pressure even more: the Knicks' next game was against Michael Jordan and the 54-6 Bulls, who owned the NBA's best record. So there'd be no relief during that bus ride back from Philly.

The challenge facing Van Gundy was the sort that generated a laser-like focus from the coach, who otherwise had a wry, self-deprecating sense of humor. He had little patience for distractions. And he thought just about anything could be a potential distraction. If a staffer wanted to iron out details in the locker room for a player to meet with a Make-A-Wish child? It needed to wait until after the game. The idea of having a chaplain praying with players less than an hour before tip-off? Absolutely a distraction. (He voiced this, but didn't ban chapel.) Van Gundy even thought the idea of having a designated Player of the Game after each contest was a distraction, and briefly fought members of the marketing and sponsorship departments on whether it was necessary. He felt singling out an individual player for his positive contributions—even after a win—could bring unnecessary headaches and jealousy.

During one such tug-of-war, Van Gundy asked Harris, the marketing director, what would happen to her job if the Knicks suddenly stopped winning. Harris said she assumed she'd be unaffected in such a case.

"That's the difference," Van Gundy told her. "You'd likely keep your job if we lost. The players want to win, but get paid regardless of whether they win or lose. And most would be back next year either way. But the coaches? We have to win. I'm not saying nobody else *wants* to win. But coaches *have* to win."

*   *   *

With a number of big names expected to be on the market, Van Gundy knew he was closer to being a long shot than a shoo-in to keep the job heading into the offseason. "50,000,000-1 [odds]; maybe in another lifetime," wrote *Daily News* columnist Mitch Lawrence about Van Gundy's early candidacy.

What Van Gundy didn't know was the Knicks gave real thought to making fellow assistant Don Chaney, a former NBA Coach of the Year, Nelson's replacement. "I was there when the decision was made to elevate Jeff, and there was some controversy over it. Dave expressed concern that he wouldn't want to have to fire Don if he hired him, because Don was [Black]," recalls Ed Tapscott.

Tapscott said he urged Checketts and Grunfeld to judge Chaney and Van Gundy on their merits alone, and that the executives reached the conclusion that Van Gundy might be a better choice since he'd long worked with the players, and didn't seem shy about pushing them—something the more agreeable Chaney seemed less likely to do.

During Van Gundy's second game as head coach, against the Bulls on NBC, the network aired an interview with Bulls coach Phil Jackson, in which he fielded a question about his own future. Jackson was asked whether Nelson's firing might alter his mind-set about extending his contract with Chicago.

But rather than give the politically correct response—"No"—Jackson instead spoke candidly.

"Of course it changes things," Jackson said.

The speculation, and Jackson's disinterest in quelling it, annoyed Van Gundy, who took Jackson's comments about the job as a sort of ethical breach within the NBA coaching fraternity. Yet any trepidation Van Gundy felt over that issue—or that New York felt about its ten losses in fourteen prior outings—faded for a few hours during that March 10 meeting with Chicago at the Garden.

In what was easily their best performance of the season, the Knicks blew the doors off the Bulls, handling the historically dominant club a 104–72 drubbing that registered as Chicago's worst of the year.

In winning by 32, the Knicks had beaten Chicago by nearly as much in one game as the other six teams who'd taken down the Bulls had, combined. Ewing looked rejuvenated, throwing down a monstrous, left-handed dunk over Chicago's Luc Longley, and unleashing a scream that looked as if it sought to shake the Knicks from their two-and-a-half-month malaise under Nelson in one fell swoop.

As the game ended, Derek Harper grabbed hold of the ball so he could bring it into the locker room and present it to Van Gundy, to mark his first win. "We had our hardest practice of the year [before this], and it carried over into today," Harper said, crediting Van Gundy, who finished the campaign 13-10 as coach.

By no means did the win suggest the Knicks would derail Jordan and Chicago that season. The Bulls would go on to eliminate New York in five games in the second round, and they eventually capped their record-breaking 72-win campaign with yet another NBA title—their fourth of the decade.

Still, the blowout win over Chicago—and the Knicks' first-round sweep of Cleveland—did show something important: that an old dog could benefit from some of its old tricks under Van Gundy's leadership.

But even if the old style still had a place with the Knicks, the team itself needed to get younger. And it needed to do it quickly.

16

DOWN IN FLAMES

Ed Tapscott figured he needed to take a slightly different approach this time around.

As the person responsible for overseeing the Knicks' scouting efforts, Tapscott normally spent the month of June holding predraft workouts for college upperclassmen who were on the cusp of joining the league. But over a three-day span in June of 1996, Tapscott welcomed a pair of wildly talented high schoolers into the team's practice facility to show what they could do.

He wanted to make sure he could get the best possible read on their talent, which meant helping the teenagers work through whatever jitters they might have before the sessions that could alter the rest of their lives.

During the first of those workouts, with 6-foot-11 power forward Jermaine O'Neal, Tapscott laid out all the pertinent information. The Knicks merely wanted to see what he was capable of, and that if he was confused by anything—NBA-level terminology, or how to do a drill—they were more than happy to help him. Then Tapscott threw out an icebreaker for the 17-year-old from small-town South Carolina.

"I want to ask you something," Tapscott said to O'Neal. "You've been to the prom, right?"

O'Neal was confused. "Excuse me?"

"You went to your senior prom, didn't you?" Tapscott asked again.

"Yes, sir—I went to my prom."

"Oh, okay. Good," Tapscott replied. "We don't work anybody out unless they've been to their prom."

With the joke, O'Neal smiled and loosened his shoulders some. He went on to give a fantastic workout; one so good Tapscott and the Knicks were certain they wanted him with the No. 18 pick. "We would've taken him right then and there if we could have," Tapscott says.

Two days later, when the Knicks hosted another high schooler, Tapscott rolled out the same spiel. He used the same icebreaker, asking whether the youngster had attended his school prom one month earlier.

Seemingly confused, Kobe Bryant raised his eyebrows.

"Yeah—I took Brandy to my prom," Bryant said, referring to the teenage, platinum-selling R&B singer.

Bryant's response for Tapscott had a *How could you not know that?* tone to it, as their prom plans had made national news in some cases. But it also spoke to Bryant's supreme confidence, even as a youngster. He didn't need to get butterflies out. He never had any to begin with. "Jermaine was 17 going on 18, and Kobe was 17 going on 30," Tapscott recalls. "Kobe didn't need to ease into anything, because he was already so self-possessed. And frankly, his workout was one of the best I'd ever seen. He finished, and [the scouts] looked at each other and said, 'He ain't falling to us.'"

Team scouts vividly remember Bryant coming in with what appeared to be a manicure and a clear coat on his fingernails—perhaps fitting for how polished his workout was that day at the age of 17.

The Knicks were in a strange spot that summer. Because of the deal they'd made months earlier to offload Charles Smith to San Antonio, and due to the tampering settlement with Miami, New York owned three first-round picks: No. 18, 19, and 21. Since the Knicks had a few picks to play with—and because they were the NBA's oldest club, with their top three players north of 30—they figured this was the time to take a swing.

"We wanted to take one or both of the high schoolers. We were set on that," scout Phil Hubbard says. "No one that far down in the draft was going to help us right away anyway. So this would be our way to add upside and athleticism without having a top pick to work with. Ernie Grunfeld had already told us that's what we were doing. We just needed the board to fall our way."

But the club, unwilling to part with any core players to move up, watched Bryant go No. 13, then saw O'Neal get taken one pick too early, by Portland, with the No. 17 pick. So after missing out on a pair of future franchise players, New York ended up with a trio of forwards—Syracuse's John Wallace, Kentucky's Walter McCarty, and Mississippi State's Dontaé' Jones—in the draft instead.

The process hadn't played out the way the Knicks hoped. Still, making the roster younger remained New York's top priority when free agency rolled around.

Unless, of course, the best player in the world was available.

Urban legend goes something like this: Michael Jordan, the archnemesis of all things New York, gave long, hard thought to the notion of leaving the Bulls for the Knicks.

Wanting to be paid his full market value, Jordan laid down a stunning ultimatum for Bulls owner Jerry Reinsdorf: you'll either agree to pay me $25 million for this coming season like the Knicks claim they will—and you'll make it happen within the next twenty-four hours—or else I'll sign a deal with the enemy.

If it seemed a bit drastic, there was a reason. By then, Jordan had won four titles, including the most recent one, and had just finished an eight-year, $25 million deal—one he'd laughably outperformed several times over. So now, after being vastly undercompensated for years, he wanted Reinsdorf and the Bulls to pay up.

And while it's true that Jordan's agent, David Falk, had an arrangement with Dave Checketts concerning Jordan—that the Knicks would spend every last penny of the $12 million they had in available salary cap room to sign him—there was never any indication things got close. "People love to think there's a story there, but there isn't one, really," Checketts says, adding that no serious conversations took place about how New

York could realistically compensate him to the tune of $25 million per year. "I never thought he was leaving Chicago."

The Knicks would have gladly deviated from their free-agent summer plans if it meant getting Jordan. Honestly, who wouldn't have? But Checketts also didn't mind being used here some. He saw value in giving Jordan leverage so it would hurt the Bulls' pocketbook, which might make it harder to keep the rest of the Chicago roster together. (Reinsdorf ultimately ended up paying Jordan a record $30 million in that year alone.) Meanwhile, New York got to make use of the plan it had banked on all along, targeting younger players who could shoulder some of the scoring pressure Patrick Ewing and John Starks had been saddled with.

Members of the front office took the team plane from Washington, DC, where they had a fruitless meeting with free-agent star Juwan Howard, to Detroit to pitch 25-year-old Allan Houston, a 6-foot-6 off-guard and deadeye perimeter shooter from the Pistons.

The talks with Houston marked the first time the Knicks sought to pull out all the stops during a free-agent process. Aside from picking up Houston, his family, and his agent to bring them back east on the team plane, the club also made a stop back in Washington to pick up Ewing, who had never taken part in free-agent pitches before. (Ewing's wife, Rita, also participated and spoke with Houston's fiancée.) Houston had never enjoyed an all-out recruiting process before, as he'd played for his father at the University of Tennessee, making him a lock to end up there.

So it left an impression on him when the team placed Houston's Knicks jerseys on every plane seat. He received two crystal apples from Tiffany & Co., one for his fiancée and another for his mom. It was still the early days of Photoshop, but the Knicks managed to drape a huge poster of Houston in a New York uniform along the side of the team's practice facility. And there were videos from celebrity fans urging him to join the Knicks. To top it all off, the club arranged a stay for him and Tamara, his soon-to-be wife, in the Cartier suite of the prestigious St. Regis Hotel in Midtown.

It was an experience so convincing that Houston took New York's seven-year, $56 million offer without allowing Detroit a chance to counter—a choice that angered Grant Hill and his other Pistons team-mates so much they ended up skipping Houston's wedding the following month. But for all the Pistons' frustrations, the Knicks were overjoyed to be adding a sharpshooter who'd just poured in almost 20 points a game.

The team then followed up by reaching a deal with Nets free agent Chris Childs, a 28-year-old floor general who'd averaged 13 points and seven assists in his lone season as a starter, for six years and $24 million. It was a hefty contract for a player, particularly one from a losing team, with such limited experience in a key role. Yet in Childs, the Knicks were getting someone who wasn't scared of anything on the court—during his New York tenure, he would go on to throw punches at Bryant and nearly came to blows with Jordan—largely because of what he'd faced away from it.

Childs, who had grown up with several family members who struggled with alcoholism, began spiraling himself the night of the 1989 draft. That evening started with an abundance of friends and relatives he had invited over for a pool party; all of whom were curious to see where he'd start his pro career. It ended with Childs going undrafted, and locking himself in his apartment for five days without answering his phone.

He bounced around the Continental Basketball Association, playing for four teams in five seasons—and watching his backups get promoted to the NBA—as he lost control with his drinking and occasionally got suspended because of it. One of his coaches recommended Childs get help at a program run by John Lucas, a former No. 1 pick who'd battled substance abuse problems of his own. But Childs's issues persisted. "One time I went out and had twenty-four Heinekens, smoked four joints, and had five or six shots of cognac," he said. "I got back at seven in the morning, and [our program] had a meeting at eight. I didn't sleep, eat, or shower."

The troubled point guard, once described as "a player only a bartender could love" in the words of one writer, turned his story around at a Miami rehab facility. Childs had his last drink on June 26, 1993, and made the most of his chance in the NBA the next year. And now he'd be running the show for the Knicks.

Yet New York's biggest acquisition during that busy free-agent period wasn't even a free agent.

Taking advantage of a relatively new, small-market club that no longer wanted to pay for star talent, the Knicks dialed up the Hornets. Just three years earlier, Charlotte had inked Larry Johnson, the physically imposing forward and former No. 1 pick, to the richest deal in sports history, at $84 million over twelve seasons. Hornets owner George Shinn had dealt 25-year-old Alonzo Mourning to Miami after declining to meet his long-term salary demands in 1995. Now, one year later, he was seeking to trade the 27-year-old Johnson.

The Knicks, of course, were a deep-pocketed, big-market club, one that not only sold out its 20,000-seat arena every night and had a season-ticket waiting list backed up for almost a decade, but also managed to do so at premium prices. Ticket and concession revenues, at about $1 million per game, afforded New York the ability to absorb a pricey talent like Johnson, a two-time All-Star who'd battled recurring back injuries, but was coming off a year in which he averaged a solid 20.5 points, 8.4 boards, and 4.4 assists.

Because Johnson's contract was so big, the teams took the unusual step of meeting to discuss the trade, as opposed to merely talking over the phone. Members of New York's front office went down to Charlotte and laid out an offer—to potentially send point forward Anthony Mason, backup power forward Brad Lohaus, and some cash in exchange for Johnson—before the Hornets said they'd like to give it thought.

As the Knicks prepared to leave the meeting, Tapscott pulled out his flip phone—still a new phenomenon at the time—to call for a car to pick up the contingent of New York executives. Tapscott noticed Shinn seemed to be interested, if not mesmerized, by his mobile device.

"Is that your phone?" a curious Shinn asked in his long, southern drawl. When Tapscott said it was, Shinn held out his hand, wanting to examine the technology. "Lemme have a look at that booger," he said.

As the Hornets further examined the Knicks' offer, they did have one key question that held up the deal momentarily. Shinn told the Knicks he wasn't sure whether he wanted to make the trade anymore after talking with Hornets coach Dave Cowens. The reason: Cowens had gotten a troubling report from his longtime friend, ex–Knicks coach Don Nelson, about how difficult Mason was to deal with.

Specifically, Nelson told Cowens of Mason's sudden outbursts, suggesting—without firm evidence—they might have been fueled by steroid use. "We were a little concerned [after Nelson suggested that]," Cowens says. "Me and Mase ended up getting along just fine. But before you make a deal, you always want to do your homework to make sure you know exactly what you're getting into."

Mason, the Queens native who'd blossomed into one of the NBA's most versatile players for his hometown team, was hurt over being moved; particularly just twelve months after signing a six-year contract to stay put.

But by giving up Mason, the Knicks now had three 20-point-per-game scorers, including two who were substantially younger. In replacing Derek Harper with Childs, they'd also gotten younger at the point of attack. And for good measure, New York added 36-year-old Buck Williams, a solid, veteran power forward, and re-signed backup center Herb Williams, whose locker-room voice had been key the year before.

On paper, the team looked to be a contender again. "We feel like we hit the jackpot," Grunfeld said.

As Pete Favat stepped onto the elevator, he worried his heart might beat out of his chest.

To that point, in 1991, the 25-year-old creative director had begun to make a name for himself in the advertising world. And he'd just been handed the biggest project of his young career: to conceptualize a shoe commercial for Converse around rookie star Larry Johnson. Even without taking into account Converse's desire to gain ground on Nike, which was basking in its otherworldly success with Jordan, the choice to hand the account to Favat represented a level of faith he had never been trusted with.

Now Favat was about to take that endowment of faith to pitch the muscle-bound Johnson on the idea of . . . dressing up as an elderly woman, complete with glasses, a flowing wig, pillbox hat, and floral-print dress?

It was bizarre. Preposterous. But in Favat's mind, it was also necessary—if only to drum up attention for Converse. He simply didn't know how Johnson, who'd just been taken No. 1 in the draft, was going to feel about it all. "I was scared shitless," Favat says. "I timed it out in my head beforehand to figure out how long it'd take me to hop off the couch and run to the elevator in case he hated the idea and wanted to kill me."

It's impossible to overstate how much of a can't-miss prospect Johnson was. He had been far and away the best player on perhaps the best team in modern college basketball history. In 1990, his colorful, controversial UNLV squad put up 103 points in the national title game to beat Duke by 30, which to this day stands as the most lopsided score in NCAA title game history. Johnson and the Runnin' Rebels followed that with an undefeated regular season in 1991 before falling in the Final Four to finish 34-1.

And for how fearsome the Jerry Tarkanian–coached team was, Johnson might have been even more scary as an individual player. He possessed the physique of a body builder, and had the leaping ability of someone whose legs came installed with pogo sticks. At 6-foot-6, he had a special blend of perimeter shooting ability to go with his unbelievable quickness in the post to do damage from both locations.

So sitting in Johnson's Dallas penthouse that day, Favat walked him through the safer of the two commercial concepts he'd created, one that featured Larry Bird and Magic Johnson, the brand's biggest endorsers. Bird and Johnson would be mad scientists in a lab, building a freak athlete who takes on the best of their attributes—and parts of their respective names—to make an unstoppable player. Then, as they put final touches on their experiment, a Frankenstein-like "Larry Johnson" would emerge from a gurney as the finished specimen.

Johnson said he was fine with the first idea, and liked it. But he was eager to see the second. So Favat flipped over his storyboard, which used a *Vanity Fair* photo of a 71-year-old Ella Fitzgerald taken by Annie Leibovitz. Fitzgerald's look—with the retro glasses, old-lady hat, and a dress—was the aesthetic Favat had in mind for Johnson in the commercial. Specifically, he wanted to get across that Johnson's Converse shoes would be so lightweight that even a grandma could dominate while sporting them. And he wanted to get it across by having Johnson, with his Zeus-like build, dressed up as a grandma.

As he wrapped his presentation with Johnson, there was a brief pause.

Favat's heart pounded again, as he was unsure of how Johnson would feel about the unorthodox idea. But after a moment or two, Johnson flashed his trademark grin, with the glimmering gold tooth. "We're doing this one for sure!" Johnson said, repeatedly tapping the sheet with the Fitzgerald mock-up. "We *gotta* do this one. I love it."

Even after Favat warned Johnson that it would be a risk, and that he might become inextricably linked to the image if they shot a commercial with him as a cross-dressing grandma, the forward was all for it.

Years after the marketing effort, which became a sales and pop culture hit in the early 1990s, what Favat recalls most is how easy it was to work with Johnson. "You go in thinking, 'This guy was such a badass at UNLV,' and have no clue how he'll be. He could've easily said, 'No, I *don't* want to be in a dress to start my career, because I won't be taken seriously as a player,'" Favat says. "But of all the guys I worked with—Magic, Bird, Kevin Johnson, Laimbeer—Larry Johnson was the most jovial. Just a fun, fun dude."

Johnson's commercial exploits prior to becoming a Knick were a microcosm for how easily he would get along with his New York teammates. (And a contrast from Mason, whose increased role under Nelson had begun souring his relationship with Ewing.) Similarly, players on the retooled roster seemed to genuinely like each other, perhaps because so many of them were new. In a shift from how things had operated in the past, the Knicks often sought to do activities as a larger group.

Eight or nine players from the team would always meet to have dinner on the road. While in Vancouver, the team gathered in a hotel ballroom to watch the heavyweight bout between Mike Tyson and Evander Holyfield. During a West Coast trip much later in the season, after a double-overtime win over the Lakers, the players partied in Los Angeles, even convincing Ewing, who rarely hung with teammates, to go to the Century Club for a night on the town. A sizable portion of the team prayed together, with six or seven players holding frequent Bible-study sessions led by Charlie Ward on road trips. The Knicks even *gambled* together far more during the 1996–97 campaign than they had in prior years.

Oakley, who enjoyed gambling more than anyone and carried around a brown duffle bag with a minimum of $50,000 in cash most trips, had grown annoyed when younger, lesser-paid Knicks said they didn't have enough cash on them to wager in the six-figure card games during flights. To get around the "I don't have enough cash" excuse, Oakley bought a credit-card imprint machine—and a pad of carbon-paper slips—to help facilitate teammates' bets that way instead. "It was one of those old, metal machines that went *click-click*," says Childs, referring to the credit-card scanner. "Let's say you owe him $2,000. He'd charge a fee for using the machine, and make it like $2,300. Basically a shylock. He was the Bank of Oak."

For all the risk involved with shaking up the roster—dealing away a key piece like Mason; making Starks, the onetime All-Star, a backup; bringing in Johnson, who theoretically could've challenged the 34-year-old Ewing as a No. 1 option—things went over smoothly because the players enjoyed each other, with very little drama.

Johnson, a player so unselfish that his high school and junior college coaches often chided him for passing too much, took a step back on offense by going from 15 shots a night to just under 10 that season. And Starks had no problem with coming off the bench for Houston, putting together an efficient campaign to win the Sixth Man of the Year award.

With their new weapons and a more balanced, less predictable offense to go with their stellar defense, the Knicks reeled off seven-game win streaks in both February and March. New York won 57 games that year and split four contests with Jordan and the defending-champion Bulls, with the two losses coming by a combined three points.

"We were really peaking at the right time. We were starting to roll," Grunfeld said. "Everything leading up to that point, it just really felt like that year was going to be our best shot to win."

With Charlotte's sellout crowd on its feet hoping to witness a late-game comeback in the final minute, Johnson drilled a dagger triple, deflating the same Hornets fan base he once dazzled.

As the forward backpedaled toward the Knicks' bench on the other end of the floor—all but having clinched a first-round sweep of his former team—he glared at the Charlotte sideline. All year, Johnson had heard about how Mason was outplaying him, and how the Hornets had gotten the better end of the deal. But at this moment, with Johnson having 22 points in a closeout game, revenge mattered far more.

"You get a lot of guys in this business who have just been spoon-fed," Oakley said. "But Larry? You can tell somewhere down the line Larry had to learn to eat soup with a fork." The by-any-means-necessary mentality made Johnson a solid fit with New York, even if he wasn't the dominant force he'd once been.

Following the first-round win, Johnson and the Knicks rolled their revenge tour into Miami, where they'd square off with ex-coach Pat Riley and the No. 2 seed Heat, winners of 61 games, in the semifinal round.

The backstories and relationships between the two sides were almost too many to count. Aside from Riley, there was Alonzo Mourning, who was close with Ewing (a fellow Georgetown alum), but had clashed with Johnson in Charlotte—a market that was ultimately too small for the two of them. There was the fact that Jeff Van Gundy's brother, Stan, was one of Riley's assistants. And there were the eerie similarities: Miami and New York, ranked No. 1 and No. 2 in defense, respectively, both thriving off their rugged physicality. Between those things, and their nearly identical play calls, the teams were carbon copies.

Now the sibling rivals were about to square off in the conference semifinals. "I hate them with all the hate that you can hate with," said Tim Hardaway, the All-Star point guard Riley had traded for one season earlier. "Can you hate more than that? If you can, I hate them more than that."

Like a pair of fighters who could anticipate each other's punches, Miami and New York slogged their way through the first four games, with neither club managing to score 90 points in a contest over that span. After splitting the first two battles, the Knicks took Game 3, then comfortably won Game 4, giving them a 3–1 series lead that put them on the cusp of matching up with the Bulls in the Eastern Conference Finals.

Being that close to getting another crack at Chicago had Starks daydreaming. "You know what it's like? It's like that toy you've wanted your whole life," Starks said of potentially winning an NBA championship.

"That's the only way you can describe it. We're getting too close now. We can taste it."

By contrast, Miami was on edge, feeling desperation. The day of Game 5, the Heat held a morning shootaround as Riley explained the stakes for his players. He asked if they were simply going to lie down.

"You guys are gonna have to scrap! You're gonna have to fight!" Riley urged his players.

Heat power forward P. J. Brown, in particular, was listening intently.

"I'm sitting right next to P.J. as Pat's putting that stuff in our heads," says Isaac Austin, a backup center on that Miami club and a friend of Brown's. "Then, Pat walks off and P.J. says, 'Man, if somebody does something to me [tonight], I'm gonna go off.' And you already know the story of what happened next."

Ask anyone and they'll tell you Brown was a gem of a human. One who visited libraries multiple times a year to read to children, and not only paid for, but also helped cook food for the homeless. Every third home game, Brown paid for dozens of underprivileged kids to be able to sit in the stands. "Maybe the nicest guy I ever dealt with," says Steve Popper, a writer who covered Brown and who's chronicled the sport for nearly two decades.

Brown, who won the NBA's Citizenship Award that season, was also a devout Christian. As was Charlie Ward. The two men, friends through their brotherhood in Christ, were in chapel praying together in the moments leading up to Game 5.

But with an 89–74 lead, and just 1:53 left to play, Miami had all but sealed a victory as Hardaway stepped to the line for a free throw. TNT cameras panned to New York's bench between the foul shots.

"Look at the Knick faces: they're all disappointed and mad, because they know the chance they had [to close this series]," said analyst Doc Rivers, the former Knick. "Now they have to fight for this series."

Just as Rivers finished that sentence, one of the more consequential fights in NBA history broke out.

Hardaway's second free throw put the Heat up by 16. But as his foul shot went down, Ward, the former Heisman Trophy winner, squatted down as he was boxing out Brown, pushing into the big man's knees. The 6-foot-11 Brown, taking issue with the nature of Ward's box-out—"He was going for my knees instead of trying to go for the rebound"—flipped out, and flipped Ward over, suplexing a player who stood nine inches shorter and weighed fifty pounds less. The reaction prompted Ward to jump to his feet and run at Brown, the man he had been praying with just three and a half hours earlier.

The explosive nature of the incident and the sheer size mismatch led many Knicks, just twenty feet or so from the action, to hop off the bench and have Ward's back. After all, this was the tight-knit New York club that did everything together. How could they *not* back up one of their leaders in a moment like this?

"It's literally a seven-footer coming in, picking on someone half his size," recalls John Wallace, who was in the game when the skirmish broke out, and was the first Knick to grab Brown in an effort to break things up. "Obviously, I'm just trying to protect my guy. I think that's all any of us were trying to do, honestly." (Miami's bench was on the other end of the floor from the incident, making the Heat players less inclined to get involved in the skirmish.)

The problem here, of course, was that in the years leading up to Game 5, the league had been cracking down on players leaving the bench to take part in fights. And between Greg Anthony hopping off the bench to throw a sucker punch in street clothes in 1993, and the brawl with Harper and Jo Jo English in 1994, the Knicks had played a bigger role than any other NBA team in those rules against fighting being fortified.

In Game 5, a few Knicks—Starks, Houston, and Johnson—ran all the way over from the bench to stifle the altercation. So did Van Gundy, who raced in, but now says he regrets not staying on the sideline to hold his players back. The ordeal lasted about thirty-five seconds. But much like Ward, New York's season got turned upside down in that moment.

With the Knicks leading the series 3–2 now, the question the following day was simple: which players, aside from Brown and Ward, were going to be suspended for their roles in the incident?

In the immediate aftermath of the incident, Starks, Houston, and Johnson came up in conversation, as they'd left the bench. It wasn't until much later that night of Game 5, though, that reporters started wondering about something else. Alternate angles and replays showed Ewing had also left the bench momentarily.

"We all said, 'Oh shit, really?' The rules were still new, and no one had really been held out or suspended just for leaving the bench before," recalls *New York Post* columnist George Willis. "In Patrick's case, he almost meandered onto the court, just to see what was going on. He clearly had no intention of instigating anything, or even to pull anyone apart. He just kind of wandered."

The Knicks pushed the following day's practice to early evening so they would definitively know who all would be allowed to play in Game 6. They were beside themselves when the league's ruling came down around 5 p.m.: six players were being suspended, with five of those suspensions being handed to New York.

Making matters worse, the penalties impacted the Knicks' most important players. Ward, Starks, Johnson, and Houston had all been docked a game. And it turned out that Ewing wouldn't be spared, either. Despite not getting anywhere near the altercation, the big man would be forced to sit out one game.

New York's punishments, the most severe penalty handed down in postseason history at the time, were so drastic that the suspensions would need to be split alphabetically—with three being served in Game 6, and two in Game 7—just so New York would have enough available players for each contest.

With about twenty-six hours until Game 6, the Knicks had their team of attorneys collaborate with lawyers from the National Basketball Players Association in hopes of getting the suspensions delayed the following morning in a Manhattan courtroom.

The high-profile situation put Jeffrey Kessler, the union's chief lawyer—who happened to be an enormous Knicks fan himself—in the spotlight. "I had this vision: we're gonna get the temporary restraining order, the players will be able to play, the Knicks will win, and I'll be able to revel in getting some justice for the players. That I would be able to say I contributed to the victory in a way," Kessler recalls years later.

Kessler and others worked overnight to prepare arguments that the league's leaving-the-bench rule was being enforced too harshly, and in a way that would irreparably harm the Knicks. Upon making the case for the players in front of District Judge Jed Rakoff—also a Knicks fan—Kessler felt he'd done all he could. Dozens of reporters were present when Rakoff emerged from his chambers with a decision two hours later. Rakoff went over his ruling point by point, taking almost twenty-five minutes to get through it all.

"There were basically five hurdles we needed to get over to get the restraining order," Kessler recalls. "He tells us that we met the criteria for the first hurdle. And the second hurdle. And the third hurdle. And the fourth hurdle. But then by the time he gets to the final one, he says our argument comes up short. We were completely crushed. And then of course I had to go call Patrick, and he was absolutely crushed."

In the end, Rakoff ruled the Knicks had clearly left the bench, something the union itself acknowledged.

And because the NBA rulebook was clear on what punishments would be doled out in such cases, the rules were the rules—even if they seemed excessive. "It was a legal question of whether David Stern was acting within his power and discretion. And the answer was yes: he had broad power to issue the suspensions," says Rakoff, whose wife told him not to come home that night, as their daughter's boyfriend was angry about his choice. "It wasn't the ruling I wanted to make, but it was also pretty clear."

Even with the suspensions, New York held its own early in Game 6 without Ewing, Houston, or Ward. The Knicks led, 66–64, at the Garden after three periods. But the shorthanded club, relying on seven men, ran out of gas in the fourth, allowing Miami to knot the series at three games each.

Ewing exploded for 37 points and 17 boards in his Game 7. But with Starks and Johnson forced to sit out, the Knicks weren't nearly as competitive as they'd been in Game 6. New York simply didn't have the horses, and fell, 101–90, in the series finale.

And with that, an entire campaign—one where the Knicks had outplayed a 61-win Miami team at full strength, and had played the defending-champion Bulls evenly all year—was down in flames. Another year the aging members of the core had come close, but fallen short in the postseason.

Houston openly wept into a towel in the visiting locker room after Game 7. A depressed Ewing stared blankly in the locker room, wondering what might have happened if not for the suspensions. "The commissioner took away a golden opportunity from me and my teammates," he said.

Not knowing how else to cope with the season-ending defeat, Van Gundy beat many of his players out to the team bus. Rather than take his seat at the very front like he usually did, Van Gundy instead stood behind the vehicle, crouching over a curb. Unsure of what the coach was doing, rookie forward John Wallace walked a little closer to him to get a better sense.

"He'd grabbed these pebbles off the ground that he was lining up on the curb. And based on how he was positioning them, you could tell he was diagramming our offense," Wallace recalls. "Our season ended an hour ago, and he's already looking at what we could've done differently. That's just how Jeff was wired."

The team's promising season earned Van Gundy a two-year extension. But the added job security didn't seem to help him sleep better. "It's not getting any easier," Van Gundy said weeks after the series loss to Miami. "Even with time, I don't know if [the pain of this loss] is something that totally goes away."

If there was any consolation, it was that New York's nucleus—starting with Ewing, their co-captain and twelve-year mainstay—looked strong, and seemed capable of making another run the following season.

17

SHATTERED

After a while, even metronomes found themselves in awe of Patrick Ewing's consistency.

At the suggestions of their coaches, Knicks rookies would usually arrive an hour early for practices to get shots up. The youngsters assumed they would be the first ones to punch the clock each morning. "But you'd get there, and you'd see Patrick. And you'd see two wet shirts on the floor, in the corner, because he'd sweat through them already," says forward John Wallace. "Hardest worker I've ever been around."

Ewing maintained that first-to-the-gym mindset in prosperous times as well as heartbreaking ones—like the morning after the Knicks lost the Charles Smith game in 1993, their most devastating defeat of the era. "He was there with a purpose: sending a message to the other players that there was no time for sulking," ex-teammate Doc Rivers said. "He knew it was a moment to step up and show the way."

The extent to which Ewing led—had to lead, really—was noteworthy.

Looking back at the entirety of that decade, few stars, if any, were surrounded by less firepower than Ewing. No, Reggie Miller—a far more one-dimensional player who had five All-Star appearances to Ewing's eleven—wasn't flanked by explosive teammates in Indiana early on. But he had a permanent mismatch, 7-foot-4 Rik Smits, to dump the ball to. Houston's Hakeem Olajuwon once griped and asked for a trade out of town, but that was before he and a near-perfect cast of Rockets role players beat the Knicks in 1994. (The next year, he partnered with Hall of Famer Clyde Drexler, his college teammate, to win it all again.) And while David Robinson had little around him in San Antonio, his broken foot in 1996 sank the Spurs to the bottom of the standings, allowing them to win the 1997 draft lottery—a victory that landed them Wake Forest's Tim Duncan, a generational player to pair with Robinson.

So if Ewing *wasn't* the NBA's most heavily relied-upon offensive player of the 1990s, the big man—who shot 50 percent and averaged 24 points during the decade up to that point—was very close to it.

By the fall of 1997, it had been six years since Ewing recommitted himself to the franchise after the Pat Riley hire. In that span, only once— during that first year with Riley—had the club finished with an offense that performed better than league-average. New York's attack, dubbed "The Gang That Couldn't Shoot Straight" by *Sports Illustrated*'s Jack McCallum, was the NBA's most predictable. "Windshield wipers offer more variety than the Knicks' offense," mused *New York* magazine writer Chris Smith.

For many years, their possessions often went something like this: a guard would dribble down to the wing and dump an entry pass into Ewing on the block. The center, forced to deal with the spacing of a crowded Twister mat, would turn and face the basket, deciding instantly whether he had enough time to get off a shot before a second and third defender could swarm. If he didn't have a good look, he would kick the ball out to reset the offense, or, in what was often a victory for the defense, set up a wide-open perimeter try for a shooting-deficient teammate. "If this were football, every time [his teammates] shoot, they'd be accused of intentional grounding," *New York Post* columnist Peter Vecsey wrote.

Every now and then, there was a pick-and-roll mixed in, or a cross screen to shake things up. When the universe allowed, a Ewing kick-out would lead to a made jumper by one of the guards. But even when players misfired, Ewing was often there to corral the miss, then gracefully put it back for a score. If his teammates were leaving messes, the 7-footer was the Bounty paper towel cleaning up after them.

So it wasn't surprising when Ewing simply decided to put the team on his back after the Knicks sputtered to an 11-9 mark to open the 1997–98 season. Feeling under the weather ahead of a December 11 game—hacking, coughing, and trying to plug a runny nose—Ewing brushed aside the flu-like symptoms to paint a masterpiece. In the third quarter of the home contest against Minnesota, he sank one rainbow jumper after another, after another. That period alone, the 35-year-old hit seven of his eight tries, all from ten feet out or more. He finished with 34 points, 12 boards, and three blocks, and New York won, 107–103.

Ewing's soft touch in the victory—which kicked off a stretch in which the Knicks stabilized, winning four of five—was the sort of feathery display that'd made him one of the best jump-shooting 7-footers in NBA history. Some, like Pulitzer Prize–winning writer David Halberstam, argued Ewing grew almost *too* skilled and comfortable with his outside shooting, saying it might have hindered the progression of his all-around game. "Like most professional basketball players, he chose to practice what he was already good at, shooting, rather than what was obviously hard for him, passing," Halberstam wrote.

Even without superior passing ability, Ewing was a rarity. He'd been a No. 1 pick who entered the NBA with the biggest expectations in fifteen years due to his showstopping defense. But then he exceeded those individual forecasts by turning out far better than expected on offense. He had no reputation whatsoever as a jump shooter coming out of Georgetown. But as an NBA rookie, Ewing put on a shooting clinic during a practice, effortlessly draining jumpers as Knicks scout Dick McGuire looked on, flabbergasted.

"Where the hell did you get that jump shot from?" asked McGuire, a Hall of Fame player and ex-coach with the franchise. "I thought all you could do was block shots, rebound, and dunk."

It wasn't an unfair assumption. When Ewing began his college career at Georgetown in 1981, coach John Thompson told Ewing he wanted him as close to the rim as possible. "[Coach Thompson] diagrammed a play where I'd run out to the corner and miss the shot on purpose, toward the front of the rim, so Patrick could grab the miss and dunk it," recalls Eric

"Sleepy" Floyd, Ewing's ex-teammate and Georgetown's all-time leading scorer. "I spent hours practicing missing from the corner. And I still tease Patrick about it to this day."

While Ewing wasn't allowed to shoot from outside the paint at Georgetown, he refined his stroke there behind the scenes, and kept working on it upon reaching the NBA. After hundreds of hours of before-practice sessions, Ewing had largely perfected the jumper. The right big toe pointing inward. The ever-so-slight dip and bend at the waist. The soft, waiter-like cradle of the basketball in his right, shooting hand. The high-arching, catapult-like release as the ball bid adieu from his fingertips.

And, perhaps most important: the effortless, split-second flick of the right wrist.

Strange things often happened with Ewing when Milwaukee popped up on the schedule.

There was the game against the Bucks, in which Charles Oakley barreled out of bounds for a loose ball; the kind of reckless, all-out effort Oakley always gave. But in this case, when he dove into the sea of courtside seats at the Garden, the 6-foot-9, 245-pound forward ended up in the third row, landing on top of Ewing's wife, Rita. (A Knicks physician escorted her to the locker room, and Patrick, who was seated on the bench, quickly joined them to ensure she was okay. She suffered a sore neck, but turned out to be fine.)

There was the fact that Ewing didn't sleep well during the club's trips to Milwaukee. Specifically, he wasn't a fan of the Pfister, the city's luxury hotel. The historic, century-old venue was known for its Romanesque style and world-class collection of Victorian art. But as far as the superstitious Ewing was concerned, the building was also known throughout league circles for being haunted by a ghost.

"Patrick was scared to death of the place. He said he'd heard ghosts there and stuff during his playing years," said coach Stan Van Gundy, Jeff's brother, who years later hired Ewing as an assistant with the Orlando Magic. "He complained about going to that hotel every time. In fact, because of him, one year we changed it up and actually stayed in another place in Milwaukee. . . . It's kinda funny. This big guy, who's very mature and very serious. But yeah, he was absolutely convinced that this hotel was haunted."

Ewing's worst Bucks-related memory, on the night of December 20, 1997, would turn out to be far scarier.

In the closing seconds of the first half at Bradley Center, guard Charlie Ward spotted Ewing open near the basket and took the rare step of throwing him an alley-oop. But just as Ewing had taken flight to dunk home the pass, Bucks forward Andrew Lang, a step behind on defense, inadvertently pushed the airborne Ewing just enough to throw off his balance under the rim, sending the franchise player clattering to the floor. On the way down, the 7-footer tried to brace for the fall by putting his right hand down first. But the descent was awkward and violent, spreading the impact of the thud between his hand and tailbone.

Ewing howled and writhed on the ground in pain, unable to move his right wrist as trainers raced onto the floor to help him. He'd lie on the ground nearly four minutes before going to the line to try to shoot his free throws left-handed. Both missed badly, forcing the Knicks to intentionally foul to get Ewing off the court.

As the shell-shocked Knicks walked into the locker room for halftime moments later, Ewing was already leaving the arena to get X-rays at a Milwaukee hospital with trainer Said Hamdan. They rode in the back of a van, with Hamdan taking stock of his condition. Hamdan took note of the player grimacing, sweating more profusely than usual, holding a white towel over his wrist; all signs of how searing the pain must be. He sensed Ewing was a bundle of nerves, perhaps wondering whether the injury might be career-ending.

The timing of the bad news, just before the half, helped the club get an important head start for team doctors back in New York, who would have more time to make sense of X-ray images that had been faxed in from Milwaukee before the Knicks' flight home. The images gave specialists a few hours to sketch out a surgical plan. But the damage shown on the radiographs left doctors stunned.

X-rays showed Ewing's right wrist, the one that had poured in more points than any other player in team history, had shattered. Doctors said the damage was so extensive that the break looked like the kind you might see in football, a car accident, or a fall from a third-story window. And with how bad things were, doctors would need to operate on the rare break, known as a right lunate dislocation, as soon as possible.

Time was critical because with a fracture dislocation, Ewing was at risk of not getting enough blood to the tissues around his wrist—a problem that could result in scarring and bone death. "The supporting structures of the wrist were totally destroyed and torn," recalls Dr. Susan Scott, one of Ewing's surgeons. Fixing it all was obviously a tall task. Aside from the small bones in his hand, his nerves, tendons, and ligaments had to be examined closely, since underlying damage to any one of those three groups could make it tougher for Ewing to enjoy the same sort of clutch, grip, and feel for the ball once he recovered.

At about 4 a.m., after Ewing got wheeled onto the second floor of the Beth Israel Medical Center–North Division and put under by an anesthetist, Dr. Scott and Dr. Charles Melone numbed the area around Ewing's wrist to ensure he'd feel no pain. There on the surgical table lay the Knicks' franchise player, covered by sterile drapes and illuminated by the room's bright overhead lights. The surgeons applied a tourniquet to his upper arm to temporarily stop blood from clotting around the hand as they prepared to go inside. Doctors drew on either side of Ewing's wrist to mark where they would make their incisions.

Over a span of two hours, the surgeons were able to repair the ligaments and piece Ewing's wrist back together. They put him in a cast he would be forced to wear for the better part of three months to make sure things healed. As the center woke from his drug-induced slumber, the surgeons told him the procedure had been successful, but that they weren't sure whether he would have the same range of motion he'd enjoyed before. It was too soon, they said, to know exactly when he'd be able to play again. They argued it made sense to proceed as if the Knicks star would miss the rest of the 1997–98 season.

Outside of Ewing himself, no one felt more lost than Jeff Van Gundy, who'd gone straight to the hospital once the team made it off the flight. He had a great fondness for Ewing, both because of his incredible work ethic, and because he'd always let Van Gundy—a little-known guy without the reputation of a Pat Riley—coach him, dating back to his days as a junior assistant.

From a work standpoint, Ewing's prognosis obviously wasn't music to Van Gundy's ears. One night earlier, he'd already seen what life might be like without the big man. Listless and lost in their star's absence, the Knicks fell apart after halftime in Milwaukee, losing by 20 points to the sub-.500 Bucks. Van Gundy tried throwing out a few strategic tweaks in the second half, using three- and sometimes even four-guard lineups for stretches. But neither alignment looked all that promising in the defeat.

After talking with Ewing in his hospital room briefly after the center's surgery, Van Gundy walked back into the waiting room at Beth Israel, where his assistants were sitting. The coach silently pondered what might become of Ewing's career due to the injury. How much time would he miss? Skill-wise, would he be the same after he finished what figured to be an arduous rehabilitation? All things that would become a bit clearer once more time passed. But then, as Van Gundy looked at his sleep-deprived coaches, he thought about his most immediate concern, one that would define the rest of the club's season.

"How are we supposed to win now?" Van Gundy asked the assistants.

In 1991, after years of effort, Pastor John Love thought he'd finally broken through.

In the years he'd served as New York's team chaplain, Love had established relationships with just about all the players—so much so that pregame prayer meetings were regularly near capacity. "It felt like the only guy not coming to chapel was Patrick," recalled Love, who considers Ewing a friend.

But on this day, just as Love and a number of players had gathered to begin a pregame session, Ewing came bursting in through the door. Before Love could even say how big a pleasure it was to have Ewing there, the big man—holding a double-cheeseburger in his right hand—clarified the reason he'd come. He wasn't looking to pray, or even be part of a prayer—he'd merely been looking for a safe place to devour the less-than-healthy pregame meal without trainers finding out. And, not knowing exactly what time chapel began, Ewing thought he'd made it to the room early enough to eat before the session started.

This was the fishbowl life of Patrick Ewing, where even eating a cheeseburger in private was a struggle.

One of the first times Ewing went out for a night on the town in New York City, to nightclub Studio 54 in 1985 with fellow teammate and draftee Fred Cofield, he had an amazing time. The Big Apple had an energy he'd never experienced. "He talked about how much fun he had for a couple of days," Cofield recalls.

But Ewing's euphoria from that night out wouldn't be replicated much, if at all. Instead, he'd quickly grow frustrated with how much his celebrity prevented him from being able to go a few minutes without being asked for a handshake, picture, or autograph. In the early days, he generally smiled and obliged. Yet the experience wore him down in a way. Cofield sensed Ewing—the No. 1 pick and the player expected to serve as the Knicks' savior at the time—had decided as a rookie that occasional nights out weren't worth the hassle anymore. He had become too much of a public figure to truly enjoy his time in public.

Teammates occasionally razzed him for not signing autographs when fans approached. So one time at Newark International Airport—just before the Riley era, when the Knicks would get their own plane—a young child walked up to Ewing in the terminal with a pen and piece of paper, asking for his signature. Ewing smiled, but politely said no. His teammates egged him on to sign, because it was a child.

Under pressure, Ewing made an exception to his rule, signing the autograph for the boy. Yet before he could finish, between twenty and thirty other kids in the area had begun making their way over to him to have things signed. "*This* is why I don't sign things," Ewing muttered under his breath to his teammates—players who ultimately couldn't relate to his level of fame or the demands on his time.

People often refer to Ewing as shy, and earlier in his life, that might have been true. In the fall of 1980, he took a recruiting trip to the University of North Carolina as the nation's most coveted high school player. (Not coincidentally, the school had a prospect named Michael Jordan visit campus that same weekend.) When Ewing had breakfast at a campus hotel with Roy Williams, then a Tar Heels assistant, the big man grabbed two thin, miniature glasses of orange juice as he walked through the cafeteria line.

"Big fella, go get more juice if you'd like," said Williams, who saw Ewing as an extremely quiet, polite kid, and knew the glasses weren't enough to quench Ewing's thirst. "Have as much juice as you want."

"Really? I can get as much as I want?" a smiling Ewing asked, just to be sure.

About a minute later, Ewing came back to the table with a tray filled with eighteen orange juice glasses on it. "He drank every single one of 'em, too," Williams recalls with a laugh. "He was thirsty that morning."

If there was a reason for Ewing's quiet nature, it stemmed from his upbringing and emigration from Jamaica. Born in 1962 as the fifth of Carl and Dorothy Ewing's seven children in Kingston, Patrick initially struggled with reading English and found it difficult to shed his strong Jamaican accent, which he got teased for at times upon moving to Cambridge, Massachusetts, as a 12-year-old. He took part in the Upward Bound program over summers in hopes of getting up to speed.

Boston wasn't the easiest place to be a young Black person in the 1970s. A 1976 Pulitzer Prize–winning photo titled *The Soiling of Old Glory*, which illustrates a white man trying to spear a Black man with the sharp end of an American flagpole, summed up the city's climate.

"This was during the turbulent time of forced busing in Boston to desegregate the city's schools," ESPN's Ian O'Connor wrote. "[Ewing's high school team] was a team of African-American students with an African-American coach, traveling to play in the largely white suburbs. Many who lived in those suburbs, Ewing's coach Mike Jarvis said, 'were folks who had left Boston. They were part of the white flight. Maybe it was too black for them in Boston, and it was very racist at the time.'"

Ewing enjoyed a dominant four-year run at Cambridge Rindge and Latin, going 77-1 en route to three state championships. But he and his teams also endured hatred. The tires of their team bus were slashed, and bus windows were smashed out by bricks people had thrown at them. Ewing, still new to life in the United States, eventually asked friends what the N-word meant after having the epithet hurled at him a handful of times as a teenager. Understandably, all of these things played a role in Ewing choosing to play at Georgetown for Thompson, a Black man strong in his convictions.

Thompson, whose societal awareness matched his towering, 6-foot-9 stature, had played for the Boston Celtics. So he had a sense of what Ewing had been subjected to before setting foot on campus, and what sorts of bigoted slights were sure to come at Georgetown. Among the worst: a "Ewing Can't Read 'Dis'" sign at a game at Providence; a bedsheet at Villanova that read, "Ewing Is an Ape"; and at the same game, a banana peel that a fan threw at Ewing's feet as starting lineups were being announced.

"When my father first played for the Celtics, the fans called him 'chocolate boy,' 'coon,' 'nigger.' You name it, he was called it. Almost three decades later, Patrick Ewing was facing the same sort of treatment, and in a way, I was reliving my father's experiences by watching it happen," wrote Karen Russell, a Georgetown classmate of Ewing's and daughter of Celtics great Bill Russell, whom Ewing drew frequent comparisons to.

All these things—the undeniable racism, the slights about his intelligence at a young age—played into Ewing being a more guarded, enigmatic figure. Thompson's efforts to keep the media at arm's length at Georgetown likely influenced this, too. With the Knicks, Ewing was standoffish with writers, saying, "That's it, fellas," when he abruptly ended media scrums. He barked at cameramen to watch his toes as they tiptoed through narrow locker room walkways far more than he ever offered a revealing detail about himself. ("I stepped on his foot by mistake once. I remember thinking, 'I'm a dead man,'" *New York Times* columnist George Vecsey says. "Instead, he smiled, and said it was okay. He was a much warmer guy than you'd think.")

So reporters had no idea that, early in his career, Ewing paid for each of his teammates to come down to spend a few days with him in his native Jamaica during the offseason. Or that Ewing would regularly tell the younger players to buy whatever they wanted at Friedman's Shoes during trips to Atlanta, because he'd pay for it. Or that when he learned the wife of Chris Jent—someone he was teammates with for just three months in 1996—developed a brain tumor, he and Van Gundy sent checks the next week to cover the entirety of her chemotherapy and radiation treatments.

Ewing was beloved by most teammates. But because his actions were behind the scenes, there were almost never fuzzy, humanizing portraits in the media about him. That made it tougher for fans to feel a connection with him, a contrast with less talented players like Oakley, John Starks, or Anthony Mason, who wore their hearts on their sleeve. "Patrick's greatest trait as a player was invisible: his loyalty. It's hard for people to appreciate a trait they can't see every day," says Selena Roberts, a Knicks beat writer.

That Ewing valued privacy and sought no credit for his good deeds likely made it even more difficult for him when a number of embarrassing stories about his personal life came to light around that time.

Earlier in 1997, he and Oakley were accused of sexually harassing a pair of flight attendants who served on the team plane. Both players denied the allegations, but the Knicks paid a six-figure settlement in the case, which played a role in the league mandating sensitivity seminars for every organization.

Years later, Ewing was dragged into testifying in a federal racketeering case that he'd accepted sexual favors, including oral sex, multiple times at the Gold Club strip joint in Atlanta, beginning in 1996. (Ewing enjoyed gentlemen's clubs, particularly in Atlanta. Bob Salmi, the assistant coach, said he once spotted Ewing from across the room at the Cheetah. As a prank, Salmi paid a woman to do a table dance for Ewing, telling her to say it was "paid for by Coach John MacLeod." Mortified by the idea that his head coach had seen him there, Ewing surveyed the club before seeing a laughing Salmi, a man much closer to him in age, instead. "Fuck you, Bob! That's not funny!" Ewing shouted.)

But the most damaging revelation emerged about a month after Ewing injured his wrist, in January 1998, when an extramarital affair he was having with a Knicks team dancer became tabloid fodder.

Though dancer-player relationships were technically forbidden by the organization, such relationships weren't all that unusual. Players often used ball boys to deliver phone numbers to dancers they found attractive. And in Ewing's case, there were multiple dancers he had relationships with over time.

The affair was a nonstarter for Rita, his wife of eight years, who quickly initiated separation proceedings. She hired a powerhouse divorce attorney three weeks later, and later that year published a novel with Crystal McCrary—then the wife of Greg Anthony—about the challenges of being an NBA spouse. (Surely it was mere coincidence the novel was built on the temptation swirling around a New York superstar, who plays for a clothes-obsessed coach and is represented by a powerhouse sports agent.)

His wife's decision to leave weighed heavily on Ewing. One woman he saw in the aftermath of the breakup says Ewing never so much as ventured toward the master bedroom of his home with female company. He viewed that room, the one he had shared with Rita, as sacred; almost museum-like.

Between his devastating wrist injury, isolating four-hour-a-day rehab sessions he had to endure to have any chance of returning for the playoffs, and his marriage blowing up publicly, it had been by far the most challenging year of Ewing's career. "Patrick was intensely private, and in looking at him, you could just sense that it all had taken something out of him," Roberts says. "He seemed hurt. Distant."

After years of carrying the Knicks on his back, the roles had finally reversed for Ewing.

Just before the season, he'd been elected president of the players union, a role that required him to monitor the situation involving Warriors star Latrell Sprewell, who'd initially been suspended for a calendar year—later reduced to the remaining sixty-eight games—for attacking coach P. J.

Carlesimo. In a way, there was more tangible work for Ewing to do in that role than there was with the Knicks, who simply needed him to heal. The center had a huge cast on his right arm through mid-February 1998. So Ewing had Oakley, who had served as his enforcer for a decade, fasten his ties in the locker room before each game.

The process of picking up the regular-season slack for Ewing wasn't easy for the Knicks. Van Gundy acknowledged there was a brief period of mourning within the team following their star player's injury. And while New York didn't fade into obscurity after losing him, the club had become painfully mediocre, alternating wins and losses for fifteen consecutive games at one point. At 32 years old, Starks was in the midst of his worst season as a Knick, struggling to play through heavy emotions, as his grandmother, who helped raise him, entered the final stages of a bout with breast cancer. Center Chris Dudley, who replaced Ewing, broke his foot in February, leaving the Knicks so thin that a sweat-drenched Van Gundy sometimes served as a tenth man in workouts so the team would have enough bodies to practice with.

If there was a bright spot for the Knicks, it was that they learned they could squeeze more out of certain players when needed. Together, Allan Houston and Larry Johnson went from combining to score 25.1 points per game before Ewing's injury to averaging 37.5 points in his absence, a nearly 50 percent boost. The contributions were just enough for New York to secure a playoff spot in its second-to-last game. And as a seventh seed with a 43-39 mark, the Knicks drew a rematch with rival Miami in the opening round—perhaps their best matchup as a low seed, since they already knew the Heat so well to begin with.

Van Gundy placed Ewing on his postseason roster even though he had just begun taking contact in practice again, and was a long shot to play in the Miami series. There was temptation to throw him in the mix when the Heat took a 1–0 lead in the best-of-five, and again after the Heat went up 2–1 after Game 3.

Then came the bizarre events of Game 4.

New York was on the brink of elimination, with a number of headwinds—Ewing's absence, Starks flying back in just before the game after his mother had emergency surgery, and Alonzo Mourning and Tim Hardaway catching fire—making it even more of an uphill battle. Yet while the Knicks allowed Mourning and Hardaway to score 29 and 33, respectively, they clamped down elsewhere, preventing any other Heat players from tallying double digits. In the closing seconds, it became clear the Knicks were going to prevail to send the series back to Miami for a decisive Game 5.

With six seconds left, and the Knicks up five, Hardaway fired up a prayer of a triple that missed badly. Starks grabbed the rebound, and the Garden crowd exploded before an array of whistles went off.

Mourning, who'd taken exception to a neck-level box-out from Johnson, had swung an unsuccessful right fist at Johnson's head. Which then prompted Johnson to swing, and miss, with a right hook of his own. The duo would trade two more punches—a right from Mourning, and a left from Johnson—that also connected with nothing but air. It was a lackluster display from Mourning (six-inch height advantage) and Johnson (five years boxing in a Dallas police-athletic league as a kid), who'd had bad blood for years, dating back to their days as jealous star teammates with the Hornets.

Van Gundy might've had the most embarrassing role in the scrap, though.

As the clock stopped with 1.4 seconds left in the contest, the diminutive coach came racing onto the scene to break up Mourning and Johnson. But it was an incredibly short-lived effort. As Van Gundy ran from the sideline to enter the fray, he nearly got clocked by Johnson's second swing. After narrowly avoiding the punch, he grabbed hold of Mourning with everything he had, sliding down the center's left leg as if it were a fireman's pole, then clinging to it to avoid being trampled at the bottom of a growing pile.

Oakley, maybe the NBA's toughest player, helped break things up before reaching down to save Van Gundy, who'd shown he'd do anything to stick up for his players.

"I get why people plead temporary insanity now, because I have no idea what I was thinking going in there," Van Gundy recalls years later.

Much like the fight between the Knicks and Heat the year before, this rumble took place in front of New York's bench. But unlike the previous time—when Ewing, Johnson, Starks, and Allan Houston left the bench, drawing one-game suspensions that cost the Knicks the series—the players largely stayed put in this instance. (Backup Chris Mills got suspended, but was the lone person to get dinged for leaving the bench area.)

For the second season in a row, Johnson would be forced to sit out the deciding game in Miami due to a suspension. The Heat got the worst of it, though, as they would have to sit Mourning—a big hole to fill for a team like Miami, where points were often hard to come by. Hardaway played all 48 minutes of Game 5 for that reason, but finished with just 21 points on 8-for-20 shooting. Houston, playing like a No. 1 option, finished with 30 points, while Starks and Oakley poured in 22 and 18, respectively.

With their 98–81 victory in Game 5, the Knicks had exacted some level of revenge, knocking off Riley and the 55-win Heat in the first round of the postseason despite not having Ewing available for the series.

After beating Miami, New York's hope was to bring Ewing back against Indiana midway through the semifinals, preferably after the Knicks jumped out to a series lead. After all, New York was familiar with the Pacers, too, having met them in the playoffs three times in the four prior postseasons. So matching up with a stylistically similar rival might benefit the Knicks again.

But these weren't the same old Pacers anymore. By the 1997–98 season, Indiana had improved considerably on offense, posting the league's fourth-most-efficient attack—up from a middle-of-the-pack No. 15 ranking the year before. Aside from the usual suspects—Reggie Miller, Rik Smits, Antonio Davis, and Dale Davis—the Pacers now had veteran sharpshooter Chris Mullin and slasher Jalen Rose, best known as the brash ball handler who'd played for Michigan's Fab Five teams. Even on nights where they didn't score a ton, the Pacers had a depth and diversity to their offense that hadn't always been there. And that was more than the Knicks could say for themselves as the East semifinals began.

Indiana took Game 1 by 10 points. Based on that result, Ewing then decided he would play Game 2—something he'd later admit might've been a bit rushed, due to the Knicks being behind in the series.

After going 138 days without real action, Ewing's game was in dire need of some WD-40. He quickly learned that the postseason, against a 58-win club, is a challenging place to try to knock off the rust. The defense looked like a bigger challenge to start, as he picked up two fouls in a little over three minutes, earning him a quick trip to the bench in the first quarter. Ewing then landed a third personal shortly after getting another opportunity in the second period, meaning he'd enter halftime without a basket, at 0-for-4.

The second half was marginally better, but had its share of lowlights. In one sequence, Ewing was being rejected at the rim. In another, he was pickpocketed by Smits, a glacially slow defender, which led to a layup on the other end of the floor. Ewing finished just 3-for-11 with 10 points as the Knicks—overly stagnant in his return—mostly stood around and watched. The Pacers won again, 85–77, to go up 2–0.

Things were certainly better in a Game 3 victory at the Garden, where Ewing had 19 points on 16 shots, a commendable effort given how serious his wrist injury had been four and a half months earlier. But unfortunately for New York, the fourth and fifth games of the series played out more like Game 2.

In the end, after Indiana took down the Knicks in five games to end their season, the airwaves in New York City lit up like a Christmas tree, with callers wanting to discuss an array of issues. Houston's 33-point showing in the closeout loss seemed to suggest his readiness for a bigger offensive role. The *Daily News* reported that Starks brought golf clubs to Indianapolis for Game 5—and that some of his teammates were incensed by it—while the Knicks were in a 3–1 series hole. But the 7-foot elephant in the room involved Ewing, and whether the 35 percent shooting against the Pacers was merely a function of rust, or if this was the new reality for an aging star who might not ever be the same after his wrist injury.

"To me, it was never a question of whether we were better with or without him. We *always* had a better chance with him," Van Gundy says decades later. "But while it wasn't a career-ending injury for Patrick, it was certainly career-altering. His body was healthy, but his wrist was forever altered after that."

18

HEART TRANSPLANT

After four consecutive second-round playoff exits, something needed to change.

That had become clear in the Eastern Conference semifinals, as Indiana sliced and diced its way through the Knicks in five games. The more-athletic Pacers had gotten to the line almost 60 percent more often in the series—disheartening for the Knicks, who'd spent big two years earlier to get younger and quicker.

By the summer of 1998, the Knicks were the league's fifth-oldest team, with all four of the older clubs—the Rockets, Bulls, Sonics, and Magic—having reached the Finals more recently than New York in 1994.

Thirty-six-year-old Patrick Ewing, who held the NBA's highest salary at $20 million after Michael Jordan's retirement in 1998, was still getting used to his surgically repaired wrist. He wasn't at risk of being traded. But in Ernie Grunfeld's mind, just about everyone else on the club's aging roster was fair game.

So, on June 24, the afternoon of the 1998 draft, Grunfeld picked up his phone. He dialed Glen Grunwald, the general manager of the Toronto Raptors, a fourth-year franchise that had logged just 16 wins the prior season—15 fewer wins than the second-to-last-place 76ers.

Grunfeld knew it had been a tough go for the Raptors during their brief existence. The organization, which drew its mascot from a 1994 fan vote influenced by hit film *Jurassic Park* a year earlier, had an uphill climb out of the gate. After the Orlando Magic won the NBA's draft lottery two years in a row, in 1993 and 1994, league officials told the expansion Raptors and Vancouver Grizzlies they wouldn't be eligible to land the No. 1 pick in 1996, 1997, or 1998.

So even though Toronto won the lotto drawing in 1996, the Raptors were relegated to the No. 2 spot (Marcus Camby), instead of the top pick (Allen Iverson), which went to Philadelphia. The expansion draft, which allowed the Raptors to pull players from other rosters to help establish their own, wasn't ideal, either. Toronto took B. J. Armstrong with the No. 1 pick, but the three-time NBA champion refused to report to camp, because . . . who really wanted to move to Canada to go play for a brand-new team?

"It was like going from the NBA to a [junior varsity] team. Or from a first-class operation to an operation that was still trying to figure out what it should be doing," says John Wallace, who'd been traded from the Knicks to the Raptors the year before. "There were times I'd get into it with [coach Darrell Walker], because I'd want to practice—and we needed practice, because we weren't good—but instead we'd just get another day off. We had talent. But we were young, and didn't practice much. And it showed."

The Raptors desperately needed veterans who could help establish a winning culture in Toronto. Knowing this, Grunfeld began making his sales pitch to Grunwald. Specifically, he wanted to know whether Grunwald would consider dealing the 24-year-old Camby, a highly kinetic big man who had just led the league in blocks, in exchange for the ever-reliable Oakley, who'd spent a decade with the Knicks as the face and linchpin of their stout, Wrestlemania-style defense.

It took some restraint for Grunwald to not shout "Yes!" upon hearing New York's offer. Between Oakley's toughness, durability, leadership, and accountability, he was exactly the sort of player Toronto needed on its roster to make a jump. Nonetheless, the Raptors' general manager opted to let his coach, Butch Carter, join the phone discussion with Grunfeld. And then something strange happened: rather than talk up Camby, as a way to extract more out of the Knicks in a swap, Carter actually began doing the opposite.

Sure, Camby had obvious talent, and would almost certainly reach greater heights as he entered his prime years. But he also was a player who, in Carter's mind, lacked the maturity and discipline a contending team like the Knicks would require. "This was a guy who was smoking up every tree in Toronto," Carter says. "He lived in the condo above me, but sometimes would just decide to not come to practice. He was injury-prone. Literally none of that stuff fit the culture that'd been built in New York."

Without saying too much, Carter asked Grunfeld if he was totally sure he was ready to swap one of his touchstone players for Camby. "Ernie was a friend and an old teammate of mine who had taught me so much about life," Carter says, recalling an eye-opening book Grunfeld had given him about Eastern European Jews immigrating to America in the late 1800s and early 1900s. (Grunfeld, born in Romania in 1955, was the son of Holocaust survivors.) "I was trying to save him from taking Marcus."

But Grunfeld wasn't interested in being talked out of the deal. So after brushing off Carter, he asked Grunwald if the general managers could complete the talks on their own. Soon after, they did just that, making a swap that would officially send Camby to New York for Oakley, the 44th pick (Sean Marks), and cash, to help the financially strapped Raptors cover a portion of Oakley's $10 million salary.

Seconds after Grunwald completed the call and hung up the phone, Carter looked at his boss and spoke bluntly. "Glen, I'm telling you right now: this trade is gonna end up costing Ernie his job," Carter said.

Charles Oakley didn't take the news well. He was trying not to take the news at all.

Sure, the 34-year-old forward had heard about the deal happening. But he still hadn't come to grips with the fact he'd be leaving New York. So he did the only thing he could do. As Grunfeld sought to phone and officially inform him the trade was being completed, Oakley repeatedly dodged Grunfeld's calls.

Oakley didn't make the process any easier for the Raptors. Later that week, after the team bought him a flight to Toronto, Grunwald and Carter waited to greet Oakley at Pearson International Airport as passengers exited their aircrafts. But the big man was nowhere to be found.

In another situation, a no-show could perhaps be seen as a mere mix-up. But that wasn't the case here. Grunwald knew Oakley wasn't happy about being a Raptor. He also knew the clock was ticking, loudly, on the deal, and that the league would void it in twenty-four hours if Toronto couldn't get Oakley to report for a physical.

So with the deadline looming—a lockout would begin one night later, prohibiting NBA teams from contacting their players—Grunwald and Carter flew down to Atlanta themselves to get Oakley.

When they arrived at Hartsfield-Jackson International Airport, they didn't have a direct line to Oakley, but managed to reach one of his acquaintances, who shared the power forward's whereabouts. Racing against the clock, Grunwald and Carter found Oakley inside the Atlanta Ritz-Carlton's fitness center, bench-pressing.

In the weight room, Grunwald and Carter pleaded with Oakley to make the trip back to Toronto with them. "He didn't want to leave the Knicks. And we told him we could fully appreciate and understand why he might not be excited about being traded to us, but that we really needed him," Grunwald recalls.

After a half hour, Grunwald and Carter won the arm-wrestling contest with the iron-willed hulk. Then, the trio left for the airport, officially cementing the Knicks' longtime glue guy as a Toronto Raptor.

As the Knicks turned the page on Oakley, the NBA owners officially locked out their players, setting the stage for a work stoppage that figured to impact New York more than most clubs. First, the wait to get back on the floor would make an old team even older whenever things ramped back up. And Ewing, as president of the players association, wouldn't have the time to get back in a rhythm with his wrist due to the long days at the negotiating table his role would require.

Money was at the heart of the lockout. Specifically, the question of whether revenue was being split fairly between owners and players, whose contracts were skyrocketing. Were huge deals—like Shaquille O'Neal's for seven years and $120 million, or Kevin Garnett's for six years and $126 million—giving stars too much power? Or was it better for more power to be held by David Stern and the owners?

In a way, that question had uncomfortably bubbled to the surface a year earlier, after three-time All-Star Latrell Sprewell choked Warriors coach P. J. Carlesimo at a practice in December 1997. The attack took place moments after Carlesimo told Sprewell to start throwing crisper passes to teammate Muggsy Bogues during a shooting drill. Sprewell had grown tired of Carlesimo's critiques and felt provoked by them. After Sprewell reacted, Carlesimo kicked him out of practice. "I'll kill you," Sprewell said at one point, confronting the coach before grabbing Carlesimo by the neck, which was left scratched and rubbed raw.

Sprewell then left the court to go to the locker room before coming back out minutes later and going after Carlesimo a second time. As a result, Stern issued Sprewell a one-year suspension, the longest penalty in NBA history for a non-drug-related offense.

When the lockout ended on January 20, 1999—after 204 days of gridlock and the longest labor dispute in league history—it was inevitable Golden State would trade Sprewell to give both sides a fresh start.

Knowing this, members of the Knicks front office wondered whether New York should be the place for Sprewell to do it.

The 28-year-old swingman stood 6-foot-5, with cornrows and a sinewy build, and possessed undeniable talent on both ends. He'd been named to the NBA's All-Defense team once, and averaged 20 points per night for his career. He could take over games. He logged 41 points in a showing against the Knicks' top-rated defense in 1994—a performance so dominant that it prompted Pat Riley to draw a brief comparison to Michael Jordan during his postgame remarks to reporters. Someone of Sprewell's ilk could absolutely help the Knicks get over their stubborn second-round hump.

Yet talent wasn't the question here. Even though Grunfeld and Jeff Van Gundy wanted him badly, the idea of bringing Sprewell—perhaps the nation's most demonized athlete at the time—to New York was a risk of epic proportions. And given the unusual nature of the scenario, Dave

Checketts said he wouldn't give his blessing for such an acquisition without having a face-to-face conversation with Sprewell first.

So after some mid-January haggling between the Knicks and Warriors on a potential trade package for Sprewell, the teams reached a preliminary agreement on a deal. But prior to finalizing the trade, Checketts made a highly unusual request of Stern: can we sit down with Sprewell before officially completing the deal?

Golden State was fine allowing it if it meant helping the deal along. But Stern had reservations about allowing the Knicks to set up the meeting; so much so that Checketts began wondering whether the commissioner was against the idea of having a polarizing player like Sprewell in the league's biggest media market.

But one day later, Stern circled back and said he'd allow the Knicks to talk with Sprewell. "Honestly, if I was running a team, that's a conversation I would want to have, too," Stern told Checketts.

Upon making it to Sprewell's modest three-bedroom home in Milwaukee on January 17, 1999, Ed Tapscott, Grunfeld, Van Gundy, and Checketts shook the swingman's hand and sat in his living room.

Van Gundy asked for a Diet Coke before giving a spirited description of how he saw Sprewell fitting the rest of the roster from an X's-and-O's standpoint. Grunfeld explained what all the organization did on a day-to-day basis to make its players feel at ease, both while in New York and on the road. Tapscott used his opportunity to walk Sprewell through how he could use the massive market, and the Garden in particular, as a canvas to paint a new life portrait and move on from the run-in with Carlesimo.

Then Checketts, who hadn't said much yet, politely asked the other three team representatives if they'd go sit out in the car so he could talk one-on-one with Sprewell. He didn't have any sales pitches to make. More than the other three men, Checketts wanted a sense of whether Sprewell had truly reflected on his mistakes.

Of course Checketts wanted to know if Sprewell was remorseful for going after Carlesimo. But he'd also been bothered by a story from a few years earlier, when one of Sprewell's pit bulls attacked his four-year-old daughter, severing her right ear in the process. The issue that didn't sit well with Checketts: when asked by reporters about that traumatic episode in 1994, Sprewell responded, "Shit happens."

"Look, I'm a father with six kids, and they mean more to me than anything," Checketts said to Sprewell, saying he found the player's response to be callous. "I told myself, '[Sprewell] is totally out of touch.'"

At that point, Sprewell got up and walked into a separate room before coming back out to the living room with his daughter. By this point, she was eight years old, with long, flowing braids and wearing a dress. With Sprewell looking on, Checketts spent ten minutes or so talking with the girl about her school and her interests, gathering that she was a happy, well-adjusted child. Then she walked back to her room.

Sprewell looked Checketts in the eye. "If you think I wasn't mortified by this, or that this didn't absolutely destroy my family, you really don't understand," he said of the dog's attack on his daughter. Sprewell then went into detail about the work it took to repair his little girl's physical and mental scarring.

As for the "shit happens" response Sprewell gave, he explained he'd said it only to limit the amount of detail the media had. He wanted his daughter to be able to maintain a degree of privacy after the accident.

Sprewell said he wished he could go back and change what he'd done the day of the Carlesimo confrontation, adding that he'd spoken to the coach multiple times since the episode to reiterate how out of line he was for attacking him.

After forty-five minutes, the men wrapped their talk. Checketts was walking to the door when he noticed something he still remembers about that day. Framed near the entrance of Sprewell's home was the poem titled "Footprints in the Sand," a religious work in which two sets of footprints—God's and a believer's—merge into one set, leading the believer to question why God would abandon her at a clear time of need.

Why was God no longer beside her?

As despair settled back over her, she began to cry.

Then the inner voice of God softly spoke and said,
"I have not left you. The one set of footprints is mine."

Checketts, of strong Mormon faith, asked Sprewell about the poem. About its takeaway—that God picks up believers and carries them through their toughest moments—and the notion that perhaps God had just carried Sprewell through a highly tumultuous year. He then shook Sprewell's hand and left, feeling far more at ease about bringing the controversial player to New York. Latrell Sprewell would be a Knick.

The move came with a cost, though. Along with Terry Cummings and Chris Mills, the club had to part ways with guard John Starks, who for eight seasons had served as the team's emotional heart and soul.

A couple of days before the trade became official, Starks's young son, John Jr., heard the deal being rumored in the media, and asked his dad if it meant he'd have to leave his school.

"Yeah, maybe," the elder Starks told him. "I'm not sure."

"But Dad, we've already been out to Golden State," the boy contended.

So much had changed since that initial, rookie stint with the Warriors. Starks had been the embodiment of the Good (the dunk over Michael Jordan and Horace Grant in 1993), the Bad (the costly 2-for-18 performance in Game 7 of the Finals in 1994), and the Ugly (the Reggie Miller headbutt in the 1993 playoffs). He'd gone from nearly being cut to becoming an All-Star and the second-most-important player on a title contender. He'd gone from having a coach who trusted him to a fault to one who loathed him.

Yet for all the guard's ups and downs, no one could ever question Starks's heart.

"Later on down the line, I'll probably shed a tear or something," Starks told reporters after the deal.

Yet even if Starks didn't shed a tear in that moment, it's a safe bet that plenty of Knicks fans did. Within months, two of the team's three decade-long mainstays had been shipped to other addresses. And given the roster overhauls and the Jordan-less, lockout-shortened season, no one knew what to expect next.

*   *   *

Dating back to the Riley era, the Knicks had committed to being the NBA's most conditioned team.

Those clubs accomplished the feat a few different ways. There were the unforgiving, running-intensive two-a-day training camp practices to kick off every season. And aside from the six or seven hours those workouts ate up, players were expected to lift weights each day, too, or else they'd face $500 fines.

Even prior to those camp workouts, members of those veteran rosters were expected to keep themselves in shape over the summers. The team monitored that process by having Greg Brittenham, the strength and conditioning coach, visit and work out with each player four separate times—and in Ewing's case, once every single week—in the summer, regardless of where they spent their offseason.

But in 1999, after dealing away long-standing vets like Oakley and Starks—and with team officials prohibited from communicating with their players during the lockout—the notion of collectively keeping the Knicks in shape was far more difficult this time around. Especially with just eighteen days between the end of the lockout and the regular-season opener.

Van Gundy knew this would be the case. He tried his best to motivate his players through the media by praising rival Indiana for gathering as a team to stay in shape and establish cohesion in the time away.

A few Knicks showed up totally prepared. Allan Houston had been diligent with his workouts. So had Larry Johnson, who'd dropped twenty-five pounds, both to be health conscious and to observe Ramadan.

Still, by and large, the Knicks were looking much larger than they should have on the first day back to work. Ewing in particular stood out, having ballooned at least twenty pounds or so; the result of being stuck in players association negotiations during the six-month lockout. "With Patrick, it's tough, because he's a guy that's prone to weight gain," says Said Hamdan, an assistant trainer that season, referencing Ewing's metabolism. "In his case, we worked really hard to keep him within a target weight, because we needed to. We didn't want him carrying the extra weight on his ankles, his knees, his calves, or his Achilles."

Sprewell hadn't picked up weight. But he also hadn't played organized basketball in fourteen months, and grew winded quickly early on. It was a departure from his usual stamina, which, according to college teammates, allowed him to use the StairMaster for an hour at the highest level without even sweating hard.

Camby, another high-profile newcomer, physically looked the part after hiring a personal trainer to help him build muscle following the trade. But Van Gundy was less than pleased with Camby's effort in the first week of workouts, at one point saying that "his work capacity, previous to today, was not acceptable"—a jarring critique to hear about the man who'd replaced Oakley, who often begged coaches to practice more.

Yet the player in the worst shape during camp was rotund free agent Dennis Scott, a three-point specialist who'd shot 40 percent from three in his career alongside O'Neal and Penny Hardaway in Orlando.

Scott had long struggled with his weight, dating back to his first two years of college, when he went from being 210 pounds as a high school senior to 260 pounds as a sophomore at Georgia Tech. As he grew heavier, Scott became more reliant on his jumper, which often worked, since he'd become proficient from deep. Nonetheless, Bobby Cremins, his college coach, threatened to bench Scott if he didn't slim down.

Dropping the pounds made Scott more explosive and versatile again, and he'd enjoyed an eight-year career, averaging 14 points a game, prior to joining the Knicks. But from New York's very first team workout, Scott looked closer to the 260-pound version of himself—perhaps even heavier—than the 230 pounds he'd settled at as a professional. Based on that, everyone knew it'd be a while before he could contribute in a meaningful way. "Obviously, he needs to get in a lot better condition before he can play," an annoyed Van Gundy said of Scott after watching the 30-year-old suck wind throughout the practice.

*   *   *

As one might expect, given the lack of preparedness and conditioning, bodies gave out quickly.

That was the case throughout the NBA, but especially in New York. Just two games into the season, Sprewell was on the shelf, the result of a stress fracture in his right heel that'd keep him out four weeks. Johnson needed an MRI scan on his left knee after the Knicks' ninth game, and gave thought to the idea of sitting out because of how diminished he was in the minutes he played. And by Game No. 18, Ewing was in so much agony he had to take himself out of a contest just twenty-nine seconds in. He'd limped over to the bench with a sore left Achilles tendon, an ailment that would keep him out for nearly a week and a half.

But time was something New York didn't have much of. Not in a lockout-shortened year, which saw teams playing fifty games each over an eighty-five-day span. Never before had the calendar been this unforgiving. In one particular stretch, the Knicks had five games slated in six nights, spread across four different cities.

The team's defense worked hard, and was among the NBA's best, like always, holding opponents to 38 percent shooting through twenty games. But the offense—first with Sprewell out, then Ewing—played like a group of complete strangers, and was often brutal. In a March 12 game against the lowly Bulls, who were now without Jordan, Scottie Pippen, and Dennis Rodman, the Knicks somehow mustered just *five* points in the second quarter. New York entered the fourth period with 33 points. And, in scoring only nineteen baskets in the 76–63 defeat, the club tied a record for the fewest field goals in a shot-clock-era game in NBA history.

After the disconcerting loss, which dropped the Knicks to an underwhelming 11-9 on the year, the team held a thirty-minute players-only meeting in the visiting locker room. In the somber summit, Johnson, a co-captain, owned his showing: 1-for-5, while struggling to defend Toni Kukoč, who'd finished with 25 points.

During the team's flight back home to New York, Scott—who played ten scoreless minutes and was shooting 30 percent and averaging 2.9 points through his first fifteen games—sought to lighten the mood, cracking jokes on the plane. In a way, this was who Scott had always been: a lighthearted person who often looked for ways to laugh in overly tense situations.

By contrast, that was *not* who Van Gundy was. The coach, often miserable in normal circumstances, was far more miserable after losses. Following home defeats, those who traversed the Garden's hallways knew they might hear Van Gundy shouting, tipping over his desk, or punching a wall in his office. And whenever the Knicks played on the road—win or lose—Van Gundy usually had limited patience for outbursts on the team plane.

"We were on a flight coming back from a preseason [win], and I got in trouble for yelling, 'Yes! Let's go Mets!' after they clinched a spot in the World Series [in 2000]," says Hamdan, the club's assistant trainer. "The next day, he calls me into his office and says I need to have more respect for the sanctity of winning and losing. And I told him: 'Jeff, the sanctity of winning and losing is why I yelled "Let's go Mets!" They just made the World Series!' And he just looks at me and says, 'Get the fuck outta my office.'"

Van Gundy let Hamdan slide with a warning. But Scott wouldn't enjoy that same grace. Seeking to send a message, the coach made a bold, unilateral choice to bypass Grunfeld and cut Scott from the team the morning after the flight.

The move evoked a feeling that *something* had to give for these Knicks, who were barely .500.

And soon, something would.

19

LONG-TERM PARKING

April 9, 1999, had great potential to be the day Jeff Van Gundy lost his job.

Heading into their game in Atlanta that night, the Knicks had lost seven of their last ten; the most recent being a 24-point thumping by the Hornets, a 13-20 team New York had dominated in the two seasons prior.

The Knicks were disastrous on offense in the first quarter, tallying just 12 points as Charlotte built a 17-point edge. New York's defense resembled Swiss cheese in the second, falling even further behind despite the Knicks shooting 11-for-19 in the period. The team's effort was ghastly in the third, leading Van Gundy to shout profanities at Allan Houston, who'd given up on a play by letting Hornets guard Eddie Jones cruise in for an uncontested transition layup. And by the fourth, the game was so over, Van Gundy never even bothered to sub in Patrick Ewing, his best player that night. There was no point.

Making matters worse: the embarrassing defeat, at the hands of a Charlotte team that had lost five straight, came after a pregame meeting in which the imperiled Van Gundy pleaded with his players to leave everything they had on the court. Yet instead of a passionate showing, the coach had gotten one that was empty. "I would say just by watching [us] play . . . that we are teetering," Van Gundy said.

Teetering mentally. Teetering emotionally. And, in tenth place with an 18-17 record despite having the NBA's highest payroll, teetering in the Eastern Conference playoff race with just fifteen games left to play.

Against that backdrop, it was completely conceivable, if not expected, that Ernie Grunfeld would suggest firing Van Gundy if the team dropped its next contest, a Friday night road tilt against the 22-14 Hawks.

If things reached that point and Grunfeld pulled the trigger, there would have been a backstory to it all.

The shortened season began on a head-scratching note, when Marcus Camby—who along with Latrell Sprewell was one of the team's glitzy offseason acquisitions—logged less than six minutes of playing time over the first two games of the campaign. (The Knicks losing both those contests didn't help matters much.)

Van Gundy had certainly been critical of Camby's lack of conditioning in the first few days of the big man's New York tenure. Camby was "treating drills at room temperature as if they were suicide sprints in the Mojave," columnist Ian O'Connor wrote of the 24-year-old. Days later, Camby sat out a preseason game, complaining of a blister on his foot—the sort of marginal injury that wasn't exactly endearing him to Van Gundy.

"He still has a ways to go, but you can't change [bad] habits in three or four days. He's going to be a work in progress the entire year," Van Gundy said of Camby just before the regular season began.

Then, literally five minutes into his home debut as a Knick, Camby nearly collapsed in the second period on the way to the sideline, telling Van Gundy he was too exhausted to stay on the floor. Annoyed by Camby getting winded that quickly, the coach never even bothered subbing him back in later in the game.

In just a week's time, Camby had shown multiple ways—the blister, and the exhaustion after just five minutes—in which he wasn't Iron Man Charles Oakley, who once put off the idea of surgery as he played through a dislocated toe, and stayed in a game after breaking a bone in his left hand.

Fair or not, this was Van Gundy's gripe. Between Oakley's leadership, punishing defensive style, and punch-the-clock mentality, he was a singular player in the coach's eyes. It was why Van Gundy never wanted to part with Oakley in the first place, even if he was 35 and in the twilight of his career.

The coach had voiced his preference to keep Oakley prior to the deal being made. But some in the organization felt Van Gundy's stance on the situation became far more critical after the trade took place.

"Jeff noticed early in camp that we were in trouble without some of the intangibles that Oakley brought. But it wasn't like he'd laid on the tracks and said 'Over my dead body' when we discussed trading Oak. If he'd said something like that, we probably don't do the deal," says Dave Checketts. "But he didn't."

Camby possessed incredible athletic ability and arms that extended seemingly forever. But without Van Gundy's trust, he averaged just eighteen minutes per game off the bench the first two months of the season. It put Van Gundy and Grunfeld at odds, with the coach quietly stewing over losing Oakley's reliability while the general manager grew increasingly annoyed at not seeing the player he'd traded for get more of a chance from one night to the next. And the team's season sinking into disarray only ratcheted up the frustration.

"From my standpoint, I could've done a much better job communicating," Van Gundy says decades later. "At that point, I was so indebted to Oakley, and still really didn't know all that much about Marcus yet."

The clash, which took place in the city's tabloids largely through anonymous sourcing, amplified in April, with reports being floated about the flimsiness of each man's job security. And on the night of that game in Atlanta, Checketts did nothing to put either person at ease. "I don't think there's anyone who escapes scrutiny as we look at the situation around us," he said, leaving all options on the table.

Ironically, in that must-win game for Van Gundy in Atlanta, Camby, of all people, returned from a three-game injury absence to spark the Knicks. His nine points, five rebounds, and stout rim protection in nineteen minutes helped New York outscore the Hawks by nine points in the time he was on the floor—key contributions in an eight-point road victory that helped Van Gundy see another day as coach.

Much like the Road Runner had always outfoxed Wile E. Coyote, Van Gundy consistently staved off the grim reaper. Each time he seemed to run out of real estate, the coach escaped by starting a mini win streak. And sure enough, the triumph in Atlanta would be the first of three straight wins for the Knicks.

Every morning, at around 6:45, team public relations official Sammy Steinlight would arrive in the office to begin going through the seven local newspapers that covered the Knicks each day.

After reading each piece—"every day, every clip, every word," he says—Steinlight and his coworkers would begin the process of photocopying them all in order to create enormous media packets with the day's Knicks coverage in each one. They would then distribute the packets. Some would go to reporters, both local and ones from out of town, to cover whomever the Knicks were playing. Some went to the coaches. Some went to Grunfeld and Checketts, if they cared to look. Then copies of these packets would be prepared for those who cared most about the media whispers: the team's ownership.

About two years earlier, in March 1997, there had been a meaningful shift within the club's ownership structure. ITT sold its 50 percent stake in Madison Square Garden properties to corporate partner Cablevision, the massive, Long Island–based cable system operator and programmer. The deal paved the way for Cablevision and its controlling family, the Dolans, to own the Knicks outright.

It didn't take long at all for Van Gundy to realize how different things would be under Cablevision.

Months after the playoff-altering skirmish between Charlie Ward and P. J. Brown in 1997, Van Gundy, his coaching staff, and members of the front office were in Charleston for training camp when they had lunch with Marc Lustgarten and James Dolan, the chairman and vice chairman of Cablevision, respectively.

The expectation was that it'd be more of a lighthearted, getting-to-know-you lunch, since Van Gundy and the other coaches hadn't spoken with the men at length before. Instead, minutes after they'd all finished eating and gotten the small talk out of the way, Dolan grew shockingly direct.

"I just want to say that if anything like that Miami [fight] ever happens again—where we lose control of the team—I will hold you directly responsible for it," Dolan said, looking at Van Gundy as he spoke.

Van Gundy defused things by owning the criticism. "We could've handled it better," he told Dolan.

Still, Checketts seethed. Dolan's comment had blindsided everyone, especially Van Gundy. Most team owners didn't engage coaches so directly. That's what management was for: to serve as a sort of buffer.

But Dolan represented a different sort of owner.

The son of Charles Dolan, who came into billions after founding HBO and wiring Manhattan for cable television, Jim struggled to find his way. He had his first drink at 14, and suffered from alcoholism and substance abuse that threatened to scuttle his role within the family business before getting treatment at a Minnesota clinic in 1993, at age 38. Just two years later, Dolan's father named him chief executive of Cablevision.

"Mostly, it was because no one else [among my six kids] wanted it," Chuck told *New York* magazine.

Jim had a passion for sports, and had run one of his father's sports radio stations in Cleveland before. He also developed a passion for—if not an obsession with—the media. So as the back-and-forth between Grunfeld and Van Gundy drew more and more headlines, Dolan began to worry it was hurting the team as a whole.

Checketts made efforts to tamp things down. "I went to [Grunfeld and Van Gundy] and said, 'Look, guys: you've gotta straighten this stuff out. Because if you can't, it's going to be a problem,' " says Checketts.

But the talking-to didn't help matters. Even before the divide created by the Camby-Oakley situation, there was already a bit of an unspoken history between Van Gundy and Grunfeld. They had been assistant coaches together with the Knicks ten years earlier. In *Just Ballin'*, a book by reporters Frank Isola and Mike Wise chronicling the Knicks' tumultuous 1999 season, the authors detailed some of that tension.

"There was a mutual understanding: *I don't trust you, you don't trust me*," the book reads. "Van Gundy always respected Grunfeld as a family man, but believed he was too enraptured by Garden politics and too worried about surviving to excel as a general manager."

The belief stemmed from Van Gundy feeling that Grunfeld, as an assistant, had privately sought to undermine head coach Stu Jackson in the run-up to Jackson getting the ax in 1990. (Van Gundy had a friendship with Jackson dating back to their time at Providence.) And by 1999, with Grunfeld suddenly popping up more at team practices as the Knicks struggled, Van Gundy figured it meant he needed to watch his back.

Some of Van Gundy's paranoia stemmed from conversations he'd had with then–Jets coach Bill Parcells. In one instance, the men were speaking on the phone when Parcells asked if the line was secure. When Van Gundy asked him what difference that made, Parcells responded, "If you don't think [management is] listening to what you're saying, you're an idiot," before telling Van Gundy to call him back on a cell phone instead.

Aside from whatever talking Van Gundy and Grunfeld did with the media behind the scenes, a pair of members from the team's PR staff were also divided on the situation. One team flack quietly supported the coach, while the other backed the executive—a situation that led the publicists to give different beat writers different information depending on which man the staffers ultimately stood behind in the dispute.

To this day, Van Gundy and Grunfeld say they coexisted just fine.

"Jeff and I got along well," Grunfeld says. "Not in that one situation with Camby, necessarily. But generally, we got along well."

But the disagreement over Camby had created a mess. And tabloids love a mess.

The team's ownership, however, did not like messes, and was getting more fed up with each passing day. So sometime on April 17, Checketts met with Lustgarten about where things stood. "I told him, 'I want to make sure I have your support on this: that if [Grunfeld and Van Gundy] don't immediately stop the sniping that's going on, they're both gone,'"

Checketts recalls, saying he initiated the conversation as a way of buying time, since the season looked to be slipping away.

Lustgarten agreed with Checketts, saying ownership would take a wait-and-see approach in hopes of things improving. But less than an hour after that talk, Lustgarten called Checketts to reverse course.

"Actually, look," said Lustgarten, who'd just finished speaking with Dolan. "We think one of these guys has to go right now."

Stunned, Checketts said he thought that was an extreme, premature step. He argued that Phil Jackson and Bulls general manager Jerry Krause had stayed together in Chicago and won six championships despite not getting along.

But the argument didn't work. Dolan, who'd come into power earlier in the year, had already made up his mind. "We look like fools because we haven't done anything [about the sniping]," Lustgarten said, relaying Dolan's message to Checketts, who now would have to choose which man to terminate.

From where Checketts sat, it was an impossible task to consider: to fire the coach who'd often watch film of the previous night's game multiple times, and still manage to be at his desk by 5 a.m.? Or take out the general manager who perennially fielded solid teams, and who'd not only been a part of the club for seventeen years, but was also a close and long-time family friend?

Checketts had no earthly idea what to do.

Yet it didn't take long—a day or two at most—for others to give Checketts their two cents. And Ewing might have been first to do so.

Beginning the call by asking Checketts whether the media whispers were true, Ewing then argued passionately in favor of Van Gundy, ticking off a number of different reasons.

First, Ewing said, there were no problems in the locker room. The players liked each other—a rarity with clubs perceived to be underperforming. Second, while tons of teams had leaned on the "We haven't had a chance to jell" excuse before, there was actual truth to that with the Knicks, who'd seen one key player after another be sidelined with an injury. (As a memorization exercise, Van Gundy sometimes went over the ailments on his team's injury report with his two-year-old daughter, Mattie, who could, in turn, recite to her father what body part was hobbling each player.) Last, from where Ewing sat, Van Gundy was among the best coaches he'd ever played for—perhaps even better than Riley, whom Ewing respected, but privately felt pushed the Knicks too hard at times.

"If you have to choose, I want you to know: we play for Jeff," Ewing said. "We're committed to him."

After thanking Ewing for sharing his perspective, Checketts then got calls from two other players, Houston and Charlie Ward, voicing the same thought: that Van Gundy's job should be spared.

Checketts walked away from the calls feeling he had clarity, and held out hope that Dolan and Lustgarten would back off their demand with the team having won three in a row. But then the team's three-game win streak bled into a four-game losing streak in mid-April. And by that point, there was no more wiggle room in Dolan's mind. So on April 20, Checketts's phone rang again. It was Lustgarten.

"Jimmy wants it to be Ernie," Lustgarten said, in a line that sounded like an ordered hit straight out of *The Sopranos*.

Checketts asked for an explanation, wanting to know not only why Grunfeld was the choice, but why ownership was forcing him to make a move at all. "This is the first time since I've been here that a decision's been taken out of my hands," Checketts said. "Not with Rand Araskog. Not with Stanley Jaffe. So this is a real departure. This is important. I need to understand why you all are telling me to do this."

Lustgarten responded to the question about Grunfeld first, suggesting that Dolan, like Checketts, had heard from players who wanted Van Gundy to remain in place as the coach. Then, Checketts says, Lustgarten explained Dolan had become highly annoyed with how Grunfeld's wife, Nancy, carried herself inside the arena's celebrity lounge, Suite 200. "He thinks she acts way too much like she's the queen of New York in controlling that room," Lustgarten said. "He doesn't like how she acts."

Dumbfounded that Grunfeld's wife would carry any weight in such a key decision—"All I cared about was, 'What gives us the best chance to win?'" Checketts says—he pressed the other question. Why was ownership opting to pull the trigger now, rather than allowing Checketts to make the call himself?

"We're one hundred percent owners now, and Jimmy will probably be a bit more involved than the previous regimes have been," said Lustgarten, who had worked with Checketts for the two years prior.

Checketts still thinks about that talk with Lustgarten. "It was a sign that life was changing fast with Dolan taking over, and that he was going to be asserting himself more and more," he says now. "And I worried that if it happened, that could be the end of [the Knicks' run of success]."

When Checketts asked Grunfeld to have dinner with him on April 20 at Gregory's Restaurant in White Plains, a place they had dined several times before, the general manager thought nothing of it.

And why would Grunfeld have thought anything of it? He and Checketts had worked closely together for eight years, a span in which their families hung out and got to know each other socially. "This is one of my best friends," Checketts says of Grunfeld. "I guess I could have waited until the next morning, and then just walked into his office and said, 'Go ahead and get your stuff—this is your last day.' But he and I knew each other so well, and were so close. I just couldn't see doing it that way."

So as they each arrived at the two-story, 1940s home that had been converted into an Italian restaurant, Checketts and Grunfeld took a seat at their usual spot, table 21, which was in a highly secluded area of the eatery, on a separate porch. The restaurant's owner, Bill Losapio, had previously held the table open for famous patrons like Frank Sinatra, Dean Martin, Sammy Davis Jr., and Liza Minnelli, among others.

The executives split an order of penne vodka pasta before having cuts of steak for their entrees. Over the meal, they spoke for between an hour and an hour and a half about where the Knicks stood, and about the challenges the 21-21 club faced in trying to reach the playoffs with eight games remaining.

Shortly after their biscotti and assorted fresh fruit arrived, Checketts finally explained the actual purpose of the meeting. "Ernie, I'm sorry to have to tell you this. But I have to let you go," he said, souring the dessert plans.

Grunfeld chuckled initially, thinking Checketts was making a joke; particularly after the ninety-minute talk. But the look on Checketts's face made clear that he was completely serious, leaving Grunfeld astounded.

Just as Checketts wanted the "why" from Lustgarten, Grunfeld asked Checketts for an explanation. Checketts told him Dolan had ordered the dismissal. "Then he said, 'And after this [season] is over, I'm gonna make a change in the coaching ranks,'" Grunfeld recalls.

Technically, the move with Grunfeld would be termed a reassignment, a phantom role as a special consultant. He'd eventually receive a multimillion-dollar severance. Still, the news took the air out of the 44-year-old, who, as a working adult, had only known the Knicks.

After finishing a five-year run in the organization as a player, Grunfeld retired in 1986 and became an analyst with the club's broadcast crew for three years. The Knicks added him to Stu Jackson's staff before Grunfeld transitioned into the front office, where he'd later become general manager. Grunfeld was in so deep with the Knicks that he even named his dog Nicky.

Around 7 a.m. the next day at 2 Penn Plaza, Steinlight, the public relations employee, pieced together the day's news clips. As he worked, he noticed Grunfeld had come into the office unusually early. "I remember thinking, 'He *never* gets here this early,'" Steinlight says. "He said hello and kept it moving. But he'd always treated me really well. So for him to be that abrupt, I kind of wondered if something was off. By that point in the day, I had no idea about what had happened the night before. None of us knew."

For Grunfeld, who was getting a jump on cleaning out his office, it was a solid seventeen-year run that had been tossed aside in part because of how the media feasted on the organizational rift that existed. Or, more accurately, because of how the new ownership group responded to the media coverage of the rift.

But the razor-sharp wheels of the New York City media cycle weren't going to stop turning just because of Grunfeld's axing. There were still eight consequential games and a boatload of drama left to play out.

20

BEATING THE ODDS

Someone could have easily mistaken New York's locker room in 1999 for the set of *Ricki Lake*.

Aside from Jeff Van Gundy wondering if an anvil was going to drop from the sky in light of the team's four-game losing streak, there were countless other distractions hovering over the .500 club.

Guard Charlie Ward touched off a controversy by handing teammates copies of an opinion piece written in the *Wall Street Journal* by ex–NFL star Reggie White, which advocated banning female reporters from the locker room. Larry Johnson—who'd just been the focal point of an ugly *Sports Illustrated* piece about NBA players having multiple children with women out of wedlock—was now being investigated by the league for an alleged sexual harassment incident, in which he was said to have exposed himself to Lori Hamamoto, the team's public relations director, in the locker room. (He denied the allegation, while Hamamoto said she and Johnson were on good terms and that the alleged incident wasn't an issue.) And even when the polarizing Latrell Sprewell wasn't making headlines anymore, his agent, Robert Gist, was. Prior to Ernie Grunfeld's demotion, Gist—frustrated with his client coming off the bench as the sixth man—had been quoted calling for the Knicks to oust either Van Gundy or the team's management.

The team's laundry list of issues was enough to fill an entire New York sports section on its own. But Dave Checketts made a rare trip to practice that would quickly shift the Knicks' scattered focus.

Upon getting there, he told the players that one night earlier, he'd fired a good man in Grunfeld, a consequence that stemmed from the team's disappointing year to that point. And if there was any notion such a move would reduce pressure, Checketts dispelled it quickly, saying the opposite was true. Every person in the organization—from Checketts, to Van Gundy, down to each of the players—would be at risk if the club couldn't turn the corner over the final eight games.

The New York Rangers, who'd won the NHL's Stanley Cup in 1994, hit a rough patch toward the end of the decade and had just missed the postseason for a second consecutive year at the time of Grunfeld's demotion. That meant Madison Square Garden would lose more than $1 million per game in ticket revenue by not having home playoff contests that were usually a given in the summer months. That shortfall would now double or triple if the Knicks met the same fate—an unacceptable outcome for a $69 million roster that carried the NBA's heftiest price tag. And certainly an unacceptable result for new owner Jim Dolan.

Knowing this, Checketts decided he'd be traveling with the team over the final two and a half weeks of the campaign. He wanted an unvarnished look at everything, from how they worked in practice to how they interacted, to evaluate what, if anything, needed to change for the following season.

Players quickly realized the importance of the last eight games. Johnson told reporters he thought he'd be traded after the season if the Knicks missed the playoffs. Marcus Camby, who'd lost his biggest advocate with Grunfeld's dismissal, figured he'd now have to do even more to prove his worth to Van Gundy.

Nonetheless, after taking one more day off, New York beat the Hornets. Then the Knicks squeezed past Miami without Ewing. Then came another victory over Charlotte and, after a loss to the Hawks, wins in three of the club's last four contests. It ensured the Knicks would earn the Eastern Conference's eighth and final playoff spot.

While it was an unfamiliar spot to be the last team in the dance, the Knicks' first-round opponent was as familiar as could be.

About one year earlier, David Stern took a highly unusual step to tone things down between the Knicks and the Heat just after each team's postseason concluded. He summoned Pat Riley and Van Gundy to his office at the league's headquarters to demand the coaches stop fueling their fiery rivalry.

The NBA commissioner lectured Riley for an hour, then spoke with Van Gundy shortly after. His message was crystal clear: you and your teams are hurting the league's image with how you conduct yourselves.

The first playoff series between the clubs, in 1997, was turned on its head after P. J. Brown and Charlie Ward got tangled up, emptying the Knicks' bench and triggering an array of suspensions that sunk New York's chances of winning the series. And in 1998, Johnson and Alonzo Mourning threw punches at each other in the final seconds of Game 4, a scuffle that left both men suspended for the deciding Game 5. After the incident, Riley escalated things even more, saying his only regret in the fight was that none of Mourning's punches landed—a comment that infuriated the image-conscious Stern.

Though Riley apologized for the remark after the meeting with Stern, there was a certain truth in his original statement. These teams despised one another. "To me, [Knicks-Heat] is the definitive rivalry when it comes to hatred between two teams. It's the level of hatred I want in my rivalries. I don't think we've seen anything like it since," says reporter J. A. Adande, who covered those series each year.

While some NBA fans reveled in watching the brawls between the clubs, others felt the fights overshadowed the actual basketball being played. Conference crowns hadn't been on the line in either matchup. And the offense was hard to come by from one game to the next. Still, the series in 1997 and 1998 had each gone the distance, showing the teams were evenly matched.

"Maybe it offended your sensibilities, since it was almost an NHL style of basketball," says Phil Taylor, who covered the series for *Sports*

Illustrated. "But in some ways, it was maybe even better than the Knicks-Bulls rivalry, because the Bulls were clearly the better team and the Knicks were the team that was just not quite good enough. With Knicks-Heat, it really was two teams looking at each other in the mirror. Each time they played, you really felt like either team could win."

The third installment of the series had a chance to change that, though. The Heat entered as the No. 1 seed, finally with no Jordan and no Bulls in their way. And while there wasn't a ton expected of New York going into the series, Van Gundy—who figured to be on the chopping block with a first-round exit—had every incentive to pull off the first-round upset.

Again showcasing how evenly matched the clubs were, the Knicks and Heat split the first four games of the series, 2–2, to set up a winner-take-all showdown between them for the third consecutive year.

To call Miami Arena a hostile environment for the Knicks in Game 5 was an understatement. The building boomed with electricity, with fans chanting so loudly that one of Riley's friends, seated courtside, wore earplugs. The Heat fed off that energy, jumping out to a 13-point advantage early before things seesawed over the last forty minutes of action.

After eight lead changes and ten ties in the contest, Ewing, gutting through his Achilles pain and some sore ribs, collected a key offensive rebound and got fouled on a follow. He'd knock in two free throws with just under forty seconds to play to bring the Knicks within a point, 77–76. On Miami's following trip down the floor, Sprewell stripped a driving Hardaway, forcing a turnover and giving New York an opportunity to take the lead with about twenty seconds left.

The Knicks nearly squandered their chance when Sprewell lost the ball out of bounds with five seconds to go. But officials ruled Miami's Terry Porter touched it last, leaving New York with one final chance.

Ward inbounded from the sideline as his four teammates—Sprewell, Ewing, Johnson, and Allan Houston—stood in a box configuration around the corners of the painted area; a play call named "Triangle Down." As the official handed Ward the ball to pass it in, Johnson ran from the free-throw line toward the corner, clearing the top of the key for Houston, who got a screen from Ewing.

Open for a brief moment, Houston caught the ball off-balance, with one foot inside the three-point arc. Dan Majerle, the man defending him, chased but was a half step behind due to Ewing's screen. He didn't have a good angle to stop Houston once the Knick dribbled into an abrupt floater from 15 feet.

Majerle, who'd later say he recognized the play call—it was almost identical to a set Miami had in its own playbook—did everything in his power to get back into the play from behind, extending his right arm to try to block Houston's shot from behind. Instead, he connected with the back of Houston's head.

Houston's leaner found its way into the air with two seconds left on the shot clock and almost three seconds left in the game. It stayed airborne for one of those seconds, then bounced hard off the front rim before colliding with the backboard for the other. "It seemed like it hung for two minutes, not two seconds," said Houston, who'd connected on just one of his first seven shots to start that Game 5.

The future of the franchise—certainly Van Gundy and a number of the high-priced players—hung in the balance along with Houston's floater. But when it finally came down and trickled through the net, putting the Knicks up 78–77 with 0.8 left on the clock, the Miami crowd went church-silent as the Knicks grew euphoric, knowing they were on the cusp of pulling off a historic upset against a bitter rival.

After Miami regrouped during a timeout to let Riley draw up a final play, Porter caught the inbound, dribbled once, then fired a 40-footer that barely misfired, launching the Knicks into celebration mode.

But not Van Gundy. The coach made a beeline for official Ed F. Rush, questioning how a player could possibly catch, dribble, and line up a jumper in just 0.8 seconds without the shot attempt being waved off.

Even a few minutes after the victory—which marked just the second time a No. 8 seed had knocked off a No. 1 seed in NBA playoff history—the Knicks were in the locker room waiting to hear from their coach, who was nowhere to be found. As Checketts searched for Van Gundy, he eventually found him out on the court, still jawing with referees about Porter's missed shot being allowed.

When the executive asked Van Gundy why he was continuing to lobby the officials, even after the win, Van Gundy gave him a matter-of-fact response.

"I'm coaching the next round, too, Dave. I've gotta put these [referees] on notice," Van Gundy told him.

Van Gundy might have saved his job that day. But his actions never suggested he'd grown overly comfortable. Given the expectations, it was the correct mindset for him to have.

A couple of days after the Game 5 victory, when Van Gundy made it to his hotel room in Atlanta for the Knicks' second-round series, there was a telegram waiting for him. It had come from Riley in Miami.

The letter held deep meaning for Van Gundy. For starters, it broke the ice and was an attempt to bury the hatchet. He and Riley had gone almost a year without speaking following Riley's comments that took a shot at him for wading into the fight between Johnson and Mourning. And it wasn't lost on Van Gundy that Riley had addressed the telegram to "Coach Van Gundy," with the word "Coach" underlined. For his entire career, Riley had always referred to Van Gundy as "Jeff." So the shift here was meant as a clear sign of respect—to acknowledge Van Gundy had come into his own.

Yet while Riley recognized Van Gundy as a capable coach, it wasn't safe to assume he'd done enough to keep his job with the Knicks—even after taking out Miami for the second time in three postseasons.

Checketts had already quietly begun the process of considering possible replacements in case Van Gundy failed to carry the Knicks to the playoffs, or if they'd lost to Riley's Heat in the first round. Back in April, as the regular season wound down, he'd had Phil Jackson—a free-agent coach after leaving the Bulls the year before—and agent Todd Musburger at his home to gauge Jackson's interest in joining the Knicks.

The conversation was top-secret, with Checketts's secretary putting a pseudonym for Jackson in the executive's appointment calendar. Similarly, Checketts opted to have the meeting in his living room rather than out on his porch despite there being picture-perfect weather. He feared someone would see him talking with Jackson—something that would appear ruthless, given that Van Gundy was already in place.

Because of the Knicks' bitter rivalry with the Bulls, Checketts says he wasn't a huge fan of Jackson's. Still, he realized Jackson was a fantastic basketball mind who had a deep history with the Knicks. He felt he needed to at least explore the possibility of bringing Jackson back to the team he began his NBA career with, particularly since there were rumors of him speaking with the Nets, who were just across state lines.

"He knew a lot about our team, but he wasn't sure what he wanted to do. And about an hour in, I began to think that it was more about having leverage to get better money elsewhere than it was about wanting to join us," Checketts recalls, saying no offer was made. (In an email, Jackson—who ended up joining the Lakers that summer—says he never had real interest in coaching New Jersey, yet flirted with the Nets anyway. He added that he only took the meeting with Checketts after being talked into it by his agent.)

That the meeting was ultimately fruitless only made things more awkward when the Knicks breezed through the fourth-seeded Hawks in the second round. By then, with New York finally humming, it was clear Van Gundy had done enough to return the following season. But in the middle of the series, word of Checketts's April meeting with Jackson leaked to *New York Times* beat writer Mike Wise.

When Wise asked Checketts about it, the Garden executive denied that a sit-down had ever taken place. "I made a public relations mistake by lying to him about it," Checketts says, adding that he wanted to protect Van Gundy from looking endangered, and to stop Jackson from looking like a potential job poacher.

Checketts, who prides himself on ethics and still regrets not being truthful initially, apologized for the lie in a news conference ahead of Game 4. He also spoke with Van Gundy in an effort to clear the air, though the coach later said Checketts had every right to speak with Jackson.

As the final minutes ticked down in the Knicks' four-game sweep of Atlanta, fans at the Garden began chanting *Jeff Van Gun-dy!* to throw their support behind their scrappy coach, who'd endured job-security ru-mors for the better part of four years.

The massive chant prompted Van Gundy's wife, Kim, to openly weep in the stands. The coach himself blinked back a few tears, too, taking a sip of Diet Coke on the sideline to mask his emotions. After the final buzzer sounded, and the players entered the locker room, the Knicks reestablished the chant for Van Gundy, who'd somehow man-aged to outrun the grim reaper yet again to show he belonged.

"Over time, many moments run together and blur," Van Gundy says today of the chants. "But that one, though? That one stuck with me then, and it still stays with me now. That meant the world."

One year earlier, as the Indiana Pacers took just five games to end the Knicks' season, Patrick Ewing was out of sorts.

After four months of protecting his rebuilt right wrist like it was Fort Knox, Ewing was thrown directly into a four-alarm fire, returning in the middle of a second-round matchup against an abusively physical Pacer defense, which ranked fifth in the league.

Ewing was healthy but rusty once he rejoined his teammates, who'd forgotten how to play alongside him. "I'm not sure if his presence helped us," Van Gundy said during that 1998 series, "or if all the attention was a distraction for us."

This time around, as Ewing and New York prepared to square off with Indiana for a spot in the NBA Finals, things were a little differ-ent. Yes, the Pacers, who hadn't lost a home playoff game in four years and who were riding an eleven-game win streak, were still tough as nails. But unlike the 1998 postseason matchup, Ewing was banged up this time, occasionally struggling to even walk at times because of the searing pain in his left Achilles tendon, which had bothered him for months.

That didn't stop him from making a huge impact late in Game 1, when he scored six of the team's last nine points over the final two min-utes, including the go-ahead free throws that decided it. Ewing finished the contest with 16 points and a game-high 10 boards, even as he limped through much of the 93–90 victory.

During a walk-off interview, NBC sideline reporter Jim Gray asked Ewing about the pain. "How have you managed to play?" he asked. "We've seen several times today where you can't even jump, can you?"

"My Achilles is bothering me, but this is what it's all about: to get to the Finals, and hopefully win it. So I've gotta gut it out, and let Spree, Allan, and the guys go get me a championship," said Ewing, somehow smiling after logging forty minutes in the game.

Two days later, as the team took the court and began warming up for Game 2, Ewing felt a pop in his lower left leg, and ran back into the locker room to get retaped. He decided not to mention anything about feeling the popping sensation he'd felt until well after the matchup began. As he limped badly over the course of the game, he finally told Dr. Norm Scott of the pain, but then got the okay to play on.

Knicks villain Reggie Miller hit a pair of free throws to put the Pacers up two, 88–86, with two seconds left. And, like so many other times in the previous thirteen seasons, Ewing would have the ball in his hands for the final shot. Ward, the Heisman Trophy–winning quarterback, fired a full-court rocket of a pass that found a wide-open Ewing at the opposing free-throw line. Upon catching it, the big man turned, shot, and watched with the other 16,600 people at Market Square Arena as the ball floated toward the rim.

But while Ewing's shot was on-line, it hit the back iron and bounced out, just like his finger roll had in the series finale against Indiana four years earlier.

And after the Knicks lost the game, they found out they'd lost even more than that. Ewing's MRI scan in New York showed he'd partially torn his Achilles tendon.

On the one hand, it was a blessing for Ewing the tendon hadn't ruptured entirely, as it could have ended his career. On the other, even without surgery being necessary, the center's recovery would require being in a walking boot for six weeks, meaning he would have to miss the remainder of the postseason.

"It's frustrating to be so close to something I've dreamed about for so many years," said Ewing, who was two months from turning 37 years old. With the injury, he'd now have to do what he'd joked about with Gray: rely on Sprewell, Houston, and his other teammates to carry him to a ring.

If any one player sought to pick up the slack after Ewing went down, it was Larry Johnson, who would finish with a season-high 26 points— more than twice his average—to help New York stay within striking distance in Game 3 despite being vastly outplayed at the Garden. The Pacers led, 91–88, with just under twelve seconds left in the game when Van Gundy called timeout to draw up a play.

As Indiana coach Larry Bird implored his players to coax the Knicks into taking a two-point shot—"No threes! Don't give up any threes!" he shouted from the huddle—Van Gundy wanted to go for the tie.

He told his players to run Triangle Down, the same play that beat Miami on Houston's runner. As Ward looked to inbound the ball to Houston, the Pacers sent two defenders at the guard, forcing Ward to go elsewhere with a pass. He saw Johnson—who was filling Ewing's spot in the play—flash open, throwing him a pass that nearly got stolen by Indiana's Jalen Rose. Upon catching it on the left wing, Johnson jab-stepped three times, then pump-faked Antonio Davis to get him off-balance.

"To me, he was on skates," Johnson says. "He was out of his element trying to guard me that far away from the basket."

Johnson dribbled once to his left, absorbed minimal contact from Davis, then launched a 24-foot triple.

There was a low hum among the sold-out Garden crowd of 19,763 as Johnson's shot hung in the air. And piercing that noise was the sound of referee Jess Kersey's whistle, which he blew as Johnson's shot found the bottom of the net—tying the score at 91, and, because of the Davis foul, giving New York a chance to take the lead with a four-point play.

The Garden boomed, uncorking its loudest eruption since the John Starks jam against Chicago in 1993.

The foul call was dubious. Davis hardly touched Johnson on the play, and any contact he made came well before Johnson rose for the shot, meaning the three-pointer shouldn't have been counted. "The shot goes in, and I'm thinking, 'We can't count that.' But then Jess counted it, and I'm thinking, 'Oh my God,'" recalls referee Steve Javie, one of Kersey's officiating partners in that game. "I blame myself, too, and wish I'd been more aggressive in overruling him. Not being the crew chief that night, I think I took a backseat. . . . You watch it over again, and Jess never even reported the number of the guy who committed the foul. Guys at the scorer's table looked at me for the call, because Jess was uncertain in the moment."

Kersey himself acknowledged the mistake, and kept a prominent photo of the play in his office as a sort of penance. "I knew right away I had screwed that play up," Kersey told *ESPN The Magazine* in 2000. "I took something away from a team that didn't deserve to have it taken away."

With the Garden still rattling after Johnson's game-tying triple, Chris Childs grabbed the forward by the shoulders and told him to calm himself before going to the line. After a deep breath, Johnson sank the free throw, which put the Knicks ahead by one, 92–91. On a play where Bird wanted his players to surrender a two in hopes of avoiding a game-tying three, the Knicks somehow managed to come away with four.

New York sealed the win on the next play, when Pacers guard Mark Jackson missed a jumper at the buzzer, giving the Knicks a 2–1 lead in the series.

Indiana managed to even things at two games apiece in Game 4. But the Knicks made Grunfeld look like a genius in Game 5. Sprewell logged 29 points and Camby had 21 to go with 13 rebounds and six blocks to push New York within one victory of history: to be the first No. 8 seed to make the Finals.

Given everything that was on the line going into Game 6, nerves easily could have been a factor for the Knicks. But in at least one case, the opposite was true. "I had a peace about me that game; just a weird, real peace," Houston said. "My wife was pregnant, and we knew that the next day, she would have the baby. It actually made me relax that whole game, and took so much pressure off me."

The guard came up huge in the Knicks' Game 6 win, particularly after Johnson suffered a knee sprain and needed to be helped off the court a few minutes before halftime. Houston, who'd hit just 35 percent of his tries in the first five games of the series, shot 70 percent in Game 6, logging 32 points while hitting eight of his nine attempts in the second half. It was a stark contrast from Miller, who connected on three of his eighteen attempts for just 8 points.

In their series with the Pacers, the Knicks lost their franchise player *and* their clutch-performing emotional leader. Yet somehow none of it mattered. Against all odds, the Knicks, who had barely reached the postseason in the first place, were now headed back to the NBA Finals.

21

THE CLOCK STRIKES MIDNIGHT

The Knicks showcased a handful of traits during their unlikely journey to the 1999 NBA Finals.

They displayed heart and resolve, showing they could sidestep distractions to sneak into the playoffs with their beloved coach's back against the wall. They certainly had talent, much of which shined even brighter after Patrick Ewing succumbed to an Achilles injury early in the conference finals.

Yet overlooked in New York's historic run was the notion of familiarity. With the Knicks having played Miami in two straight postseasons, and Indiana in four of the last six playoffs, the club's coaching staff had a slight advantage compared to other underdogs, since it had a better sense of what to prepare for.

That wouldn't be the case in the Finals, though. Where the Heat and Pacers held a ton in common with the Knicks from a roster and game-plan standpoint, the San Antonio Spurs were the polar opposite.

The Western Conference champions, who'd earned the top seed after tying for the league's best mark at 37-13, represented the smallest media market in the NBA. New York, which snuck into the dance as a No. 8 seed, obviously represented the NBA's biggest market. Between the Latrell Sprewell acquisition and the litany of locker room controversies at the Garden, there was no such thing as the Knicks flying under the radar. Meanwhile, the buttoned-up Spurs were quiet—not only touting perhaps the league's most fundamentally sound, yet least flashy star in second-year power forward Tim Duncan—and usually operated with militaristic precision. The Spurs' attention to detail fit the bill, given they were coached by Gregg Popovich, an Air Force Academy alumnus. And they were led on the court by David Robinson, a future Hall of Famer nicknamed "the Admiral," because of his service time with the Naval Academy.

Clear stylistic differences between the clubs existed, too. The less-than-healthy Knicks had come to rely on their wing scorers far more than in years past, particularly without Ewing available. By contrast, the Spurs were something of a throwback, sporting two elite big men in Robinson and Duncan. The dominant combination helped power San Antonio to an 11-1 postseason record heading into the Finals. That mark included second- and third-round sweeps, respectively, over the Shaquille O'Neal– and Kobe Bryant–led Lakers and the Trail Blazers, who had won 70 percent of their games during the shortened campaign.

At most, two similarities were present in the title-round matchup: both teams fielded stellar defenses, and both Popovich and Jeff Van Gundy had fended off job-security questions to survive the hot seat.

After San Antonio began the season with a disappointing 6-8 mark, Popovich asked Robinson and point guard Avery Johnson to stop by his home during an off day in March. Neither player made much of the request, or saw it as a formal meeting. Robinson showed up for the sit-down eating Popeyes Chicken.

"Boys, we've got to win this [next] game in Houston," said a blunt Popovich, whose team was coming off a 101–87 loss to Utah. "If we don't, there could potentially be a coaching change."

The following day, as the team's bus pulled up for a morning shoot-around in Houston, Johnson asked each of the players to stay behind to meet privately as coaches and other staffers exited the vehicle. Without mentioning the meeting at Popovich's house, Johnson relayed the same message his coach had: if San Antonio didn't beat Houston that night, a coaching change—likely ex-Knick and onetime Spurs guard Doc Rivers taking over for Popovich—would almost certainly take place afterward.

Johnson's message clearly resonated with his teammates. The Spurs beat the Rockets on the road by 17 that night, and wouldn't lose again for almost three weeks. From the time of that meeting to the Spurs' run to the Finals, San Antonio had been a machine, winning forty-two of its last forty-eight contests.

If the Knicks were going to win a title, they had some extremely tall odds they'd have to reckon with.

The Spurs' top-ranked defense, powered by their All-Star bigs, blocked more shots than any other team in the league in 1999—a daunting enough reality for the Knicks when they were at full strength, let alone when they were shorthanded. Ewing's absence in a matchup like this one particularly stung.

The Knicks did get Larry Johnson back after his hospital visit during the Game 6 clincher against the Pacers. But he was still banged up, between his knee and back problems. It also wouldn't help matters that he'd be at a four- or five-inch height disadvantage against Duncan in the post.

Backup center Chris Dudley, Ewing's fill-in, would be tasked with defending Robinson. Yet the Knicks had to scramble after Dudley was forced out of Game 1 with a hyperextended right arm mere minutes into the contest.

The series had just begun, and New York was already running out of big bodies against the much-taller favorites.

"It was a feeling of David against Goliath," guard Allan Houston recalled years later. "In every series we played, we had so much confidence, and knew the other team could sense they were in a fight—that [the Knicks] were a team that was hungry and dangerous. And we'd win the first game of every series, on the road, and it would change the whole series."

New York hoped to pounce on the fact that San Antonio had been off for ten days between series, twice as long as the Knicks. The Spurs got out of the gate a little slow, missing a couple of defensive rotations that helped the Knicks tally 27 first-quarter points. But then New York barely scored the rest of the night.

It might have been the team's struggles with depth perception on jumpers in the cavernous Alamodome, or the almost forty thousand screaming fans in attendance (double that of a Garden crowd). It might have been that short-range shots were hard to come by once the Spurs' elite rim protectors tightened up. But whatever the reason, the Knicks tallied just 50 points over the final three quarters and fell, 89–77.

Things were even worse for New York in Game 2, when Sprewell had 26 and Houston had 19, but no other Knick logged more than six points. The top-heavy performance resulted in an 80–67 Spurs victory. It registered as a gut punch for a team that usually drew confidence by jumping out to early series leads.

The Spurs, who hadn't lost consecutive games in almost four months, were now up 2–0 to start the series.

"As things progressed, it started feeling like it was going to take every single [Knick] having the game of his life each night to win the series," *New York Times* reporter Selena Roberts recalls. "You weren't gonna beat that Spurs team with will and scrappiness."

The Spurs knew they were the better team, too. But they'd also been instructed to not take their foot off the pedal. "We weren't idiots. Of course they couldn't match up with us on paper," says Will Perdue, Robinson's backup on that San Antonio team. "At the same time, they were an eighth seed that had just beaten the odds to make it to the Finals. So Pop said he'd dress us down immediately if he ever got the sense that we weren't taking [the Knicks] seriously."

New York showed heart at the Garden in Game 3, getting 34 from Houston and forcing 20 turnovers in an 89–81 win, trimming the series deficit to 2–1. But the momentum was brief. The Spurs won Game 4, pushing the Knicks to the brink and threatening to turn their Cinderella ride to the Finals into a pumpkin.

*   *   *

Late in the afternoon, just hours before Game 5 was set to tip off at the Garden, Van Gundy popped out of his arena office, curious to figure out why there was so much noise coming from the court.

By the time he made it to the entrance of the Garden tunnel, he had his answer. NBA staffers were on the floor performing a run-through of how the championship trophy presentation—complete with the gleaming, sixteen-pound prize itself—would be handled if the Spurs clinched the title later that evening.

For nearly half an hour, Van Gundy stood in the corner of the arena, helplessly watching the display. He could draw up an ace game plan, and his players could leave every last ounce of effort they had on the court. But only so much could be done to close the enormous size and talent gap without Ewing playing.

"That Finals was the toughest one; tougher than [1994]," Ewing said. "Because I couldn't play. I was there, but I couldn't play."

There would be no Willis Reed moment, when the injured Knicks star gave his team a shot in the arm by suiting up unexpectedly. Instead, the Knicks took the floor in Game 5 without their franchise player.

They withstood a 13–0 San Antonio run to stay in the hunt. At one point, Sprewell handled the scoring all on his own, embarking on an incredible back-and-forth with Duncan, in which the men accounted for 28 of the contest's 29 points over a six-minute stretch. Game 5 featured twelve ties and twelve lead changes, with neither team pulling ahead by more than three points in the fourth. New York held a one-point edge, 77–76, with just over fifty seconds left when the Knicks swarmed Duncan with a double team in the post.

He flung the ball out to the perimeter for Sean Elliott, who pump-faked Chris Childs, then dribbled once before finding Avery Johnson wide open in the left corner inside the arc. The guard squared his shoulders and unleashed a perfect 18-footer that gave the Spurs a 78–77 lead and silenced the once-raucous crowd.

As Van Gundy called a timeout, Avery Johnson and the Spurs excit-

edly raced to their sideline, knowing they were one step away from winning a title. Meanwhile, Childs—who'd blown the assignment in leaving
Johnson open—and the Knicks walked over to their bench slowly, with
slumped shoulders.

On the ensuing play, Sprewell missed a jumper, before the Knicks got
the ball back by making a stop on defense. They would get one final crack
at extending the series. Again, the opportunity would go to Sprewell, the
player who'd polarized fans of the sport eighteen months earlier, but now
had the full-throated support of the Garden faithful as New York poured
the last of its hope into the talented swingman.

With 2.1 seconds left to play, Charlie Ward uncorked a nearly perfect 40-foot inbound pass to Sprewell underneath the basket. But upon
catching it, Sprewell—who had a game-high 35 points—got trapped by
Duncan and Elliott along the baseline. Knowing time was running out,
he dribbled once to his left to get to the other side of the basket, and
bounded into a fadeaway jumper from the left block. Robinson and Duncan each hounded him, nearly blocking the shot, which fell short of the
rim as the buzzer sounded.

Spurs 78, Knicks 77.

It was over. The clock finally struck midnight on New York's surreal, exhilarating season. The Spurs were NBA champions. The scrappy
Knicks again finished as the bridesmaid rather than as the bride.

The average football fan wouldn't know it, but Super Bowl losers receive
rings, too.

They aren't nearly as gaudy or expensive as the ones the champions
receive. And recipients rarely wear them. But they do exist, and not just
in the NFL. Major League Baseball clubs have long had runner-up rings
made after losing the World Series, too.

After New York came up short against the Spurs, Dave Checketts had
something similar in mind.

Checketts thought back on 1994, and how Pat Riley's agitation with how those Finals manifested. The coach had been adamantly against the idea of doing anything to honor the team's effort that season.

"He said he didn't want a single dinner, a pleasant conversation, a pat on the back. Nothing," Checketts recalls. "And I said, 'Pat, you have your rings already. The rest of us don't. This is still a special thing.'"

Still, knowing how Riley felt, Checketts stood down, and ultimately didn't do anything to mark the occasion.

Against that backdrop, Checketts had already made up his mind to commemorate the 1999 Finals run somehow. By then, he knew how hard it was to make that climb, particularly as an eighth seed. And players like Ewing, at 36, weren't getting any younger. So he sat down with a number of people to ask what sort of keepsake might be most appropriate. Rings, to honor the team's conference title, were one consideration.

But when he spoke with Van Gundy about it, the coach made one request.

"I really don't mind if you do something. But if you do, *please* don't make it rings," Van Gundy urged Checketts. "Because a championship ring is a championship ring. Let's not make runner-up rings."

So Checketts scaled things back, instead giving each member of the organization a silver-band, blue-face Movado watch that was engraved, "New York Knicks: 1999 NBA Eastern Conference Champions."

Van Gundy's mindset was understandable. Being handed a ring after losing could be interpreted as satisfaction with coming up short. Especially since New York was used to making deep runs—including the Finals run five years earlier. Plus, with Ewing coming back healthy and a full season for the roster to jell, it would have been fair to think New York was positioned even better to win it all the following year.

"I remember thinking, 'We'll make it back to this point [in 2000],'" says Sammy Steinlight, who worked in the team's public relations department at the time. "Then that year went by. And the next year. And the next year. . . . I have a greater appreciation now for what it takes just to make the playoffs. And I think a lot about how it would have been really nice to have gotten a ring that season, rather than a watch."

As badly as the Knicks and their fans wanted to wrap themselves in the warmth of a title—and as cruel as it might've felt to get that close, only to fall short again—the 1999 Finals loss was apt in a number of ways.

The defeat marked the sixth time in the 1990s New York had been knocked out of the playoffs by the eventual champion. And much like their 1991 playoff defeat against the Bulls took place at the beginning of Chicago's dynastic run, the Knicks' loss to the Spurs paved the way for an enchanted run of success in San Antonio. The Spurs' title in 1999 would mark their first of four over an eight-year run, as Duncan transformed into the greatest power forward ever.

Tellingly, the Knicks made it to the Finals twice during that decade, with each trip coming immediately after Michael Jordan left the sport. Between the Bulls and Spurs, the era was bookended by dynasties that kept the Knicks out of the winner's circle. They never did manage to win the championship; a feeling the Jazz, Pacers, Sonics, Suns, and Blazers can all relate to. And there's no shame in that reality.

More than any of those clubs, though, the Knicks stood out because of how many times they charged back up the mountain after being turned back at the summit. They knowingly punished their bodies, and at times subconsciously tortured their souls, by getting as close as they did without tasting immortality.

Without rings to validate their place in history, it's impossible to consider the Knicks the focal point of the NBA's golden era. Yet it's fitting they stand just outside the limelight. Those blood-inducing, bandage-causing clubs were far more interested in making their presence felt rather than seen anyway.

EPILOGUE

When Hall of Fame basketball scribe Harvey Araton thinks of the 1990s Knicks, another sport comes to mind.

"To me, the Knicks were that boxer that just pummeled at your midsection," Araton says. "They never could beat Michael, but they always administered some pain. And you always felt they were one big left hook away from winning."

In 1992, New York became the first club to push Jordan and the title-era Bulls to a seventh game. The Knicks followed that up with the wrenching defeat in 1993, after the winnable Charles Smith sequence. They were a 2-for-18, Game 7 John Starks performance away from winning the whole thing in 1994. A Game 7, Patrick Ewing finger roll at the buzzer away from beating Indiana to make the conference finals in 1995. A bench-clearing dustup against the Heat from getting one last good crack at Chicago in 1997. And then a Ewing Achilles injury away from having the size to go toe-to-toe with the Spurs in 1999.

It was a lifetime's worth of close calls; ones that gnawed at players and fans alike. Yet the near-misses also illustrated the strength and consistency of the organization. It's not easy to get *that* close so many times.

Something was being done the right way.

But not everyone felt that way. Toward the end of the 1999 lockout season, owner James Dolan ordered the dismissal of general manager Ernie Grunfeld, the first time that decade a Knicks owner had issued such a directive. Then, immediately after the move—but not necessarily because of it—the Knicks went on a run, winning six of their final eight games to reach the postseason as the East's eighth seed.

"The worst part of that entire thing was Marc [Lustgarten] and Jim thinking we made that run because they chose to fire Ernie," says Dave Checketts, who argues it was merely the Knicks getting healthy and jelling in that shortened season. "I think Jim was emboldened by the adrenaline of [the run]."

In a number of ways, 1999 marked the end of an era. It turned out to be the year New York reached a deal with free agent Charlie Ward, a first-rounder in 1994, to sign for five years and $28 million. Somewhat unbelievably, it would take 23 years for the Knicks to re-sign one of their own first-round picks to stay on a multiyear deal—a fact that highlights just how much turnover took place in the two decades that followed.

During the 1999 draft, the Knicks used the No. 15 overall pick to take the man who theoretically should have been their center of the future: 7-foot-2 Frenchman Frederic Weis. But it didn't pan out that way.

In one of the bigger draft misfires in history, Weis never graduated beyond playing in summer league with the club, and failed to log a single minute of NBA playing time. Weis experienced hardship away from the court years later, driving to a French rest stop and taking a box full of sleeping pills in January 2008. He woke up ten hours later, which prompted him to stop drinking and reconcile with his wife.

Yet it was arguably the mishandling of Ewing that set off the chain of instability most. Feeling underappreciated after a fifteen-year run, he asked the Knicks to trade him following the 1999–00 campaign, after New York got bounced in the conference finals by the Pacers. Rather than make the best of the 37-year-old's time left in New York—he had just one year and $17 million left on his expiring contract—the team dealt him for a smorgasbord of mediocre, redundant pieces that added almost $90 million in long-term salary. (It would be the first of dozens of head-scratching stumbles—including the 2002 deal for Antonio McDyess, the 2004 swap for Stephon Marbury, the 2005 barter for Eddy Curry, and the Andrea Bargnani trade in 2013—that bloated the Knicks' books without adding helpful, sustainable talent. And in a handful of these franchise-altering moves, including the Bargnani trade and the 2011 one that brought Carmelo Anthony to the franchise, Dolan was said to have gotten personally involved in the transactions.)

After trading Ewing to Seattle in a four-team blockbuster in 2000, the other organizational mainstays weren't far behind. Sensing Dolan wanted to exert his power as owner, Checketts resigned as Garden chief in May 2001.

Checketts said the final straw for him was Dolan's decision to spend more than $330 million on Nobody Beats the Wiz, a failing New York–based consumer electronics chain, and a glut of area movie theaters, which Dolan then placed under Checketts's purview.

"Eventually I said, 'Why don't I get out of your way? It's clear you don't want me [handling these assets], and I hate doing it, because it's a distraction,'" he recalls. "And he said, 'I think you're right.'"

Six months later, coach Jeff Van Gundy, the last true tie to the rugged roots of that 1990s era, abruptly left the team. And the Knicks went on to lose more games than any other NBA franchise in the two decades that followed his exit.

It didn't take the Knicks long to realize Anthony Mason could be difficult to deal with.

Just minutes into Pat Riley's first practice as coach, he'd punched teammate Xavier McDaniel. And just one year into his tenure with New York, Mason pulled a prima-donna move that even Ewing would've taken heat for.

It was 1992, and the Knicks were hosting their first annual summer camp for youngsters. Like many camps with professional teams, the club wanted to have one of its players make an appearance for a day. Not someone like Ewing, a star who had too many demands on his time already. But not someone from the end of the bench, either. So they asked Mason—basically still new to the NBA—if he'd appear for $1,500.

The forward said yes, and the team provided him with a limousine to the camp that day. Mason had his window rolled down as the vehicle arrived, and the kids hovered around it like paparazzi, wanting to catch a glimpse of him up close. Yet Mason stayed in the car. First for two minutes. Then five. Then almost fifteen.

Finally Ed Tapscott, then the club's administrative director, came outside. He'd been responsible for Mason's appearance at the camp that day, and couldn't figure out why Mason wasn't making his way inside the gym.

"I'm not getting out of the car for anything less than $2,000, bro. And I want cash," Mason told him.

Tapscott figured he was joking at first. But Mason was completely serious. Sure, he'd agreed to the $1,500 figure before, but now—with an army of young, excited kids waiting inside—he had the leverage to play hardball.

Tapscott said he wasn't even sure he could realistically get access to that much cash that soon. "I had to give one of our staffers my ATM card," he recalls. "What choice did I really have in a situation like that?"

With assurance of the pay increase, Mason hopped out. He played in a couple of scrimmages with the children. But, in classic Mason fashion, he couldn't turn off his competitiveness. While playing, Mason inadvertently elbowed a kid, knocking the child out cold and breaking his nose, which gushed with blood.

When the boy regained consciousness, he woke to find a worried Mason hovering over him. The child smiled and asked the Knick to sign his bloody T-shirt. Meanwhile, Tapscott said he and others running the camp were merely happy to escape the situation without the threat of a lawsuit.

When it all ended, and Mason prepared to get back in the limo to head home, he left Tapscott with one final message. "By the way: after I get dropped off, I'm gonna have the car take my mom shopping," Mason told him. That, Mason explained, was the reason he'd demanded the extra money from Tapscott to begin with.

Then Mason rode off.

Simply put, he hadn't always been the easiest personality. But by the time Mason left the Knicks in 1996, he'd either built solid relationships or made amends with most people he'd rubbed the wrong way before.

Which is why, when Mason tragically died at age 48 following a heart attack in February 2015, Ewing, Starks, and Charles Oakley were all there at the Greater Allen A.M.E. Cathedral in Queens for his funeral.

And despite their high-profile clashes, so was Riley. In fact, the coach was among those who eulogized Mason at the service.

That frigid, snowstorm-filled morning of the funeral, Mason's mother, Mary, was assisted by wheelchair to the front of the church pulpit, where the player's casket stood. Seeing Mason's mother—who'd been to nearly every home game during that run in New York—Riley knelt down on one knee and put a hand on her shoulder to speak with her. When he stood up minutes later, Riley's face streamed with tears.

Riley and the Knicks ended on terrible terms. But while he and his Miami teams struggled to take down New York—Van Gundy and the Knicks won three of those four playoff series from 1997 to 2000—the Heat would enjoy wild success in the following years. Riley led Miami to its first title in 2006, then, as an executive, pulled off a free-agent heist in 2010, convincing LeBron James and Chris Bosh to play alongside Dwyane Wade. It shifted the league's balance by giving star players newfound power, and yielded four Finals runs and two more championships for the Heat.

Still, at the funeral, it was clear that a piece of Riley's heart remains with many of his ex-Knicks players.

It's far less clear whether there's ever been true closure for someone like Charles Smith.

In 1996, he filed a grievance against the Knicks through the players union, alleging team doctors withheld medical information about the depth of his knee problems. (He later dropped the grievance.) Just over a year after being traded from New York to San Antonio, Smith played his final NBA game, at 31.

Smith had an odd stumble in his post-NBA life. In 2014, he made a trip to North Korea along with a Dennis Rodman–led group to play a game in front of Kim Jong-un for the dictator's birthday, in hopes of creating what Rodman called "basketball diplomacy." Looking back on the excursion—which didn't have the backing of the NBA or US State Department—Smith suggested he had regrets for being part of the effort, which got widely panned despite his intentions.

Only Smith knows whether he's ever fully gotten over the what-ifs surrounding that fateful Game 5. Even if he has, Smith seemingly struggles at times with the fact that it's what other people remember him for.

When Araton contacted Smith to interview him for a memoir about deceased Knicks fan Michelle Musler—who sat courtside during those years and befriended players, coaches, and reporters alike—the conversation was warm and reflective. Then Araton mentioned how deeply Musler admired Smith, and how she felt almost protective of him, in part because of the heartbreaking nature of Game 5.

"He became almost unhinged at the very mention of [Game 5]," Araton says, adding that Smith initially berated him and sought to take back his quotes for the book before later apologizing for overreacting. "Charles is very smart. Very well-spoken. But I think he's become very protective and sensitive to that whole Game 5 experience in part because he worries that it continues to color the way people see him."

If there's someone who's had the opposite experience, and not been frozen in their worst moment, it's Starks, who remains one of the most beloved players in the franchise's history. Despite his historically brutal performance in Game 7 of the 1994 NBA Finals, he generates nothing but warm feelings among the fans. "They still ask me about it [on the street] *every* single day," Starks said, referring to the famous, nearly thirty-year-old dunk against Chicago, rather than the awful shooting night in the deciding game of the Finals.

For just about everyone, there was more than enough good to outweigh Starks's bad—even though the low point took place on the biggest stage. His passion stayed with fans more. "I always thought if you looked at Starks closely enough, you could almost see his heart beating, because that's how he played," Hall of Fame Knicks announcer Mike Breen said of the guard, who now works for the team in its alumni relations department.

Van Gundy, after resurfacing to coach the Rockets from 2003 to 2007, enjoyed greater day-to-day visibility than anyone from those clubs. From 2007 to 2023, he worked as an analyst alongside Breen and ex–Knicks point guard Mark Jackson as part of ESPN's lead NBA broadcast team. Then, shortly after leaving ESPN, Van Gundy took a job in the Celtics' front office as a senior consultant—a role that earned him a title ring when Boston won it all in 2024.

The most uncomfortable relationship all these years later is the one between Oakley and the Knicks.

In February 2017, Oakley, the former co-captain who'd long spoken his mind on the state of the team and had his differences with Dolan, was a courtside spectator at the Garden. Midway through the first quarter of the game he was attending, a security guard approached Oakley, asking him to leave. Oakley asked why—a number of fans sitting near him said they didn't understand the reasoning, either, as they hadn't seen him do anything wrong—and soon found himself encircled by guards.

As Oakley angrily pleaded to stay in his seat, one of the guards grabbed his left arm, which Oakley responded to by shoving the guard in the chest twice. A group of no less than six men dragged the fan favorite out into the bowels of the arena. Later that evening, Oakley was arrested for his role in the incident.

Adding fuel to the fire, the Knicks released a statement, saying Oakley "behaved in a highly inappropriate and completely abusive manner" before adding "we hope he gets some help soon." Oakley took issue with the last line's implication, saying he'd had a few drinks before the contest, but that he wasn't an alcoholic. (A recovering alcoholic himself, Dolan said during a radio interview he believed Oakley had an anger problem and possibly an alcohol problem. The Knicks owner offered no proof to back the assertions.)

Oakley's misdemeanor charges were dropped, but bad blood still lingers. He hasn't been back to the Garden since—the team barred him—and in December 2020, Oakley sought to add Dolan as a defendant in a suit he'd filed against the Garden, arguing that Dolan ordered his removal from the venue that night.

The instance, a low moment for a club that's had any number of them since those 1990s years, left Oakley feeling ostracized. It prompted him to take stock of which of his former teammates have publicly voiced support for him. The lack of vocal backing from Ewing, his most meaningful running mate, stung Oakley, who in turn became increasingly critical of Ewing's leadership with the Knicks in the 1990s as a result.

As for Ewing—the most decorated Knick, and the man who knew all too well what it was to wait for his moment in the sun—he spent much of his time after those New York years waiting. He never did win a championship with Seattle, or with the Orlando Magic. In 2002, he took a job as an assistant coach with the Washington Wizards—the team Jordan, his longtime friend, played for—staying for one season.

He bounced from there to Houston, where he worked as an assistant under Van Gundy for four years, then latched on as an assistant for five years with Orlando, where Van Gundy's brother, Stan, was head coach. Ewing took the title of associate head coach when he went to Charlotte, where he reunited with Jordan, who'd taken over as the owner of the Bobcats.

After paying fourteen years' worth of dues as an assistant, Ewing finally got his shot in the lead chair. He was handed the reins at his alma mater, Georgetown, in 2017. And at the end of his fourth season in the job, Ewing led the Hoyas—who'd entered their conference tourney with a 9-12 mark—to four victories in four days to both win the Big East Tournament title and clinch a spot in the 2021 NCAA Tournament.

It wasn't exactly the championship Riley tried to get Ewing to envision on that day back in 1991. (And the euphoria didn't last long, with Ewing eventually being dismissed from the job in 2023.) Still, it was championship confetti raining down on Ewing at the Garden—a proper tribute for the Knicks legend; particularly as the coach at Georgetown, only months after the passing of mentor John Thompson.

Now, with Ewing reaching a winner's circle of sorts, the question is when the Knicks will do the same.

They went off the rails time and time again with big, accomplished names like Isiah Thomas and Larry Brown at the helm. Even Phil Jackson, who'd been part of those title-winning teams from the 1970s before becoming a Hall of Fame coach with the Bulls and Lakers, crashed and burned as team president from 2014 to 2017.

Yet after decades of dysfunction and losing, things were finally looking up for the Knicks by the mid-2020s.

In their first season under coach Tom Thibodeau, a former Knicks assistant under Van Gundy, New York shocked the league by finishing with a 41-31 mark, storming into the playoffs for the first time in eight years. It marked a stunning turnaround from 2020, when the Knicks went 21-45, and finished ranked 23rd on the defensive end. Under Thibodeau—who, like Van Gundy, prioritizes getting stops—New York rose all the way to fourth in the NBA on defense. The season was a turning point, as New York—led by point guard Jalen Brunson and forward Julius Randle—has now made the postseason three times in four years. The Knicks finished with the No. 2 seed in the Eastern Conference with a 50-win campaign in 2024, regularly drawing standing ovations from the Garden faithful for the otherworldly effort. During that 2024 playoff run, a number of Knicks from the nineties era—including Ewing and Starks—even sat courtside to cheer on their new-school counterparts.

The current club has a tough-as-nails identity, predicated on defense and offensive rebounding, and looks as if it could be a factor in the postseason for years to come. Much of the credit belongs to Leon Rose, the team president who overhauled New York's front office. A lot of it also belongs to Thibodeau, a tireless man who knows how to win only one way: by outworking the competition every day.

Van Gundy recalled a time in 2000, when he let Thibodeau run a pair of summer workouts, which were scheduled for 10 a.m. to noon, and 4 to 6 p.m., with lunch in between.

"By the time Thibs let them out of the first practice, it was 3:15," Van

Gundy said. "He tells them, 'Get off your feet. Get some rest. Get something to eat.' I'm like, 'Tom: it's 3:15. They've only got 45 minutes.'"

Thibodeau's maniacal focus on conditioning at the time certainly sounds out of place within the context of modern-day NBA standards. Nowadays, teams are more mindful of giving players time to rest and recover.

In that sense, the 1990s Knicks were almost prehistoric, hard-hat-wearing dinosaurs. Back in the days when they roamed the Garden and left their opponent's blood on the hardwood, the Knicks routinely put their bodies on the line. Shattered teeth. Fractured toes. Broken hands. Broken hearts. It's the price they paid in hopes of winning a title.

And even if the story didn't have a happy ending, it's one nearly all the players—and their millions of fans, who've longed for a team like that ever since—would gladly relive.

ACKNOWLEDGMENTS

Almost no book happens without the help and support of countless others. And in my case, I never would have written *Blood in the Garden* without the suggestion and urging of two people.

My literary agent, Daniel Greenberg, just knew there was a hunger among the Knicks' enormous fan base for more information on those colorful 1990s teams. He just needed to find the right author to tell the story.

So back in 2018, he called another person he'd worked with before—Jonathan Abrams, a brilliant *New York Times* best-selling author who has covered the NBA for years—for advice about whom to target for the project. Despite my having met Jonathan maybe only once or twice, he passed my name along to Daniel, saying he thought I'd do a great job painting a portrait of those teams, despite having been a mere four-year-old when Pat Riley first joined the Knicks.

To say I was standoffish when Daniel approached me would be putting it gently. My dad—who'd been my gateway into sports as a kid unexpectedly passed away six months earlier. And I'd told anyone who'd listen that I needed a break from everything. Mentally. Physically. Spiritually.

But then I thought about how, for years, my dad had passed along book ideas for me to pursue. About how he wanted me to write one. And how this chance to write—without a family of my own yet—might not ever present itself again. So, I told Daniel: I'd be a fool *not* to write this book.

I worked with a fantastic editor, Amar Deol, who kept reassuring me that I'd uncover the right details and strike the proper tone with the most challenging aspects of the story. Amar read through versions 1.0 through 27.0 before we tweaked and tweaked and tweaked to reach the finish line with this manuscript. He's extraordinarily patient. And anyone would be fortunate to have someone who believes in them as much as he believes in me.

I had fantastic friends in the writing industry in Ty Wenger and Mirin Fader, who read through the roughest versions of my roughest chapters and made invaluable suggestions. They helped immensely, and I would have been lost without their help at times.

In Andrew Donlan, I had a researcher who somehow was more excited about this book than even I was. He reached out shortly after it went public that I'd be doing the project (and as he was finishing his master's degree), asking if he could help with it in any way. Each time he'd come by with a new binder of research, it would turn into a two-hour conversation about how surreal and bizarre those Knicks were. It validated the notion that they were a fascinating club.

To the 204 people who spoke with me for this project—from the secretaries, season-ticket holders, and security people to the players, coaches, and executives—thank you so much for trusting a relative stranger with your stories and recollections. A handful of folks told me they created private Facebook groups for ex–Knicks staffers to do their homework on me before agreeing to interviews. Was I asking fair questions? Was I only looking for dirt? Could anyone vouch for my credibility? I don't blame anyone for having those concerns, but I couldn't be more grateful that so many people eventually put them aside to open up about their time with the club. It helped make the book so much better.

Some folks truly went above and beyond in trying to help me. In particular, Dave Checketts, Ernie Grunfeld, Ed Tapscott, Jeff Van Gundy, Bob Salmi, Jeff Nix, Mike Saunders, Doc Rivers, and Derek Harper all spoke with me several times, for hours at a time, to give me the proper context and detail.

Separately, I'd be remiss if I didn't say a special thank-you to the close friends and family of Anthony Mason. I've said countless times that, perhaps more than anything, I felt a responsibility to accurately capture his story and all the complexities that come with it. I hope that level of care came across in the text.

To the Knicks fans, who treated me so warmly in my years as a beat writer for the *Wall Street Journal* covering those far-less successful clubs from 2012 to 2016, I say thank you and that I hope this book is everything you hoped it would be. I will always feel grateful for all the support during those years in New York, when I initially doubted my own voice as a writer.

To my bosses over the past few years, who hung in there with me when I couldn't be as available to write or travel because of the book, thank you so much. You helped me reach the finish line much sooner than I otherwise would have. And helped safeguard my sanity.

For my family and my friends, whom I care about most in this world: I ended up taking more than two years away from you all to finish this thing. Thank you for being patient, and not hating me anywhere near as much as you could have. If I ever write another book, I'll find a way to do it without going off the grid as much as I did the first time.

And for my parents, who aren't here anymore, but whom I think of every hour of every day: if this made you proud of me for even a second, I wouldn't change anything about the process it took to get it done. I love you, and I miss you. Thank you for everything.

A BRIEF NOTE ON SOURCING

The vast majority of the information in this project stems from interviews with just over two hundred people tied to those Knicks clubs. Participants included an array of players, coaches, executives, rank-and-file employees, spouses, friends, agents, relatives, opponents, high school and college teammates, league executives, television executives, and team dancers and doctors, among a variety of others.

In a handful of cases, interviewees asked to go on background to discuss more sensitive subjects, and avoid being identified as the source of the information. To the best of my ability, and in the interest of transparency, I've laid out a chapter-by-chapter accounting of what information comes from each corresponding interview I've done.

For other details, I've provided references laying out which books, newspapers, articles, podcasts, video clips, and films I've pulled my information from. There were several works I drew from more frequently, and wanted to list here, as they were particularly helpful in my research.

Those works are as follows:

Wright Thompson, "Pat Riley's Final Test," ESPN.com, April 25, 2017. https://www
.espn.com/espn/feature/story/_/ld/19233570/why-miami-heat-president-pat
-riley-leave-nba.
Dan Klores, *Winning Time: Reggie Miller vs. the New York Knicks*, March 14, 2010.
Ken Berger, "Forgotten Finals: Remembered for All the Wrong Reasons," CBS
Sports.com, May 26, 2014. https://www.cbssports.com/nba/news/forgotten
-finals-remembered-for-all-the-wrong-reasons/.

Dennis D'Agostino, *Garden Glory: An Oral History of the New York Knicks*.

Doc Rivers and Bruce Brooks, *Those Who Love the Game*, 1993. Henry Holt.

Jeff Pearlman, *Showtime: Magic, Kareem, Riley, and the Los Angeles Lakers Dynasty of the 1980s*, 2014. Gotham Books.

Mark Heisler, *Lives of Riley*, 1994. Macmillan.

Spike Lee with Ralph Wiley, *Best Seat in the House: A Basketball Memoir*, 1997. Crown.

John Starks and Dan Markowitz, *My Life*, 2004. Sports Publishing, LLC.

Chris Smith, "Knicks Go for the Grand Slam," *New York*, May 31, 1993.

Chris Smith, "Hoop Genius," *New York*, November 27, 1995.

Mark Jacobson, "The Beloved Anthony Mason," *New York*, November 28, 1994.

Frank Isola and Mike Wise, *Just Ballin': The Chaotic Rise of the New York Knicks*, 1999. Simon & Schuster.

Stefan Marolachakis and Jesse Williams, "Open Run podcast with Doc Rivers," January 18, 2017. https://podcasts.apple.com/us/podcast/doc-rivers-president -and-coach-of-the-la-clippers/id964872681?i=1000380143540.

Mark Kriegel, "Escape from New York," *Esquire*, December 1, 1995.

Mike Wise, "Book Is Closed on the Knicks-Riley Saga," *New York Times*, September 8, 1995.

NOTES

PROLOGUE

The majority of the information in this section comes from interviews with Said Hamdan (12/30/20), Pam Harris (6/21/19), and Sammy Steinlight (1/9/21).

1. SPEAKING A NEW LANGUAGE

2 **Details about McDaniel tripping Mason on the first day of training camp in 1991 and Mason's reaction to the tripping** came from an interview with Patrick Eddie (2/8/19).

3 **Sideways plane seats:** Phil Jasner, "Mason Thinks He Deserves Some Credit," *Philadelphia Daily News*, June 17, 1994.

3 **Language barriers and social isolation:** Mark Jacobson, "The Beloved Anthony Mason," *New York*, Nov. 28, 1994.

3 **Details about McDaniel wrapping a towel around his manhood in Seattle** came from an interview with Frank Brickowski (12/9/20).

4 **McDaniel fighting with Reggie King:** Bruce Newman, "X," *Sports Illustrated*, February 11, 1991.

4 **Constant sparring in McDaniel's rookie year:** Sam McManis, "X Marks the Spot," *Los Angeles Times*, May 12, 1989.

4 **Boy chasing Riley with butcher knife:** Mark Heisler, *The Lives of Riley*, p. 12, 1994. Macmillan.

5 **Riley's first date with Chris Rodstrom:** Riley's Hall of Fame speech, 19:45

mark of YouTube video. Published by OfficialHoophall. https://www.you tube.com/watch?v=RXy6o7hm9qM

5 **Loud noises at Knicks' first practice:** John Starks and Dan Markowitz, *My Life*, p. 97, 2004. Sports Publishing, LLC.

5 **Details about Riley laying out his game plan on Day 1 of camp** came from an interview with Gerald Wilkins (11/12/19).

6 **Details about Riley's "easy run"** came from an interview with Jeff Sanders (8/8/19).

6 **Details about the court being wet from the lack of air-conditioning** came from an interview with Jeff Van Gundy (multiple conversations).

Relevant interviews for this chapter included: Patrick Eddie, Xavier McDaniel, Ed Tapscott, Tim McCormick, Frank Brickowski, Bernie Bickerstaff, Dan O'Sullivan, Jeff Sanders, Brian Quinnett, and Jeff Van Gundy.

2. THANK GOD THEY DIDN'T HAVE HAND GRENADES

9 **PA announcer pleading with fans:** Roy S. Johnson, "Fans Hurl Posters in Defeat," *New York Times*, March, 18, 1987.

9 **"Thank God . . . they didn't have hand grenades":** Dave Anderson, "Seeds of a Knick Revolt," *New York Times*, March 19, 1987.

10 **One of the Knick players having a PhD:** William C. Rhoden, "Too Late; Fall Back, Baby," *New York Times*, Feb. 26, 1991.

10 **Bill Bradley being a U.S. senator:** Peter Kerr, "Bradley, Heavily Favored, Narrowly Defeats Whitman," *New York Times*, Nov. 7, 1990.

10 **Jerry Lucas being able to memorize parts of the phone book:** Scott Cacciola, "A Thinking Man's Player Never Stops Thinking," *New York Times*, April 6, 2013.

10 **Jackson's admission that the Knicks of the 1970s used to deflate basketballs slightly:** Sam Smith, "Call It Deflating, Scuffing, Cutting—or There's a Better Word: Cheating," *Chicago Tribune*, Nov. 30, 1986.

11 **FBI investigation into Knicks:** Gary Buiso, "Knicks Fixed Games for Drug Dealers: FBI Probe," *New York Post*, September 14, 2013.

11 **Walker-Brown confrontation:** Roy S. Johnson, "Brown-Walker Rift Continues to Strain the Knicks," *New York Times*, Feb. 2, 1986.

11 **Detail about a member of the coaching staff having an extramarital affair,**

and it annoying players came from a pair of players who asked to be on background.

12   **Record-breaking injury totals:** "Knicks Top Even Themselves for Injuries," Associated Press, April 6, 1986.

12   **Idea of issuing fines for poor rebounding:** Roy S. Johnson, "Knicks Pathetic Again, Dropping 13th in Last 16," *New York Times*, Feb. 17, 1987.

12   **Cartwright and Bogues rebounding at same rate:** Peter May, "Knicks Are Facing a Very Long Haul," *Hartford Courant*, Nov. 17, 1987.

12   **Walker's pivot struggles:** Rick Pitino and Bill Reynolds, *Born to Coach: A Season with the New York Knicks*, p. 39, 1988. New American Library.

13   **Failures of Knicks management:** Spike Lee with Ralph Wiley, *Best Seat in the House: A Basketball Memoir*, p. 155, 1997. Crown.

13   **Mistrust between Pitino and Bianchi:** Harvey Araton, "As Bianchi Leaves, Bitterness Lingers," *New York Times*, April 5, 1991.

16   **Riley asking for book and movie deals:** Chris Smith, "Knicks Go for the Grand Slam," *New York*, May 31, 1993.

17   **Potential tampering charges against Warriors:** Harvey Araton, "Knicks May Charge that Warriors Tampered," *New York Times*, July 9, 1991.

18   **The Knicks having entertained trade offers for Ewing previously:** Paul Knepper, *The Knicks of the Nineties*, p. 7, 2020.

19   **List of Ewing's preferred trade destinations:** "Knicks Are Considering Trading Ewing," *Baltimore Sun*, August 23, 1991.

Relevant interviews for this chapter: Brendan Malone, Paul Westphal, Butch Beard, Butch Carter, unnamed players from the 1980s, Bob Hill, Curtis Bunn, Harvey Araton, Al Bianchi, Jehudith Cohen, Dick Evans, Dave Checketts, David Falk, Dick Rosenthal, and Ed Tapscott.

3. THE REINVENTION OF PAT RILEY

20   **Riley's love for "My Girl":** Wright Thompson, "Pat Riley's Final Test," ESPN.com, April 25, 2017.

20   **Detail about Riley using "This Old Heart of Mine" as his entrance music at the Garden** came from an interview with Billie Streets (10/24/19).

21   **VanDeWeghe bracing for practices:** Clifton Brown, "Vandeweghe Enjoys Job as Backup to McDaniel," *New York Times*, Oct. 13, 1991.

23   **Riley's unimpressive first day of practice with San Diego:** Mark Heisler, *The Lives of Riley*, p. 25, 1994. Macmillan.

24   **Riley jumping center:** Mark Heisler, *The Lives of Riley*, p. 20, 1994. Macmillan.

24   **"His number one task was to beat to the hell out of me":** Jerry West and Jonathan Coleman, *West by West: My Charmed and Tormented Life*, p. 129, 2012. Back Bay Books.

24   **Riley's five siblings:** Mark Heisler, *The Lives of Riley*, p. 9, 1994. Macmillan.

24   **The Riley home's heat register:** Wright Thompson, "Pat Riley's Final Test," ESPN.com, April 25, 2017.

24   **Lack of affection in the home:** Wright Thompson, "Pat Riley's Final Test," ESPN.com, April 25, 2017.

25   **Tommy Lasorda entertaining Riley as a toddler:** Mark Heisler, *The Lives of Riley*, p. 10, 1994. Macmillan.

25   **Riley's father burning his baseball memorabilia:** Mark Heisler, *The Lives of Riley*, p. 10, 1994. Macmillan.

25   **Riley's father's businesses fizzling out:** Mark Heisler, *The Lives of Riley*, p. 10, 1994. Macmillan.

25   **Riley's father running onto the court:** Mark Kriegel, "The Father Within Pat's Dad Is Here and Now," New York *Daily News*, Sept. 5, 1995.

26   **Being denied entry into Lakers' pressroom:** Mark Heisler, *The Lives of Riley*, p. 40, 1994. Macmillan.

26   **Riley's drifting phase:** Mark Heisler, *The Lives of Riley*, p. 42, 1994.

26   **Riley's start as a broadcaster with Chick Hearn:** Mark Heisler, *The Lives of Riley*, p. 43, 1994. Macmillan.

26   **Riley's salary as an analyst:** Jerry Crowe, "As Hearn's Sidekicks, They Got a Kick Out of Their Jobs," *Los Angeles Times*, May 25, 2009.

26   **Hearn intervening to help Riley get signed as a Laker:** Mark Heisler, *The Lives of Riley*, p. 30, 1994. Macmillan.

27   **Riley wanting assurances he could get his old job back:** Mark Heisler, *The Lives of Riley*, p. 51, 1994. Macmillan.

27   **Jerry West's lack of interest in the Laker job:** Jerry West and Jonathan Coleman, *West by West: My Charmed and Tormented Life*, p. 131, 2012. Back Bay Books.

28   **"He just let us play":** Mark Heisler, *The Lives of Riley*, p. 66, 1994. Macmillan.

28   **Trademarking the phrase "three-peat":** Scott Ostler, "Champions Enter-

ing a New Phase as Riley Impels by Word of Mouth," *Los Angeles Times*, June 6, 1989.

28   **Riley's control and attention:** Mark Heisler, *The Lives of Riley*, p. 141, 1994.

28   **"What happened was, he made more money, commercials, and things than players":** Mark Heisler, *The Lives of Riley*, p. 146, 1994. Macmillan.

28   **Riley trying to plant a story:** Mark Heisler, "Showtime Goes to Broadway: Happy Days Are Here Again for Pat Riley," *Los Angeles Times*, Oct. 31, 1991.

29   **Riley's reluctance to do Coach of the Year award press conference:** Jeff Pearlman, *Showtime: Magic, Kareem, Riley, and the Los Angeles Lakers Dynasty of the 1980s*, p. 388, 2014. Gotham Books.

29   **Detail about Riley requiring scouts to get permission in advance to watch practice** comes from an interview with Phil Hubbard (7/25/19).

30   **Detail about Riley making the comment concerning a hostage** cames from an interview with Spencer Checketts (12/12/19).

31   **Riley initially learning to watch film as an analyst:** Jim Luttrell, "Video Viewing Becoming Vogue in the NBA," United Press International, Oct. 19, 1985.

33   **Riley taking sleeping pills after tough losses:** Curtis Bunn, "Riley Remains Critical," *Newsday*, Jan. 21, 1992.

33   **Riley seeing acupuncturists for stress:** Sam McMannis, "A Winner from the First," *Los Angeles Times*, Jan. 21, 1990.

33   **Riley's smoking habit:** Dr. Jack Ramsay, "Riley Kept his Word to Van Gundy," ESPN.com, Oct. 25, 2003.

Relevant interviews in this chapter: Billie Streets, Gerald Wilkins, Jerry Albig, Bob Salmi, Xavier McDaniel, Mike Meola, Howie Lorch, Dave Pryzbylo, Gil Brandt, Warren DeSantis, Larry Conley, Dennis DeNovio, Dave Checketts, Pastor John Love, Swen Nater, Frank Gardner, Spencer Checketts, Ernie Grunfeld, Ed Tapscott, Brian Quinnett, and Tim McCormick.

4. KNOCK MICHAEL JORDAN TO THE FLOOR

34   **Detail about a scuttled poster idea featuring Riley** came from interviews with Pam Harris (6/21/19) and Mark Pannes (7/31/19).

34 **Balsam and Chenfeld as playlist creators:** John Anderson, "Going for the Gusto of '70s Nostalgia," *Newsday*, July 26, 1990.

34 **Itzler creating Knicks' anthem:** William C. Rhoden, "Hip-Hop in Orange and Blue," *New York Times*, Feb. 18, 1995.

34 **Detail about Jaffe throwing notebooks in response to seeing an example of how the Knicks' team dancers would perform** came from an interview with Pam Harris (6/21/19).

35 **"Assault" nickname:** Jan Hubbard, "Young Guards Are Impressing Riley," *Newsday*, Oct. 27, 1991.

35 **McDaniel's frequent pump fakes:** Curtis Bunn, "X-Man Falls Short: Punchless McDaniel Not Meeting Expectations," *Newsday*, March 12, 1992.

36 **Detail about VanDeWeghe claiming to go "3-for-5"** came from an interview with Brian Quinnett (2/15/19).

36 **Riley's "clique" meeting in Oakland:** Chris Smith, "The Knicks Go for the Grand Slam," *New York*, May 31, 1993.

37 **Details about the races between Oakley and Mark Jackson** came from an interview with Patrick Eddie (2/8/19).

37 **Team's $50,000 card games:** Robby Kalland and Martin Rickman, "Dime Podcast, Ep. 4: Greg Anthony Talks Fights at Knicks Practice and Lemon Pepper Wings," Oct. 19, 2017.

39 **Franchise-worst 61 points:** Curtis Bunn, "Hold That Team! Defense Key for Knicks," *Newsday*, April 24, 1992.

39 **Scoreless over final 3:41 versus Atlanta:** Curtis Bunn, "Self-Destruction; Scoreless Last 3:41 Drops Knicks into Tie for 1st," *Newsday*, April 16, 1992.

40 **Losing sole possession of first place:** Curtis Bunn, "Self-Destruction; Scoreless Last 3:41 Drops Knicks into Tie for 1st," *Newsday*, April 16, 1992.

40 **Detail about Holzman gently correcting Checketts** came from interviews with Ed Tapscott (multiple conversations).

41 **Only team in history to blow such a lead:** ESPN Stats & Information research; original reporter query.

41 **Putting Ewing further from the basket:** Clifton Brown, "Stomping at the Garden, Knicks Win in a Waltz," *New York Times*, April 25, 1992.

41 **Trapping Isiah Thomas:** Jan Hubbard, "Brainpower Gives Knicks Better Look," *Newsday*, April 25, 1992.

41 **Strategy to contain Rodman:** Sam Smith, "Few Shots (Clank!) on Playoffs," *Chicago Tribune*, April 28, 1992.

41   **Six technical fouls:** Curtis Bunn, "Ewing Steps Up; Leads Knicks to Thrill-
     ing OT Win, 2–1 Lead," *Newsday*, April 29, 1992.

41   **Four techs and a flagrant:** Sam Smith, "Knicks, Pistons Get Down and
     Dirty," *Chicago Tribune*, May 1, 1992.

42   **"When push came to thug":** Bruce Newman, "Rough and Tough," *Sports
     Illustrated*, May 11, 1992.

42   **Pippen wishing Oakley good luck:** Sam Smith, "There's No Escaping Back-
     to-Back Weekend Games in New York," *Chicago Tribune*, May 5, 1992.

43   **"Knicks' Best Hope? Look Good Losing":** Chris Smith, "The Knicks Go for
     the Grand Slam," *New York*, May 31, 1993.

43   **Pippen's ankle sprain:** Sam Smith, "X-Rated Encounter for Pippen," *Chi-
     cago Tribune*, May 9, 1992.

43   **Three Bulls needing to be bandaged in one quarter:** Joe Gergen, "Bulls
     Take a Licking but Keep Ticking," *Newsday*, May 10, 1992.

44   **"Thrown around like a rag doll":** Alan Greenberg, "Pippen Makes It Tough
     on Bulls," *Hartford Courant*, May 28, 1993.

44   **Bulls' drives to the basket in Game 5:** Anthony Cotton, "Bulls Repel Knicks
     on Jordan's Drives," *Washington Post*, May 13, 1992.

44   **Details from the locker-room tape shown to the team before Game 6** came
     from interviews with Bob Salmi (multiple conversations), Gerald Wilkins
     (11/12/19), and Patrick Eddie (2/8/19).

45   **"I expect my head to be taken off":** Melissa Isaacson, "Jackson Says He Saw
     It Coming," *Chicago Tribune*, May 15, 1992.

46   **Knicks forcing Jordan's game to the perimeter:** Curtis Bunn, "Knicks Live!
     Limping Ewing, Starks Lead Awesome Effort," *Newsday*, May 15, 1992.

46   **Knicks' five flagrants to Chicago's zero:** Lacy J. Banks, "Bulls Know Cava-
     liers Can't Be Taken Lightly," *Chicago Sun-Times*, May 19, 1992.

47   **Ewing's three fouls in four minutes in Game 7:** Steve Jacobson, "All Hail
     Michael! No Excuses for Average Patrick," *Newsday*, May 18, 1992.

Relevant interviews in this chapter: Dave Checketts, Pam Harris, Mark Pannes,
Cliff Chenfeld, Stanley Jaffe, Bob Salmi, Jeff Nix, Brian Quinnett, Gerald Wilkins,
Mike Saunders, Patrick Eddie, Tim McCormick, Ed Tapscott, and Xavier Mc-
Daniel.

5. CHALK OUTLINE

48 **Detail about Riley's misinterpretation of the poster mock-ups** came from an interview with Pam Harris (6/21/19).

48 **Chalk outline on a printout:** Sam Smith, *The Jordan Rules: The Inside Story of One Turbulent Season with Michael Jordan and the Chicago Bulls*, p. 422 (Kindle version).

49 **Indestructible ticket material:** Eric Fisher, "Knicks Take Plastic, Not Paper, for New Anti-Counterfeit Tickets," *Washington Times*, Dec. 12, 1992.

49 **Knicks' offer for Harvey Grant:** David Hutchison, "Grant Offer Tops $17 Million," *Washington Times*, July 3, 1992.

50 **Stanley Roberts holding up the trade:** Barry Cooper, "Roberts Agrees; Deal Done," *Orlando Sentinel*, Sept. 23, 1992.

50 **Boston signing McDaniel:** Peter May, "X Marks His Spot: McDaniel, Celtics Team on 3-yr Deal," *Boston Globe*, Sept. 11, 1992.

51 **Roberts being swayed by Sterling's party:** Barry Cooper, "Roberts Agrees; Deal Done," *Orlando Sentinel*, Sept. 23, 1992.

51 **An O where their X used to be:** Joe Gergen, "A Big 'X' Carved in Checketts' Reputation," *Newsday*, Sept. 11, 1992.

52 **Oakley's siblings:** Mike Wise, "The Knicks' Family Man," *New York Times*, Nov. 22, 1995.

52 **Oakley's flagrant total:** Harvey Pollack and Joe Favorito, "1993–94 NBA Media Guide and Statistical Yearbook," p. 188, Oct. 1993.

52 **Oakley hitting Silas in the chest:** Mike Cranston, "Former NBA Enforcer Charles Oakley Takes Tough-Guy Persona to Charlotte," Associated Press, Jan. 21, 2011.

53 **Detail about team staffers sitting their families away from the courtside seats, to avoid them being run into by Oakley** came from interview with Said Hamdan (12/30/20).

53 **Oakley's father dying at 35:** Mike Wise, "The Knicks' Family Man," *New York Times*, Nov. 22, 1995.

54 **Oakley's early wake-up calls:** Shaun Powell, "He Got His Toughness from Cleveland's Inner City and His Work Ethic from Rural Alabama," *Newsday*, May 8, 1994.

54 **Oakley's grandfather's lack of equipment:** Shaun Powell, "He Got His Toughness from Cleveland's Inner City and His Work Ethic from Rural Alabama," *Newsday*, May 8, 1994.

54 **Oakley washing cars:** Phil Taylor, "Charles Oakley Made His Name Under the Boards with His Elbows and His Heart," *Sports Illustrated*, Jan. 24, 2000.

54 **Oakley's plainspoken riddles:** Chris Jenkins, "Ewing's Shots Irk Knicks," *San Diego Union-Tribune*, June 17, 1994.

54 **Oakley's Starburst-like clothing:** Richard Sandomir, "Inside the Closet of Charles Oakley," *New York Times*, March 12, 1995.

54 **Refusing to wear the same thing as a teammate:** Richard Sandomir, "Inside the Closet of Charles Oakley," *New York Times*, March 12, 1995.

56 **Oakley's $10,000 fine:** Clifton Brown, "No Harm, No Foul? Oakley Is Fined $10,000," *New York Times*, Jan. 1, 1993.

56 **"The way a defensive back pops a receiver":** Clifton Brown, "No Harm, No Foul? Oakley Is Fined $10,000," *New York Times*, Jan. 1, 1993.

56 **"Just because there's glass in the road":** Doug Smith, "The World According to Oakley," *Toronto Star*, July 27, 2007.

57 **Knicks' meeting with the league office:** No byline, "Fine to Oakley Is Questioned," *New York Times*, Jan. 12, 1993.

57 **flagrant fouls:** Harvey Pollack and Joe Favorito, "1993–94 NBA Media Guide and Statistical Yearbook," p. 188, Oct. 1993.

57 **97 technical fouls:** Harvey Pollack and Joe Favorito, "1993–94 NBA Media Guide and Statistical Yearbook," p. 199, Oct. 1993.

59 **Frisbee-catching dog named Whitney:** Curtis Bunn, "Pitiful Showing Extinguishes Glow of Win over Bulls," *Newsday*, Sept. 30, 1992.

59 **"We just followed suit":** Curtis Bunn, "Pitiful Showing Extinguishes Glow of Win over Bulls," *Newsday*, Sept. 30, 1992.

59 **15 consecutive misses and 11-minute drought:** Curtis Bunn, "Pitiful Showing Extinguishes Glow of Win over Bulls," *Newsday*, Sept. 30, 1992.

59 **Video with car crashes and rams head-butting each other:** Stefan Marolachakis and Jesse Williams, "Open Run" podcast with Doc Rivers, Jan. 18, 2017.

59 **"Fire coming out of his eyes":** Stefan Marolachakis and Jesse Williams, "Open Run" podcast with Doc Rivers, Jan. 18, 2017.

60 **Hack opponents early and often:** Stefan Marolachakis and Jesse Williams, "Open Run" podcast with Doc Rivers, Jan. 18, 2017.

60 **Kenny Anderson breaking his wrist:** Mike Freeman, "Broken Wrist Sidelines Anderson and Angers Nets," *New York Times*, March 2, 1993.

60 **The narrative around the Suns being "soft":** No byline, "Suns Have Plenty of Punch Left, Pound Knicks," Associated Press, March 24, 1993.

62   **Greg Anthony returning to practice one day after breaking his jaw:** No byline, "Anthony Inspires No. 2 UNLV," *Orlando Sentinel*, Feb. 28, 1990.

62   **Anthony charging at a referee:** Howard Blatt, "Knicks Get Win, Barely Greg Leads Grizzlies Against Former Team," New York *Daily News*, Nov. 20, 1995.

62   **Six ejections and 12 technical fouls:** Clifton Brown, "Six Ejected in Knicks-Suns Wild West Slugfest," *New York Times*, March 24, 1993.

63   **Unprecedented fines:** Mark Heisler, "Brawl Costs Knicks, Suns $294,173.97," *Los Angeles Times*, March 25, 1993.

63   **"We're either gonna win the game, or win the fight":** Dan Klores, *Winning Time: Miller vs. The Knicks; ESPN 30 for 30* film, 2010.

Relevant interviews in this chapter: Pam Harris, Mark Pannes, Dave Checketts, Ernie Grunfeld, Dr. Norm Scott, Elgin Baylor, Xavier McDaniel, Bob Salmi, Loren Olson, Tim McGee, Said Hamdan, Stu Jackson, Jeff Nix, Greg Butler, Brendan Malone, David Cain, Donnie Walsh, Billie Streets, Bobby Goldwater, Ken Munoz, Rod Thorn, Joel Litvin, Russ Granik, Doc Rivers, Mike Saunders, Kenny Anderson, Steve Javie, Ed T. Rush, Jerry Colangelo, and Curtis Bunn.

6. THE BUTTERFLY AMONG THE BUFFALOES

64   **Paul Evans named Pitt coach:** Pohla Smith, "Pitt Names Evans Coach," United Press International, March 26, 1986.

65   **Smith being 5-foot-10 as a high school freshman:** Mark Whicker, "Smith's Style Finally Fits in with Clippers," *Orange County Register*, Jan. 22, 1990.

65   **Then growing to 6-foot-7 by graduation:** Mark Whicker, "Smith's Style Finally Fits in with Clippers," *Orange County Register*, Jan. 22, 1990.

65   **Smith's interests in other things:** Scott Howard-Cooper, "Smith Knows His Stuff on the Court," *Los Angeles Times*, March 28, 1990.

65   **Stocks and world affairs:** Scott Howard-Cooper, "Smith Knows His Stuff on the Court," *Los Angeles Times*, March 28, 1990.

65   **Smith's disinterest in watching game film with his father:** Scott Howard-Cooper, "Smith Knows His Stuff on the Court," *Los Angeles Times*, March 28, 1990.

66   **Smith's 52-point game:** Scott Howard-Cooper, "Smith's 52 Tie Record in Clipper Win," *Los Angeles Times*, Dec. 2, 1990.

66 Smith's hair loss due to stress: Ben Sin, "Checking In with Charles Smith," *New York*, Dec. 13, 2011.

68 Starks's short fuse: Larry McShane, "Malik and the Missing Playbook: A True Story," Associated Press, April 30, 1993.

68 Ref telling Starks to shut up and play: Sam Morrill, "John Starks Reminisces About Battles with Reggie Miller," YouTube video, MSG Network, July 26, 2017, https://www.youtube.com/watch?v=UFqQ7f2xBQs.

69 "Wanted to take my fist and put it through his face": Sam Morrill, "John Starks Reminisces About Battles with Reggie Miller," YouTube video, MSG Network, July 26, 2017, https://www.youtube.com/watch?v=UFqQ7f2xBQs.

69 "I'm gonna cut [Miller's] dick off and make him eat it": Frank Isola and Mike Wise, *Just Ballin': The Chaotic Rise of the New York Knicks*, p. 223, 1999. Simon & Schuster.

69 Starks's mother's frustration with Ewing: Dan Klores, *Winning Time: Miller vs. The Knicks; ESPN 30 for 30* film, 2010.

70 Detail about the hard-hat worker cussing out Phil Jackson from the upper deck of MSG came from an interview with Will Perdue (12/19/20).

71 Disparity in credential requests: Bob Ryan, "City is Basking in its Basketball," *Boston Globe*, May 26, 1993.

72 Jordan's struggles: Jan Hubbard, "Jordan Is Human, at Least for Now," *Newsday*, May 24, 1993.

72 Starks's training camp dunk attempt that kept him on the roster: John Starks and Dan Markowitz, *My Life*, p. 83, 2004.

73 Horace Grant's ankle injury: Lacy J. Banks, "Big Apple No Fun City for 'No-Show Grant,'" *Chicago Sun-Times*, May 26, 1993.

73 Jerry Krause passing on chance to sign Starks: Mike Mulligan, "Anthony Foul Angers Jordan," *Chicago Sun-Times*, May 26, 1993.

73 The report on Jordan's gambling in Atlantic City mid-series: Dave Anderson, "Jordan's Atlantic City Caper," *New York Times*, May 27, 1993.

74 Van Gundy on New York's blown opportunity to go up 3–0: Dennis D'Agostino, *Garden Glory: An Oral History of the New York Knicks*, p. 231, 2003.

74 Smith dropping weight to play small forward: Clifton Brown, "Smith Learning Less Can Mean More," *New York Times*, April 16, 1993.

74 Teams opting to leave Smith open unless he was under the basket: Sam Smith, "Knicks' Smith No Softie," *Chicago Tribune*, May 27, 1993.

75 Knicks' 27-game winning streak at the Garden: Ira Winderman, "Knicks Get Down and Dirty; Jackson Annoyed by Physical Tactics," *South Florida Sun-Sentinel*, May 26, 1993.

76 "Like the sudden death of a family member who was perfectly healthy": Doc Rivers and Bruce Brooks, *For Those Who Love the Game*, p. 147, 1993. Henry Holt.

77 Rivers seeing Herb Williams at a gas station after Game 5: Doc Rivers and Bruce Brooks, *For Those Who Love the Game*, p. 148, 1993. Henry Holt.

77 Rivers seeing Smith pulled over by the police after Game 5: Doc Rivers and Bruce Brooks, *For Those Who Love the Game*, p. 148, 1993. Henry Holt.

77 "Maybe this is the defining moment of this team's life": David Moore, "Bulls Plan a Quick Ending for Knicks," *Dallas Morning News*, June 4, 1993.

77 Smith and Knicks reaching a tentative agreement on a deal between Games 5 and 6: Clifton Brown, "Large Step for Knicks, but It's Small Solace," *New York Times*, June 6, 1993.

78 "We had a championship team. We really did": Dennis D'Agostino, *Garden Glory: An Oral History of the New York Knicks*, p. 230, 2003. Triumph Books.

Relevant interviews for this chapter: Steve Maslek, Paul Evans, Reggie Warford, Ed Tapscott, Doc Rivers, Jake O'Donnell, Mike Wise, George Whittaker, Will Perdue, and Dave Checketts.

7. DAYLIGHT

79 Riley family traveling for vacation to Wailea: Jason Hehir, *The Last Dance: The Untold Story of Michael Jordan and the Chicago Bulls*, unused research material shared by Hehir, who directed the ESPN documentary, April 2020.

80 Ewing learning of Jordan's retirement: Rachel Nichols, "The Jump," interview with Patrick Ewing, ESPN, May 12, 2020.

80 "It helps us": Steve Jacobson, "Never Going to Be the Same," *Newsday*, Nov. 3, 1993.

80 Team begins season at 12:01 a.m.: David Steele, "Up Before Dawn: Riley Starts Work Ethic at Midnight," *Newsday*, Oct. 9, 1993.

80 The new rules around flagrant fouls: No byline, "NBA to Enforce New Flagrant Rule," United Press International, Nov. 5, 1993.

81   Detail about Smith's tooth being knocked out by Oakley during a training-camp practice came from an interview with Lewis Geter (7/30/19).

81   Bonner being bruised up in camp: Clifton Brown, "Bonner Muscling His Way into Knicks' Picture," *New York Times*, Oct. 17, 1993.

81   Knicks being on the road to start the season: David Steele, "Knicks Handle Road, Ailments," *Newsday*, Nov. 19, 1993.

81   A number of Knicks being unhappy with their places in the rotation: Clifton Brown, "Not All Knicks Are Happy Campers," *New York Times*, Oct. 8. 1993.

82   Hornacek being able to predict New York's offense: Frank Lawlor, "Surprise! Sixers Pull a Trap on the Knicks," *Philadelphia Inquirer*, Jan. 24, 1994.

82   Anonymous quotes: Mark Heisler, "Riley Has a New Project: Find Locker Room Rats," *Los Angeles Times*, Jan. 30, 1994.

82   Ewing's and Starks's shooting woes: No byline, "Rockets Win 15th in a Row," *Los Angeles Times*, Dec. 3, 1993.

83   Smith having had knee surgery just months earlier: Clifton Brown, "Knee Surgery Will Sideline Smith for Six Weeks," *New York Times*, Dec. 7, 1993.

83   MRI confirming more bad cartilage: Clifton Brown, "Knee Surgery Will Sideline Smith for Six Weeks," *New York Times*, Dec. 7, 1993.

83   Smith having an array of celebrity nicknames: Steve Bulpett, "All Celtics See No Stars," *Boston Herald*, Feb. 2, 1994.

84   Doc Rivers tears his ACL: Clifton Brown, "Injury to Rivers the Cloud in Ewing's Silver Lining," *New York Times*, Dec. 17, 1993.

85   Greg Anthony can't find his belt: Tim Layden, "Differences Are Easy to Pinpoint," *Newsday*, Dec. 22, 1993.

85   Knicks had tried to acquire Harper before: Jan Hubbard, "Knicks' Deal for Harper Rejected," *Newsday*, Feb. 25, 1993.

86   Courtside fan taunting Harper: Dennis D'Agostino, *Garden Glory: An Oral History of the New York Knicks*, p. 235, 2003.

87   Riley's worst loss: Clifton Brown, "Sonics Blast Knicks, and So Does Riley," *New York Times*, Feb. 23, 1994.

87   The Knicks' West Coast struggles: Clifton Brown, "Sonics Blast Knicks, and So Does Riley," *New York Times*, Feb. 23, 1994.

Relevant interviews in this chapter: Jason Hehir, Lewis Geter, Rolando Blackman, Mike Saunders, Brig Owens, Will Perdue, Mike Wise, Doc Rivers, Dr. Norm Scott, Derek Harper, Phil Hubbard, and Scott McGuire.

8. THIRTY-SIX HOURS IN RENO

91 **"They all had their hands out"**: Ira Berkow, "The Plot Thickens for Knicks and Bulls," *New York Times*, May 10, 1994.

91 **Harper pocketing his money**: Dennis D'Agostino, *Garden Glory: An Oral History of the New York Knicks*, p. 230, 2003. Triumph Books.

91 **Riley changing his starting lineup**: Clifton Brown, "Knicks Respond Favorably to Riley's Changes," *New York Times*, March 3, 1994.

92 **Starks not thrilled with bench role**: Clifton Brown, "What, Starks Worry? Game 7 Is Buried," *New York Times*, Oct. 9, 1994.

92 **Holding eight straight opponents under 90 points**: Michael Arace, "Knicks Step Up Defense," *Hartford Courant*, March 20, 1994.

92 **Riley paying players for charges**: Dennis D'Agostino, *Garden Glory: An Oral History of the New York Knicks*, p. 236, 2003. Triumph Books.

92 **Eric Anderson trying to draw a charge**: Dennis D'Agostino, *Garden Glory: An Oral History of the New York Knicks*, p. 236, 2003. Triumph Books.

94 **Starks missing rest of regular season**: Robert McG. Thomas Jr., "Knee Surgery Puts Starks on Sidelines for Six Weeks," *New York Times*, March 15, 1994.

94 **"We needed scoring"**: Clifton Brown, "This Finishing Stretch May Be Finishing the Knicks," *New York Times*, April 20, 1994.

95 **"That's what [Riley] said?"**: Clifton Brown, "This Finishing Stretch May Be Finishing the Knicks," *New York Times*, April 20, 1994.

95 **"Defines offense a different way than I define it"**: Mike Freeman, "Riley Fires Back and Suspends Mason Indefinitely," *New York Times*, April 22, 1994.

95 **"You're either in, or you're out"**: Mike Freeman, "Riley Fires Back and Suspends Mason Indefinitely," *New York Times*, April 22, 1994.

96 **Mason attending game while suspended as a spectator**: Sandy Keenan, "Knicks Shake It Off, Slam Sixers," *Newsday*, April 22, 1994.

96 **Davis thinking a fight was happening in the stands**: Sandy Keenan, "The Last Word Belongs to Pat; Hands Mase Indefinite Suspension," *Newsday*, April 22, 1994.

97 **"You're banned! You're barred! You're not part of this organization!"**: Mark Jacobson, "The Beloved Anthony Mason," *New York*, Nov. 28, 1994.

Relevant interviews in this chapter: Corey Gaines, Anthony Bonner, Derek Harper, Mike Saunders, Jeff Van Gundy, Dave Checketts, Don Cronson, and Ernie Grunfeld.

9. THE ENIGMATIC LIFE OF ANTHONY MASON

98 Details about Mason's Senior Night came from interviews with Nico Childs (10/9/19) and Wayne Bell (multiple interviews).

99 Details about Mason nearly being kicked off the team after sneaking into the girls-only dorm numerous times, and borrowing team staffers' cars came from multiple interviews with Wayne Bell.

102 **Mason struggling with Turkish food:** Mark Jacobson, "The Beloved Anthony Mason," *New York*, Nov. 28, 1994.

102 **Fouls hardly ever getting called in Turkey:** Mark Jacobson, "The Beloved Anthony Mason," *New York*, Nov. 28, 1994.

102 **Improving his quickness in Venezuela:** Mark Jacobson, "The Beloved Anthony Mason," *New York*, Nov. 28, 1994.

102 **Averaging 28 points and 11 rebounds for USBL team:** Joe Krupinski, "Surf Stint Could Pay for Mason," *Newsday*, June 24, 1994.

102 **Ed Krinsky suggesting to Fuzzy Levane to sign Mason:** Harvey Araton, "Tough Knick Anthony Mason Was True to the City," *New York Times*, Feb. 28, 2015.

102 **Mason's 36 points that day:** Harvey Araton, "Tough Knick Anthony Mason Was True to the City," *New York Times*, Feb. 28, 2015.

102 **Detail about Mason's teeth being knocked out overseas and Mason's offer to play for an Israeli team before joining the Knicks** came from an interview with Latifa Whitlock (multiple interviews).

103 **Riley watching Mason at summer league:** Dennis D'Agostino, "Remembering Anthony Mason," NBA.com, March 2015.

105 **"Was about 8-to-1 in favor of chicks":** Eddie Mata, "NY Knicks Anthony Mason Where Are They Now in Sports," YouTube video, Jan. 24, 2015. https://www.youtube.com/watch?v=--PYkdAZUxw&t=131s.

107 **Detail about Mason's wild night out with Hubert Davis** came from an interview with Ed Tapscott (multiple interviews).

108 **Mason's legal troubles from 1996 to 2000:** Jenna Fryer, "Hornets' Mason Sorry About Arrest," Associated Press, July 7, 2000.

108 **Cop tried to shake down Mason:** No byline, "Report: Cop Tried to Shake Down Basketball Player," Associated Press, April 16, 1997.

108 **Mason charged with statutory rape:** Mike Wise, "Mason Denies Charges in Statutory Rape Case," *New York Times*, Feb. 9, 1998.

109 **Five hours of police questioning:** No byline, "Mason Faces Rape Charge," Associated Press, Feb. 9, 1998.

109 **Felony charges dropped:** No byline, "Felony Charges Dropped Against Mason," United Press International, June 25, 1988.

110 **"Anthony's what I'd call an oxymoron":** Mark Jacobson, "The Beloved Anthony Mason," *New York*, Nov. 28, 1994.

110 **Detail about Corey Kelly being ticketed in the wake of Mason's auto accident** came from an interview with Anthony Kelly (9/16/19).

111 **Mason's mother was a bookkeeper:** Mark Jacobson, "The Beloved Anthony Mason," *New York*, Nov. 28, 1994.

111 **Detail about Mason enduring physical abuse while trying to protect his mother** came from multiple interviews with Latifa Whitlock.

111 **Detail about Mason leaving thousands of dollars on his mother's dresser** came from an interview with Gary Waites (8/2/19).

112 **Detail about Mason staying at the strip club to engage writers after nearly all his other teammates left** came from an interview with David Steele (10/2/19).

112 **Mason asking people if they were Christians, too:** Mark Jacobson, "The Beloved Anthony Mason," *New York*, Nov. 28, 1994.

113 **Detail about Mason being critical of Ewing for regularly turning down interview requests** came from interviews with Patrick Eddie (2/8/19), Freddy Avila, (8/28/19), and Anthony Kelly (9/6/19).

113 **Visiting the dying child in the hospital:** Ian O'Connor, "Mase's Greatest Assist," New York *Daily News*, March 28, 1995.

114 **"Joey had his moment before he died":** Ian O'Connor, "Mase's Greatest Assist," New York *Daily News*, March 28, 1995.

Relevant interviews in this chapter: Nico Childs, Wayne Bell, George Lester, Judon Roper, Latifa Whitlock, Cordell Johnson, Monica Bryant, Ed Krinsky, Bob Salmi, Ed Tapscott, Gary Waites, Patrick Eddie, Freddy Avila, Anthony Kelly, Antoine Mason, Don Cronson, Dave Checketts, David Steele, Curtis Bunn, Chris Smith, Fred Kerber, Frank Isola, Pastor John Love, and Ed Oliva.

10. STANDING OUT IN THE CROWD

115 **The Knicks having a 15,000-person season-ticket wait list:** Richard Sandomir, "How Knicks Drummed Up Business," *New York Times*, Sept. 26, 2002.

115 **Daryl Hannah and JFK Jr. breaking up:** Bill Zwecker, "JFK Jr. Nicked by Breakup," *Chicago Sun-Times*, Nov. 16, 1994.

115 Detail about JFK Jr. requesting season tickets of his own came from interviews with Maggie McEvoy (8/19/19) and Dave Checketts (multiple interviews).

116 Derrick Coleman needing stitches for his lip: Al Harvin, "The Playbook Vanishes, and Other Nets' Riddles," *New York Times*, April 30, 1994.

116 Nets doctor being delayed on the way down to the locker room: Al Harvin, "The Playbook Vanishes, and Other Nets' Riddles," *New York Times*, April 30, 1994.

117 "We want the Bulls!" chant: David Steele, "Ewing, (36) Knicks Dismiss Nets, Get Shot at Bulls," *Newsday*, May 7, 1994.

118 Starks jawing with the daughter of a Bulls minority partner: Ed Sherman, "Like It or Not, Fans Get into Fight Action," *Chicago Tribune*, May 14, 1994.

118 Courtside fans wearing helmets at the following game: Steve Rosenbloom, "Ahmad & the Unapproach-a-Bull," *Chicago Sun-Times*, May 16, 1994.

118 Knicks trailing by 22 before tying the score late in Game 3: Mike Lupica, "Harper and Pippen: A Tale of Two Quitters," *Newsday*, May 15, 1994.

118 Pippen's refusal to go back into the game: Mike Lupica, "Harper and Pippen: A Tale of Two Quitters," *Newsday*, May 15, 1994.

118 Greg Anthony's 2-for-13 performance in Game 4: David Steele, "Nasty Whippin' by Pippen: Great Scottie, 21 Turnovers Destroy Knicks," *Newsday*, May 16, 1994.

118 B. J. Armstrong's go-ahead jumper in Game 5: Lacy J. Banks, "Heady Armstrong Steps Up in Big Way," *Chicago Sun-Times*, May 19, 1994.

119 Anthony telling Hubert Davis to be ready to shoot: Dennis D'Agostino, *Garden Glory: An Oral History of the New York Knicks*, p. 237, 2003. Triumph Books.

119 "What happened? Who fouled?": J. A. Adande, "Hollins' Call Still Resonates After 15 Years," ESPN.com, May 29, 2009.

119 Garretson calling Hollins's call "terrible": Melissa Isaacson, "Ref Admits that Pippen Foul Wasn't," *Chicago Tribune*, Oct. 13, 1994.

120 "[The Knicks] are gonna win those sorts of games": Harvey Araton, "Knicks: A Train that Could (or Couldn't)," *New York Times*, March 16, 1994.

121 "They're a copy; we're the real thing": Clifton Brown, "Knicks Score 100 Against Pacers to Pass First Test," *New York Times*, May 25, 1994.

121 Ewing's two air balls and one point in Game 3: Peter May, "Knicks' Chances Go by the Boards; Rebounding the Key in Game 4," *Boston Globe*, May 30, 1994.

121 Ewing's scream out of frustration: David Steele, "Just Another Game 3 Loss, but This One Is New Mark for Futility," *Newsday*, May 29, 1994.

121 Knicks break record for fewest points by a team in shot-clock-era playoff game: David Steele, "Just Another Game 3 Loss, but This One Is New Mark for Futility," *Newsday*, May 29, 1994.

121 Spike Lee skipping his father's jazz concert to attend Game 7 of the Finals: Spike Lee with Ralph Wiley, *Best Seat in the House: A Basketball Memoir*, p. 62, 1997. Crown.

122 Actress Cheryl Burr telling Lee they needed to talk: Spike Lee with Ralph Wiley, *Best Seat in the House: A Basketball Memoir*, p. 105, 1997. Crown.

122 "Spike, it's over between me and you": Spike Lee with Ralph Wiley, *Best Seat in the House: A Basketball Memoir*, p. 107, 1997. Crown.

122 "Time for commitment": Spike Lee with Ralph Wiley, *Best Seat in the House: A Basketball Memoir*, p. 107, 1997. Crown.

122 Lee's first time buying season tickets, landing in Section 304: Spike Lee with Ralph Wiley, *Best Seat in the House: A Basketball Memoir*, p. 107, 1997. Crown.

122 Detail about Lee taking Knicks players to Shark Bar with other celebrities came from an interview with Patrick Eddie (2/8/19).

122 Lee getting financial help from prominent Black celebrities to finish *Malcolm X*: Lena Williams, "Spike Lee Says Money from Blacks Saved 'X,'" *New York Times*, May 20, 1992.

123 Lee's betting arrangement with Reggie Miller: No byline, "Spike and Reggie Hug and Make Up," Associated Press, June 6, 1994.

123 The agreement to cast Miller's wife in a Lee film if Pacers won series: Jared Zwerling, "Miller Enters Hall with Spike Lee Motivation," ESPN.com, Sept. 7, 2012.

123 "Are we in trouble here?": Spike Lee with Ralph Wiley, *Best Seat in the House: A Basketball Memoir*, p. 212, 1997. Crown.

124 "My wife was right there!": Dan Klores, *Winning Time: Miller vs. The Knicks; ESPN 30 for 30* film, 2010.

125 Starks calling a players-only meeting before Game 6: Clifton Brown, "Drive Time for Starks; Knicks Hope Mercurial Guard Has Post-Season Rebound," *New York Times*, April 16, 1995.

125 Knicks taking a 1-6 postseason road record into Indiana: Clifton Brown, "It's Do or Done Tonight for Knicks Era," *New York Times*, June 3, 1994.

127 Checketts asking that the Larry O'Brien Trophy be given to the Knicks in the conference finals round to motivate the players, and Riley saying it was a bad idea: Dennis D'Agostino, *Garden Glory: An Oral History of the New York Knicks*, p. 238, 2003. Triumph Books.

128 **"There's Patrick coming out of the sky"**: Mike Lupica, "Magic from the Big Guy; Patrick's Game 7 a Story of Soaring," *Newsday*, June 6, 1994.

128 **Miller openly weeping in the locker room after Game 7**: Bruce Jenkins, "Ewing Leads Knicks into NBA Finals," *San Francisco Chronicle*, June 6, 1994.

128 **Starks saying the NBA Finals will be a "breeze" compared to the Indiana matchup**: J. A. Adande and Lacy J. Banks, "After Some Clarification, Starks Breezes into Opener," *Chicago Sun-Times*, June 9, 1994.

Relevant interviews in this chapter: Pam Harris, Maggie McEvoy, Dave Checketts, Butch Beard, Derek Harper, Russ Granik, Rod Thorn, Brian McIntyre, Phil Jackson (via email), Larry Brown, Patrick Eddie, Anthony Bonner, Donnie Walsh, Corey Gaines, Jeff Nix, J. A. Adande, and Ed Tapscott.

11. THE DREAM, THE CHASE, AND THE NIGHTMARE

129 **Starks getting into a fight on his first day of middle school**: John Starks and Dan Markowitz, *My Life*, p. 27, 2004. Sports Publishing LLC.

129 **Principal telling Starks to leave school grounds**: John Starks and Dan Markowitz, *My Life*, p. 27, 2004. Sports Publishing LLC.

129 **Starks's effort to take the bus back home**: John Starks and Dan Markowitz, *My Life*, p. 27, 2004. Sports Publishing LLC.

131 **Starks requesting thirty tickets each for Games 1 and 2 of the NBA Finals**: Harvey Araton, "Starks Is Left Walking Mental Balance Beam," *New York Times*, June 10, 1994.

131 **Starks's uncle dying**: Clifton Brown, "What Do the Knicks Need? Some Easy Hoops Off the Fast Break," *New York Times*, June 10, 1994.

131 **Starks flying in from Tulsa**: Harvey Araton, "Starks Is Left Walking Mental Balance Beam," *New York Times*, June 10, 1994.

131 **"[His passing] didn't have anything to do with my performance"**: Jerry Bembry, "Starks Is Pretty Angry Over Ugly Start," *Baltimore Sun*, June 10, 1994.

132 **Starks saying he got kicked off his high school team:** John Starks and Dan Markowitz, *My Life*, p. 34, 2004. Sports Publishing LLC.

132 **Starks growing up with six siblings:** John Starks and Dan Markowitz, *My Life*, p. 1, 2004. Sports Publishing LLC.

133 **Starks playing at four different colleges:** Jacob Lewis, "Starks Elevates His Game," *Washington Post*, Nov. 21, 1997.

133 **Starks taking a minimum-wage job as a cashier at Safeway:** John Starks and Dan Markowitz, *My Life*, p. 46, 2004. Sports Publishing LLC.

133 **The 10.5-foot beams in the store:** John Starks and Dan Markowitz, *My Life*, p. 47, 2004.

133 **Playing in a local tournament against the likes of Karl Malone and Dennis Rodman:** John Starks and Dan Markowitz, *My Life*, p. 53, 2004. Sports Publishing LLC.

133 **Starks trying cocaine, telling himself he'd never do it again:** John Starks and Dan Markowitz, *My Life*, p. 48, 2004. Sports Publishing LLC.

134 **22 points in one half on his wedding night:** John Starks and Dan Markowitz, *My Life*, p. 59, 2004. Sports Publishing LLC.

135 **Hakeem Olajuwon being in pain because of Anthony Mason:** Phil Taylor, "Competitive Edge, Toughness Made Anthony Mason One to Remember," *Sports Illustrated*, Feb. 28, 2015.

136 **Starks's double-digit fourth quarter in Game 3:** Clifton Brown, "Pressure Points: Knicks Surge Past Rockets in 4th," *New York Times*, June 16, 1994.

136 **Ewing breaking record for most blocked shots in an NBA Finals series:** NBA Series Finals Leaders and Records for Blocks, Basketball-Reference.com.

137 **Ahmad Rashad sitting on Garden hay bales, weeping:** Tim Rohan, "Michael, Murray and . . . O.J.? Ahmad Rashad Has Kept His Friends Close—Most of Them, Anyway," *Sports Illustrated*, June 29, 2018.

137 **O. J. Simpson serving as Rashad's best man:** Tim Rohan, "Michael, Murray and . . . O.J.? Ahmad Rashad Has Kept His Friends Close—Most of Them, Anyway," *Sports Illustrated*, June 29, 2018.

137 **Rashad being mentioned in Simpson's note the day of the chase:** Tim Rohan, "Michael, Murray and . . . O.J.? Ahmad Rashad Has Kept His Friends Close—Most of Them, Anyway," *Sports Illustrated*, June 29, 2018.

138 **Kenny Smith being preoccupied by the Simpson chase during Game 5:** Charles Curtis, "Kenny Smith: Rockets Talked O.J. During '94 Finals," *USA Today*, Oct. 16, 2016.

139 **NBA's television ratings being down considerably without Jordan:** No by-line, "NBA Finals Gets Lowest Ratings," Associated Press, June 20, 1999.

139 **NBC affiliates' use of the split screen during the chase:** David Barron, "Juice on the Loose: When O.J. Stole the Rockets' Thunder 25 Years Ago," *Houston Chronicle*, June 14, 2019.

140 **Starks scoring 11 of his 19 in the fourth quarter of Game 5:** Sam Smith, "Title-Starved Knicks a Step from the Top," *Chicago Tribune*, June 18, 1994.

141 **Starks's appearance in the 1992 dunk contest:** Dan Devine, "Dunk History: John Starks, the Chicago Bulls and 'The Dunk,'" *Yahoo Sports*, August 18, 2014.

142 **"Standing at the free-throw line, running down the middle wide open, and you didn't throw it to me":** Ken Berger, "Forgotten Finals: Ewing on Game 6," YouTube video clip with Ewing, June 2, 2014. https://www.youtube.com/watch?v=n8ZFjgpJT_4.

142 **"When it left my hand, it was money":** John Starks and Dan Markowitz, *My Life*, p. 167, 2004. Sports Publishing LLC.

142 **Details about the planning in case the Knicks won Game 6 in Houston** came from interviews with Pam Harris (6/21/19), Stu Crystal (7/18/19), and Mike Saunders (multiple interviews).

142 **The parade for the New York Rangers, who'd won the Stanley Cup:** James Barron, "New Yorkers Bury the Rangers' Curse in a Sea of Confetti," *New York Times*, June 18, 1994.

142 **The Rockets "confiscating" the Knicks' champagne ahead of Game 6:** Dennis D'Agostino, *Garden Glory: An Oral History of the New York Knicks*, p. 241, 2003. Triumph Books.

142 **Riley's comment to Butera about his belief in Starks** came from multiple interviews with Butera.

143 **Starks having a third straight game with a double-digit fourth quarter:** Michael Arace, "Starks Makes Big Plays, but Olajuwon Makes Biggest," *Hartford Courant*, June 20, 1994.

143 **"Look, please let's just play tomorrow and get this over with":** Dennis D'Agostino, *Garden Glory: An Oral History of the New York Knicks*, pp. 241–42, 2003. Triumph Books.

143 **Detail about the pregame chapel meeting in a weight room before Game 7** came from an interview with Pastor John Love (7/30/19).

144 **Starks turning down the Spurs' contract offer in 1988:** John Starks and Dan Markowitz, *My Life*, p. 72, 2004. Sports Publishing LLC.

149 **The preplanned party in Riley's suite after Game 7, win or lose:** Dennis
     D'Agostino, *Garden Glory: An Oral History of the New York Knicks*, p. 243,
     2003. Triumph Books.

149 **Herb Williams walking back to the team hotel, instead of taking the bus:**
     Dennis D'Agostino, *Garden Glory: An Oral History of the New York Knicks*,
     p. 243, 2003. Triumph Books.

149 **Details about players being crestfallen as they showered after Game 7:**
     came from interviews with Jeff Van Gundy (multiple interviews), Jeff Nix
     (multiple interviews), Derek Harper (multiple interviews), Rolando Black-
     man (8/18/19), Neil Best (9/26/19), and David Steele (10/2/19).

149 **"Biggest mistake I ever made":** Fran Blinebury, "Heat Coach Returns to
     State Where He Originally Shined," *Houston Chronicle*, June 13, 2006.

149 **Almost no writers present for Starks' postgame interview, because of how
     long he took:** Neil Best, "The Aftermath: A Cold, Starks Reality; Says Mea
     Culpa After Poor Game," *Newsday*, June 24, 1994.

149 **"I blame myself":** David Steele, "It All Ends in Anguish: Knicks' Bid for a
     Title Comes Up Short in Game 7," *Newsday*, June 23, 1994.

149 **Starks's inability to sleep or focus on his kids:** David Steele, "The After-
     math: Starks Deals with the Pain," *Newsday*, June 25, 1994.

Relevant interviews in this chapter: Butch Fisher, Ken Trickey Jr., Hakeem Olaju-
won, Rudy Tomjanovich, Bob Salmi, Derek Harper, Curtis Bunn, Dave Robbins,
Dick Ebersol, Bob Costas, David Steele, Dave Checketts, Bo Kimble, Ed Tap-
scott, Stu Crystal, Pam Harris, Mike Saunders, Dick Butera, Anthony Bonner,
Pastor John Love, Larry Brown, Greg Butler, Scott Brooks, Rolando Blackman,
Doc Rivers, and Jeff Nix.

12. COMMITMENT ISSUES

150 **Details on Mason's blind-date introduction to Latifa Whitlock and even-
     tual engagement to her** came from interviews with Anthony Kelly (9/16/19)
     and Latifa Whitlock (multiple interviews).

151 **Mason arranging to join the Nets:** No byline, "Deals," Associated Press,
     Jan. 26, 1990.

152 **Checketts touching base with Riley during the offseason concerning an
     extension:** Clifton Brown, "Checketts Continues to Look for Offense," *New
     York Times*, Sept. 10, 1994.

152 **A deal that would have doubled Riley's salary:** Mike Lupica, "Quit Being So Thin-Skinned," *Newsday*, March 23, 1995.

153 **Rod Thorn stopping by a Knicks training camp practice:** Clifton Brown, "While Ewing Takes Dip, Knicks Enlist at Camp Riley," *New York Times*, Oct. 8, 1994.

153 **NBA three-point line getting moved in:** Sam Smith, "Seeking Extra Points, New NBA Rules Favor Scoring," *Chicago Tribune*, Sept. 14, 1994.

153 **Harper appearing in the league's hand-checking demonstration video:** Clifton Brown, "While Ewing Takes Dip, Knicks Enlist at Camp Riley," *New York Times*, Oct. 8, 1994.

153 **NBA's television ratings being down:** No byline, "NBA Finals Gets Lowest Ratings," Associated Press, June 20, 1999.

154 **The Knicks playing the longest postseason in NBA history at that time:** Mark Heisler, "It Wasn't Pretty, but It Was Compelling," *Los Angeles Times*, June 23, 1994.

154 **Ewing's offseason knee clean-out procedure:** Clifton Brown, "While Ewing Takes Dip, Knicks Enlist at Camp Riley," *New York Times*, Oct. 8, 1994.

154 **Riley joking with Smith, telling him to ice his newborn baby's knees:** David Steele, "Doc Hopes to Make Grade," *Newsday*, Oct. 11, 1994.

155 **Oakley's toe discomfort in camp:** Clifton Brown, "Oakley, the Indestructible Man, Is Hurting," *New York Times*, Oct. 18, 1994.

155 **Tapscott feeling Ward could improve considerably by focusing on solely basketball:** David Nakamura, "FSU's Ward Has Sights Set on June's NBA Draft," *Washington Post*, May 27, 1994.

156 **Monty Williams's thickened heart muscle being a risk:** David Haugh, "Rumors Haunting Monty Williams," *South Bend Tribune*, June 18, 1994.

157 **Viacom preparing to sell the Knicks, other MSG properties:** Julie Sanchez, "Viacom Eager to Sell Off Knicks, Rangers," Reuters, June 13, 1994.

157 **Riley's extension offer being for five years, $15 million:** Mike Lupica, "Focusing on Dotted Line: Checketts Prefers to Keep Pat, but Not as Lame Duck," *Newsday*, June 1, 1995.

158 **Riley feeling he'd gotten assurances in exchange for staying silent about his plans to resign:** Mike Wise, "Knicks Are Said to Have Asked for Riley's Silence," *New York Times*, Sept. 1, 1995.

158 **ITT and Cablevision partnering to buy Knicks, MSG for more than $1 billion:** Murray Chass, "ITT-Cablevision Deal Reported to Buy Madison Square Garden," *New York Times*, August 28, 1994.

158 **Details on Riley's comment about being owed $10,000 during Arask-og's first board meeting after taking over the Madison Square Garden properties** came from interviews with Araskog (7/19/19), Bob Gutkowski (9/30/19), and Dave Checketts (multiple interviews).

159 **Starks's $13 million deal:** Joe Donnelly, "Starks Pleased, but Not Mason; Mase Rejects Offer, Will Be Free Agent," *Newsday*, Nov. 9, 1994.

159 **"When you run from something for so long, it can catch up with you":** Sam Smith, "Nighttime Soap Opera Plays Big in N.Y.," *Chicago Tribune*, Dec. 18, 1994.

159 **Riley's dilemma with Doc Rivers in 1994:** Clifton Brown, "Will Oakley Show? Checketts Optimistic," *New York Times*, Oct. 1, 1994.

159 **Details on Riley's blowout with Rivers:** came from multiple interviews with Rivers.

160 **Shouting match between Riley, Rivers:** Ian O'Connor, "Rivers Still Pained by Finals Loss in '94," ESPN.com, June 14, 2010.

160 **Shouting match between Ewing, Starks in Atlanta:** Clifton Brown, "Who Will Step Up and Save Knicks?," ESPN.com, Dec. 18, 1994.

160 **Teammates calling Starks "Riley's son":** John Starks and Dan Markowitz, *My Life*, p. 98, 2004. Sports Publishing LLC.

160 **"Who are you to ever question *anyone's* shot selection?":** Mike Lupica, "Time to Decide Who Knicks Are," *Newsday*, Dec. 13, 1994.

160 **"The Knicks don't have the same step anymore":** David Steele, "It's Magic, . . . And Knicks Disappear in Embarrassing Loss," *Newsday*, Dec. 3, 1994.

160 **Riley chartering a jet to Aspen on New Year's Eve:** Mike Wise, "Book Is Closed on the Knicks-Riley Saga," *New York Times*, Sept. 8, 1995.

162 **ITT and Cablevision having an 85-15 ownership split of the Garden initially:** Vicki McCash, "Viacom Stock a Garden Party Pooper," *South Florida Sun-Sentinel*, Aug. 30, 1994.

162 **Araskog being a West Point graduate:** Thomas C. Haynes, "I.T.T.'s New Chief," *New York Times*, July 15, 1979.

162 **Small profits at MSG prompting layoffs under Checketts:** Mary Kay Melvin, "Strengthen Profits, Franchises: MSG's New President Sets Goals," Responsive Database Services, April 10, 1995.

164 **Riley punching a mirror and cutting his hand open as Lakers coach:** Wright Thompson, "Pat Riley's Final Test," ESPN.com, April 25, 2017.

164 **Knicks surrendering season-worst 38 points in a quarter to Pistons:** Clifton Brown, "Going from Dreadful to Simply Defeated," *New York Times*, Feb. 15, 1995.

164 **Riley punching a hole in a blackboard in Detroit as Knicks coach in 1995:** Mark Kriegel, "Riley Returns Regrets, Starks Passed on Pass," New York *Daily News*, Sept. 4, 1995.

164 **The record of phone calls between Butera and Arison shortly after Arison's acquisition of the Heat:** Mike Wise, "Book Is Closed on the Knicks-Riley Saga," *New York Times*, Sept. 8, 1995.

164 **Details on Arison's request to watch the Knicks' shootaround** came from interviews with Chris Brienza (1/28/21), and Jeff Van Gundy (multiple interviews).

165 **"The fact that he refused? I respected it":** Geoff Calkins, "Haggling Ends, Arison Closes Deal," *South Florida Sun-Sentinel*, Sept. 3, 1995.

165 **Riley and Arison meeting in a tunnel after the shootaround:** Geoff Calkins, "Haggling Ends, Arison Closes Deal," *South Florida Sun-Sentinel*, Sept. 3, 1995.

Relevant interviews in this chapter: Anthony Kelly, Freddy Avila, Latifa Whitlock, Dave Checketts, Rod Thorn, Derek Harper, Doc Rivers, Russ Granik, Ed Tapscott, Dr. Norm Scott, David Falk, Curtis Bunn, Bob Gutkowski, Ernie Grunfeld, Rand Araskog, Dick Butera, Chris Brienza, Jeff Van Gundy, and Jeff Nix.

13. WE'RE ALL A LITTLE GUILTY

166 **Fans chanting "We want Charlie!" and Riley calling the team "unprofessional":** Joe Donnelly, "What's Wrong? Riley Calls Team 'Unprofessional' After Beating Heat," *Newsday*, Feb. 18, 1995.

167 **"It'd be fake to say the victory puts that all aside":** Clifton Brown, "Knicks Walk Off with Winning Review," *New York Times*, Feb. 20, 1995.

167 **Riley sending Mason to the locker room in Denver before suspending him a second time:** Clifton Brown, "Mason-Riley Blowup Symptom of Internal Strife," *New York Times*, March 16, 1995.

167 **"They've already heard that sales pitch, and got nothing out of it":** Howard Blatt, "Doc Gives Diagnosis of Knick Ills," New York *Daily News*, March 23, 1995.

168 "I ask Pat if he wants me to leave, and he says no": Dennis D'Agostino, *Garden Glory: An Oral History of the New York Knicks*, p. 244, 2003. Triumph Books.

169 "[Mase] was our worst inbounder": Dan Klores, *Winning Time: Miller vs. The Knicks; ESPN 30 for 30* film, 2010.

169 Reggie Miller acknowledging he fouled Anthony with a shove to the back: Ian Begley, "Miller Admits He Pushed Off in 1995," ESPN.com, Sept. 9, 2012.

169 Sam Mitchell fouling Starks: Dean Schabner, "Pacers 107, Knicks 105," United Press International, May 7, 1995.

170 "Did this dude just did [*sic*] this?": Dan Klores, *Winning Time: Miller vs. The Knicks; ESPN 30 for 30* film, 2010.

170 "You lose the edge when you start losing big games": Dennis D'Agostino, *Garden Glory: An Oral History of the New York Knicks*, p. 244, 2003. Triumph Books.

170 Ewing's game winner in Game 5 victory over Pacers: Mike Freeman, "After Game 5, Traveling Tune Is Pacers' Song," *New York Times*, May 18, 1995.

171 Knicks holding Miller without a basket through three quarters in Game 6: Rob Parker, "Miller Goes Flat, Bottled by Knicks," *Newsday*, May 20, 1995.

172 Details of Riley's phone conversation about leaving New York immediately after the Game 7 loss to Indiana: came from multiple interviews with Dick Butera.

174 Riley's demand for a $300-a day-per diem from Arison: Mike Wise, "Book Is Closed on the Knicks-Riley Saga," *New York Times*, Sept. 8, 1995.

174 Butera not wanting to let go of the memo: Mike Wise, "Book Is Closed on the Knicks-Riley Saga," *New York Times*, Sept. 8, 1995.

174 Riley asking Van Gundy to bring his things from the office to his Connecticut home: Dennis D'Agostino, *Garden Glory: An Oral History of the New York Knicks*, p. 244, 2003. Triumph Books.

175 Details concerning Riley quietly telling his assistants first of his plan to resign came from multiple interviews with Mike Saunders.

176 Riley's resignation letter: Mark Heisler, "Riley Abruptly Leaves Knicks; Rejecting a $3 Million Per Year Deal, Coach Says He Wanted Control Over Personnel," *Los Angeles Times*, June 16, 1995.

177 Riley leaving for Greece the same day his resignation letter was faxed to the Knicks: No byline, "Riley Suing Knicks?" *South Florida Sun-Sentinel*, June 27, 1995.

177 The memo between Riley and Arison being dated ten days before Riley's

resignation from the Knicks: Mike Wise, "Book Is Closed on the Knicks-Riley Saga," *New York Times*, Sept. 8, 1995.

177 **David Stern hearing arguments during the tampering case:** Ira Winderman, "Knicks: Riley Deal Has Hit Impasse; Compensation, Tampering Unsettled," *South Florida Sun-Sentinel*, August 24, 1995.

177 **Knicks, Heat reaching a settlement, with New York getting $4 million and Miami's first-round pick:** Mike Wise, "Book Is Closed on the Knicks-Riley Saga," *New York Times*, Sept. 8, 1995.

177 **The vast monetary difference between the Knicks' offer and Miami's offer for Riley:** Barbara Barker, "Heat's Off Heat: Knicks Drop Riley Charges, Get Draft Pick and $1M," *Newsday*, Sept. 2, 1995.

177 **Riley being "miserable" in New York:** Mark Kriegel, "Escape from New York," *Esquire*, Dec. 1, 1995.

177 **"I could have seen myself ending my career in New York":** Dennis D'Agostino, *Garden Glory: An Oral History of the New York Knicks*, p. 245, 2003. Triumph Books.

178 **Riley being introduced on a ship named *Imagination*, inside a lounge called Dynasty:** Mike Wise, "Riley Back in Spotlight and Back at the Helm," *New York Times*, Sept. 3, 1995.

178 **"We're all at least a little guilty":** Mike Wise, "Book Is Closed on the Knicks-Riley Saga," *New York Times*, Sept. 8, 1995.

Relevant interviews in this chapter: Derek Harper, Donnie Walsh, Dick Butera, Bob Salmi, Jeff Van Gundy, Dave Checketts, Mike Saunders, Ernie Grunfeld, Ken Munoz, Larry Pearlstein, and Mike Wise.

14. WHACK-A-MOLE

179 **Nelson's call for the final shot being questioned in Vancouver loss:** Mike Wise, "For Nelson, Unpleasant Loss, Unpleasant Questions," *New York Times*, Jan. 22, 1996.

180 **Details of the team's plane ride back from Vancouver** came from multiple interviews with Jeff Nix.

181 **Nelson growing up on a farm:** Jeff Mayers, "Bucks Coach Hopes to Score for Farmers," Associated Press, Feb. 20, 1995.

182 **Nelson's fish neckties:** Lisbeth Levine, "Comeback of the Year," *Chicago Tribune*, Dec. 14, 1995.

182 Tommy Hilfiger's deal to outfit Nelson for the season: Lisbeth Levine, "Comeback of the Year," *Chicago Tribune*, Dec. 14, 1995.

182 The Knicks' meetings with Chuck Daly: Mike Wise, "Daly Tells the Knicks: Thanks, but No Thanks," *New York Times*, June 24, 1995.

182 Details about the Knicks' efforts to keep their meeting with Daly under wraps came from multiple interviews with Ed Tapscott.

182 Daly's tight-knit relationships with his players: Alan Goldstein, "Players Walk Tightrope of Stardom," *Baltimore Sun*, Feb. 17, 1993.

182 Daly's relationships with the Dream Team players: Jack McCallum, "Remembering Chuck Daly," *Sports Illustrated*, May 9, 2009.

183 Daly's wife reportedly being opposed to him taking another job, due to potential stress: Neil Best and Shaun Powell, "Wanted Man: Daly Figures to Get Knicks' Offer Today," *Newsday*, June 22, 1995.

183 "It had to be the most seductive drink that's ever been placed in front of me": Mike Wise, "Daly Tells the Knicks: Thanks, but No Thanks," *New York Times*, June 24, 1995.

183 Grunfeld being drafted by and playing for Nelson in Milwaukee: No byline, "Nelson, Knicks Get Close," Associated Press, July 4, 1995.

183 Nelson's reputation as an offensive innovator: Chris Ballard, "Genius of a Mad Scientist," *Sports Illustrated*, April 5, 2010.

184 Nelson's first question for Grunfeld being about Mason's free-agent status: Clifton Brown, "Holding On to Mason Was the Only Move," *New York Times*, Sept. 22, 1995.

184 Mason winning the prior season's Sixth Man of the Year award: Clifton Brown, "Holding On to Mason Was the Only Move," *New York Times*, Sept. 22, 1995.

184 Nelson asking Oakley and Ewing to occasionally bring the ball up to create different looks, and Ewing hating it: Bill Fay, "League Regaining Its Stability," *Tampa Tribune*, Oct. 15, 1995.

184 Riley using blue, card-stock paper for his notes: Tom D'Angelo, "Welcome to . . . Camp Riley," *Palm Beach Post*, Oct. 1, 1995.

185 "We're not a running team": Amy Shipley, "Knicks' Nelson Tries to Make a Point," *Miami Herald*, Oct. 15, 1995.

186 Ewing and Nelson's first conversation being awkward: Mike Wise, "In Collapse of Chemistry, Nelson and Ewing Failed to Mix," *New York Times*, March 10, 1996.

186 **Nelson joining the Knicks as the sixth-winningest coach in NBA history:** No byline, "Nelson, Knicks Get Close," Associated Press, July 4, 1995.

186 **Webber opted out of his Warriors contract after his rookie season:** No byline, "Webber's $74.4 Million Deal Doesn't Guarantee Loyalty," Associated Press, June 29, 1994.

186 **Golden State trades Memphis State's Penny Hardaway and three future No. 1 picks for Webber:** Ric Bucher, "Warriors Get Top Pick Chris Webber in Draft Night Trade," *Mercury News*, June 30, 1993.

187 **"I have no love for Don Nelson":** Mark Heisler, "Eyed by the Birds, Then Gored by the Bulls," *Los Angeles Times*, Nov. 27, 1994.

187 **Nelson suggesting players could blame Webber's salary for their stalled contract negotiations:** Clara Morris and Ryan Simmons, "Chris Webber's Beef with Don Nelson Was a Power Struggle that Ruined the Warriors," Secret Base (YouTube video), August 23, 2020. https://www.youtube.com/watch?v=HPlOefnhiRw&t=288s.

187 **"About the toughest guy I ever coached":** Alex Williams, "Retired NBA Coach Don Nelson Talks Playoffs, Poker and, Uh, Weed," *New York Times*, April 30, 2018.

187 **Nelson spending five days in the hospital and thirteen at home during midseason bout with viral pneumonia:** Leigh Montville, "The Crash: Battling Fractious Players and Illness, Golden State Coach Don Nelson Has Seen His Dream Season Ruined," *Sports Illustrated*, Jan. 16, 1995.

187 **The Warriors' media guide image, with Nelson leading the elevator ride:** Leigh Montville, "The Crash: Battling Fractious Players and Illness, Golden State Coach Don Nelson Has Seen His Dream Season Ruined," *Sports Illustrated*, Jan. 16, 1995.

187 **Nelson leaving the job midseason with a 14-31 mark:** No byline, "Nelson's Future Uncertain," Associated Press, Feb. 13, 1995.

188 **Knicks being tied for the NBA's second-best record through 12 games:** Basketball-Reference.com's historical league standings tracker, on Nov. 26, 1995.

188 **Headlines praising the Knicks:** Eddie Sefko, "Riley Is Gone, but New-Look Knicks Still Tough," *Houston Chronicle*, Nov. 25, 1995.

188 **Second headline praising the Knicks:** Curtis Bunn, "D-Lightful Are Don's Knicks," New York *Daily News*, Nov. 5, 1995.

188 **Knicks offering Charles Oakley and Charles Smith for Mourning:** Mark

Heisler, "Core Truth as New York Fans Set the Fax Straight, and in Fewer Words," *Los Angeles Times*, Dec. 20, 1995.

188 **The Knicks countering with Starks, Mason, and a first-round pick:** Howard Blatt, "Zo Close, Yet Zo Far: Last-Minute Knick Offer Almost Lands Mourning," New York *Daily News*, Nov. 7, 1995.

188 **New York's offer being the runner-up to Miami's, according to Hornets coach Allen Bristow:** Howard Blatt, "Zo Close, Yet Zo Far: Last-Minute Knick Offer Almost Lands Mourning," New York *Daily News*, Nov. 7, 1995.

189 **Riley's name still being taped onto the remote control after Nelson took over:** Chris Smith, "Hoop Genius: Don Nelson Looks Like a Jovial, Beer-Drinking Sports Fan. Until He Gets Mad. Can He Succeed Where Pat Riley Failed?" *New York*, November 27, 1995.

189 **"After an hour and a half, we'd be out of practice":** Dennis D'Agostino, *Garden Glory: An Oral History of the New York Knicks*, p. 247, 2003. Triumph Books.

190 **Nelson's practice quizzes, which fined players $10 per wrong answer, and yielded $600 for charity in a single session:** Chris Smith, "Hoop Genius: Don Nelson Looks Like a Jovial, Beer-Drinking Sports Fan. Until He Gets Mad. Can He Succeed Where Pat Riley Failed?" *New York*, November 27, 1995.

190 **Charlie Ward going from a career-best performance in Nelson's Knicks debut to not playing most nights:** Tim Potvak, "Royal Challenge: Fill In for Grant," *Orlando Sentinel*, Dec. 22, 1995.

190 **"I wonder if we're all really, really accepting [the sacrifice]":** Howard Blatt, "A Matter of Minutes for Knicks," New York *Daily News*, Nov. 27, 1995.

191 **"I think he should be in jail!":** YouTube video, titled "NBA Pat Riley Returns to MSG as Miami Head Coach Pregame 1995," posted by tdreadedkaz, Aug. 5, 2020. https://www.youtube.com/watch?v=w_8qgJ6nNoc&t=442s.

191 **Riley intentionally having the Heat players arrive at MSG late, to avoid the media glare:** Curtis Bunn, "Lost on Planet Pat," New York *Daily News*, Dec. 20, 1995.

191 **Heat fined $25,000 for not having players speak to media before game in New York:** Ira Winderman, "NBA Fines Riley $10,000 for Tirade About Officiating," *South Florida Sun-Sentinel*, Jan. 13, 1996.

192 **Starks, Harper, and Ewing embracing Riley before the game began:** Don Amore, "Hot Knicks, Raining Boos Dampen the Life of Riley," *Hartford Courant*, Dec. 20, 1995.

192 Knicks being shut out for first five minutes of Riley's return game: Don Amore, "Hot Knicks, Raining Boos Dampen the Life of Riley," *Hartford Courant*, Dec. 20, 1995.

192 Riley asking if a cough drop at the Garden was safe for him to have: Barbara Barker, "All Riled Up: Knicks Pull Away for Emotion-Filled Victory," *Newsday*, Dec. 20, 1995.

193 Doug Christie making it known he wanted to be traded: Frank Isola, "Christie Tries to Swing Trade," New York *Daily News*, Nov. 29, 1995.

193 "If there's dissension and there's a problem, you don't go to the newspaper. You talk it out": Mike Wise, "Knicks Have No Trouble Expressing Themselves," *New York Times*, Dec. 31, 1995.

193 Mason questioning Nelson and the team's direction: Frank Isola, "Mase: What's Going On Here?" New York *Daily News*, Jan. 3, 1996.

194 Details of the note Mason left for Nelson came from interviews with Jeff Nix and Bob Salmi.

195 Detail concerning Nelson needing new fittings for his Hilfiger-made suits came from Ed Tapscott, who took part in multiple interviews.

195 "It was a team loaded with veterans, that I thought I could be more passive with. It didn't work": Frank Fitzpatrick, *Miami Herald*, March 1, 1997.

196 Oakley's broken thumb: Mike Wise, "Oakley to Miss Six Weeks with a Broken Thumb," *New York Times*, Feb. 16, 1996.

196 Knicks trading Williams and Christie to Toronto: Mike Wise, "Cash and Carry On at Trader Knick," *New York Times*, Feb. 19, 1996.

196 "Everybody thought he'd be a good coach. But sometimes nightmares happen": Michael Wilbon, "A New Day for Knicks of Old," *Washington Post*, March 12, 1996.

196 Starks being benched immediately after making a three-pointer against Phoenix: Shaun Powell, "Nelson, You're Not a Teflon Don," *Newsday*, Feb. 29, 1996.

197 Starks having a fruitless meeting with Nelson: Shaun Powell, "Nelson, You're Not a Teflon Don," *Newsday*, Feb. 29, 1996.

197 "Hubert is the better player": Frank Isola, "Nellie's Stark Answer: Davis," New York *Daily News*, Feb. 29, 1996.

197 Team's first winless four-game road trip in ten years: Barbara Barker, "No Zest Out West: Knicks Lose to Jazz, Wind Up 0-4 on Trip," *Newsday*, March 2, 1996.

197 Nelson getting booed during starting-lineup intros at MSG: David Steele, "Starks-Nelson Feud Turns Nasty," *Newsday*, March 5, 1996.

197 **"I didn't think he had very much left in the tank":** Bryant Gumbel, *HBO Real Sports with Bryant Gumbel*, interview with Don Nelson in June 25, 2019, episode.

198 **Nelson's meeting with Dolan:** Bryant Gumbel, *HBO Real Sports with Bryant Gumbel*, interview with Don Nelson in June 25, 2019, episode.

198 **"It got back to [Ewing], and once that happened, I was toast":** Bryant Gumbel, *HBO Real Sports with Bryant Gumbel*, interview with Don Nelson in June 25, 2019, episode.

198 **Detail about Nelson calling his players "assholes"** came from an interview with Willie Anderson (7/26/20).

198 **Knicks sign free agent Matt Fish:** No byline, "Knicks Sign Forward Matt Fish to 10-day Contract," Associated Press, Feb. 24, 1996.

198 **Ewing being sidelined with an ankle injury and flu-like symptoms:** Barbara Barker, "Herb Back with Team," *Newsday*, Feb. 29, 1996.

199 **"I loved everything except the team":** Jackie MacMullan, "Van's the Man Relieved to Be Rid of Don Nelson; the Knicks Blew Away the Bulls for New Coach, Jeff Van Gundy," *Sports Illustrated*, March 18, 1996.

199 **"As a coach, you can't just say, 'That's it.' Some guys may need a little more explaining":** Frank Isola, "Christie Says Starks Is Legit in Complaint," New York *Daily News*, March 7, 1996.

Relevant interviews in this chapter: Jeff Nix, Ed Tapscott, Ernie Grunfeld, Dr. Norm Scott, Derek Harper, Charlie Ward, Chris Brienza, Bob Salmi, Don Chaney, Willie Anderson, and Matt Fish.

15. BACK TO BASICS

200 **Details on Van Gundy spending nights at Providence's basketball office** came from an interview with Stu Jackson (8/20/19).

201 **Van Gundy drinking a half-dozen Diet Cokes per day:** Percy Allen, "Revived Van Gundy Back in NBA Action; Sonics Notebook," *Seattle Times*, Oct. 9, 2003.

201 **Van Gundy being in room 1814 at the Ritz-Carlton:** Dave D'Alessandro, "Van Gundy Young, Game," *Bergen Record*, March 10, 1996.

201 **Van Gundy being NBA's youngest head coach by seven years:** Dave D'Alessandro, "Van Gundy Young, Game," *Bergen Record*, March 10, 1996.

201 **Van Gundy's father being fired a number of times:** George Vecsey, "Van Gundy: Like Father, Like Son, Like Son," *New York Times*, March 10, 1996.

201 Van Gundy's lone head-coaching experience being at McQuaid Jesuit: George Vecsey, "Van Gundy: Like Father, Like Son, Like Son," *New York Times*, March 10, 1996.

202 Van Gundy telling his parents he planned to transfer from Yale to a junior college: Ira Berkow, "Born to Coach Basketball: From a Scouting Assignment at Age 10, Van Gundy Has Risen to the Top," *New York Times*, April 21, 1997.

202 Van Gundy reaching the Division III Elite Eight as a player: Scott Pitoniak, "Van Gundy's Connection to Nazareth Remains Strong," *Rochester Business Journal*, Oct. 23, 2019.

202 "Working with Huggies to develop a disposable coach": Tony Kornheiser, "Making Sales Calls," *Washington Post*, May 28, 1991.

203 Details on Van Gundy occasionally playing the role of babysitter came from an interview with Pat Hazelton (8/12/19).

204 Details on Van Gundy's end-of-season exit meeting with Riley came from multiple interviews with Van Gundy himself.

204 Van Gundy's daughter, Mattie, having the middle name "Riley": Dave Hyde, "Two NBA Coaches and One Torn Family," *South Florida Sun-Sentinel*, May 5, 2000.

204 Van Gundy asking Riley for some time away after his wife's miscarriage: Ian O'Connor, "Van Gundy a Playoff-Winning Coach with Perspective and Compassion," *Journal News*, April 26, 2001.

204 "I wanted at least one Van Gundy with me": Ira Berkow, "From a Scouting Assignment at Age 10, Van Gundy Has Risen to the Top," *New York Times*, April 21, 1997.

205 Sixers had lost 11 of 12, and had a league-worst record of 11-47 entering the game: Raad Cawthon, "Sixers Ambush Knicks; the Knicks Had a New Coach, but the Sixers Were the Ones Who Looked Rejuvenated," *Philadelphia Inquirer*, March 9, 1996.

205 Pinckney comparing the win over New York to Christmas miracle: Raad Cawthon, "Sixers Ambush Knicks; the Knicks Had a New Coach, but the Sixers Were the Ones Who Looked Rejuvenated," *Philadelphia Inquirer*, March 9, 1996.

205 Van Gundy being too nauseated to eat his Philly cheesesteak: Dennis D'Agostino, *Garden Glory: An Oral History of the New York Knicks*, p. 248, 2003. Triumph Books.

205 Van Gundy's preoccupied mishaps with his car: Mike Wise, "From Team to Car, Woe Is Van Gundy," *New York Times*, May 19, 2000.

206 **Van Gundy's criticism of the team chaplain:** Chris Broussard, "Coach Criticizes Knick Chapel in Article," *New York Times*, April 6, 2001.

206 **Details about Van Gundy's opinions on "distractions"** came from interviews with Pam Harris, Mark Pannes and Ed Oliva.

207 **"50,000-to-1 [odds]":** Mitch Lawrence, "Unusual Suspects," New York *Daily News*, March 9, 1996.

207 **Don Chaney winning Coach of the Year:** No byline, "Rockets Fire Coach Don Chaney," United Press International, Feb. 18, 1992.

207 **"Of course it changes things":** Lacy J. Banks, "Lost in New York: Knicks Job Interests Phil—and Michael," *Chicago Sun-Times*, March 11, 1996.

208 **Ewing's dunk over Longley:** Terry Armour, "New York Nightmare: Knicks 104, Bulls 72; Knicks Return to Old Ways in Rout over the Bulls," *Chicago Tribune*, March 11, 1996.

208 **Harper giving Van Gundy the game ball after win over Bulls:** Mike Wise, "Knicks Get Ball Back in Their Own Court," *New York Times*, March 12, 1996.

208 **Bulls winning fourth title after notching league-record 72 wins in regular season:** Terry Armour, "Michael Jordan Named MVP as Chicago Bulls Win 1996 Title over Seattle Supersonics," *Chicago Tribune*, June 17, 1996.

Relevant interviews in this chapter: Stu Jackson, Jeff Van Gundy, Ernie Grunfeld, Don Chaney, Pam Harris, Pat Hazelton, Patrick Eddie, Brendan Malone, Ed Oliva, Mark Pannes, Pastor John Love, Ed Tapscott, Derek Harper, and Dave Checketts.

16. DOWN IN FLAMES

209 **Details about the Jermaine O'Neal and Kobe Bryant draft workouts** came from multiple interviews with Ed Tapscott.

210 **The Knicks getting a pick from the Spurs for Charles Smith:** Mike Wise, "Knicks Deal Smith, and His Salary, to San Antonio," *New York Times*, Feb. 9, 1996.

210 **The Knicks getting a pick from Miami in the Riley tampering case:** Ira Winderman, "Barring Late Trade, Heat to Sit Out Draft," *South Florida Sun-Sentinel*, June 14, 1996.

211 **New York taking Wallace, McCarty, and Jones in the first round of the 1996 draft:** Clifton Brown, "Knicks Sign Their Three First Rounders," *New York Times*, August 7, 1996.

211 Michael Jordan laying out an ultimatum to Jerry Reinsdorf and the Bulls: Sam Smith, "How Close Did Michael Jordan Come to Joining the Knicks?," *Chicago Tribune*, August 13, 1997.

211 Jordan's previous contract paying him $25 million over eight years: Sam Smith, "How Close Did Michael Jordan Come to Joining the Knicks?," *Chicago Tribune*, August 13, 1997.

211 Jordan getting a $30 million deal for the 1996–97 season: Sam Smith, "How Close Did Michael Jordan Come to Joining the Knicks?," *Chicago Tribune*, August 13, 1997.

212 Detail about Houston never having experienced a true recruitment came from multiple interviews with Ed Tapscott.

212 Houston playing for his father at Tennessee: No byline, "Tennessee Basketball Coach Wade Houston and Son Allan Can Team Up, NCAA Rules," June 24, 1989.

212 Houston leaving Pistons in free agency without letting them counter New York's offer: Mitch Albom, "Houston's Sudden Departure Just Another Sign of NBA's Greed," *Detroit Free Press*, July 14, 1996.

212 Grant Hill, other Pistons not attending Houston's wedding: Sam Smith, "Houston's Departure to Knicks Changes Course for Pistons," *Chicago Tribune*, Dec. 24, 1996.

213 Chris Childs taking on both Jordan and Kobe Bryant: "Hoop Stories, Ep. 1: Chris Childs Stood Against Kobe Bryant and Michael Jordan," YouTube video, posted by Oldskoolbball, Dec. 30, 2018.

213 Childs having family members who suffered from alcoholism: Ira Berkow, "Childs Thinks He Can . . . and So Do the Nets," *New York Times*, Feb. 19, 1996.

213 Childs having a pool party on the day he expected to be taken in the draft, then spiraling for days when he wasn't drafted: Shaun Powell, "From Drunk to Knick, Chris Childs Took the Long Road to NBA," *Newsday*, Oct. 13, 1996.

213 "A player only a bartender could love": Shaun Powell, "From Drunk to Knick, Chris Childs Took the Long Road to NBA," *Newsday*, Oct. 13, 1996.

213 "I went out and had twenty-four Heinekens, smoked four joints, and had five or six shots of Cognac": Shaun Powell, "From Drunk to Knick, Chris Childs Took the Long Road to NBA," *Newsday*, Oct. 13, 1996.

213 Johnson's twelve-year, $84 million deal being the biggest in sports history at the time: Ed Hardin, "$84 Million: Hornets' Johnson Gets Plateful; Contract Will Run Through 2005," *News & Record*, Oct. 5, 1993.

214 **Charlotte trading Alonzo Mourning to Miami:** Mark Heisler, "Mourning Turns Up With Heat; Center Is Traded for Rice, Reeves, and Geiger After Turning Down Hornets," *Los Angeles Times*, Nov. 4, 1995.

214 **Johnson's back problems in Charlotte:** Phil Taylor, "The Sting Is Back; Propelled by Revitalized Larry Johnson, the Hornets Are Buzzing Around Top of the Central Division," *Sports Illustrated*, March 6, 1995.

214 **Details on Charlotte's concern over Mason's purported steroid use:** came from an interview with Dave Checketts. A separate interview with Dave Cowens confirmed the Hornets' initial concerns, with Cowens saying Nelson first raised the question in a conversation with him.

215 **New York signs veteran big men Buck and Herb Williams:** Selena Roberts, "Knicks Seal Up Buck Williams," *New York Times*, July 27, 1996.

215 **"We feel like we hit the jackpot":** Clifton Brown, "Quick as 1-2-3, the Knicks Grab a Shot at a Third Championship," *New York Times*, July 15, 1996.

215 **Details on Pete Favat's initial meeting with Larry Johnson in which he introduced the concept of Grandmama to him** came from an interview with Favat himself (11/6/20).

217 **Details on the relationships between teammates that season** came from interviews with Charlie Ward, Chris Childs, Eric Leckner, and John Wallace.

218 **Starks winning the Sixth Man award:** No byline, "Sixth Man Award for Starks," *New York Times*, April 23, 1997.

218 **Johnson's revenge dagger in Charlotte:** Steve Adamek, "Buzz Off! Knicks Swat Hornets; Miami Next?" *Bergen Record*, April 29, 1997.

219 **"A lot of guys in this business have been spoon-fed. But Larry? . . . Somewhere down the line, Larry had to learn to eat soup with a fork":** Barbara Barker, "Johnson Has Come a Long Way Since Tough Background," *Newsday*, Oct. 27, 1996.

219 **"I hate them with all the hate you can hate with":** Selena Roberts, "Haranguing Above the Rim Begins," *New York Times*, May 2, 2000.

219 **"It's like that toy you wanted your whole life":** Mal Florence, "It's So Close, Yet So Far Away for the Knicks," *Los Angeles Times*, May 20, 1997.

220 **P. J. Brown cooking and serving for the homeless, paying for underprivileged children to attend games, and reading to kids at libraries:** Ira Winderman, "Brown to Receive Citizenship Award for Community Work," *South Florida Sun-Sentinel*, April 25, 1997.

220 Detail about P. J. Brown having been in chapel with Charlie Ward shortly before that fateful Game 5 came from multiple interviews with Ward himself.

221 "He was going for my knees instead of trying to go for the rebound": Barbara Barker, "Tempers and Heat Rising; Knicks Brawl, Fall in Miami," *Newsday*, May 15, 1997.

222 The Knicks having five players suspended to Miami's one for the altercation: Frank Hughes, "NBA Punches Out Game 5 Battlers; Heat, Player, Five Knicks," *Washington Times*, May 16, 1997.

222 New York having so many players suspended that they had to split the penalty over two games, and use alphabetical order to determine who would sit out first: Chris Sheridan, "NBA Sets Down Five Knicks; Heat's Brown," Associated Press, May 16, 1997.

224 "I don't feel like the best team won": Barbara Barker, "Emptiness Crushing Disappointed Knicks," *Newsday*, May 20, 1997.

224 "The commissioner took away a golden opportunity from me and my teammates": Frank Isola, "Into a Long, Hot Bummer; Ewing Offers Stern Parting Words," New York *Daily News*, May 20, 1997.

224 Van Gundy arranging pebbles in the sand to diagram the offense right after the Knicks got bounced: Katie Baker, "It Was Like True, True Disdain for Each Other," *Ringer*, May 15, 2017.

224 "Even with time, I don't know if this is something that totally goes away": Frank Isola, "Van's the Man with a Finals Plan," New York *Daily News*, May 31, 1997.

Relevant interviews in this chapter: Ed Tapscott, Jerry Albig, Phil Hubbard, Ernie Grunfeld, John Wallace, Dontaé Jones, David Falk, Dave Checketts, Russ Granik, Joel Litvin, Chris Childs, Jeff Van Gundy, Dave Cowens, George Willis, Pete Favat, Charlie Ward, Eric Leckner, Fletcher Cockrel, J. D. Mayo, Dennis Helms, Isaac Austin, John Crotty, Jeff Kessler, Judge Jed Rakoff, and Steve Popper.

17. SHATTERED

225 Ewing being first to the gym the day after the Game 5 loss: Doc Rivers, *For Those Who Love the Game*, p. 149, 1993.

226 **David Robinson's broken foot:** No byline, "Spurs' Robinson Breaks His Foot," Associated Press, Dec. 24, 1996.

226 **Spurs winning the lottery to get Duncan:** Tarik El-Bashir, "Spurs Win the Tim Duncan Sweepstakes," *New York Times*, May 19, 1997.

226 **The Knicks' lone season with a league-average offense:** Basketball-Reference.com's Knicks' page for the 1991–92 season has the team offensive rating ranked 12th out of 27 teams.

226 **"The Gang That Couldn't Shoot Straight":** Jack McCallum, "Rough . . . but Ready?," *Sports Illustrated*, Feb. 1, 1993.

226 **"Windshield wipers offer more variety than the Knicks' offense":** Chris Smith, "Hoop Genius: Don Nelson Looks Like a Jovial, Beer-Drinking Sports Fan. Until He Gets Mad. Can He Succeed Where Pat Riley Failed?" *New York*, November 27, 1995.

226 **"They'd be accused of intentional grounding":** Peter Vecsey, "Clippers Will Gain a Coach, Lose a Shot at Luring Barkley," *USA Today*, Feb. 5, 1992.

227 **Ewing playing through flu-like symptoms:** Sandy Keenan, "Ewing of Old: 34 points, 12 Rebounds for Knicks Leader," *Newsday*, Dec. 12, 1997.

227 **Ewing hitting seven of eight jumpers in one quarter:** Steve Adamek, "Ewing's 34 Cage Timberwolves," *Bergen Record*, Dec. 12, 1997.

227 **"He chose to practice what he was already good at":** David Halberstam, "Changing NBA Game, Greatness Passes Ewing," ESPN.com, March 2001.

227 **"Where the hell did you get that jump shot from?":** Russ Bengtson, "King of New York: Patrick Ewing Ruled New York. Ew Heard?," *Slam Magazine*, Dec. 14, 2010.

228 **Oakley crashing into Ewing's wife:** Sandy Keenan, "Squanderers: Knicks Again Blow Late Lead, Lose in OT," *Newsday*, Jan. 30, 1998.

228 **Historic nature of the Pfister Hotel:** No byline, "Roster of Historic American Hotels Expands," *Chicago Sun-Times*, Feb. 21, 1993.

228 **"He'd heard ghosts there and stuff":** LeBatard Show, "Ewing Is Scared of Haunted Milwaukee Hotel," YouTube clip, Feb. 7, 2014. https://www.youtube.com/watch?v=S_RV0dzBMg4&t=2s.

229 **Left-handed free throws:** Selena Roberts, "Horror Show for Knicks as Ewing Injures Wrist," *New York Times*, Dec. 21, 1997.

230 **Ewing injury resembling one seen in car accidents:** Susan Ferraro and Frank Isola, "How Well He'll Recover Is Hard Call for Docs," *New York Daily News*, Dec. 23, 1997.

230 **Right lunate dislocation:** Susan Ferraro and Frank Isola, "How Well He'll Recover Is Hard Call for Docs," New York *Daily News*, Dec. 23, 1997.

230 **The detailed description of what took place at the hospital during Ewing's surgery** came from an interview with Dr. Susan Scott (12/2/20), who operated on him.

231 **Three- and four-guard lineups:** Selena Roberts, "Horror Show for Knicks as Ewing Injures Wrist," *New York Times*, Dec. 21, 1997.

231 **Van Gundy's "How are we supposed to win now?" question** was relayed in interviews with Brendan Malone and Jeff Nix.

232 **Details on Ewing being frustrated having to sign autographs for several children at Newark Airport** came from an interview with Brian Quinnett (2/15/19). **The detail about Ewing putting all his teammates up in Jamaica** also came from Quinnett.

233 **Ewing and Michael Jordan being on the same recruiting trip at UNC:** Jimmy Black and Scott Fowler, *Jimmy Black's Tales from the Tar Heels*, p. 99, 2006. Sports Publishing LLC.

233 **Ewing being one of seven children:** Ralph Wiley, "The Master of the Key: After Years of Relying on Others to Unlock Doors for Him, Georgetown's Center Patrick Ewing Will Soon Go Off on His Own," *Sports Illustrated*, Jan. 7, 1985.

233 **The turbulence around Boston's desegregation:** Ian O'Connor, "Patrick Ewing Has the Floor," ESPN.com, Nov. 1, 2017.

234 **Ewing's high school going 77-1:** Chip Malafronte, "The Day Wilbur Cross Beat Patrick Ewing," *New Haven Register*, June 29, 2013.

234 **The overt racism Ewing faced:** Noah Perkins, "Ewing, Jarvis Rewind the Time," *Milford Daily News*, June 25, 2020.

234 **Racist signs at Big East games, and the banana peel:** Gary Pomerantz, "Ewing Under Siege," *Washington Post*, Feb. 9, 1983.

234 **Parallels between Ewing and Bill Russell:** Karen Russell, "Opinion: Growing Up with Pride and Prejudice," *New York Times*, June 14, 1987.

235 **Details about Ewing covering young teammates' purchases at Friedman's** came from Greg Butler (8/13/19), and **the detail about him paying for a sizable chunk of Chris Jent's wife's brain-tumor treatment** came from Jent himself (10/31/20).

235 **Ewing's sexual harassment allegation:** No byline, "Ewing Denies Allegations," Associated Press, April 17, 1997.

235 **The detail about the six-figure settlement the Knicks paid in response to those allegations** came from multiple interviews with Dave Checketts.

235 **Ewing testifying in a racketeering case:** David Firestone, "In Testimony, Patrick Ewing Tells of Favors at Strip Club," *New York Times*, July 24, 2001.

236 **Ewing's extramarital affair:** Kevin Merida, "NBA Wives' Tale," *Washington Post*, Oct. 27, 1998.

236 **The detail about Ewing having slept with more than one team dancer, and dancers getting the numbers of players from ball boys** came from an interview with a team dancer, who agreed to be interviewed for the book on background.

236 **Ewing's wife starting divorce proceedings:** Joanna Molloy, Michele McPhee, and Virginia Breen, "End of a Romance? Ewing and His Wife Head for Splitsville," New York *Daily News*, Feb. 13, 1998.

236 **The number of coincidences between the novel and real life:** Kevin Merida, "NBA Wives' Tale," *Washington Post*, Oct. 27, 1998.

236 **Ewing's spending four hours a day on wrist rehab:** Dave D'Alessandro, "Ewing's Prognosis: Playoffs," *Newark Star-Ledger*, March 18, 1998.

237 **Oakley tying Ewing's ties for him:** Mike Lupica, "Ewing Connects," New York *Daily News*, Jan. 18, 1998.

237 **Brief period of mourning:** Joe Schad, "Ewing Won't Accept Bad News," *Newsday*, Dec. 22, 1997.

237 **Starks having multiple family members dealing with cancer:** Mike Wise, "For Starks No Gloves; Just Heart Amid Mother's Fight with Cancer," *New York Times*, May 1, 1998.

237 **Dudley breaking his foot:** Mike Wise, "Dudley Is Injured in Dismal Knick Loss," *New York Times*, Feb. 25, 1998.

237 **Van Gundy filling in as team's tenth man at practice:** Ohm Youngmisuk, "Knicks Ailing, Van Gets the Point," New York *Daily News*, March 14, 1998.

238 **Starks's mother needing surgery:** Mike Wise, "For Starks No Gloves; Just Heart Amid Mother's Fight with Cancer," *New York Times*, May 1, 1998.

238 **Larry Johnson's childhood background in boxing:** Tom Withers, "Boxing Led to Hoops for Rebels' Johnson," United Press International, April 1, 1990.

239 **Chris Mills being the lone Knick suspended:** Lisa Dillman, "TKO in Fight Night at Garden," *Los Angeles Times*, May 2, 1998.

240 **Two fouls in three minutes:** Mike Wise, "Lost in the Return: The Motion Offense," *New York Times*, May 8, 1998.

240 **Starks bringing golf clubs to Indiana:** Frank Isola, "Starks Bringing Golf Clubs to Indy Has . . . Knicks Teed Off," New York *Daily News*, May 15, 1998.

Relevant interviews in this chapter: John Wallace, Eric "Sleepy" Floyd, Andrew Lang, Said Hamdan, Dr. Susan Scott, Dr. Norm Scott, Jeff Van Gundy, Pastor John Love, Fred Cofield, Brian Quinnett, Roy Williams, Karl Hobbs, Craig Esherick, Bill Stein, George Vecsey, Filip Bondy, Curtis Bunn, Greg Butler, Chris Jent, Selena Roberts, Dave Checketts, Bob Salmi, and unnamed team dancer.

18. HEART TRANSPLANT

241 **The Pacers getting to the free-throw line almost 60 percent more than the Knicks in 1998 playoff series:** Basketball-Reference.com page; 1998 NBA Eastern Conference Semifinals Knicks vs. Pacers page.

241 **New York being the fifth-oldest team:** Basketball-Reference.com page; 1997–98 NBA Season Summary page, under the Miscellaneous Stats section.

241 **Ewing's $20 million salary, and it becoming the NBA's highest salary after Jordan's departure:** L. C. Johnson, "Owners Willing to Try a Tax; Proposal Would Affect More Player Contracts, However if It Doesn't Hold Down Salary Growth, It Calls for a Hard Cap," *Orlando Sentinel*, Oct. 17, 1998.

242 **The Raptors essentially getting their name from *Jurassic Park*, and through a fan contest:** Doug Smith, *We the North: 25 Years of the Toronto Raptors*, p. 30 (Kindle version), 2019. Viking.

242 **Orlando Magic winning the lottery for a second-straight season:** Tim Povtak, "It's Magic! Orlando Wins Lottery Again; An Astonishing Upset, the Magic Beat Long Odds to Choose the Cream of the College Crop. Will It Be Webber? Bradley?," *Orlando Sentinel*, May 24, 1993.

242 **The Raptors and Grizzlies not being eligible to win the lottery in 1996, 1997, or 1998:** Phil Jasner, "Lotto Luck: Sixers Emerge from Draft Lottery with No. 1 Pick," *Philadelphia Daily News*, May 20, 1996.

242 **The Raptors' lotto ball coming up first in 1996, but them being given the second pick:** Phil Jasner, "Lotto Luck: Sixers Emerge from Draft Lottery with No. 1 Pick," *Philadelphia Daily News*, May 20, 1996.

242 **The Raptors picking B. J. Armstrong first in the expansion draft:** Sam Smith, "Toronto Picks Armstrong; May Not Trade Him," *Chicago Tribune*, June 25, 1995.

242 **Toronto trading Armstrong after he refused to report to the team:** Blake Murphy, "Why the 15th Anniversary of the Vince Carter Trade Is the Perfect Time to Put It into Its New and Complete Perspective," *Athletic*, Dec. 17, 2019.

242 **Camby leading the league in blocks per game in 1996–97:** Barbara Barker, "Oak Leaves Knicks; Toronto Gets Him in Deal for Camby," *Newsday*, June 26, 1998.

243 **The Knicks sending cash to Toronto in the deal for Camby:** Selena Roberts, "Knicks Part Ways with Oakley to Get Toronto's Camby," *New York Times*, June 25, 1998.

244 **Specific details on Oakley's decision not to report to Toronto right away** came from an interview with Glen Grunwald (12/13/20).

244 **Oakley pushing things close to the lockout deadline by not reporting to Toronto in the aftermath of the trade:** Selena Roberts, "Knicks Near Deadline in Trade Bid," *New York Times*, June 30, 1998.

245 **Sprewell attacking Carlesimo:** Mike Wise, "Sprewell Attack Stuns League," *New York Times*, Dec. 3, 1997.

245 **Sprewell receiving the longest non-drug-related suspension in NBA history at the time:** Don Markus, "NBA Star Benched for Rest of Season," *Baltimore Sun*, Nov. 22, 2004.

245 **NBA lockout lasting 204 days:** Chris Sheridan, "NBA Lockout Officially Ends," Associated Press, Jan. 20, 1999.

245 **Sprewell being named to the All-NBA team for defense:** Nathan Tidwell Jr., "Sprewell: A Diamond in the Rough Before Heading to New York," *Daily Press*, May 28, 2000.

245 **Riley drawing a comparison between Sprewell and Jordan back in 1994, after coaching against him:** Clifton Brown, "Sprewell's 41 Points Sting Knicks," *New York Times*, Feb. 11, 1994.

246 **The Knicks getting permission from David Stern to meet Sprewell before finalizing a trade for him:** Mike Wise, "How the Heat Missed Landing Sprewell," *New York Times*, May 7, 2000.

246 **Van Gundy asking for a Diet Coke before going through X's and O's for Sprewell at the swingman's home:** Frank Isola and Mike Wise, *Just Ballin': The Chaotic Rise of the New York Knicks*, p. 16, 1999.

247 **Checketts requesting an explanation for Sprewell's "Shit happens" comment:** Frank Isola and Mike Wise, *Just Ballin': The Chaotic Rise of the New York Knicks*, p. 23, 1999. Simon & Schuster.

248 **"But Dad, we've already been out to Golden State":** Mike Wise, "A Piece of New York Is Leaving the Knicks," *New York Times*, Jan. 20, 1999.

249 **Riley's mantra during the early 1990s about wanting the Knicks to be**

the hardest-working, best-conditioned team: Jan Hubbard, "Knicks Try Tough Way," *Newsday*, Oct. 8, 1991.

249 Greg Brittenham visiting Knick players regularly during offseason to track their conditioning: Clifton Brown, "Camp Riley's Regimen Is More Like a Boot Camp," *New York Times*, Oct. 13, 1993.

249 Van Gundy mentioning Indiana's teamwide conditioning plan during the lockout as a way to motivate the Knick players: Frank Isola, "Van Gundy to Team: Work It Out; Wants Knicks Together," New York *Daily News*, Nov. 19, 1988.

249 Larry Johnson dropping twenty-five pounds during the lockout: Alan Greenberg, "Is One Ball Enough on Ewing's Knicks?" *Hartford Courant*, Feb. 5, 1999.

249 Ewing's weight gain: Kevin Kernan, "Out-of-Shape Ewing Worries Checketts," *New York Post*, Jan. 8, 1999.

250 Detail about Sprewell being able to keep up on StairMaster at highest level for a considerable amount of time during college came from an interview with Gary Waites (8/2/19).

250 Camby hiring a personal trainer following the Oakley trade, in an effort to put on muscle: Frank Isola, "Camby Pumped Up for Season," New York *Daily News*, July 29, 1998.

250 "His work capacity, previous to today, was not acceptable": Kevin Kernan, "He's Jeff Van Grumpy: Coach Already Worried About Knick Effort," *New York Post*, Jan. 27, 1999.

250 Dennis Scott being out of shape for camp: Brian Lewis, "Scott's Debut Breathtaking," *New York Post*, Jan. 25, 1999.

250 Scott's struggles with his weight before turning pro: Anthony Cotton, "A Light Scott Now Carries More Weight," *Washington Post*, March 3, 1990.

250 Scott's college coach threatening to bench him if he didn't lose weight: John Romano, "For Ga. Tech's Scott, Results Were Worth the Weight Loss," *Tampa Bay Times*, March 23, 1990.

250 "Obviously he needs to get in a lot better condition before he can play": Selena Roberts, "Sprewell & Co. Ponder Roar of Garden Crowd," *New York Times*, Jan. 27, 1999.

251 Sprewell having stress fracture in heel: Brian Lewis, "Sprewell Setback: He'll Miss 3–6 Weeks with Fractured Heel," *New York Post*, Feb. 10, 1999.

251 Larry Johnson needing MRI on knee during first month of season: Selena

Roberts, "Knicks' Johnson Hoping to Play with the Pain," *New York Times*, Feb. 23, 1999.

251 Ewing limping off the court after twenty-nine seconds with Achilles pain: Selena Roberts, "Fright Night: Ewing Hurt in Loss," *New York Times*, March 10, 1999.

251 Knicks having five games in six nights, in four different cities: Chris Sheridan, "Bucks 87, Knicks 86," Associated Press, March 9, 1999.

251 Johnson taking blame in Knicks' awful offensive showing in Chicago: Selena Roberts, "Knicks Offer Apologies, but No Explanations," *New York Times*, March 14, 1999.

251 Scott being cut by Van Gundy after making jokes on the team plane following bad Chicago loss: Selena Roberts, "As Boat Rocks, Grunfeld Is Pushed Overboard," *New York Times*, April 22, 1999.

252 Van Gundy reportedly not consulting Grunfeld about the move beforehand: Selena Roberts, "As Boat Rocks, Grunfeld Is Pushed Overboard," *New York Times*, April 22, 1999.

Relevant interviews in this chapter: Ernie Grunfeld, Glen Grunwald, Butch Carter, John Wallace, Charlie Ward, Kurt Thomas, Chris Childs, Dave Checketts, Jeff Van Gundy, Said Hamdan, Gary Waites, and Selena Roberts.

19. LONG-TERM PARKING

253 The blowout nature of the Knicks' April 7 loss in Charlotte: Selena Roberts, "Knicks Are All Out of Answers," *New York Times*, April 8, 1999.

253 Van Gundy shouting profanities at Allan Houston for his lack of effort: Frank Isola and Mike Wise, *Just Ballin': The Chaotic Rise of the New York Knicks*, p. 136, 1999. Simon & Schuster.

254 "I would say . . . that we are teetering": Kevin Kernan, "Back Up the Van Gundy; Jeff's Knicks Fall to 10th Place After Embarrassing Loss to Hornets," *New York Post*, April 8, 1999.

254 Grunfeld reportedly being prepared to fire Van Gundy if the Knicks lost to Atlanta that night: Ian O'Connor, "Van Gundy, Camby Patch Things Up and Get the Last Laugh," *Journal News*, June 7, 1999.

254 "He was treating drills at room temperature as if they were suicide sprints in the Mojave": Ian O'Connor, "Van Gundy, Camby Patch Things Up and Get te Last Laugh," *Journal News*, June 7, 1999.

254 **Camby sitting out due to a blister on his foot:** Frank Isola, "Van Gundy Gives Camby a Blistering," New York *Daily News*, Jan. 30, 1999.

254 **"He's going to be a work in progress the entire year":** Mark Kriegel, "Oak a Tough Act to Follow for Camby," New York *Daily News*, Feb. 2, 1999.

254 **Oakley playing through a dislocated toe as a Knick:** Mike Wise, "Oakley Edges Closer to Having Toe Surgery," *New York Post*, Dec. 26, 1994.

254 **Oakley playing three more quarters in a game after breaking his hand:** Curtis Bunn, "Breaks Go Against the Knicks," *Newsday*, March 24, 1990.

255 **"I don't think there's anyone who escapes scrutiny as we look at the situation around us":** Selena Roberts, "Garden's Checketts Losing Patience with Losing Knicks," *New York Times*, April 10, 1999.

255 **Camby, of all people, standing out in a game that likely would have cost Van Gundy his job:** Ian O'Connor, "Van Gundy, Camby Patch Things Up and Get the Last Laugh," *Journal News*, June 7, 1999.

256 **ITT selling its half of the Garden properties to Cablevision:** Richard Sandomir, "ITT Sells Cablevision Control Over Madison Square Garden," *New York Times*, March 7, 1997.

257 **Dolan warning Van Gundy and the team's other assistants that they'd be held responsible if anything like the 1997 Miami incident transpired again:** Harvey Araton, "Dave Checketts Reflects on Tenure with Knicks and Spots Similarities," *New York Times*, Dec. 14, 2015.

257 **Jim Dolan's struggle with alcoholism and timeline leading up to his becoming Cablevision CEO:** Ian O'Connor, "James Dolan, Unplugged," ESPN.com, Dec. 17, 2018.

257 **"Mostly, it was because no one else wanted it":** Joel Siegel, "Oedipus at the Garden," *New York*, March 18, 2005.

258 **The men "had a mutual understanding: *I don't trust you, you don't trust me*":** Frank Isola and Mike Wise, *Just Ballin': The Chaotic Rise of the New York Knicks*, p. 59, 1999. Simon & Schuster.

258 **Where Jeff Van Gundy's paranoia came from:** Paul Knepper, *The Knicks of the Nineties*, p. 186, 2020. McFarland.

258 **Van Gundy's call with Bill Parcells:** Adrian Wojnarowski, podcast with Jeff Van Gundy, Feb. 10, 2016.

259 **Ewing going to management to say Van Gundy needed to stay on as coach:** William C. Rhoden, "Checketts Stays Afloat Over Mess He Created," *New York Times*, April 12, 1999.

259 Van Gundy's two-year-old daughter memorizing the Knicks' injury report: Mike Wise, "Van Gundy Produces Patchwork Surprise," *New York Times*, March 2, 1998.

261 Gregory's Restaurant being Checketts and Grunfeld's place: Frank Isola and Mike Wise, *Just Ballin': The Chaotic Rise of the New York Knicks*, p. 160, 1999. Simon & Schuster.

261 The history behind table 21, the restaurant's secluded area where Checketts and Grunfeld had dinner: Frank Isola and Mike Wise, *Just Ballin': The Chaotic Rise of the New York Knicks*, p. 161, 1999. Simon & Schuster.

262 Grunfeld's rise through the Knicks' organization: No byline, "Knicks Promote Grunfeld," United Press International, July 21, 1993.

262 Grunfeld's dog being named Nicky: Paul Schwartz, "Ernie's Plan Lookin' Good; Knicks Proving Grunfeld Right," *New York Post*, May 20, 1999.

Relevant interviews in this chapter: Dave Checketts, Ernie Grunfeld, Jeff Van Gundy, Ian O'Connor, Steve Popper, and Sammy Steinlight.

20. BEATING THE ODDS

263 Charlie Ward backing Reggie White's opinion on women reporters being in the locker room: Mike Wise, "Getting the Word Out," *New York Times*, May 1, 1999.

263 Larry Johnson denying allegation: Mark Cannizzaro, "Furious Johnson Fires Back," *New York Post*, April 22, 1999.

263 Sprewell's agent calling for a change in coach or GM: Kevin Kernan, "Free Spree—Or Else! Agent Blasts VG, Ernie over Latrell's Role," *New York Post*, April 21, 1999.

264 Checketts announcing the move at practice: No byline, "Knicks President, GM Reassigned," Associated Press, April 21, 1999.

264 Rangers miss postseason for second straight season: Joe LaPointe, "After Flopping Twice, What Will Rangers Do?," *New York Times*, April 9, 1999.

265 Stern meets with Van Gundy and Riley: Selena Roberts, "Van Gundy, Riley Get Lecture from Stern," *New York Times*, May 20, 1998.

265 Riley saying he wished Mourning's punches landed: Charlie Nobles, "Seething Riley Says Van Gundy Lost Control," *New York Times*, May 3, 1998.

266 Eight lead changes and 10 ties: Play-by-play log on Basketball-Reference.com.

266 **Ewing's rib and Achilles injuries:** Kevin Kernan, "Ewing Hurts His Rib-cage," *New York Post,* May 17, 1999.

266 **Knicks running Triangle Down play:** Dennis D'Agostino, *Garden Glory: An Oral History of the New York Knicks,* p. 271, 2003. Triumph Books.

267 **Dan Majerle knowing the play call beforehand:** Brian Biggane, "The Frantic Final Seconds: Heat Were Ready for 'Triangle Down,'" *Palm Beach Post,* May 17, 1999.

268 **Van Gundy's telegram from Riley:** Dennis D'Agostino, *Garden Glory: An Oral History of the New York Knicks,* p. 272, 2003. Triumph Books.

268 **Details on the steps Checketts took to keep the meeting with Jackson secret** came from separate interviews with Checketts: Maggie McEvoy (8/19/19) and Clare Gluck (9/10/19).

268 **Checketts meets with Jackson and Musburger:** Mike Wise, "Amid Turmoil, Knicks Talked with Jackson," *New York Times,* May 23, 1999.

269 **The meeting being reported on:** Mike Wise, "Amid Turmoil, Knicks Talked with Jackson," *New York Times,* May 23, 1999.

269 **The meeting being reported on:** Dennis D'Agostino, *Garden Glory: An Oral History of the New York Knicks,* p. 273, 2003. Triumph Books.

269 **The Garden chanting Van Gundy's name:** William C. Rhoden, "For Knicks, It's Turmoil and Success," *New York Times,* May 26, 1999.

270 **Van Gundy's wife moved to tears:** Chris Sheridan, "Knicks' Future Uncertain," Associated Press, June 6, 1999.

270 **Ewing's Achilles being a problem for months:** Kevin Kernan, "Ewing Asks Out—Sore Achilles Sends Patrick to Hospital," *New York Post,* March 10, 1999.

271 **"Let Spree, Allan and the guys go get me a championship":** Emanuel-Knicks, "NBA 1999 Eastern Conf. Finals: Knicks at Pacers gm 1, part 18," YouTube, uploaded Feb. 21, 2008. https://www.youtube.com/watch?v=MR RUzStx55U&t=168s.

271 **Ewing feeling a pop in his lower leg:** Frank Isola and Mike Wise, *Just Ballin': The Chaotic Rise of the New York Knicks,* pp. 225–28, 1999. Simon & Schuster.

271 **Dr. Scott allowing him to keep playing:** Frank Isola and Mike Wise, *Just Ballin': The Chaotic Rise of the New York Knicks,* pp. 225–28, 1999. Simon & Schuster.

271 **The diagnosis after the game:** Frank Isola and Mike Wise, *Just Ballin': The Chaotic Rise of the New York Knicks,* pp. 225–28, 1999. Simon & Schuster.

271 "It's frustrating to be so close to something I've dreamed about for so many years": Selena Roberts, "Ewing to Miss Rest of Playoffs with Torn Achilles' Tendon," *New York Times*, June 3, 1999.

272 Detail about Larry Bird imploring his players to let the Knicks have a two-pointer, rather than giving up a three: came from a courtside observation by reporter Steve Adamek (2/16/21).

272 The Knicks running the Triangle Down play again: Dennis D'Agostino, *Garden Glory: An Oral History of the New York Knicks*, p. 273, 2003. Triumph Books.

272 Larry Johnson filling Ewing's place in the play call: Dennis D'Agostino, *Garden Glory: An Oral History of the New York Knicks*, p. 273, 2003. Triumph Books.

273 "I knew right away I screwed that play up": David Teel, "Peninsula Icon, Former NBA Referee Jess Kersey Remembered for 'Magnetic Personality,'" *Daily Press* (Virginia), April 22, 2017.

273 "I had a peace about me that game": Dennis D'Agostino, *Garden Glory: An Oral History of the New York Knicks*, p. 275, 2003. Triumph Books.

274 The Houston-Miller dynamic: Frank Isola and Mike Wise, *Just Ballin': The Chaotic Rise of the New York Knicks*, pp. 222–23, 1999. Simon & Schuster.

Relevant interviews in this chapter: Dave Checketts, J.A. Adande, Phil Taylor, Maggie McEvoy, Clare Gluck, Phil Jackson, Mike Wise, Jeff Van Gundy, Chris Childs, Charlie Ward, Kurt Thomas, Steve Adamek, and Steve Javie.

21. THE CLOCK STRIKES MIDNIGHT

276 Popovich being an Air Force alum: No byline, "Spurs & NBA—97–98 Spurs Staff; Special Section," *San Antonio Express-News*, Oct. 30, 1997.

276 The Spurs going 11-1 in the postseason run-up to the Finals: Kelley Shannon, "City Goes Wild over Spurs' NBA Finals Berth," Associated Press, June 6, 1999.

276 Beginning with a 6-8 record: Jonathan Feigen, "Awaiting Finals, Spurs Feel They Haven't Done Anything Yet," *Houston Chronicle*, June 9, 1999.

276 Robinson bringing Popeyes Chicken to Popovich's home: Jackie Mac-Mullan, "Bubble Asterisk? The Champion '99 Spurs Say It Shouldn't Exist," ESPN.com, July 22, 2020.

276 **Popovich warning of his possible dismissal:** Jackie MacMullan, "Bubble Asterisk? The Champion '99 Spurs Say It Shouldn't Exist," ESPN.com, July 22, 2020.

276 **Avery Johnson relaying the message:** Chris Broussard, "Victories, Not Vindication, for Spurs' Popovich," *New York Times*, June 15, 1999.

277 **Doc Rivers looked likely to replace Popovich:** Marc Stein, "Timmy and Pop:NBA Power Couple," ESPN.com, July 11, 2016.

277 **Spurs winning 42 of 48 games at one point:** Chris Broussard, "Victories, Not Vindication, for Spurs' Popovich," *New York Times*, June 15, 1999.

277 **Larry Johnson getting an MRI in the hospital during Game 6:** Michael Wilbon, "Knicks Rush In, Pacers Roll Out," *Washington Post*, June 12, 1999.

277 **Dudley's elbow overextended:** Paul Schwartz, "Dudley Injury Pains Knicks," *New York Post*, June 19, 1999.

277 **"It was a feeling of David against Goliath":** Dennis D'Agostino, *Garden Glory: An Oral History of the New York Knicks*, p. 276, 2003. Triumph Books.

279 **Van Gundy coming out to the Garden floor to find a noise:** Frank Isola and Mike Wise, *Just Ballin': The Chaotic Rise of the New York Knicks,* p. 262, 1999. Simon & Schuster.

279 **Ewing's despair in not being able to play during the Finals:** Dennis D'Agostino, *Garden Glory: An Oral History of the New York Knicks*, p. 276, 2003. Triumph Books.

279 **Play-by-play showing 12 lead changes and 12 ties:** Jackie MacMullan, "Bubble Asterisk? The Champion '99 Spurs Say It Shouldn't Exist," ESPN.com, July 22, 2020.

280 **Knick fans being solidly behind Sprewell:** Michael Hunt and Tom Enlund, "Sprewell's at Home in Garden: Knicks Forward Is No Longer an Outcast As He Becomes a Favorite Among the Fans," *Milwaukee Journal Sentinel*, June 15, 1999.

Relevant interviews in this chapter: Selena Roberts, Will Perdue, Antonio Daniels, Charlie Ward, Kurt Thomas, Dave Checketts, Jeff Van Gundy, and Sammy Steinlight.

EPILOGUE

284 **Ward re-signs in 1999:** No byline, "Dudley and Ward Stay Knicks," *New York Times*, Jan. 21, 1999.

284 **Knicks draft Frederic Weis:** Kevin Kernan, "Knicks Take Big Gamble, Shock Draft by Choosing Weis, 7-2 French Center," *New York Post*, July 1, 1999.

284 **Weis's struggles after being drafted:** Sam Borden, "For Frederic Weis, Knicks' Infamous Pick, Boos Began a Greater Struggle," *New York Times*, July 14, 2015.

284 **Ewing asking for trade out of New York:** Marc Berman, "Why Ewing Wanted Out of New York," *New York Post*, Dec. 9, 2001.

284 **$90 million in long-term deals in return for Ewing:** Kenny Ducey, "Five Worst Trades in Knicks History," *Sports Illustrated*, June 22, 2016.

285 **Dolan reportedly getting personally involved in the Bargnani trade:** Howard Beck, "Phil Jackson Could Be Perfect Mentor for Ailing Knicks," *Bleacher Report*, March 12, 2014.

285 **Dolan getting involved in the deal for Anthony:** Frank Isola, "James Dolan Tries to Close Deal for Carmelo Anthony by Negotiating with Nuggets Owner Directly," New York *Daily News*, Feb. 8, 2011.

285 **Cablevision spending $330 million on the Wiz:** Richard Katz, "Cablevision Buys the Wiz," *Variety*, Jan. 27, 1998.

285 **Cablevision buying dozens of theaters in August 1998 for $240 million:** David W. Chen, "Cablevision to Buy 20 More Movie Theaters in Region From Loews Cineplex," *New York Times*, Aug. 28, 1998.

285 **Details on how difficult Mason was at the beginning of his tenure with the Knicks:** came from multiple interviews with Ed Tapscott.

287 **Mason's funeral held in Queens:** Nick Forrester and Corky Siemaszko, "Mason's Private Funeral Attended by Ex-Knicks Coach Pat Riley, Teammates Patrick Ewing, John Starks," New York *Daily News*, March 6, 2015.

287 **Charles Smith filed a grievance against the Knicks:** Clifton Brown, "Smith and Knicks: Bad Blood Still Flows," *New York Times*, Dec. 28, 1996.

288 **Charles Smith acknowledging his regrets with making trip to North Korea:** No byline, "Ex-Knick Regretting North Korea Participation," Associated Press, Jan. 7, 2014.

288 **"[People] still ask me about it *every* single day":** "Twenty-three years later, John Starks asked about epic dunk 'every day,'" KJRH-TV news segment, pulled from YouTube clip, Jan. 22, 2016.

288 **"If you looked at Starks closely enough, you could almost see his heart beating":** Mike Breen, "John Starks' Dunk Over Michael Jordan in 1993 Playoffs," MSG Network, YouTube clip, May 14, 2020. https://youtu.be/g8jY8fHuXnQ?t=210.

289 **Oakley's arrest at the Garden:** Mike Vorkunov, "Former Knick Charles Oakley Arrested After Altercation at Madison Square Garden," *New York Times*, Feb. 8, 2017.

289 **The Knicks' statement on Oakley:** Emily Shapiro, "Charles Oakley Calls Knicks' Statement 'a Slap in the Face,'" ABC News, Feb. 9, 2017.

289 **Oakley's effort to add Dolan as a defendant in his lawsuit:** Tim Daniels, "Charles Oakley Wants Knicks' James Dolan Named in Assault and Battery Lawsuit," *Bleacher Report*, Dec. 17, 2020.

290 **Ewing, Georgetown winning the Big East Tournament:** Joseph Salvador, "Patrick Ewing–led Georgetown Completes Big East Run to Steal NCAA Tournament Bid," *Sports Illustrated*, March 13, 2021.

290 **Coach John Thompson's passing:** Richard Goldstein, "John Thompson, Hall of Fame Basketball Coach, Dies at 78," *New York Times*, August 31, 2020.

290 **The Knicks having the most losses from 2001 to 2020:** Data from Basketball-Reference.com's Stathead query system.

291 **Thibodeau's intense summer league workout:** Ian O'Connor, "Is New York's Tom Thibodeau Too Tough for the Toughest Job in Sports?" ESPN.com, Dec. 21, 2020.

Relevant interviews in this section: Harvey Araton, Dave Checketts, Ed Tapscott, Patrick Eddie, Latifa Whitlock, and Don Cronson.

ABOUT THE AUTHOR

Chris Herring is a *New York Times* best-selling author and senior writer for ESPN. He previously spent eight years writing about the NBA for *Sports Illustrated* and FiveThiryEight, and prior to that spent seven years at *The Wall Street Journal*, where he covered the New York Knicks. He lives in New York. You can follow him on X @Herring_NBA.